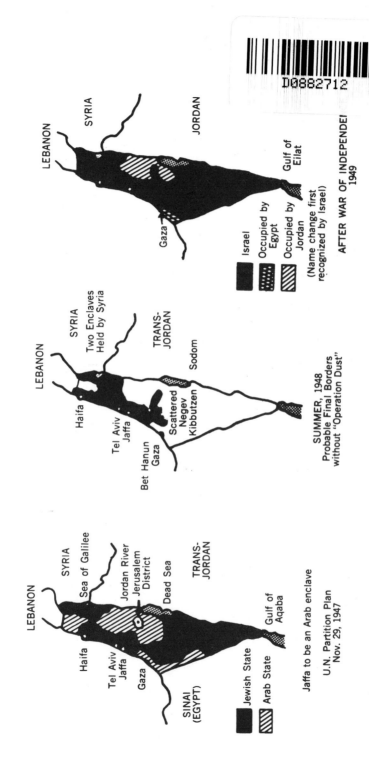

BOUNDARIES OF ISRAEL

First map (left):

LEBANON
SYRIA
Sea of Galilee
Jordan River
Jerusalem District
Haifa
Tel Aviv
Jaffa
Gaza
Dead Sea
TRANS-JORDAN
SINAI (EGYPT)
Gulf of Aqaba

Jaffa to be an Arab enclave

U.N. Partition Plan
Nov. 29, 1947

Jewish State
Arab State

Second map (middle):

LEBANON
SYRIA
Two Enclaves Held by Syria
TRANS-JORDAN
Haifa
Tel Aviv
Jaffa
Bet Hanun
Gaza
Scattered Negev Kibbutzen
Sodom

SUMMER, 1948
Probable Final Borders
without "Operation Dust"

Third map (right):

LEBANON
SYRIA
JORDAN
Gaza
Gulf of Eilat

Israel
Occupied by Egypt
Occupied by Jordan
(Name change first recognized by Israel)

AFTER WAR OF INDEPENDENCE
1949

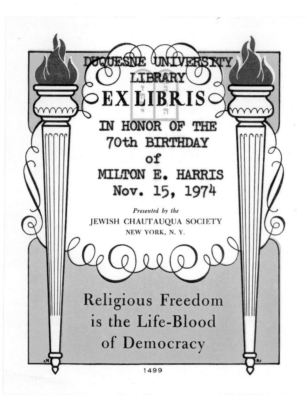

American Volunteers
and Israel's
War of Independence

They also serve who only stand and wait.
—"On His Blindness" by John Milton

Be strong as the leopard, light as the eagle,
swift as the deer, and mighty as the lion, to do
the will of your Father in Heaven.
—*Mishna Nezikin,* Tractate 9, 5:20

God helps them that help themselves.
—*Poor Richard's Almanac* by Benjamin Franklin

American Volunteers
and Israel's
War of Independence

A. Joseph Heckelman

(1)

KTAV PUBLISHING HOUSE, INC.

NEW YORK

Library of Congress Cataloging in Publication Data

Heckelman, A. Joseph.
  American volunteers and Israel's war of independence.

  Bibliography: p.
    1. Israel-Arab War, 1948-1949—American participation. I. Title.
DS126.9.H42   956'.042   74-4015
ISBN 0-87068-266-0

CONTENTS

Foreword

Hagalgal ḥozer. Turning, the wheel returns.

The events of October 1973 have suddenly turned this into a work of topical importance. Until then, it was an engaging study of the infancy of the State of Israel—a period long since transcended, a different world. But the Yom Kippur War wrenched us back to 1948. Consider these duplications:

> Serious, simultaneous attacks by the armies of different countries, on separate fronts.
> Syrian tank forces broke through primary Israeli defense lines, were stopped near the Sea of Galilee primarily by their own timidity.
> Israel, finding itself without adequate military supplies, becomes totally dependent on an emergency airlift, by American planes, for the tools of survival.
> Crisis of leadership: Are the leaders leading? Where are we going?
> Crisis of direction: Peace is necessary—but is it possible? Is Arab hatred truly metaphysical and unreachable? Is it merely a political tactic which has gotten out of hand? Is it more complex, but somehow reachable?
> Post-war recession, malaise, uncertainty.
> Sense of ultimate dependence on others.
> Initiating the identical, unusual "wedge" tactic to defeat a seemingly invulnerable Egyptian army on the identical date (October 15) exactly 25 years apart. (See chapter 15).

The infant has grown to be a sturdy adult, with obvious major developments over the past quarter century. Yet, the eye-opening discovery of the writer's probing visit to Israel at the very end of 1973, was the astonishing extent to which, indeed, 1973/1974 was again 1948/1949. And, so our study of the War of Independence takes on a new immediacy.

Hagalgal ḥozer. Turning, the wheel returns.

May the God of Israel enable Medinat Yisrael to transcend this, and all future times of trial, fulfilling the symbolism of its name, "who has struggled with God and man and has prevailed."

Many thanks to all those who cooperated with the writer, among them Samuel E. Alexander, Israel Amir, Ralph Anspach, Shaul Avigur, Avraham Avi'hai, David Baum, Elihu Bergman, Eugene Blum, Jerold Bobrow, B. Bressloff, Moshe Brodetzky, Samuel Burstein, Irving Calic, Shoshana (Kliers) Carmeli, Mendel Cohen, Jules Doneson, Adina Dorfman, Ben Dorfman, J. J. Doyle, Harry Eisner, Mike Feingood, Joe Feldman, S. Finard, Leonard Fine, Miriam K. Freund, Eli Freundlich, David Gen, D. Glassman, Hannah Goldberg, Moshe Goldberg, Stanley E. Green, Reuben E. Gross, David Hanovice, Matityahu Harris, Valia Hirsch, Ed Kaplansky, Harold Kates, Benno Katz, Sam Katz, Rose Kaufman, Abraham Kenny, Samuel Z. Klausner, Harold Kraushar, Aaron Lebow, Lou Lenart, William Lichtman, Netanel Lorch, Jesse Zel Lurie, David Macarov, Will Manolson, I. Meltzer, Ben Ocopnick, Yosef Oren, Victor Perry, Felix M. Putterman, Isidor Rabinovich, Sidney Rabinovich, Aharon Remez, Gershon Rivlin, Mordecai Rubin, Moses B. Sachs, Milton Sackin, Nadav Safran, Robert St. John, Jack Schaffer, Avraham Schenker, Gidon Shimoni, Shlomo Shulkiss, Akiva Skidell, Shlomo Sokol, Leslie Solomon, Yehuda Solter, Theodore J. Stern, Moses Stambler, Morris Swartz, Julian Swing, Tom Tugend, Murray N. Weisberg, Eliezer Whartman, Israel Winkelman, Zvi Moshe Zohar. Also, Janus Martha Olear, Angelika Wolff, Ruth Glushanok.

My late father, Jacob C. Heckelman ל״ז, and Dr. Norman Schanin (then, of Brooklyn; now, of Jerusalem) provided the documentary assistance which made possible the first link in the chain of events ultimately leading to this work: Acquiring an American passport at the height of the State Dept. ban on travel to the Middle East. And the Tel Aviv apartment of Moshe and Sylvia Ettenberg (he, the volunteer with overall responsibility for Israel radar; she, in process of becoming a mother) was a most welcome oasis to us, and to numerous other young Americans.

Please note that there is no implication that the above-named individuals agree with any of the developments or conclusions of this work: Full responsibility is that of the author alone.

10 Tevet 5734

A. Joseph Heckelman
Waterbury, Conn.

Preface

The End and The Beginning

March 28, 1948, it was all over.

The Arabs apparently had won. The Jewish state was dead. There was scarcely even a possibility that a Jewish state might arise, for the yishuv was no longer a viable community. The outlying villages had long been beseiged; now it was clear that there was not enough strength to reinforce sizable settlements hardly an hours' drive from the major cities.

This was made brutally clear March 28, by two disasters.

On the 26th, a heavily armored convoy had succeeded in breaking through to Jerusalem from the coast. The next day, most of those precious armored vehicles were sent south, to share some of their supplies with the beleaguered Etzion group of Kibbutzim guarding the southern approach to Jerusalem. Since this was a Sabbath, the move was not expected by the Arabs, and the convoy reached its destination without serious difficulty. But the way back was totally blocked at Nebi Daniel (an Arab village named for the prophet Daniel). By the second day of fighting, March 28th, with ammunition almost gone, there was no choice but to accept the terms offered by the "neutral" British: Surrender of all weapons and vehicles, in return for safeconduct back to Jerusalem for all survivors. Not only were a significant part of Jewish Jerusalem's weapons, together with a majority of its armored vehicles, thus lost to the Jews—but the British promptly gave all this material to the Arabs.

That self-same day, an armored convoy from Haifa, the major Jewish city in that region, attempted to reach Kibbutz Yeḥiam in northwestern Galilee. A single vehicle got through; all the others were turned back, with the shocking loss of forty-two lives: In effect, the convoy was destroyed.

Not only were the major cities not able to reinforce their outposts, but they themselves were isolated and coming under seige—to such an extent that contact with their own suburbs was haphazard at best.

Arab irregulars continued to enter the country at will, as they had been doing for months, bringing with them whatever they wished in the way of military supplies. Although the British occupation was being wound down, British power continued to be used to prevent the Jews only from receiving military supplies. And the Jews were pitifully underarmed to begin with: Whatever arms they possessed were the miscellaneous result of several years of smuggling, reduced by loss in use and periodic seizure by the British mandatory power.

Indeed, it was finished. Eighteen hundred years after the Romans eradicated the last vestiges of Jewish sovereignty in the Holy Land,[1] 50 years after modern Zionism had spurred a purposeful return to the Land, 3 years after the almost total destruction of European Jewry because there was no homeland for them—a Jewish state would *not* arise: Not in our time.

Six weeks before it was officially to see the light of day, the Jewish state was dead.

Three nights later, the resurrection began.

That night, an American aircrew delivered a single planeload of Czechoslovak arms to a tiny Palmach unit which had briefly "liberated" the ostensibly Arab-held airstrip at Bet Darras in southwestern Palestine. The American four-engined transport plane refueled, turned around, and was on its way back to Prague airport well before dawn.

Like a ghostly bird, Hassida (the Stork) had come and gone.

Unlike a ghost, the wispy imprint left by Hassida hardened into a pattern: A permanent pattern of American intertwining with the military realities of the State of Israel. This pattern predates the official proclamation of the State of Israel, and has continued to the present day.

The state of Israel came terrifyingly close to being strangled at birth. Three factors intertwined to perform the rescue. Its own absolute determination, forged on the anvil of a long and bitter history and fixed in the flames of the just extinguished European Holocaust; funds and supplies from abroad; and volunteer fighters and military technicians from overseas.

Of these three basic elements, the first two—the steadfastness of the Jews of Israel and material support from abroad—were expected; the third—participation of overseas volunteers—could be neither expected nor assumed. After all, overseas volunteers gratuitously risked life, limb, and domestic citizenship. Presumably they were desperately needed—or were they? How vital *was* their contribution? And how many volunteers were there? Where did they come from? What did they actually accomplish?

For the writer, this question of the real value of overseas volunteers is not only a matter of abstract curiosity—it is also a deeply personal question: My wife and I were married less than half a year, when extreme pressure on my part launched us towards Israel, so that my special military skills (such as they were) could be available to the army of Israel and/or so that we could simply be there then. I was then 22, and my wife barely 20.

World War II training in the U.S. Navy had made me a radar technician, with special competence in antiradar, and I believed that such skills would be in desperately short supply in Israel. Still, volunteering had involved our transcending the usual serious parental misgivings, verbalized in part as the argument that there was "more important work to be done here now," that by going later (when it would be physically safe) one would be making a "more significant contribution."

My particular prejudice had been: The direct participant at the point of action is truly indispensable. The distant supporter may provide tools, may promote a climate of opinion—but cannot effectuate results.

This work is an outgrowth of my doctoral thesis entitled: "What If? . . . An Attempt to Evaluate the Significance and Participation of Overseas Volunteers in Israel's War of Independence." The doctorate was issued by the Jewish Theological Seminary of America, New York, N. Y., in 1971. Its specialized research extended over many years, including correspondence and written and oral interviews with countless individuals (some of which was initiated through special questionnaires circulated by the Association of Americans and Canadians in Israel, and the American Veterans of Israel, in the United States). There was careful study of virtually all available written material on and about the War of Independence, in English and in Hebrew, published and archival.

Some of the developments and conclusions may well be controversial. There is no implication that any individual or sources necessarily support any particular conclusion: Full responsibility rests with the author alone.

Introduction

The response of the world and the worldwide Jewish community to the crisis in Israel in May and June 1967 recalls to mind the situation nineteen years earlier—a situation vastly different in some respects, and rather similar in others: Similar in that in 1948, as in 1967, Israel was attacked by its Arab neighbors; in 1948, as in 1967, the world professed concern, but remained officially aloof. While preparations were made to destroy the Jewish state, they acted only to reduce the fighting after shooting had already started—and then focused on "fighting" as the essential evil, rather than on the context which made fighting necessary: that of self-proclaimed aggression and intended victim.

The differences, too, are significant: The Jewish state of 1967 was no longer an 1800-year-old ghost; it had nineteen years of very real, solid, healthy existence behind it; Israel of January 1967 was a viable state of two-and-a-quarter million Jews and a quarter-million Arabs—whereas pre-Israel of January 1948 was a Jewish community of little more than a half-million Jews, intermingled with an Arab population at least as large; Israel, then, was economically agricultural with a rudimentary industry; today, it stands in the forefront of science and technology; militarily, pre-Israel of January 1948 was without an air force, without tanks, without artillery, without a navy, desperately short of rifles and ammunition and of men to shoot the rifles it did not possess. Israel today has one of the most modern and effective armies in the entire world. In 1948, just as Israel had to import the beginning of the makings of a modern army to enable it to fight successfully for its first breath as a state, it also imported some military technicians to operate some of this equipment, and train others in its use.

In 1948 Israel barely managed to survive—in 1967 it was its own forebearance alone that kept Israel from occupying the capitals of its would-be destroyers. In 1967 Israel had no need of non-Israeli overseas volunteers; as a matter of fact, it could not use them efficiently. In 1948, it actively recruited such overseas volunteers.

What is an overseas volunteer? Is this term just a euphemism for

xiii

the pejorative word "mercenary"? Is one a "volunteer" if he is unskilled and serves without pay—and, necessarily, a "mercenary" otherwise?

The latter suggestion is one that the writer rejects out of hand. The clear implication of this usage of "mercenary" is that the mercenary is a tool, bought for money, unimplicated and unconcerned with the cause for which he is fighting. That, since the money was available, if a particular individual or group did not take advantage of it, another would have. To regard the volunteer as a mercenary in this sense is ungracious, unfair—and untrue. In general, the sums of money paid were smaller than the volunteers were earning as civilians in their home countries; and they were substantially smaller than some of them could have earned working for the other side. (For example, George "Buzz" Beurling, a Christian Canadian war ace with family responsibilities who was killed in an accident near Rome, was said to have refused an offer of $1,500 per month to fly for the Egyptians, but accepted $500 from Israel.) And, despite intensive recruiting efforts, certain skill categories remained in desperately short supply at particularly critical times.

By and large, what motivated the more highly paid volunteers—as well as the volunteers who received no special pay—was a complex combination of ideology, conscience, and a zest for adventure (the proportions, of course, varying from individual to individual). For some, the break in civilian routine may have been welcome. For almost all, however, service meant an interruption in a normal life (including career and family) recently resumed (or just begun) after years of military duty in World War II. And there were even some who had not had previous military experience.

There is, however, one category of non-Israeli whom we do exclude from our definition of overseas volunteer. This is the individual—and there were such—who considered himself hired for a specific, limited noncombatant goal. Such an individual was not placing himself fully at the service of Israel; rather, he had a clear, limited contract which he would fulfill to the best of his ability. He might, for example, contract to ferry aircraft to Czechoslovakia, but not beyond; or he might contract to ferry aircraft to Israel, but not to do any combat flying in Israel; or he might have contracted solely to train Israelis. If the term "mercenary" is to be used at all, its use should be restricted properly to these men: skilled technicians who were paid fairly to do a war-related job. Often, one who began on a "contract" basis (a less pejorative term than "mercenary") progressed to "volunteer" status, so that only a tiny proportion of the total number of volunteers were strictly "contract" during the active phases of the war.

Our line of distinction between "mercenary" and "overseas volunteer," then, is not related to level of pay: The sole criterion is the type of participation. Therefore, we apply the term "overseas volunteer" to all overseas volunteers who took part in a war away from their home countries, whether or not they received supplementary, or even substantial, stipends; whether they were Jewish or Christian; whether or not they were actually and officially in the Army of Israel.

"Inconsistent" is probably the kindest word to apply to the pay situation in 1948. While all volunteers received standard army pay of two Israeli pounds per month (then worth almost $4 per pound) plus a supplementary country-of-origin stipend,[1] there was also a variety of individual arrangements. These were generally the mixed result of the original recruiter's enthusiasm, the Israeli negotiator's assessment of the particular volunteer's patriotism, and the latter's reactions to rumors of special "deals" with others. This chaos was regularized in early 1949, when skill categories were defined, and supplementary compensation was made both uniform and mandatory.

Not every last overseas volunteer was a great asset. As could be expected, some served in areas and in ways which do not appear to have been of special importance; and, since the need was felt to be very great and screening was haphazard, the ranks of the volunteers included some mistakes—a few bluffers, a few who refused to put up with even the modicum of discipline required, a few chronic troublemakers, a few who came only to "fight" and could not tolerate the relatively long truce intervals—and so it was with an entirely legitimate sense of relief that Israel sent some of its overseas volunteers back home, as early as the summer of 1948. However, the writer has not been able to uncover a single specific instance in which the misbehavior of an overseas volunteer led to a significant negative result.

The term loosely used in Israel for overseas volunteers was "Mahal," an acronym for "Mitnadvey huts la'arets" (literally, "volunteers from outside the country"). This designation applied essentially to overseas volunteers from the free countries of the West, primarily those from English-speaking countries (who, interestingly, were referred to in Israel as "Anglo-Saxons"). They were regarded as having come entirely of their own free will, with the likelihood that they would return to their countries of origin after the war.

In order to help protect the citizenship of the Mahal Americans, a limited oath of allegiance was administered, so that it could be said that they were serving "with" rather than "in" the armed forces of Israel. This small difference in the oath resulted in no practical difference whatever in service (rank, discipline, action, etc.). Under the then current American law, taking an abstract oath of allegiance to a foreign government (or voting in a foreign election) was clearly a cardinal offense, whereas actually risking one's life in the service of a foreign government could be presumed to be less reprehensible. The fact that some Mahal were permitted to opt out of the army at their own initiative was a practical accommodation on the part of the army—not the result of a special form of oath.

In terms of a technical definition, we should exclude as overseas volunteers those from abroad who had come before the War of Independence and had established a home in Israel (Palestine)—although in the popular mind such a sharp line probably cannot be drawn. Thus, included would be those who already were in the country on a presumably temporary basis (e.g., students), and who joined the armed forces. Generally, we include as overseas volunteers all those whom Israel classified as "Mahal" (which included such temporary residents)—excepting for technicians arriving after the fighting, who do not really concern us.

Thus, our definition of "overseas volunteers" includes all those who were not previously residents of Jewish Palestine and who served Israel directly, away from their home countries; such service being either in or with the armed forces, or in connection with procurement for the armed forces. This includes those who were designated Mahal or ATC, as well as those who came under their general definitions without specific designation, since Mahal as an administrative designation did not come into use until mid-1948 (it was established as a formal office with a detailed official definition only in February 1949), and our period begins November 29, 1947.

The official definition of Mahal, promulgated by the Mahal Committee of the Manpower Section of the General Staff, 4 Feb 49, says: Mahal are residents of the U.S., Canada, United Kingdom, South Africa, Latin America who arrived in Israel as volunteers for the army prior to 1 Jan 49; also residents of France, Holland, Belgium, Switzerland, Italy and the Scandinavian countries who arrived prior to Sept 1948; also the American students at the Hebrew University and the Technion, who had arrived on the G.I. Bill of Rights with the intention to study here and then go back home, and who left their studies after 29.11.47 and volunteered for the army; also anyone from the above countries who arrived after the respective dates specified, provided he came upon the authorized request of the army.[2]

The terms "Israel" and "Israeli" are technically correct only after May 14, 1948, when the state of Israel officially came into being. However, as a convenience, these terms will sometimes be used anachronistically to avoid a cumbersome phase like "resident of Jewish Palestine, on the side of what was later to become the Jewish state."

We follow the general consensus of historians, considering the effective dates of the War of Independence to be November 29, 1947, to July 20, 1949. The first of these is the date of the UN decision terminating Great Britain's mandate over Palestine, and providing for the emergence of independent Jewish and Arab states, to come into existence in 1948. Although the original date suggested by the UN for mandate termination was to be the autumn, Britain shortened the transition period, announcing in early December that the mandate would be terminated officially on May 15; since May 15 was a Sabbath, the existence of the State of Israel was promulgated Friday, May 14. Organized, large-scale attacks against Jewish communities and lines of communications commenced immediately following the UN decision of November 29, 1947. July 20, 1949, is the date of the signing of the armistice agreement between Syria and Israel on the island of Rhodes; Syria was the last of the belligerents to sign such an armistice agreement.

Sources: Depth reporting of any kind, from the newspaper backgrounder to the detailed history, rests on two bases: (1) Availability of sources, (2) the writer's ability to sift and weigh his materials. Facile writing is the glossy package which determines readership—but not the *nature* of what is read.

The intertwined problems of sources and sifting are greatly intensified in the Middle East, where conscious and subconscious propaganda, passion and bias continue to suffuse everybody's "facts." And there are no ultimate criteria: Neither appearance in a government archive, nor testimony by a participant, is any guarantee of the whole truth, or even part of it.[3] An excellent example is the Deir Yassin story (our chapter three).

As related in one best-selling history, this was a horrible example of rape, murder and mutilation by Jewish terrorists. Yet, this writer's careful weighing of all available evidence leads to the conclusion that none of these things happened. How can this be?

The horror story rests on a British archival report partially buttressed by the eyewitness report of a high official of the International Red Cross—and disregards all other testimony. On the contrary, we regard this particular archival report as a planted falsehood whose fictional nature would have been so obvious in 1948 that it could only be buried then, anticipating that a later generation of researchers would newly uncover this "truth." After all, the "evidence" was a report of the Civil Information Division of the British Police in Palestine—the bitterest enemies of the Irgun and the Stern groups, the minority undergrounds most directly involved in the taking of Deir Yassin. (A reading of the report indicates that the male CID investigators, purportedly interviewing bashful female survivors several days later, did not even speak Arabic!) While one would not suspect a senior Red Cross representative of a deliberate fabrication out of whole cloth, one would expect a strong antiterrorist and antiviolence bias to color what he saw and how he honestly reported it. The above considerations permitted us to weigh fully *all* of the evidence, and come to our own very different conclusions.

Language is a most important qualification in a reporter of events. Although fluency in the language of the land is hardly an assurance that one will penetrate to the core, a lack of knowledge of the language is a guarantee that one will be treated as an outsider. And an outsider has no way of knowing whether he is being used, toyed with, or treated with candor. To some degree this extends to written sources: English translations of some Hebrew sources differ in significant details from the original.

Almost without exception, the popular American books on Israel are characterized by errors—some trivial, some ludicrous, some rather important—which clearly betray the deficiencies in the author's background. Although I am reasonably fluent in written and spoken Hebrew, I am also illiterate in Arabic. Thus, the reader is forewarned that any presentation of the Arab viewpoint is, at best, second-hand. I make no pretense of Olympian objectivity. Rather, the recognition that subjectivity is never absolutely avoidable, tends to mitigate its effects—both in probing for bedrock facts and in presenting my conclusions as honestly as possible.

Gullibility is also a real problem. Those interviewed will sometimes repeat as first-hand fact that which simply reached their ears as rumor, and which they believed to be true; and sometimes information may be deliberately fabricated for a variety of reasons—including one that can best be labeled as "fun": A number of years ago, a friend who now is rather high up in Israel's educational establishment, confided to me the sad fate of a serious American sociologist. The sociologist was doing a detailed survey among Hebrew University students on their life-styles, with emphasis on sexual mores. By common impulse, a large coterie of the students invented answers much more interesting than their actual, restrained, prosaic patterns. They were vastly amused at the published results which were then accepted in the field at face value.

In general, there seems to be a tacit assumption on the part of writers and readers alike that the direct verbal interview is the best way to arrive at the truth of any and every situation. It is this writer's view that such is not at all the case. To begin with, human recollection is fallible and partial, even when the source is a witness rather than a participant. The likelihood of honest distortion increases with the extent of the source's direct involvement. Even if one's memory is refreshed by notes made at the time, such notes themselves cannot be said to be totally free of bias.

And there is a factor beyond these generalizations: A factor which operates most markedly when the person being interviewed is prominent. This is something that is perhaps best labeled direct deception. The reporter, granted a direct and sometimes lengthy interview by a present or past high official, is convinced that the friendly rapport established guarantees total honesty: A clear commitment to share the truth, the whole truth. In such friendly discourse it is easy to lose sight of the fact that particular individuals may feel a very deep stake in perpetuating a deliberately slanted view of a given event.

This is not to suggest that the verbal interview be discarded as a means of gaining information. It is to underline its limitations and pitfalls. Thus the written interview—the questionnaire—mitigates some of the looseness of the verbal interview; and there are circumstances under which one ought to be aware that interviewing is pointless or embarrassing (or both)—whereas analysis of the hard facts in the totality of a given situation may most effectively lead to startling new conclusions. A case in point is the last battle for Jerusalem in the War of Independence. Using the analysis approach, focusing on the broad parameters of the background of the battle, Chapter Six develops the conclusion that Israel's regular authorities did not really want to retake the old city of Jerusalem under the conditions prevailing in July 1948. But a bestseller, purporting to tell the entire real story by relying largely on depth interviews, is totally unaware of any such possibility. Instead, it came up with such revelations as an alleged Jewish plan to offer sacrificial sheep on the Temple mount. Of course, such a thing never could have taken place. At best, this outlandish notion was the transient thought of a single individual who happened to be Jerusalem's military commander—an individual who was something of an outsider both to Israel's Jewish religious community and to its kibbutz-oriented zionist community. Given enough persistence, the depth interview will produce color—often, artificial color—rather than historic perspective.

In this work, more weight has been given to the written than to the verbal—to pattern and fit, rather than to the unique, startling, romantic story. Thus, in putting together the Deir Yassin story (Chapter Three), there was no point re-interviewing those whom others had exhaustively interviewed—but it was of the highest importance to fully examine everyone's published results and data, in order to extract the most credible conclusions from often contradictory material.

The researcher must be a skeptic. Paradoxically, it is his informed, *subjective* judgment which is the ultimate criterion in writing *objective* history.

How can one successfully penetrate to the *real* truth? Participants distort, eyewitnesses distort, archives distort, researchers and researched books add further distortion (often in the interest of a smooth, or romantic, or exciting narrative). There is even disagreement over totally objective facts, as in the case of the rifles of "Operation Pirate" described in Chapter 12; depending on the source, one may read of 10,000 as the original number of rifles, with 8,500 salvaged; 8,000 rifles; 6,000 rifles. One may determine that certain sources are essentially reliable, yet find blatant errors stated quite serenely.

It is the writer's task to balance depth and breadth. One must probe facts deeply, recognizing that a most important test is fit: Is this part of a coherent whole? Does it make sense in *some* context—even though it may point in a direction different from one's previous conclusions?

Compounding the difficulties of piecing together the hitherto hidden picture of the participation of overseas volunteers were a combination of (1) general benign neglect and (2) a serious lack of reliable records for establishing hard facts. As we shall see, our sources disagree rather widely even in estimating the basic number of overseas volunteers: 1948 was a most unsettled time, and records simply were not kept.

Why should there have been an apparent policy of neglect of the role of overseas volunteers? There are several possible attitudes which may have made for such an approach: (1) All Jews are one people; the vast majority of overseas volunteers were Jewish; thus, to speak of such a separate category as overseas volunteers would be to introduce an element of divisiveness which is undesirable—therefore, we neither write nor think in terms of such a separate category (2) Local pride; an unwillingness to concede the possibility that there may have been genuine dependence on "outsiders." (3) Psychological warfare to support a vitally important "bluff," particularly in 1949 and 1950. There was an interim period when the volunteers had departed and Israelis had not yet fully mastered the complex tools of modern warfare which they were to use so very effectively in 1956 and 1967. During this learning period, Israel was relatively defenseless and it could have been disastrous to acknowledge this situation at that time. (4) The conviction that overseas volunteers could not have mattered and must not have mattered—since, in the future, Israel would have to rely entirely on itself. (5) Recognition that the bulk of the fighting and dying, and the living under prewar and postwar tension, were of course done by the ordinary Israeli—and the feeling that too much acknowledgment of outside assistance would, somehow, demean the truly heroic accomplishments of the Israelis.

Here is some interesting direct evidence of the minimizing of the role of overseas volunteers:

(1) *Gal-'Ade Lagiborim,* put out under the joint imprint of the Jewish National Fund and Jewish Agency in 1959, illustrates and describes every war memorial in Israel[4]—with one exception: The American Veterans Memorial Forest monument, which lists the names of those Americans and Canadians killed in Israel's War of Independence.[5]

This is a striking oversight. Equally striking is the fact that this memorial which marks a Jewish National Fund Forest about halfway between Jerusalem and Tel Aviv, was not and is not on any regular tour of any kind—although one might think that its existence would be of special interest to visiting Americans and Canadians.

(2) In early 1965, a rather high-ranking official, Mr. Israel Amir,[6] traveled in this country in order to make preliminary arrangements for the theme of Israel Independence Day 1965, to be "Mahal." Essentially, this would have meant considerable publicity in Israel on the role of overseas volunteers in the War of Independence; well before Independence Day 1965, this plan was quietly and completely shelved. It is of interest to note that this plan was put into effect after the Six Day War, for Independence Day 1968, with considerable Mahal publicity. Since the Independence Day celebration following the Six Day War for the first time genuinely publicized Mahal, perhaps the basic reason had been a problem of inner security (essentially on the part of the older generation). When one is completely sure of one's self, when one's strength has been tested successfully, then one can afford to be open. Until then there is a

tendency to insist that not only is one totally self-reliant, but that this has always been the case.

What has resulted from our perceptive awareness of special difficulties, our presumably knowledgeable digging, our judicious weighing and balancing of sometimes conflicting information? Do we really have a coherent, accurate, balanced picture of the complex, significant events contributing to the birth and early survival of the State of Israel?

This, each reader must judge for himself.

Prof. Abraham Halkin further corrects the record quoting Shaltiel to the effect that, far from sheep-sacrificing being his idea, he was appalled when the suggestion was made to him. (See page xix).

Part One:

PRELUDE AND WAR

Chapter 1

PRE-NATAL SURVIVAL

Israel's War of Independence was in many respects a peculiar little war. Perhaps this is only fitting for those whom God called (according to one translation) "a peculiar people." Most wars are fought, more or less steadily, for a respectable length of time, generally for a few years; then both sides stop fighting and begin normalizing their relationship. During the war, the advice of outsiders is resented and ignored unless the outsiders themselves become active participants.

Everywhere but in Israel.

In 1967 the war lasted just six days. And the direct peace talks—which, inevitably, were to have followed—were precluded by the intervention of the world's peace-keeping body, the United Nations, which effectively interposed itself between the combatants, making peace talks unnecessary from the viewpoint of the vanquished: A unique situation in world history.

This repeated, in part, the 1956 pattern when Israel's then allies Britain and France got nowhere militarily and Israel was forced to return to Egypt all the buffer territory it had taken in just four days of fighting (the Gaza Strip and all of Sinai to the Suez Canal). This, without any direct negotiations; and the promises of the United Nations and the United States turned out to be even less weighty than the paper on which they were written.

The 1948 war was an on-again off-again thing, fought under the benevolent eyes and rules of the UN, some of whose rules were made up as things progressed. From the first moment of statehood, the war was on for a month, and off for a month; it was on for ten days and then off for several months. There was an autumn campaign, a couple of relatively quiet months, and a winter campaign. Then the hammering out of armistice agreements between some of the combatants—and a drifting from armistice, not to peace, but to cold war. "Cold war," suggesting the kind of relationship that existed between the Soviet Union and the United States, is actually a misnomer: With no diplomatic or trade exchanges whatever, "deep freeze" would be a more accurate term.

3

Thus Israel has been the focus of a strangely supervised situation in which the paternalistic interference of outsiders (nations geographically distant) has been of the greatest importance in failing to promote peace or even in failing to permit peace to develop; in keeping the pot simmering, yet limiting the duration of the inevitable explosions.

In addition to all the other peculiarities, Israel's War of Independence actually was under way for half a year before there even was a state of Israel!

Let us go back to that beginning.

On November 29, 1947, the United Nations voted, by a better than two-thirds majority of the General Assembly, to adopt the majority report of its Special Commission of Inquiry on Palestine (UNSCOP) as the solution to the Palestine problem.

Post-World War I Palestine included not only the territory west of the Jordan River, but the area several times larger to the east of the Jordan. In 1922, the mandatory power, Great Britain, had divided the country to establish the Kingdom of Transjordan as that part of Palestine east of the Jordan River and of the Aravah (the valley connecting the southern end of the Dead Sea with the Gulf of Aqaba (Eilat); the unmarked international border was simply the lowest point in that valley for its entire length. Thus, since 1922, Palestine had been redefined as the area west of the Jordan.

The "Palestine problem" involved the rights and desires of three groups—and attitudes were by no means totally uniform within each group: First, Jews[1]—those already in Palestine, and those desperate to go there, primarily, survivors of the European Holocaust; second, Arabs[1]—among whom were some post-World War I immigrants, attracted by Palestine's relatively outstanding increase in standards of health and living. Undoubtedly, some were pleased with the modern, busy, Western presence represented by the growing Jewish communities; others were neutral and some were resentful; the latter were augmented by nonresidents whose purpose was to foster trouble; and third, Britain—the great power which had been given the mandate to establish a Jewish homeland in Palestine, but whose basic concern was not that unusual task, but rather, the presumed effect of its stewardship of Palestine on its worldwide empire.

Under the circumstances, conflict was inevitable. Jewish pressure was constant to bring in the survivors of the Holocaust who would not stay in the European graveyard, who were not welcomed anywhere else in the world—and who yearned, above all, to go to Palestine—and produced escalating violence against Britain, which resisted this pressure in clear violation of the fundamental terms of its mandate. While many Arabs were happy with the Jewish yishuv (settlement), and many were neutral— the local visible leadership was held by those who opposed it: This opposition was becoming increasingly violent in the absence of governmental restraint.

Britain was in a position which was quite untenable both morally and practically: In making its basic aim the cutting off of Jewish immigration, it found itself putting the pitiful survivors of German extermination camps into British concentration camps; and, in attempting to contain the increasing Jewish pressure, it had to put twice as many British soldiers on the soil of Palestine as there were young male Palestinian Jews of comparable age! Most sources give the ratio of British soldiers to male Jews of military age as roughly one-to-one; a detailed analysis suggests two-to-one as more nearly correct.

The essence of the UN plan, adopted November 29, 1947, was that the British mandate be terminated as soon as possible, with an orderly transfer of government to a Jewish state and an Arab state. Each state was to consist of three segments, linked at mutual crossover points (their borders were determined, roughly, by the existing populations) and Jerusalem and its environs were to be an international zone, under an international trusteeship.

May 15, 1948, was selected as the official date on which British sovereignty would cease, and the Jewish and Arab states would come into existence. (Actually, the British maintained a small military enclave in Haifa through June 30, 1948.)

This was the UN partition plan; it was accepted by the Jews and rejected violently by the Arabs.

Palestine's Arab neighbors had their own areas of conflict with each other. There was one issue on which they agreed: A Jewish state must never arise. Through the Arab League—a paper alliance formed through the inspiration of Great Britain somewhat earlier (March 22, 1945)— these six (originally, five) countries (Saudi Arabia, Iraq, Transjordan, Egypt, Syria, and Lebanon) planned military action to abort the gestating Jewish state. Their negative focus was so strong, that they failed to take any meaningful action to bring into being the intended new Arab state. (See appendix B for detailed discussion of the failure to create a Palestinian Arab state.)

On the one hand, such action might have seemed to imply approval of the partition plan as a whole, and thus, of the forthcoming Jewish state; on the other hand, Palestine's immediate neighbors coveted its territories for themselves, and a new Arab state would have foreclosed this opportunity.

So long as British sovereignty remained officially effective—that is, until May 15, 1948—the armies of the Arab countries would not act in a formal way against the Palestinian Jews. The most blatant exception was the final attack, led by the Arab Legion against the beleaguered Etzion block of kibbutzim south of Jerusalem, May 12-13. The Legion had actually entered this fight briefly on May 4, with a heavy artillery barrage against the Russian monastery; its purpose, then, was to stop Jewish sniping at Arab military traffic on the main Hebron-Jerusalem road. However, it might never become necessary to undertake such naked aggression: By effective use of terror tactics, the Arabs fully expected to make it impossible for a Jewish state to arise.

A great many Arab villages already harbored terrorists—some Palestinian, and some visitors from neighboring countries. They needed little encouragement to kill Jews wherever they might be found, so long as the Jews were unarmed or in small groups. These would be augmented by large numbers of "volunteers" from Arab countries, organized into private armies of irregulars. There were several such battalions operating in various parts of the country; the most prominent of these was the Arab Liberation Army commanded by Fawzi el Kaukji, a native of Lebanese Tripoli who had served in the Ottoman army in World War I and had been active in the disturbances of 1936–1939. These forces were to do their utmost to kill Jews, disrupt communications, and capture settlements. They lost no time in starting: The day after the partition resolution, a bus on the road to Jerusalem was fired on near Lydda Airport, killing three women and two men. In Jerusalem, Haifa, and Jaffa-Tel Aviv, Arabs rioted against Jews. On December 10, a small group patrolling the water pipeline in the Negev was wiped out by the "friendly" Arab village of Shu'ut. The next day a convoy on its way from Jerusalem to reinforce the Etzion block of settlements to the south, was ambushed, and ten were killed. Such instances multiplied—with the British often totally neutral as between armed attacker and unarmed (or underarmed) victim.

In the period preceding the UN partition plan, it was primarily the Jews who fought the British—through the IZL (Irgun Zvai Leumi) and

LHI (Lohamai Herut Israel), whose militancy was opposed by the Jewish Agency except for a period of common approach from late 1945 to mid 1946; the Arabs only attacked the Jews, whom the British did little to defend. It was thus, in effect, illegal for the Jews alone to possess arms. This need for the concealment of arms from the omnipresent British made the Jewish position far more precarious, and it severely limited the quantity of arms that the Jews were able to stockpile. The number of Jews available for "soldiering" on the eve of the war, in Autumn 1947, was far from large. The Haganah core network consisted of 420 men who received salary, plus 9,500 considered "regulars" (ages 18 to 25), and 32,000 considered "home guard" (over age 25, and women with special duties, such as first aid). Residents of the agricultural settlements were included in the home guard; each settlement was to be a strongpoint, primarily responsible for its own defense. There were close to 1,800 members of the Jewish Settlement Police (who were to suffer heavy losses in convoy escort work). The Palmach numbered 2,100 active and 1,000 reservists (including some women). The IZL membership is estimated as 2,000 to 3,000 total (including some not available for front line duty); LHI membership is estimated as perhaps 300. (One source gives IZL and LHI memberships as 5,000 and 1,000 respectively in early 1948; this appears to be an exaggeration.) Some 27,000 men had some level of military training in World War Two (far fewer had actual combat experience): Not all were included in the above figures.

With these limited numbers generally hampered by the ever-present British, those Arabs bent on destruction were relatively free to do as they chose; any deterrent would have to come from the Jewish underground. (For brief sketches of the various underground organizations, see the Glossary, Appendix A, for Haganah, Irgun Zvai Leumi (IZL), Lohamei Herut Israel (LHI), and Palmach.)

The most effective means of controlling an amoral population is to demonstrate that crime truly does not pay—that hard punishment is meted out to the criminal and his associates—while the truly innocent are unharmed. Under even moderately unstable circumstances, this method is quite effective in maintaining a reasonable level of order and stability, although it requires excellent intelligence and great personal risk.

However, following the November 29, 1947, UN partition decision, the large influx of Arab nationalist terrorists, combined with the hospitality broadly made available to them by Palestine's Arab residents, and the rapidly increasing rate of murders (often accompanied by British neutrality which, under the circumstances, was equivalent to encouragement), shortly led to such a breakdown of normal order that this kind of policing could no longer be effective, nor could it be implemented. The success of the Night Squads against the Arab attackers in the late thirties,[2] could not now be duplicated. As the number of murders escalated, guilt became more widespread, and selecting the individual guilty thus became more difficult and many times more hazardous. A Palmach error in blowing up Jerusalem's Semiramis Hotel in the course of retaliating for Arab acts of indiscriminate terror, was to poison relations with the government of Spain for years. (The *New York Times* account of January 5, 1948, lists Spanish Acting Consul M. A. Salazar Travesdo among the dead. A sense of initial outrage by Spain is understandable; however, its ongoing refusal to extend full diplomatic recognition to Israel reduces Spain's first reaction to the regrettable tragedy to a convenient excuse.)

Yet, to prevent total chaos, retaliation was a cardinal necessity. Thus, in mid-January 1948, after a relief platoon of thirty-five men for the Etzion block of kibbutzim south of Jerusalem was totally wiped out, the policy was officially revised: Henceforth, counterattacks would be carried out in terms of geographic guilt, punishing at least an equivalent number of people in the area from which attacks originated. This policy of *general* retaliation had been instituted first by the IZL some ten years earlier; at that time, under more settled conditions, it was rejected by the majority of the Jews of Palestine. Israel was now most unhappy with the harsh necessity for such a policy and as soon as reduction in the scale of hostilities permitted, later in 1948, there was a resumption of the policy of swift punishment carefully applied only to the guilty individuals and their immediate associates. Obviously, this could be applied only within Israel's borders. In the postwar years, when acts of terror originated outside Israel's borders, geographic retaliation was the only possible recourse; but it was carefully directed against soldiers (regular or irregular), with considerable care exercised, sometimes at great cost, to minimize harm to true civilians. Still, for the five months preceeding May 1948, indications are that more than twice as many Arabs as Jews were killed. This reflects a continuation of what had been an ongoing phenomenon during the normal years of the Mandate: Arab extermists taking advantage of unsettled periods to settle personal grievances and to wipe out potentially moderate leadership. (The years following the Six Day War, June 1967, saw an increasing use of the Israel air force for such retaliation, with the unavoidable result of some level of civilian casualties.)

Nevertheless, the situation deteriorated steadily. With the British generally acting as onesided umpires (there were some exceptions), the Jewish difficulties were enormous.

The course chosen by the British does not appear to have been innocently motivated: January 21, 1948, Sir Alexander Cadogan advised United Nations Special Committee on Palestine that it was "not possible" for Britain to comply with its recommendation that a major seaport be opened to facilitate Jewish immigration. On the contrary, the blockade of the coast against Jewish immigration would continue to be fully maintained. But no firm attempt was made to deter the "irregular" Arab forces from coming in to the country from the north, south, and east. Thus, General Ismail Sarwat Pasha, former chief of staff of the Iraqi army and officer commanding the entire Arab Liberation Army from its general headquarters in Damacus, was able to report that he had 8,000 men available in the North, West and South Palestine Command areas, plus an Egyptian unit at the Gaza airfield (which was under RAF jurisdiction), and an unspecified number of "bedouins, toughs, and mercenaries" in the East Palestine Command, with headquarters in Jerusalem, adjacent to the British High Command.

As the weeks passed, attacks by the Arabs increased in frequency and ubiquity, and Jewish counterattacks followed whenever possible. This fighting was essentially local; no attempt was made to coordinate attacks in one locale with those in another. The isolation of the kibbutzim in the Negev (an area whose name means, literally, "dry"; the Negev is the hot, dry, southern part of the country), of outpost settlements elsewhere, and of Jerusalem itself, proceeded from threat to fact; life in the cities with major mixed populations became increasingly hazardous, with ethnic polarization unavoidable, as was travel between Jewish settlements even in supposedly Jewish areas. March 28, 1948, was probably the blackest day in this increasingly black period: Jerusalem had already been isolated from the coast, and the Old City from the New. A substantial part of the sparse military strength in Jewish Jerusalem had been sent to escort a supply convoy to the isolated Etzion block of kibbutzim; on its way back to Jerusalem, it was stopped at Nebi Daniel by overwhelming Arab strength. A British armistice permitted the men to return to Jerusalem, but all their arms and their armored cars were turned over to the Arabs via the British. On that same day, a convoy attempting to reinforce Kibbutz Yehiam in the Galilee was destroyed, and forty-two of its personnel were killed. Even western Galilee was cut off from the coast. To attempt to travel from one town or village to another, or from a city to its own suburbs, was, quite literally, a risk to one's life.

Jewish Palestine was no longer a viable community six weeks before the Jewish state was officially to come into being.

Although, thus far, not a single Jewish settlement had fallen before the sometimes massive attacks of the Arab irregulars, local defense and local retaliation were quite inadequate to check the increasing isolation and fragmentation of the Jewish areas. Unless something positive were done, and done quickly, a Jewish state could not possibly come into being in mid-May. In order to reduce fearful destruction, it would be necessary to forego independence, and seek shelter under some form of UN trusteeship.

Action was essential and the Haganah High Command decided to seize the initiative in a major operation—to be named "Operation Nahshon"—to open the road to Jerusalem. This would involve seizing and holding all the Arab villages flanking the road to safeguard the passage of convoys. A force of 1,500 men (three times the number involved in any previous action) was to be assembled secretly, temporarily stripping other areas of needed protection. There was no alternative.

Chapter 2

NAHSHON, YEKUM PURKAN, BALAK: CODE NAMES

To the average non-Jew, "Nahshon" is simply a somewhat odd Hebrew word. A philologist might connect it with "nahash," serpent (the word also suggests overtures of subtlety and divination). But to the knowledgable Jew, it could not fail to evoke the memory of a felicitously appropriate midrashic[1] story:

Nahshon ben Aminadav, according to a hoary rabbinic tale, was directly responsible for the parting of the Red Sea immediately following the Exodus from Egypt. The Children of Israel were threatened with destruction by the Egyptians behind them, and with drowning in the deep waters ahead of them. As Nahshon entered the water, nothing happened; he went further, and nothing happened, not even when the water was at his throat. When the water was at his nostrils and he took the next step—which surely would have meant his drowning if the waters did not part—then, and only then, did the waters part.

It looked as though survival itself depended on Operation Nahshon. If it failed, not only might beseiged Jerusalem well fall, but even the coastal areas, stripped for this operation, might be doomed. If Nahshon succeeded, there was a desperately hard road ahead—but eventual success was a possibility.

Thus, to one who knew the Midrash, "Nahshon" was *the* incomparably appropriate designation for this terribly crucial operation—it was a code name that combined security with a wry touch of humor.

And then there are the Aramaic words, *Yekum purkan*; Aramaic is a language older than Hebrew. It originated in the Fertile Crescent area which once was designated Babylonia and today is called Iraq. Although Aramaic at one time was the lingua franca of the ancient world (it was, for example, the vernacular in Palestine at the time of Jesus), it is preserved today primarily because of its widespread use in the Talmud and, as a result, in a few prayers in the traditional Jewish prayer book.

Relatively late in the Sabbath morning service, there is included an ancient Aramaic prayer which asks Divine blessings for scholars and teachers. This prayer opens with the words *"Yekum purkan."* What con-

11

ceivable reason can there be for applying this label to the airlift of arms and planes from Czechoslovakia?

It happens that the next two words are *min shemaya* "from the sky." Thus, the literal translation of the first four words is, "May aid come from the sky"—in its original context, simply an invocation of Divine aid for deserving scholars and teachers. In the context of 1948, it becomes an evocation of tangible skyborne aid. What is more, only the first two words (*Yekum purkan*), which make no reference whatever to the sky, are used. Thus, the reference subtly conveys a great deal to knowledgeable Jews—and to outsiders, it conveys nothing.

Furthermore, each flight on the Czech airlift was designated "Balak" (Balak 1, Balak 2, etc.). Why? Because of the paternity of a rather obscure Biblical figure!

Towards the end of the Book of Numbers, several chapters tell of the enigmatic non-Jewish seer Balaam who was hired to curse the Israelites, but found himself constrained to bless them instead. (Among schoolchildren, he is probably most widely remembered for his difficulty in controlling his own donkey). Balaam's employer was Balak, King of Moab, who, 3000 years ago, was fearful of the approaching Israelites. Numbers 22:2 speaks of "Balak the son of Zippor"—and Zippor is the Hebrew word for "bird." Again, a subtle and appropriate designation to those who know their Bible—and a meaningless word to those who do not.

A further fun example: Israel desperately needed fighter aircraft. As we shall see, in a compounding of ironies American dollars were used to buy such aircraft from Czechoslovakia, with Soviet permission, when the East/West cold war was its most bitter—and the aircraft themselves were German Messerschmitts! Messages between Czechoslovakia and Israel (and pre-Israel) referred to these planes as *sakinim*. "Sakinim" is the innocent Hebrew word for "knives." What is the connection? In German (and in Yiddish), the word *messer* (the first half of "Messerschmitt") means "knife"!

It would be unreasonable to expect these delightful standards to prevail in the naming of all operations. Thus, although "Ten Plagues" was very apt as a description of the autumn campaign against the Egyptians, from the security point of view, it was much too obvious. And "Operation Pirate" was a colorful description of a major success at sea, but from the perspective of hindsight, it is unnecessarily pejorative. (What was involved was a legitimate act of war against an enemy arms vessel, not an act of piracy.) And, in some instances, operations were simply named for individuals—for example, Operation Danni, after Danni Maas, the leader of "The 35," killed with his entire platoon in a vain attempt to relieve the Etzion group of kibbutzim south of Jerusalem in mid-January 1948.

We now return to the sequence of events.

About April 5,[2] Operation Nahshon was launched: It lasted until April 15. As noted above, its objective was to clear the Arab villages on both sides of the highway to Jerusalem, thus lifting the siege of Jerusalem. Although the lifting of the siege was to be only temporary, the operation was most important. Not only did it provide experience in the problems of moving and coordinating men (and some women) on a relatively large scale, but it marked the vitally important shift from defensive to offensive operations. It also included the incident at Deir Yassin.

Briefly, Deir Yassin was an Arab village on the outskirts of Jerusalem, the capture of which was assigned to IZL and LHI. The village was attacked and taken April 9, with significant Arab civilian casualties.

The Jewish Agency radio (the official voice of the Jewish community) promptly and most publicly condemned the "dissident" groups for their "wanton slaughter of Arab civilians." This, in turn, was seized on, enlarged, and widely publicized by the Arabs as proof positive that all the Jews were butchers—with the totally unexpected result that, from then on, Arabs in populated areas fled like rabbits whenever the tide of battle appeared to shift in favor of the Jews. This was undoubtedly a most potent factor in the virtually total exodus of the Arab populations of the cities and from scores of villages, in the immediate aftermath of fighting—fighting which took place in the succeeding few weeks.

This unanticipated exodus of hundreds of thousands of potentially hostile Arabs from within what were to become Israel's borders, made entirely manageable what otherwise might well have become an internal security problem of monumental proportions. It will be recalled that Palestine's entire Jewish population in 1948 was approximately 600,000; 600,000 is also a bit higher than the best estimate of the number of Arabs displaced from Israel by the war, and a bit lower than what would otherwise have been its post-war Arab population. (It is also the approximate number of Jewish refugees displaced from Arab countries as a result of the hostility engendered by the war, and brought to Israel to live soon thereafter.)

The writer is indebted to Professor Nadav Safran for the suggestion that the first truce (beginning just before mid-June 1948) probably marked a shift in the approach of the Israeli leadership towards encouraging the

Arabs to stay. Before then, the general attitude favored their remaining, both in terms of ideological attitude and with the defensive thought that if the Arab armies did break through, a mixed Arab/Jewish population would be less susceptible to general slaughter than an isolated, clearly identifiable, Jewish population. With the first truce and the opportunity to digest what had happened, it was realized how greatly the internal security of Haifa, Tel Aviv, Safed, Tiberias, and much of the countryside had improved because so many Arabs had fled.

And it was simultaneously recognized that the Arab armies had lost their best opportunity to break through to Israel's populated centers, and were far less likely to do so in the future.

As this realization was internalized, local commanders on their own initiative (without needing anything as crass as a central headquarters directive) may well have felt it prudent to encourage local Arabs to leave, as later fighting engulfed new areas.

Broadly speaking, then, the attitude of the Jews to the Arabs' fleeing, ranged from reluctance to relief. Haifa represents one extreme: There, both directly and through the British, the Jewish community urged the Arabs to remain; almost all fled anyway. In some localities—particularly where there was a history of overt Arab hostility—there can be little doubt that the local Jewish population encouraged local Arabs to leave in the aftermath of the direct fighting. And in the prefighting, maneuvering naturally led to some localized shifting. As a general pattern, however, reluctance changed to relief as the calendar moved from spring to summer and beyond. As a broad estimate, we would suggest that not less than two-thirds of those later to be labeled "Arab refugees" left essentially of their own volition; and possibly as few as 100,000 left because of serious prodding by Israel. Certainly, ultimate responsibility for the very coming into being of Arab refugees, lies with the Arabs: If, instead of going to war to prevent the UN-sponsored Jewish state from coming into being under any condition, they had peacefully accepted the UN's decision to recognize a jointly interlinked new Jewish state and new Arab state in Palestine, there would have been no war—and no refugees.

But the initial thrust of the Arab exodus, and what, in all likelihood, was numerically the greatest portion, took place before the first truce, in the immediate aftermath of the taking of the village of Deir Yassin. Some feel that the specter of Deir Yassin did not reach some rural Arab villages. In this view, their evacuation in the wake of battle is simply ascribed to local native factors; it is by no means unusual for civilian village populations to flee as battle approaches.

What is beyond dispute is that Kastel (named for a ruined castle on its crest), the bitterly contested Arab strongpoint controlling the Jerusalem road several kilometers west of Deir Yassin, was abandoned by the Arabs the day following the Deir Yassin battle; and, thereafter, Operation Nahshon—temporarily reopening the Jerusalem road by clearing and/or controlling the adjacent Arab villages—went quite well. It is also true that Abd el Kader, dynamic leader of the Arab irregulars in the Jerusalem area, was killed at Kastel in the fighting immediately preceding, and many credit this loss of field leadership, rather than the image of Deir Yassin, with the Israeli local field successes which followed; others may find no connection, simply crediting the normal prowess of the Palmach.

However, the very fact that the April–May exodus of such numbers of Arabs was quite unanticipated by both Jews and Arabs, is compelling evidence that the image of Deir Yassin did create the psychological phenomenon best described by the word "panic." Virtually the entire Arab populations of cities, towns, and villages fled for their lives as the tide of local battle appeared to favor the Jews, somehow certain that if they remained they would be slaughtered as were the residents of Deir Yassin.

The *reality* of Deir Yassin was something totally different.

Chapter 3

DEIR YASSIN: THE MASSACRE THAT NEVER WAS

Operation Nahshon was a Haganah operation, largely involving Palmach personnel. With rare exceptions, Jewish defense until the final phases of British withdrawal had to be kept underground. The most obvious reason for this is that some Jews declared war on the British viewing them as the immediate enemy, since it was they who used their military might to prevent the survivors of Hitler's crematoria from entering Palestine. Actually, it was the two smaller underground groups, IZL and LHI, which had most consistently and forcefully taken this position. (See the Glossary in Appendix A for brief descriptions of these organizations.)

Following half a year of cooperation, mid-1946 saw a definite break between Haganah on the one hand and IZL/LHI on the other. From then on, public denunciations of the others as "dissidents" and "terrorists" were frequent and bitter. Such denunciations were made by the Haganah, by Jewish Palestine's quasi-governmental arm, the Jewish Agency, and by Establishment sources elsewhere in the Western world—as well as by those opposed to Zionism in any form.

Ideological differences are often far more severe between public relations people than between those directly involved in physical action. Enemy soldiers who have been engaged directly in trying to kill each other, generally fraternize quite unself-consciously once the shooting is permitted to stop—whereas their political mentors back home retain a level of violent hostility that takes a long time to mitigate.

Thus, IZL and LHI, with limited forces in Jerusalem, wanted to come aboveground, and participate in Operation Nahshon, turning their attention away from the British who clearly were committed to leave Palestine by a date certain. They called on Colonel David Shaltiel, who was then Haganah commander in Jerusalem,[1] urging that they be permitted to clear Deir Yassin. While there had been no hostile acts recently against Jews directly from the village, it did have a past history of hostility, and in the current reality even friendly Arab villages were generally unable to prevent their being taken over and used as bases by hostile Arab "irregular" forces. Although he did not mask his personal disdain for

16

IZL and LHI, Shaltiel approved their proposed taking of Deir Yassin, and confirmed this in writing. In any event, the clearing of such a village was consistent both with general Haganah policy and with the ongoing Operation Nahshon.

Thus, quite early Friday morning April 9, 1948, a force of perhaps 120 IZL and LHI personnel moved to clear the village. The approach was planned to take place from more than one direction, with the west left clear to encourage villagers to flee in that direction. Furthermore, an armored car with a loudspeaker was to enter first, warning all villagers to leave at once. Thus, there was reason to hope that the village might be emptied with little or no bloodshed—as was to be the case, for example, with the villages cleared by the Haganah between Kibbutz Hatsor in the south and what was to become the Egyptian army's advance point at Isdud (Ashdod). However, the armored car went into a ditch from which it could not be extricated on the outskirts of the village. And there was very heavy defensive firing from the village itself.

The heavy firing—most uncharacteristic of a peaceful village—probably came from a company of Iraqi irregulars who had apparently stationed themselves in the village. One of those making this suggestion was Glubb Pasha (Sir John Bagot Glubb), the Englishman who commanded Transjordan's Arab Legion in its invasion of Israel. It is also possible that some of the villagers themselves were responsible for part of the shooting, although it is not unlikely that many of the men had already left for their day's work.

Since the village was defended house by house, the attackers decided to take it house by house, using grenades or similar explosives thrown into whichever room the firing seemed to be coming from. This technique generally kills everybody in the room. Although, (perhaps, because) the fighting went slowly, no one in the village thought of surrendering. Towards the end of the fighting, with the house of the mukhtar (village chief) still holding out, a Palmach unit with 2-inch mortars volunteered its welcome assistance to the attackers.

By early afternoon, the fighting was over with most of the village's inhabitants having fled. About 120 survivors—mostly women and children —who had been trapped by the fighting were taken by IZL through Jewish Jerusalem, where they were passed through the Arab lines to East Jerusalem.

The initial population of the village was probably close to 1,000. It is likely that not more than 200 were killed, of whom about 110 were villagers, and the balance the irregulars who had defended the village. All were killed in the course of the fighting for the village.

It is a tragedy when any civilian women or children or, for that matter, men, are killed in battle. The tragedy is not diminished by the realization that in the heat of battle all moving figures tend to be shot at—whether they are civilian or military, men or women—and that when high explosives take out a room, they do not discriminate between innocent children and fighting adults.

But this is a commentary on the nature of warfare: It is a far cry indeed from cold-blooded massacre—the deliberate shooting of women and children after the shooting has stopped and the village has surrendered.

The above are the facts, as sharply and honestly as it is possible to determine them by studying and reconciling all the written sources, including the results of many interviews with participants on both sides.[2]

As for the atrocity allegations themselves, a number of the Arab survivors of the Deir Yassin battle interviewed from a perspective of twenty years, could not turn up a single claim that there was any post-battle killing of women and children. Their only "atrocity" testimony had to do with a claim that some of the killing during the battle was cold-blooded and unnecessary, and that some ten men were deliberately shot in the battle's immediate aftermath. If verifiable, either would be an unfortunate but not a unique battle occurrence for which the guilty merit severe punishment. But both are unverified: The first is vague by its nature; what participant can truly, objectively draw the line between "necessary" and "unnecessary" in the midst of battle? And the second—which is absolutely denied by all the participating Israelis[3]—involves neither women nor children. Both appear to be a pathetic attempt to salvage some semblance of "atrocity" from the Deir Yassin legend. In semi-underground pre-Israel, one ought to have expected a range of behavior essentially like that of normal armed forces everywhere, not excluding the possibility of occasional excess. But even those who continue to feel that there was some level of excess at Deir Yassin do not view it as any kind of unique horror, but rather the normal kind of horror associated with warfare in the world at large.

The one bit of written testimony to which this writer has not had direct access, is the private diary of Jacques de Reynier, representative of the International Red Cross in Jerusalem in 1948. However, its contents are reported on by both Kurzman, and Collins and Lapierre.[4] In *O Jerusalem* Collins and Lapierre claim that de Reynier entered Deir

Yassin in the immediate aftermath of the fighting; Kurzman—who, in general, is far more reliable—gives the time of the visit as the following morning. This diary apparently does report gratuitous violence—but certainly no rape. (For a direct refutation of the allegation of rape, see pp. xvii-xviii in the Introduction.)

It is possible, of course, that de Reynier was an absolutely neutral observer reporting with the accuracy and dispassion of a camera; however, it is also possible ("likely" would probably be more accurate) that the resident representative of the Red Cross—not unlike the British—was conditioned to view the Jewish "terrorists" with particular loathing, and that this is reflected in how he saw what there was to see and in how he reported it. When the Irgun left the village (it was taken over by the Haganah on the following day) it left numerous bodies outside. Some saw this as "proof" of postbattle executions. This writer is persuaded rather that there is a simple, more logical explanation: The bodies had been dragged outdoors preparatory to burial.

Perhaps the sharpest brief summation of Deir Yassin may be found in the words of Yunes Ahmad Assad, described as a prominent inhabitant of Deir Yassin who survived the battle:

> The Jews never intended to hurt the population of the village, but were forced to do so after they met enemy fire from the population which killed the Irgun commander.[5] [The Irgun commander was seen to fall—but his wound was actually not fatal.]

This is worlds removed from the reflex picture triggered by "Deir Yassin" of heavily armed gunmen entering a defenseless village and cold-bloodedly slaughtering almost every man, woman and child encountered. This kind of murder was more characteristically practiced periodically by the Arabs against the Jews. (In 1929, for example, the undefended Jewish community of Hebron was wiped out and the few survivors fled permanently, so that Hebron—one of Judaism's four holy cities, the city in which the Patriarchs were buried—was totally without Jews probably for the first time in more than 3,000 years. Jews did not return for close to forty years, resettling only in the wake of 1967's Six Day War. At the same time, there were further murderous attacks by Arabs on Jews in Jerusalem, Ramat Rahel, Moza, Hulda, Tel Aviv, Mishmar Ha'emek, Haifa, Beit She'an, Pekiin, and Safed.) Deir Yassin was war, not murder. This is not to deny that all killing is tragic. Yet, the legally, socially, and morally authorized fighting by soldiers against soldiers is vastly different from the wanton killing of an innocent woman or child by an armed marauder. That the taking of Deir Yassin, and of countless thousands of other localities throughout the world, resulted in the death of civilian men, women, and children, greatly heightens the tragedy (to the extent that the civilians were truly innocent bystanders). This is the unfortunate reality of a world that has not yet discovered how to live in peace.

It is a matter of interest as well to point out that the world has experienced "Jewish terrorists" far more negatively than any other kind. For example, the smaller of the above Jewish underground groups called itself Lohamei Herut Israel (LHI) which, in English, is "Fighters for the Freedom of Israel"; yet, from its inception a third of a century ago and throughout its existence even to the present day, the normative journalistic reference to this group is "Stern Gang." This contemptuous label is virtually universal—although their attacks were on particular enemy individuals and male soldiers in uniform. By way of contrast, the Arab outlaws whose general targets are civilians—women and children no less than men—are universally referred to by whatever official names they give themselves. For example, no one speaks of the Arab "Habash Gang"; everyone respectfully refers to PFLP ("Popular Front for the Liberation of Palestine"). Obviously, this is the result of no conspiracy; it is simply a natural, instinctive development in the world at large.

Is it not in the subtle, small things that true attitudes are most tellingly revealed?

But—if there was truly no atrocity at Deir Yassin, why the immediate official cry of "massacre" by the Jewish Agency? Why did David Ben Gurion send a wire of apology to King Abdullah of Transjordan? Further, since these are the acts which gave the massacre charge credibility in the first place—why has Israel failed forcefully to correct the public record?

The answer to this makes a fascinating study in the dynamics of intracommunal and intercommunal public relations. The mistrust and animosity that existed between the politically "right" IZL/LHI and the politically "left" Haganah/Palmach/Jewish Agency were rather deep rooted. To the normal framework of responding to ideology and politics with a European intensity, was added a fundamental difference in approach to the British. The Jewish Agency had faith that British democracy *must* lead to the triumph of morality; that the misguided Colonial Office would inevitably be corrected; and that Britain would properly carry out its obligations to the Jewish National Home. (It is interesting to note that this view had also been held by the rightist leader, Vladimir Jabotinski, who died in 1940). In this view, a Jewish "war" against Britain (in which IZL had joined LHI since 1944) could not be won: It made use of wanton terror that would necessarily result in British counteraction to weaken the Jews against the truly dangerous enemy they might soon have to face: the Arabs.

Perhaps it was the different assessment of British reaction and British power that was truly crucial—since a half year of Haganah/IZL cooperation had come to an abrupt end after the suddden imprisonment of the leadership of the Jewish Agency, Haganah, and Palmach in mid-1946. On this same "Black Sabbath" (June 29) during which almost the entire Jewish civil and military leadership was seized, the British also uncovered the Haganah's well-hidden major arms cache at Kibbutz Yagur. The message conveyed by this action apparently was "we can break you if we so choose; if you continue to cooperate with the IZL "revolt," we will surely do so." This, in turn, was followed by the round-up and de-portation of much of the IZL leadership, coupled with a continuing anti-"terror" propaganda campaign by the Jewish Agency.

We do not know whether in this instance Agency or Haganah people informed on the IZL, or whether British intelligence was very good or very lucky. Distasteful as the thought is, such informing had taken place in earlier years. One extremely reliable source gives details of each of the undergrounds informing on either or both of the others, and some-times taking direct action as well. Such acts occurred intermittently, beginning at least as early as 1941. The most public of these was 'The Season,' when Haganah acted against IZL from October 1944 to mid-1945.[6] We do know that many IZL people believed that such informing took place in the summer of 1946 and, also, that a significant portion of the populace was sympathetic to the IZL; on the other hand, many non-IZL people believed that the "terrorists" were murderers who were destroying the moral and physical foundations of the Jewish community.

Thus, there was *readiness* by sóme to see all action by IZL/LHI as murderous and, if informing, as a matter of policy, had indeed taken place, there would have been a *need* to see all IZL/LHI acts as vicious. And people tend to see as fact, that which they have prepared themselves to see. Particularly, if there is some level of doubt as to the rightness of a distasteful position to which one is committed, is there a need to view specific acts as proof of the villainy of the others—regardless of the ob-jective reality. Thus, the Jewish Agency publicists were thoroughly preconditioned to see the first IZL/LHI-Arab battle as a massacre, "proving" that these people were indeed wanton terrorists. And so, when Ramallah (Arab) radio quoted a hysterical report of the wanton slaughter of hundreds of civilians—the kind of report that normally would have been ignored as enemy propaganda—the Jewish Agency radio gave the report credibility by denouncing the "dissident terrorists" for the "massacre," and apologizing in the name of the Jewish community.

"Jewish conscience" may also have been a factor in this reaction. Jewish tradition has always been very much concerned with the sanctity of human life, and Nazi Germany's genocidal thrust, focusing largely on Jews, was a very recent and searing experience. In reaction to that degradation of human life, the deep concern for all human beings with whom Jews had dealings would naturally be reinforced. This surely strengthened the anti-"terrorist" propaganda of the preceding period, and multiplied its effectiveness.

The mainstream Zionist posture was thus one of sanitary righteousness—a position from which it was natural to denounce the "dirty terrorists" within the Jewish family. Further, there was the Zionist ideological overlay which had been stressing for decades that Jewish settlement in Palestine was of great benefit to the resident Arab population. Thus, there were added factors that paved the way for a readiness to condemn the terrorists—particularly and paradoxically at the point at which they did the right thing: open cooperation with Haganah in opening the road to Jerusalem.

Those who seek evidence of the finger of God may find a bit of added fuel here: Because of an attitude whose origin was partly admirable and partly not, the Jewish establishment authenticated an absurd Arab claim with the result that Israeli successes in the field may have been made somewhat easier, and that a Jewish state with a Jewish majority was made possible: After all, if no Arabs had left in 1948, Israel's eventual armistice borders (assuming they would have been achieved just the same, with a quiescent Arab population) would have held fully as many Arabs as Jews. By its very nature, Israel could not then have been the Jewish state since, by visceral definition, the Jewish state must be based on a population with a Jewish majority.

As pointed out by the official history of the Army of Israel, in retrospect, the Arabs themselves recognized that their publicity about "Jewish cruelty," based on the alleged "slaughter of Deir Yassin," worked against Arab interests since it encouraged Arabs in great numbers to flee from all parts of the country.[7] Yet, in the Deir Yassin story, Israel had a tiger by the tail. While in the short run, the innocent, self-righteous denunciation of something that never actually happened redounded to Israel's physical benefit—a monster had been created.

Israel's public-relations people faced a dilemma which appears to have proceeded somewhat as follows:

"The truth ought to be told; but if we say that we were wrong—that there was no massacre at Deir Yassin—don't we put in question for all time, the absolute credibility of the State of Israel? Furthermore, the truth never fully overtakes a publicized lie. Is it not likely that we would not be fully believed anyway—that it would be taken by world public opinion not as an exoneration of the participants, but rather as an extension of our responsibility for whatever they will continue to believe actually did happen? And, after all, the alleged act was perpetrated by "them"—those "dissidents and terrorists"—not by "us": We proved our innocence by condemning them then; we continue to do so by condemning them today. The most sensible, most politic course is to continue telling this story along its original line."

Making this more complex, was the psychological difficulty many of those in the Jewish Agency establishment—which later essentially became the government of Israel[8]—must have had in coming to terms with the evidence that they were wrong as regards the internal "enemy" (IZL/LHI) to whom they had reacted so harshly.

It remained for the succeeding generation, free of the experiences and the bitter, warped outlook of their fathers, to be able broadly to apply one of the dicta of the Talmud: "These and these are the words of the living God." In this context, that is to say that deeply different approaches can be necessary supplementary aspects of the same vital enterprises; one should respect the hard things that are done by those whose approach may be somewhat different. Above all, one has the duty to look beyond vested interests for the simple truth insofar as it can be ascertained factually.

Thus the advice given the writer by Israel's Foreign Office in 1968 was strikingly free of the carried-forward passions and partisanship of 1948; it was most simple and straighforward:

"The IZL carried out the operation, and it therefore appears to us that the most desirable procedure is for you to obtain facts and details from one of the heads of IZL...."[9]

Although this is the approach of Israel's younger generation—that is, those under 45 or 50 ("middle age" in Israeli national leadership, seems to be about 70)—it has thus far failed to make its mark in the English-speaking world with reference to Deir Yassin. Israelis generally tend to be direct and pragmatic; the feeling seems to be that what others misconstrue or misunderstand—particularly with regard to something in the relatively dim past—is their own concern: There are more immediate problems which require one's current energy. Thus, even those Israelis who do recognize that public opinion does have some level of importance, tend to focus on current events—not on what happened three wars ago. There is failure to recognize that a visceral American abhorrence of "unfair" violence is an inseparable component of acceptance—even applause—of "fair" violence. American consciousness of what it continues to view as the "Massacre of Deir Yassin" remains just below the surface, ready to color a lurid portrait of the savage Israeli as justification for turning away from Israel, should it become politic to do so. For the nice distinction between "considerate" Haganah and "dissident, terrorist" Irgun, on which the Establishment tendered so much effort, has simply evaporated with the passage of time. What remains in the public mind is the simple impression that whatever happened at Deir Yassin was done by the Jews as part of their fight to establish a Jewish State.

The time is, indeed, long past publicly to set the record straight: A critical study of everything in print forces the conclusion that there was no massacre and no semblance of a massacre at Deir Yassin. What happened there was the normal tragedy of a village that becomes a battleground—neither more nor less.

Operation Nahshon succeeded temporarily. By mid-April, the Jerusalem road was cleared and vital truck convoys made their way to the city. What they brought was most important in sustaining the city through May and June when it was again cut off, for there was not enough Jewish strength to hold indefinitely all the strong points necessary to protect all of the road.

Still, the corner had been turned. In the following weeks, sharp fighting between Jews and Arabs in the mixed cities (Safed, Tiberias, Haifa, Jaffa) invariably led to the wholesale flight of the Arab population, pursued by the specter of the well-publicized "Deir Yassin." Many Arab villages similarly were emptied.

And so, by mid-May, when the neighboring Arab armies officially struck with artillery, tanks, and planes, a semiviable Israel had been stitched together. To the optimists, there appeared to be a chance for survival.[10]

Chapter 4

HOLDING AND TURNABOUT

Nahshon marked the beginning of the second level of Arab failure. The first had been the failure of Arab gangs and paramilitary forces to overrun relatively small, relatively poorly armed agricultural settlements. Like any cutthroats looking for easy prey, these assailants were lacking in steadiness. Before determined defense or determined counterattacks, they broke off the engagement, hoping to do better another day.

The second level, attempted strangulation. Where frontal attack proved too costly, there was another tactic. By keeping the isolated settlements isolated with little possibility of replacing losses in people, food, and arms, the Arabs believed that, sooner or later, they would have to fall. Further, by isolating contiguous groups of settlements from each other, destroying communication between the cities, and making life difficult within them and weakening them by continual sniping, they would be able to destroy their Jewish populations. Above all, their policy was to isolate, besiege, and wipe out Jewish Jerusalem. This level has been called broadly the "battle of the roads"—and Nahshon marked the beginning of Arab failure in the battle of roads.

On May 15, the nature of the war would change alarmingly. Then, invasion by the regular armies of the Arab League states was expected, and the enemy was no longer to be only a well-armed rabble, but would be supplemented by a relatively large number of trained men with a totally new level of modern equipment: artillery, tanks, and war planes. In order for even an outside chance of survival against such an attack, not only was comparable equipment needed, but, most fundamentally, internal security would have to be established: The cities would have to become safe, and the roads passable. And the time was very short.

While Operation Nahshon was underway in the Jerusalem corridor, important events were taking place further north. From southern Galilee, Kaukji's Palestine Liberation Army struck towards Haifa by way of the Valley of Jezrael. A short distance beyond the ancient military keystone of Megiddo, stood Kibbutz Mishmar Ha'emek ("Guardian of the Valley"). From April 4 to the middle of the month a crucial battle developed here—

a battle which saw the "Liberation Army" fought to a standstill and, eventually, withdrawn. Just as Nahshon led to Deir Yassin, with most important results, the battle of Mishmar Ha'emek led to most important results with respect to the Druze.

The Druze are an Arab people with a warrior tradition. Geographically, their main base is the Jebel Druze (Mountain of the Druze), in western Syria. Many Druze live in villages in the Golan Heights, in what until June, 1967, was southwestern Syria; and a few live in villages in Galilee. By religion, they are not Moslems; they are monotheists, with certain Jewish-Moslem traditions; many of their doctrines are secret. There was no overwhelming historical reason for them to be committed ideologically to either side—and both Jews and Arabs offered to buy their services. They accepted the offer of the Arabs.

At the height of the battle for Mishmar Ha'emek, Kaukji insisted that the Druze go into action further north, hoping either for a breakthrough there, or that strength would have to be drained from the defenders of Mishmar Ha'emek to meet the new threat. True to their contract, the Druze attacked Kibbutz Ramat Yohanan from April 12 through April 14. They fought hard—and they were defeated. Digesting their defeat and that of the "Liberation Army" at Mishmar Ha'emek, they reconsidered their position, and became Israel's firm allies. Subsequently, they fought—and fought well—on the side of Israel in the War of Liberation; they have been part of the Army of Israel ever since; and their population in the Golan Heights was of significance during the Six Day War and of great importance since: Their villages in the Golan Heights are a positive factor in Israel's current occupation of this area.

Let us follow the delineations of the official army history (*Toledot*), in defining the various stages of the war. Stage I, which we have already discussed, extended from November 29, 1947 to April 3, 1948 (the start of Operation Nahshon); stage II stretched through the proclamation of the State of Israel, May 14.

Following Nahshon, Israel continued to take the initiative with the result that on April 18 the mixed city of Tiberias was captured; April 22, the mixed city of Haifa was captured; May 4 the area between the Sea of Galilee and Lake Huleh was cleared; between May 1 and 12 eastern Galilee, in the vicinity of Rosh Pina and Tiberias, was cleared; May 4 to 15, the area from the southern city of Rehovot southward to Beer-Tuvia was cleared; May 11 the key western Galilee city of Safed was liberated; May 12 the key southern Galilee town of Bet She'an was taken; May 13 the vital Arab city of Jaffa adjoining Tel Aviv surrendered (after two weeks of on-again, off-again fighting, with some British intervention on the side of the Arabs).

Our summary does not begin to indicate the extraordinary combination of daring and devotion by which, time after time, the seriously underarmed and greatly outnumbered Jews defeated their would-be destroyers. Acts of heroism were so commonplace that the very concept became an embarrassment. The price was heavy, both in casualties and in consumption of limited supplies, but a minimal level of geographic viability had been established. The optimists, led with much faith by David Ben Gurion, perceived the possibility that Israel would be able to withstand the onslaught of the regular Arab armies—and, on the eve of the Sabbath, May 14, 1948, proclaimed the State of Israel.

Stage III covered four weeks of fighting, from May 15 to the imposition of the first truce by the UN on June 11, 1948. This was a mixed period with the advantage going decidedly to the invaders. While there was some internal consolidation, there was considerable penetration by the invading Arab armies. The Arab Legion (Transjordan's British-officered army) did not wait for May 15. On the thirteenth it joined the irregulars who had been besieging the Etzion block of kibbutzim midway between Jerusalem and Hebron for half a year, and administered the coup de grâce. May 15, two isolated settlements, Beit Yaacov and Atarot, several miles north of Jerusalem, were evacuated; May 18, Bet Haarava and the Dead Sea Works on the northern shore of the Dead Sea were abandoned. The final defenses of the Old City of Jerusalem fell May 28; the New City of Jerusalem had been cut off from the coast for months (with brief, limited breakthroughs). By June 11, three separate major attacks on Arab Legion-held Latrun (a major bottleneck on the only road from Jerusalem to the coast) had failed. . . . The Egyptian army had advanced up the coast road to Isdud (Ashdod), less than twenty miles from Tel Aviv, and sent forces eastward to link up with the Arab Legion south of Jerusalem, thus strengthening the isolation of the northern Negev from the rest of the country. Three southern settlements were taken (Yad Mordechai, Nitzanim, Hartuv) and a number of others were under severe pressure.

Farther north, the narrow Tel Aviv-Haifa corridor was threatened at several points, and the northern third of the road itself was subject to attack by hostile resident Arabs.

Settlements south of the Sea of Galilee changed hands a number of times; Ein Gev, on the eastern shore, was cut off. The fate of central Galilee was most uncertain. The road to the northeastern "finger" of Galilee was threatened by the fall of Mishmar Hayarden to the east, and Malkiya to the west.

The only positive accomplishments in the field in this period, in addition to some internal consolidation, were the taking of the city of Acre May 18, and of the military camp at Sarafand May 19. Also, the Egyptian advance up the coast had been stopped at the Ashdod bridge May 29, and held there. Finally, the rough beginnings of a bypass road to Jerusalem were established which would provide a UN-acceptable legal basis for significantly lifting the siege of Jerusalem during the first truce. Thus, the end of Stage III found Israel exhausted and most seriously threatened in vital areas—but it had taken the full weight of simultaneous attack by the regular armies of the Arab states, and, thus far, it had survived.

Stage IV began with the first truce on June 11, and ended with the start of the second truce on July 19. The first truce lasted until July 9. During this period, the attitude of the United Nations was nicely balanced and totally amoral: The truce should freeze the positions of both sides in all respects, keeping the balance of forces intact; there was no consideration of theoretical categories like invader and defender, aggressor and victim—the approach was practical. There were simply two opposing sides. Enforcement of the intended freeze, too, was practical: Since policing all the harbors and airfields of Egypt, Transjordan, Syria, Lebanon, and Iraq (Saudi Arabia, the sixth member of the Arab League, did not participate significantly in the fighting) was not possible, attempted enforcement of the freeze was applied only to Israel! Quite understandably, Israel did its best to evade this one-sided enforcement.

Thus, in its commitment to correctness, the UN declared that the siege of Jerusalem must not be lifted during the truce (except for what the Arabs would permit to be taken through their lines).

Israel's reaction to what it considered to be an outrageous position set a rather important pattern for the future. She acted.

Israel continued building and improving and using the Latrun bypass (called the "Burma Road")—and then advised the UN that the activity was legal since the road had been inaugurated during hostilities (June 1). Since the UN did not have the military power to impose its will, and since many of its members must have recognized the patent unfairness of the UN's position, Israel's legal argument was, in effect, accepted. Israel had acted to establish a fact, and this established fact was then acknowledged.

Acting to establish facts was by no means restricted to Israel. For example, "unidentifiable" Arabs destroyed the Latrun pumping station (under Arab Legion control) when the first-truce terms included the provision that it be used to supply water to besieged Jewish Jerusalem during the truce. And all the attacks by "irregular" Arab forces, before and after the proclamation of the State of Israel, were similar attempts to establish facts.

The real difference was that Israel officially took responsibility for all of its bold and sometimes questionable acts, whereas those attacking Israel, particularly in the periods between wars, attempted to evade responsibility by functioning through "front" organizations, claiming to be independent of their host countries. The clear and intended implication of such independence of host countries was that there would be no national entity responsible, and thus accountable, for their violent actions. Israel has countered by insisting that host countries, by definition, are responsible for acts originating from their premises; on occasion, she has retaliated accordingly.

The ninth of July marked the end of the first truce, and the nineteenth of July, the beginning of the second truce. This limited period of hostilities was, for obvious reasons, called "The Ten Days." The Ten Days marked a radical reversal in the direction of the war: The initiative was very much in the hands of Israel, with the Arabs primarily on the defensive.

Israel was not universally successful—her attempts to open a corridor to the Negev failed, and the Egyptians took some additional territory south of Negba and the Arabs took some territory north of Jenin in the center. But Israel's gains were of major importance: The corridor to Jerusalem was significantly widened with the retaking of Ein Karem and Hartuv; additional territory extending to Gat and Negba provided an important hinterland south of Rehovot. The key towns of Ramle, Ben Shemen and Lydda (and the Lydda airport) were taken, relieving pressure on Tel Aviv. In the north, the central Galilee, including Nazareth, was taken. The Syrian bridgehead at Mishmar Hayarden was attacked, neutralizing the pressure there. And an attempt was made to liberate the Old City of Jerusalem.

While Israel's defensive posture had never been static—it's policy had always been to lash out at the enemy and keep him off balance even if the strength to defeat him was lacking—now there was the strength to succeed, at least in some areas, and to hold the enemy in the others. The tide had turned.

Chapter 5

VICTORIES IN THE FIELD

Included under Stage V, are all the events from the onset of the second truce, July 19, 1948, to the signing of the last of the armistice agreements (with Syria) July 20, 1949. The truce periods were far from being times of total inactivity, but fighting tended to be localized, small-scale and sporadic, rather than large-scale with significant territorial changes. Thus, the second truce included Operation Shoter ("Policeman") to clear the Carmel range of hills overlooking the northern section of the Tel Aviv–Haifa road. And there was considerable skirmishing in the Negev, with both sides preparing for the next round. The Egyptians continued to keep the vital road to the Negev sealed off.

Operation Yoav, October 15–21, (also called Operation Ten Plagues, evoking the first victory of Israel over Egypt some 3200 years earlier), decisively beat the Egyptian army for the first time (see Chapter 15 for details). Access to the Negev was established; considerable Negev territory was made secure; the Egyptian coastal finger pointing toward Tel Aviv was shrunk to a coastal enclave terminating at Gaza; Beersheba was taken; the broad Egyptian swath from the coast to Jerusalem was eliminated—instead, a strong Egyptian force was trapped in the Faluja area. On the night of October 22, the *Emir Farouk,* flagship of the Egyptian fleet, was sunk in the roads off Gaza by the Israeli navy.

October 29–31, Operation Hiram cleared northern Galilee, finally driving out the forces of Kaukji, and included limited, temporary occupation of a number of Lebanese villages.

November 9, the police fortress at Iraq Sueidan, guarding one of the approaches to Faluja, was taken after severe bombardment. The mandatory power had dotted the landscape with strong, concrete police fortresses (named after their designer, Teggart), and these were formidable defenses in terms of the then current military realities. This particular fortress, which was uncomfortably close to a main Negev road, had absorbed far more punishment over a far longer period of time than any other. It had been nicknamed "The Monster on the Hill." The taking of Iraq Sueidan left the police fortress at Latrun as the only one to have withstood serious Israeli attack, and Latrun was not taken until the Six Day War (June, 1967).

Operation Lot, November 24–25, occupied Kurnub and Ein Hussub without battle, opening the way to Sodom, at the foot of the Dead Sea, and extending Israel's boundaries east and south.

Operation Assaf (named for its commander), December 5–7, seized strategic strongpoints in the western Negev (some of which had earlier been taken by the Egyptians), preparatory to Operation Horev.

Operation Horev was the last major military operation of the war. Israel wanted to move from belligerence to peace. The political realities were such that the largest, most powerful foe—Egypt—would have to be the first to make peace; only then would the other Arab nations be able to do the same. But Egypt would not talk peace until she had militarily been brought to her knees—thus, the objective of Operation Horev ("Horev" is a biblical synonym for Sinai) was to force peace by resoundingly defeating the army of Egypt. A corollary objective was the clearing of all Egyptian forces from Palestinian territory. This operation was begun December 22, and continued through January 7, 1949. Because the names of many of the key localities began with the Hebrew letter "ayin," it was also called "Operation Ayin."

The operation succeeded in its major objective: The Egyptians were soundly defeated, with armistice talks following on the island of Rhodes. Egypt signed the first armistice agreement on February 24. Yet the operation was not an unqualified success. The effort to dislodge the Egyptians from the coastal strip terminating just above Gaza failed. The Egyptians had considerable fire power, and fought very well from dug in, static, defensive positions. Thus, the armistice agreement left Egypt in internationally recognized possession of the part of the Palestinian territory known since as the Gaza Strip. Israel's shooting down of four British planes which were flying with the Egyptians as (armed) "observers," on January 7, and Britain's immediate, strenuous reaction, inspired both the ending of operation Horev (January 8) and Israel's total withdrawal from northwestern Sinai—although, with Egypt's main forces destroyed or bottled up, the road to the Suez Canal was open.

Now a most important question arose: To whom would the central and southern Negev be assigned? The partition plan had allocated it to the Jewish state, but UN Mediator Count Folke Bernadotte subsequently proposed an adjustment, giving most of the Negev to the Arabs and western Galilee to the Jews; the Negev was bare of any permanent settlements, and Transjordan argued that in Arab possession it would provide an important overland link between Transjordan and Egypt. The question was settled by Operation Uvda ("Fact"). Apparently it was physical possession of an area that was of paramount importance.

The assassination of Count Bernadotte on September 17 by members of LHI in the name of a synthesized "Fatherland Front" as a means of negating his plan, served instead to give added weight to it; this revised plan also coincided with the ongoing urging of the British Foreign Office. On the other hand, the platform on which the Democratic Party had run in the November 1948 elections included the following plank: "We approve the claims of the State of Israel to the boundaries set forth in the United Nations resolution of November 29 and consider that modifications thereof should be made only if fully acceptable to the State of Israel. . . ." [1]

Since the November 29 resolution had awarded the Negev to Israel, this would seem to define the American position, except for the fact that party platforms often become just that—something to be stepped on—after an election. And, although President Truman's general personal support was clear, unless Israel could demonstrate physical possession of the Negev, it might be expecting a bit too much for him singlehandedly to roll back the Bernadotte Plan with its aura of a martyr's last testimony, further supported by committed British Foreign Office and American State Department officials. Contrariwise, since the Egyptian border had already been delineated, if Israel could now demonstrate physical possession and obtain Transjordan's agreement to delineating the Negev border as the old international boundary, pressure to take the Negev away from Israel would be resistable indeed.

Therefore, beginning March 5, Israel sent two columns south from Beersheba, one through the center of the Negev, and the other along the Aravah valley marking its eastern border. On the afternoon of March 10, Eilat/Etzion Gever, on the shore of the Gulf of Aqaba (the eastern branch of the Red Sea, subsequently to serve as Israel's only outlet to Asia and Africa) was occupied: all of the Negev was *in fact,* Israeli. At the same time (March 9) another army unit occupied King David's ancient hideaway, Ein Gedi, some thirty miles north of Sodom on the Dead Sea, placing that portion of the Dead Sea coast under Israeli jurisdiction.

The second Arab country to sign an armistice agreement was Lebanon, March 23. Transjordan followed, April 3. After much hesitation, almost leading to a resumption of hostilities, Syria became the last of the invaders to sign, on July 20, 1949. Iraq, the remaining major combatant, never did sign an armistice agreement; since it had no common border with Israel, its concluding a formal agreement of this kind was not considered to be of vital importance; it simply called its forces back home.

In establishing the armistice borders, the operating principles seemed to be that (1) all territory assigned to the Jewish state under the partition plan was to go to Israel; (2) since the projected Arab state had not come into being, its territory would remain under the control of whoever occupied it at the cessation of hostilities; (3) since the Jerusalem area, which was to have been an international zone under the original plan, was now divided between Israel and Transjordan, and since U.N. Trusteeship was fiercely opposed by both and would have been most complicated to execute, the Jerusalem area, too, was allocated on the basis of possession at the time of the last cease-fire.

For mutual convenience, there were minor territorial exchanges between Israel and Transjordan in the Jerusalem area, and an important trade of Israeli positions in the Hebron mountains for Jordanian evacuation of Wadi Aza and the Afula-Hadera road. And there were traffic and access agreements (to holy places in the Old City) which were not to be honored. As a bargaining concession to Egypt, Israel agreed that the area around Auja (a village in the western Negev which was the junction of three important roads to Sinai) would be a demilitarized zone; and the Egyptian forces besieged in the Faluja pocket were permitted to depart with all their arms and equipment.

The Israel-occupied Lebanese villages were evacuated, with small border adjustments. (Rosh Hanikra, at Israel's northwest corner, reverted to Israel). The major difficulties were with Syria. There had been no major military offensive against the Syrians, so that they emerged from the conflict without tasting defeat, and in possession of the settlement of Mishmar Hayarden. Mishmar Hayarden was small in area, but vital militarily and economically; it was within the area assigned by the partition plan to the Jewish state. The pattern of exchange of territories could not be followed with Syria, since Syria held Israeli territory while Israel held no Syrian land. Presumably, the implied threat of resumption of hostilities persuaded the Syrians finally to consent to the armistice agreement which led to their withdrawal from all occupied land; this, on the clear undertaking by Israel that half the area between the line of occupation and the international border, plus Dardara east of the Huleh and

Ein Gev east of the Sea of Galilee, would constitute a demilitarized zone.

Syria's freedom from invasion and actual defeat plus its one-sided evacuation, no doubt left it feeling both aggrieved and proprietary about the demilitarized zones—and helps explain why Syria's overtly hostile acts from then until June 1967 were so much more frequent than those of Israel's other neighbors.

Thus, the armistice agreements parceled the proposed Arab state, which had never come to fulfillment, among Egypt (the Gaza Strip), Transjordan (the west bank of the Jordan River from south of Galilee to the mid-part of the Dead Sea) and Israel (all of Galilee, plus substantial sectors elsewhere). And the Jerusalem area was divided between Transjordan (which changed its name to Jordan) and Israel. (For a discussion of the Arab military failure from the Arab perspective, see Appendix C.)

Chapter 6

DELIBERATE FAILURE IN JERUSALEM?

Daring, steadfastness, courage, bluff can go a long way toward compensating for a shortage of arms—but there are limits: As happened in the famous story of the Emperor's clothes, sooner or later the fact of nakedness must be discovered—and disaster is then inevitable. Under any circumstances, if there is great disparity in arms, the equation must be balanced in blood: the total number of Israelis killed in the War of Independence exceeded 5,000 (civilian and military) out of a population of 600,000. On a proportionate current basis, this is equivalent to 1,500,000 Americans. (The total number of Americans killed in World War II was just under 300,000.)

Not only had the British forbidden the importation of arms into Palestine by Jews under severe penalties, but they conducted exhaustive searches (sometimes very successfully) to unearth and seize whatever had been smuggled in and cached away. Thus, the outbreak of the War of Independence found Israel with a pitifully meager supply of arms, widely assorted as to type, vintage, and usability. Each underground organization and each settlement jealously guarded its scant supplies since what was actually in hand was all that could be counted on.[1] Local underground manufacture was able to turn out limited supplies of grenades, land mines, explosives and Sten guns (early Israeli artillery consisted of sacks of explosives carried to the point of impact on the backs of volunteers). The Sten was a rather crude machine pistol of quite limited range and accuracy, which had an unpleasant habit of jamming. Everything, including the raw materials for the explosives, had to be located abroad (involving local cooperation), purchased and delivered secretly: Wherever British power reached, its policy was to seize Jewish arms.

At this writing, an organized, complete study of the full picture of the flow of arms does not exist. In broad terms, we can state the obvious: The early months of 1948 were indeed busy ones for "Rehesh," Haganah's underground purchasing network which was worldwide in scope, operating with a maximum of local initiative and responsibility; its headquarters was

35

in Geneva, under Shaul Avigur. (The IZL maintained its independent network.)

While most of Europe was neutral or cooperative, on the practical, if not the official level, the United States joined Britain in zealously trying to enforce an embargo on arms to the Jewish state—paying little attention to the Arabs, who were already fully armed, yet continued to receive armaments from Britain on the grounds that she must honor her contracts.

The pressure of time was enormous—and the role of non-Israelis, crucial.

We have already seen that Operation Nahshon was the hinge upon which the very existence of the Jewish state turned: It was Israel's first large-scale offensive operation, and it led directly to the wresting of a semiviable area from Arab control, so that there existed a minimally secure foothold from which to face the invasion of the regular Arab armies on May 15. Nahshon was not launched until early April and, because of lack of arms, it came perilously close to not being launched at all.

Lorch writes that it was only the timely delivery of the first planeload of arms from Czechoslovakia (Balak 1) the night of March 31/April 1 that prevented the delay, or possibly the cancellation, of Operation Nahshon.[2]

The size of the cargo indicates how truly desperate the shortage was: It consisted of just 200 rifles, 4 machine guns, and ammunition.[3] Because of its timely arrival, the 1,500 men being held in readiness for Nahshon were not dispersed, although they were needed desperately in every part of the country. And, when the ship *Nora* succeeded in bringing 200 machine guns and 4,300 rifles to the port of Tel Aviv two days later, these, too, could immediately be utilized in the operation.

The timing of the arrival of this one little planeload of arms was of maximum importance: With the British still in control of the country, the *safe* arrival of the cargo of the *Nora* was problematical. Thus, the decision to continue holding the men in readiness for Nahshon was apparently firmed solely by the safe arrival of the cargo of Balak 1. As it is, there was precious little time to do the monumental restoration of internal security and communications that was absolutely necessary before May 15. Had the assembled forces been returned home, invaluable days would have been lost reassembling them—if, indeed, they could have been fully reassembled altogether, with road conditions deteriorating daily. Without a successful Nahshon, the Jewish state would likely not have come into being at all. And this critical plane on which all apparently hinged—was flown by an American crew.

While the problem of receiving supplies was minimized, with the ending of British hegemony (the UN enforcement on the soil of Israel of its declared quarantine on supplies during truce periods was not very effective) the problems of location of supplies, location of money, and delivery to Israel, remained. Thus, as late as July 17, Israel's attempt to retake the walled Old City of Jerusalem appears to have been defeated, at least in part, by a shortage of ammunition. The battle plan called for Haganah to break into the Old City from the south, in the vicinity of Zion Gate, while IZL and LHI invaded through New Gate to the north. Although the official formation of the Army of Israel at the end of May had promptly led to absorption of Haganah, IZL, and LHI in all other areas, this step was not taken until much later in Jerusalem because of the different status of this area under the partition plan—it was to have been internationalized. Thus, Haganah, IZL and LHI continued to retain their separate identities in the Jerusalem area, their activities being coordinated by joint agreement, with major decisions requiring GHQ/minister of defense clearance.

Only on July 16 was permission granted to attempt to retake the Old City with the full knowledge that the cease-fire—the beginning of the second truce—was to take place in Jerusalem at dawn on the morning of the 17th. It was decided to proceed with the attack nonetheless. Since Zion Gate was very heavily defended, Haganah's attack depended largely on a new "device" which was expected to blow an opening in the one- to two-yard-thick wall itself after initial artillery, machine gun and mortar softening up of the city. This was a surface device;[4] in addition, a tunnel had been dug underneath the wall, to implement a supplementary option, which was to blow an opening from below. In the event, only the surface device was used, and it failed totally—as did the Haganah attack.[5] The IZL/LHI attack succeeded in breaking through New Gate, but because of an unlucky chance occurrence, could not establish a viable foothold (which would have involved taking at least the strategic building called the College des Frères). The unforeseen event: all the reserve ammunition lay ready in three open trucks parked nearby; a random Arab Legion shell landed in one of the trucks—and the resulting explosion demolished all three vehicles and their contents.[6] With no ammunition, there was no choice but to retreat from this dearly won toehold. Although sporadic fighting did continue elsewhere (primarily, near the Mandelbaum Gate) until the evening of July 18, this was Israel's last attempt to retake the Old City until June 1967. In any event, this failure was not an unmixed loss. The fighting ended with the Jerusalem Zone divided: Old Jerusalem and its hinterland occupied by Transjordan, New Jerusalem occupied by Israel. The UN-approved armistice agreement confirmed this de facto situation, marking the beginning of an end to the paper internationalization which had been a firm part of the original partition plan. One may well speculate whether, in 1949, the UN would have been equally sanguine in accepting Israeli possession of both the New and the Old City—or whether, in *that* circumstance, it would not *then* have forcefully resurrected the internationalization scheme for the entire Jerusalem area.

We cannot avoid questioning whether the Haganah attack on the Old City was really intended seriously.

1. The attack was made totally dependent on the success of the "device": Just 300 pounds of ordinary explosives blowing a large opening through massive stone blocks three to six feet in thickness. This was not cement, not concrete, but *stone*. As any rational person should have expected, the stone was slightly blackened—but otherwise hardly damaged, much less blasted open.

2. The explosives buried near the wall could perhaps have had a diversionary effect if a serious attempt were to be made to break through at Zion Gate or to scale the wall elsewhere. Those explosives were not used, nor was there any attempt made to break through Zion Gate or to scale the walls.

3. From the beginning of the Ten Days, IZL and LHI had been urgently pressing for a combined attack. Yet, it was hardly a dozen hours before the second truce was due to go into effect that approval was given. If it was intended that the truce be obeyed, it is difficult to imagine that more than merely a solid foothold could have been gained in the Old City at best.

This seems to suggest that Haganah approval and participation in the attack essentially was a *gesture*—a gesture whose credibility was added to by the preliminary shelling of the Old City and by administrative preparations. It was suggested above that not taking the Old City was part of a deliberate—and wise—plan. A simpler possibility might well have been the calculation that there was not sufficient strength to take the Old City; that a serious attempt might yield no more than a foothold which would have to be abandoned under political pressure—in short, that it would simply be a useless sacrifice of lives. One might complete this speculative picture by suggesting the view that the "Undergrounds" (IZL and LHI) could not be reasoned with—they were emotionally too far committed to the symbolism of the Old City—and so the only practical course was to give them the opportunity they demanded; but with a minimum of hard support.

Thus, everyone would be satisfied: IZL and LHI would mount the attack on which they insisted, yet there need be virtually no Haganah losses since the attack follow-through would legitimately not take place when the explosive device failed. For this maneuvre to be acceptable to public opinion, proximity of the attack to the truce was all-important. If, for example, IZL/LHI managed to establish a real foothold in the Old City with several days of fighting still permitted, it would be shameful, disgraceful—really intolerable—for Haganah/Palmach to fail to give at least as good an accounting of itself. It appears to this writer, then, that there was deliberate Haganah holding back—holding back which, under the circumstances, was prudent and proper.

Prudent and proper, since a successful attack would very likely have been politically counter-productive. As noted above, all of Jerusalem under Jewish control *then* almost certainly would have led to an internationalized Jerusalem.

Chapter 7

THE *ALTALENA:* TO THE BRINK OF CIVIL WAR

Somewhat earlier, the supply shortage came close to destroying the infant state of Israel by bringing it to the brink of civil war.

In discussing Deir Yassin in chapter three, we saw one consequence of the hostility and mistrust between the Jewish Agency and IZL and LHI. Another consequence occurred later, with the mutual hostility and mistrust exacerbated by the Deir Yassin publicity itself. It was a near civil war, in which volunteers played crucial direct and indirect roles.

The evening of June 11, an IZL ship, the *Altalena,* left the port of Marseilles carrying some 900 passengers (including some Mahal and many Gahal), 5,000 rifles, 270 machine guns, quantities of antitank weapons, and a large store of ammunition.[1] Clearly, these supplies were urgently needed by Israel, but distrust was to prove even stronger than this very real need. Since the first truce had come into effect coincidentally with the sailing of the *Altalena,* there was some initial uncertainty: Would the public unloading of a military transport (the ship was an American surplus LST) be too blatant a violation of the truce? The decision, to which the government was a party, was against delay: The ship would not make for a major port, but would unload, preferably at night, at the secluded beach near the village of Kfar Vitkin, a settlement whose political stance was anti-Irgun. There was, however, no agreement as to how the arms were to be distributed.

The IZL account of the immediate background of the shooting claims that with no agreement as to arms distribution, the government only said it would not help in the unloading of the ship. The ship began unloading the night of June 20 (removing passengers first) and continued into the following day. Then government troops suddenly surrounded the beach area and, after some parley, began shooting. Government naval vessels bracketed the *Altalena* from the sea, and it was subsequently ordered to Tel Aviv harbor (an order which coincided with the Irgun's desire at that point) where intense gunfire set the ship afire.[2]

Bitterness was at its peak. The country, appalled at the waste of seemingly irreplaceable supplies and horrified by the knowledge that

40

Jewish soldiers had deliberately killed each other, teetered on the brink of civil war. To avert this, and to avoid a repetition of the tragedy of the Roman War when Jewish factions in Jerusalem actively fought each other while the city was under siege, the IZL leader Menahem Begin went on the radio that evening and ordered full submission by all IZL individuals and units. Thus, although there had been a tragic loss of lives and supplies, and many volunteers were deeply shaken at a situation of whose background they were ignorant, large-scale civil war was averted.[3]

What really happened? How could the situation have deteriorated so badly?

The statement that the government's initial reaction to failure to agree on the distribution of the arms was simply to suggest that the IZL would have to do the work itself, does not ring true. What is a far more persuasive hypothesis is that the government should have been expected to regard such unloading as an act of defiance, equivalent to insurrection. Thus, the Alexandroni Brigade was ordered to put a stop to what could not be tolerated: A huge arms shipment being unloaded privately on a beach ringed with IZL personnel.

Companies Thirty-two and Thirty-three were specifically detailed for this police action; Company Thirty-five, which was also available, was not employed because it included many former IZL men—twenty-one of whom actually tried to join the IZL in this action, but were arrested. After an ultimatum to surrender, there was firing between the land forces,[4] with men killed on both sides.[5] Two Israeli naval vessels appeared, the larger of which (the *Wedgewood*) ordered the *Altalena* to proceed to Tel Aviv (thus minimizing fighting on the beach). With periodic firing between the corvette *Wedgewood* and the *Altalena,* all ships involved sailed for Tel Aviv where the work of destruction was completed. Although Lorch repeats the "official" statement that the *Altalena* was set afire by the accident of a warning shell falling short,[6] St. John's detailed interviews with the captains of both ships, both of whom were American volunteers, is conclusive as to there having been much heavier shelling.[7] Ironically, among the casualties of this final stage was the fatally wounded Abraham Stavsky (also called *Palest, Abrasha, Nebraska*), purchaser of the *Altalena,* who had left Palestine more than a dozen years earlier when he was accused of responsibility for the still unsolved murder of Haim Arlosoroff in that very area.

What, actually, were the irreconcilable positions? On the one hand, since a unified army, including IZL units, had come into existence, it was not unreasonable to assume that the distribution of all arms should be completely controlled by the government. On the other hand, since the Jerusalem area had been excluded from the unified command, and since major IZL units were in Jerusalem, it was not unreasonable for IZL to feel that a substantial portion of these IZL-procured arms should go to IZL forces in Jerusalem. But there apparently *was* agreement on the latter point: 20 percent was to go directly to the IZL units in Jerusalem.[8]

With reference to the balance, however, IZL insisted that it was proper for these arms to go to IZL people who would bring them into the unified army. Here, it would appear that pride was involved: It would be truly glorious for IZL to fade out with its people being by far the best equipped in the army! Apart from practical considerations, this was an indignity that could not be permitted by the government.

And there were practical considerations: The government was something quite new; as we discussed in connection with Deir Yassin, there was very deep distrust between the Agency (whose officials had become the Provisional Government) and IZL. When there would be elections later, would everyone submit to the democratic process, or might the former dissident, militant minority find it "necessary" to use force to move the government in the "correct" direction? Would it be possible to rely on the government to distribute arms adequately, or should each interest look out for itself, and build private stockpiles?[9]

Having considered the correctness of the government's position in acting against the *Altalena* at Kfar Vitkin, we want to point to one event which seems to have been an important added factor in furthering the intransigeance and suspicion of the IZL (although none of our sources has so identified it). This was the loss of Mishmar Hayarden ten days earlier.

Mishmar Hayarden was a cooperative settlement established at the very beginning of the modern return to Zion—the date of its founding is variously given as 1884 or a few years later. Its location was historically strategic: The point at which the ancient Via Maris—the more than 4,000-year-old highway between the East and Egypt—crossed the Jordan River, just above the Bnot Yaakov bridge, between the Sea of Galilee and the Huleh. Beyond it, to the west, lay the main north-south road: north, to the "finger" of eastern Galilee, south to Rosh Pina and Tiberias. Mishmar Hayarden, the "Guardian of the Jordan," was captured by the Syrians June 10. Its capture led to frantic defensive activity by Israel which succeeded in limiting the Syrian advance (and in costly counter-offensives, which were not successful).

In attempting to understand the fall of this settlement which lay very close to a number of neighboring settlements, Lorch writes that its defense "had been neglected before and during the war. Perhaps the reason lay in the differences in outlook and the clash of interests between the old colony and the neighboring new collective settlements." In less oblique language, Mishmar Hayarden was "rightist" in ideology, and thus would not be supplied through Haganah channels but through IZL channels. Perhaps this was an instance of falling victim to one's own propaganda: Since IZL stood, above all, for militancy and military preparedness, perhaps its neighbors assumed that while everyone else may have been underarmed, this IZL-connected settlement *must* be relatively well armed. Lorch relates that on June 6 a number of kibbutzim in the area were shelled, but only Mishmar Hayarden was attacked by units attempting to occupy it. By June 8, a reinforcing Israeli Army battalion was in the area—yet, even by June 10, it had not "had sufficient time to orient itself and to take up positions." [10] Even through the final, overwhelming Syrian attack on June 10, repeated radio pleas for help were fruitless.[11]

These are the facts. We do not suggest that the army deliberately withheld assistance: It may simply have been a matter of underestimating the seriousness of the situation at Mishmar Hayarden at the time simultaneous attacks were underway elsewhere. We do suggest that the IZL leadership could readily have concluded (correctly or not) that there was anti-IZL discrimination: That the government could not be relied on fully. It would appear that this event may well have been a significant added factor in IZL stubborness over the allocation of the cargo of the *Altalena,* and in the precipitous action it took, bringing the country to the brink of civil war.

One nagging question remains: Why was the *Altalena* destroyed in Tel Aviv harbor?

We have seen the necessity for the use of force on the beach at Kfar Vitkin[12]—but why Tel Aviv? David Ben Gurion, who was then prime minister and minister of defense, claimed that the ship was still in a condition of insurrection, that it was far better to destroy the ship than have its weapons in the hands of rebels; regrettable as it may have been, "Blessed is the gun that blew up that ship." [13] This vehemence, coupled with the claim of survivors that they tried to surrender the ship in Tel

Aviv, leads to a possible cold-blooded theory: That the ship was deliberately destroyed as an object lesson. That is, it was decided that there would be minimum loss of lives in the long run and the greatest benefit to the state if maximum harshness were used at this point: The threat of rebellion could best be totally erased for all time. A corollary political benefit would be that the IZL would never be able to appeal to the electorate in the future as the savior of the state through its arms ship, if the state clearly made do without those arms by publicly destroying them.

After the fact, this view that the destruction of the ship as an object lesson was justified would find itself affirmed by seeing Begin's surrender and the subsequent lack of overt IZL/Government incidents as due to the realization after the *Altalena* experience, that the government would instantly use maximum suppressive force against any impropriety. Others, of course, may well disagree, insisting that IZL people were always prepared to submit fully to the proper decisions of the government. The validity of this most uncomfortable theory of calculated force[14] would be rather firmly established if there had been a high-command decision to bomb the *Altalena* from the air.

We mention this, not because it was a quiet rumor at the time, but because three separate works by volunteer fliers each gives significant space to this as fact. In *The Coasts of the Earth,* it is the non-Jewish pilot protagonist who is assigned this task (and, by implication, reluctantly carries it out);[15] in *The Midnighters* it is the protagonist, Marty Ribakoff (like Nevins, chief pilot of the ATC—although Ribakoff is described as the Jewish son of an anti-Zionist father, with a Christian wife) who indignantly refuses to bomb the ship;[16] and in *Between Star and Cross* it is the Jewish chief pilot, Leon Becker, who himself recoils in horror from the "order," and says that he will shoot any other volunteer who attempts to carry it out.[17]

It is true that none of these books are histories—all are what can best be described as documentary novels: A genre in which the writer has the license to fictionalize as he sees fit, but which is aimed at a public interested in its presumably authentic background rather than in its characters as individuals.

It seems highly unlikely that three separate participant-writers would invent such a story out of whole cloth, and only a little less likely that the two later writers would be inspired to repeat it because of the example of the first. Unlikely, but theoretically possible. Therefore, the writer raised the specific question of the alleged bombing of the *Altalena* in an interview in the summer of 1965 (when two of the three above-cited books were in print), with Israel Amir. In the spring of 1948 Israel Amir had been commandant of the air arm and its link with the Army High Command (at its inception the air force had been viewed simply as a special adjunct of the army). Thus, Amir would have had to be in the midst of any such presumed order. Israel Amir flatly and completely *denied* that there had been any order to bomb the *Altalena*.

This denial will probably not set the "bombing" story finally to rest: Those convinced of its underlying validity will insist that Amir's was a technical denial—that there had been no "order," but there was intent which could not be carried out because the volunteers refused to co-operate and no Israelis were available who could fly the necessary planes. There is nothing further to add beyond emphasizing that the *Altalena* was not bombed from the air, and that it was heavily worked over in the Tel Aviv harbor to some extent by the three ships on its seaward side, and most tellingly by heavy rifle, machine-gun, and mortar fire from the beach.

There is also a somewhat different way of reading the events of June 22: Not that Begin called off the incipient civil war that evening out of the greatness that comes from deep humility and self-sacrifice, but that the civil war had already taken place and had been lost during the day. In this view, Begin's radio address disguised the doubly unthinkable: That the Irgun had been in a state of revolt against the government of Israel, and that it had lost.

This approach comes from a broadening of focus from the ship, to the streets of Tel Aviv. Irgun men by the score had left their army units (many in front-line positions) to flock in to Tel Aviv for the confrontation; two IZL leaders, who were arrested en route, intended to take over the seat of government physically; others headed for the beach area and other rendezvous points; others for the Ritz Hotel—Palmach headquarters, close by the beach—which was surrounded and under fire for a time.

This indeed had the appearance of planned insurrection, though not its substance: There is no evidence that the top leadership of the IZL was interested in anything beyond unloading the arms in their way (Begin was fully occupied on the ship); it was for this purpose only the IZL men had been called in to Tel Aviv; and the idea of seizing the seat of government appears to have been the momentary inspiration of two individual IZL leaders—an idea which they undoubtedly kept to themselves when they were arrested. Yet, in the stress of a developing fire fight, one can only be guided by appearances. Yigal Alon was in overall charge of the reaction, which involved elements of Yiftach, Carmeli, and Negev Brigades (some hastily pulled back from the front). Prominent among those in action in the beach area was Yitzhak Rabin; leading those whose task was running down and arresting IZL soldiers throughout the city was Moshe Kelman. By late afternoon it was over.[18]

From the perspective of apparent actual insurrection, the harshest repression could be justified.[19] Even so, destruction of the ship would be both terribly wasteful and divisive. We prefer to set aside the "deliberate destruction" hypothesis. Considering the dynamics of rising tempers and poor communications, the explanation may well be in the misunderstanding and the confusion that prevailed. It is understandable that the *Altalena,* which had mounted an impressive number of machine guns on deck, initially for possible antiaircraft defense, should fire back with vehemence whenever it was shot at. From the initial confrontation at Kfar Vitkin through the voyage and beaching off Tel Aviv, there must have been rising bewilderment, frustration, and anger. With the ship aground some distance off the beach, with some fire from the navy (by now, three ships were involved) from the far side towards the beach, with increasing fire from the beach—it is quite likely that when the attempt to surrender was finally made, it was not clearly understood in the midst of the escalating fight. And although the shells were deliberately aimed at the ship, their purpose was to accelerate its surrender, not to destroy it. In this sense, the ship's being set afire was accidental.

Thus, the heavy firing from the beach was a blunder: It should have been realized that with the beach and city secure, the ship would surely surrender. What prevented this realization was the accumulated filter of mistrust through which the dissidents were viewed. And Ben Gurion's vehement justification of the destruction of the ship is very much the kind of reaction which ought to be expected in these circumstances, particularly on the part of one who recognizes that strong attack is the best defense.[20]

Thus, the critical supply shortage not only almost led to destruction of Israel by the Arabs—it also came very close to triggering the country's self-destruction by internal explosion.

This entire affair, which brought Israel to the brink of civil war, might not have been possible without overseas volunteers. The Captain of the *Wedgewood,* the corvette which took the lead in shepherding (and firing at) the *Altalena* from Kfar Vitkin to Tel Aviv, was Jerry Rosenberg, a Canadian volunteer from Hamilton, Ontario.[21] Could the *Wedgewood* have functioned as it did without this Captain, and without the volunteers in its crew? Perhaps—and perhaps not. It is even less likely that the *Altalena* would have been able to function without its Captain, Monroe Fein, an American volunteer from Chicago, Illinois. The *Altalena* was a war surplus U.S. Navy LST (Landing Ship, Tank), and Fein was a rare find for the IZL: He had had LST experience as a naval lieutenant in the Pacific. Furthermore, it would seem that a major portion of the arms used on the beach against the *Altalena*, would have come via the Czech air lift which, as we shall see, depended on volunteers. Thus, it appears that the *Altalena* affair, which was so deeply upsetting to the volunteers (who were totally unprepared for anything of this sort), might not have been possible without the volunteers!

With the passage of time, the supply shortage was ameliorated. The Czech airlift (which we will discuss later in detail) brought a steady flow of rifles, machine guns, ammunition, and fighter planes; heavy shipments by sea were coming through on a regular basis. Although the timely arrival of a single planeload of arms was of critical importance on the last night of March, when the Czech airlift was stopped on August 12 it was no longer vital. Similarly, while the arms on the *Altalena* were of great potential importance in mid-June (had they not been lost, it is not unlikely that gains during the Ten Days would have been greater, and perhaps, casualties lower), by the end of the summer they had been more than replaced. During the summer and early autumn there was a major buildup of supplies, some of which had been put into the pipeline months earlier. A sometimes significant local source of supplies was the capture in battle of enemy arms, which generally were put to immediate use.

Broadly, one might say that men and supplies arriving prior to the first truce and "digested" during that truce, made possible a turnaround, so that beginning with the Ten Days, the initiative against the regular Arab armies was Israel's.

Although there was a stalemate following the Ten Days, the status quo was intolerable to Israel: Egyptian forces controlled the Negev, and the Negev kibbutzim, quite cut off, were strangling. The continuing major buildup of supplies was necessary if there was to be any reasonable possibility of defeating the relatively modern, heavily equipped, defensively excellent Egyptian army. And, as we shall see, the proper prior placement of some of those supplies was to be crucial.

Procurement from the United States was of great importance; although this was largely the product of Israeli initiative and domestic (not overseas) volunteer cooperation, it is important to a full picture of events. To this our next chapter but one is devoted.

Part Two:

THE ROLE OF THE VOLUNTEERS

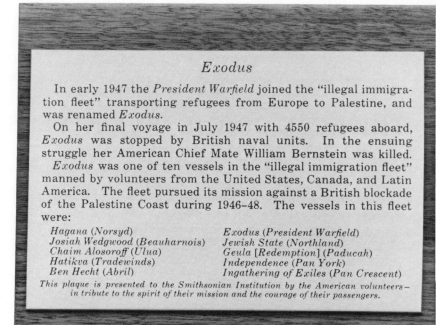

Exodus

In early 1947 the *President Warfield* joined the "illegal immigration fleet" transporting refugees from Europe to Palestine, and was renamed *Exodus*.

On her final voyage in July 1947 with 4550 refugees aboard, *Exodus* was stopped by British naval units. In the ensuing struggle her American Chief Mate William Bernstein was killed.

Exodus was one of ten vessels in the "illegal immigration fleet" manned by volunteers from the United States, Canada, and Latin America. The fleet pursued its mission against a British blockade of the Palestine Coast during 1946–48. The vessels in this fleet were:

Hagana (Norsyd)	*Exodus (President Warfield)*
Josiah Wedgwood (Beauharnois)	*Jewish State (Northland)*
Chaim Alosoroff (Ulua)	*Geula [Redemption] (Paducah)*
Hatikva (Tradewinds)	*Independence (Pan York)*
Ben Hecht (Abril)	*Ingathering of Exiles (Pan Crescent)*

This plaque is presented to the Smithsonian Institution by the American volunteers—in tribute to the spirit of their mission and the courage of their passengers.

Text of the plaque alongside a model of the ship "Exodus" in the Smithsonian Institution, Washington, D. C.

(THE SMITHSONIAN INSTITUTION)

Chapter 8

AMERICAN AND CANADIAN VOLUNTEERS KILLED IN THE WAR

These brief biographies of the 38* Americans (including Canadians) killed in the War of Independence, is intended as a tribute and memorial to them.

In addition, it also serves to concretize the extent to which Americans were active in virtually every phase and every area of the war; and to encapsulate the range of different backgrounds and approaches which prompted some very different kinds of Americans to voluntarily risk—and lose—their lives, so that the State of Israel could be born, and live.

NOTE: (1) Most of the information here is drawn from *Yizkor*, the official memorial book of the Government of Israel, "COMPRISING BIOGRAPHIES AND PHOTOGRAPHS OF ALL THE FALLEN IN THE WAR OF LIBERATION IN ISRAEL"; some from Shahan's very useful summary tables (Shahan, Avigdor. *Kanfei Hanitzahon*. Am Hassefer Publishers Ltd., 1966.); some, from other sources, including interviews with surviving veterans (a few of the names do not appear in "Yizkor" at all). Whatever errors the writer was aware of, have been corrected; it is entirely possible that other inaccuracies remain. The writer personally knew only Spence Boyd (with whom my wife and I went to the opera in Rome, less than a month before his death) and Mosie Perlstein (with whom I had attended an elementary Hebrew Day School in Brooklyn, New York). (2) Definition: The question of precisely how to define "American Volunteer" is a thorny one. Thus, the Jewish National Fund in consultation with the Army of Israel, when it first erected the American Volunteers Memorial Plaque at the Memorial Forest near Hulda, included people who were technically American citizens but who had moved to Palestine at any early age, apparently settling permanently; a number of survivors of the Holocaust whose next of kin were American; some American volunteers killed after the war in the service of Israel; some volunteers from English-speaking countries outside the Western hemisphere; and some names concerning whom no information is now available. At the urging of this writer, the American Veterans of Israel has insisted that a new plaque be erected listing as "American Volunteers" only those who in their own eyes and/or by general consensus were essentially "American" (or Canadian) at the time of their death; further, that only such

---

* In addition, two Canadian cousins, *Harvey Cohen* and *Ed Lucatch* appear to have arrived in Israel early in June 1948. There is no record of their having joined any Army unit, nor has any trace of them been found.

51

people be included who were killed during the War of Independence itself, or its prelude. For the category of American citizens who came to Palestine *perhaps* to settle permanently, an arbitrary distinction was made: Those who came before the end of World War II we regard as permanent residents and exclude from our definition (unless they served in the U.S. or Canadian armed forces in World War II), while those who came following the end of World War II, even though some may have intended to reside permanently, or may have lived in Palestine earlier, we include in our definition of American Volunteers. In no sense is there any suggestion that it is considered somehow better to have been an American Volunteer than any other kind; our sole aim is to have a sensible, working definition. Our definition is identical to that adopted by the American Veterans of Israel, as a result of joint consultation.

Stanley Andrews. Born April 13, 1923, in the Bronx, New York. At the age of 18, he graduated from College of the City of New York (CCNY) with honors, and with apparent talent in literary writing and in painting. In World War II, he served four years in the U.S. Air Force as a pilot in the Pacific area. He attained the rank of captain, and was awarded a number of decorations. After the war, he moved to Los Angeles where he studied in the art department of one of the local universities. Although he had not had a reinforcing Jewish upbringing, Israel's battle for independence reached him deeply; he sought and found the proper connection and volunteered to serve in the Israeli air force. His battle fights and his work in structuring and strengthening his unit were valuable contributions to the battlefield results in June 1948. During the First Truce, he served as air communications officer with the U.N. truce supervisory team. Upon realizing that the score with the enemy was not yet settled, Andrews requested to be returned to battle service. In the October campaign against the Egyptians in the south, he flew a great many effective fighter-bomber missions. On October 20, 1948, in an attack on the Teggart fortress at Iraq Sueidan, his Beaufighter was hit by groundfire and crashed. Although *Yizkor* states that the plane, with Andrews' burnt remains alongside it, was found near Ashdod (Isdud), Shahan's information seems more likely: that the plane landed safely in the Faluja Pocket area (of which Iraq Sueidan was a part), and that the three crew members were killed by Arabs on the ground. In addition to Andrews, the others on that ill-fated flight were Leonard Fitchett, copilot (Canadian); and Dov Sugarman, navigator (Englishman). There are indications that "Andrews" was an adopted cover name—that Stanley's real name was something like "Ankenstein."

Philip Balkin. Born February 2, 1929, in Brooklyn, New York. In 1935, the family moved to Los Angeles, where his father, a veteran leather-worker, worked in a shoe factory. From the age of nine, Phil added to the family income by shining shoes and selling newspapers. Phil entered public school, and was enrolled in an after-hours, Labor-Zionist oriented school—although he was far more interested in sports, choral singing and the theater. However, in the upper grades of the Jewish school he apparently was stirred by the heroic events in Jewish history, and in public school, he tasted a bit of contemporary anti-semitism (for example, reacting to being called "dirty Jew" by one teacher, by slapping his face). Drafted into the American army in 1946, he saw upwards of a year of service in the Far East. Phil never had had excessive zeal for the army, and his service in the American army reinforced this basic antimilitaristic thrust. However, Israel's struggle was different. On realizing what was happening there, he felt that his place must be with Israel's defenders. Phil also felt that America's Jews were not guaranteed immunity from the fate of their brethren in Europe, and argued that it might well be worse here, with more efficient use of mechanical devices. He determined to follow in the footsteps of his older brother Jerry and serve in the Army of Israel. Phil Balkin kept his decision a secret, informing his parents only on the eve of his departure in October 1948. To avoid passport difficulties, he traveled first to France and thence to Israel. He promptly volunteered for the army, and was attached to a commando unit in the armored corps. Thus, he was able to participate only in the war's last major campaign: Operation Ayin, (Dec. 1948–Jan. 1949), the final campaign against Egypt. Philip Balkin fell in the attack on Auja-el-Hafir December 27, 1948. Buried in Halutsa; July 20, 1949, he was reinterred in the cemetery in Nahalat Yitshak.

Louis Ball (Ludwig Smargad). Born March 10, 1922 in Vienna, Austria. When the Germans took Vienna, he and his brothers succeeded in making their way to Switzerland and from there to the United States. Their parents remained in Vienna, and were killed there. Living with relatives in New York, Ludwig finished high school, entered college, and completed his training in optics. At the age of 21, he became an American citizen, changed his name to Louis, and entered the American army where he reached the rank of sergeant. At the end of his service, he was stationed with the American Army of Occupation in Austria, the country of his birth. From the time of his discharge, Louis Ball had a yearning to go to the land of Israel. In this, his brother Sam had preceded him, becoming a model pioneer, and a commander in the Haganah and in the Army of Israel. Louis Ball arrived in Israel in December 1947 via Cyprus—having come on a refugee ship which was caught by the British, and with all its passengers was interred on Cyprus. His brother made arrangements for him to live on kibbutz Maayan Baruch, in order to learn the language and something of the land. From there he went to Degania, where he joined the Palmach and fought in numerous engagements in many parts of the country. He was capable and cheerful. Louis Ball fell in the first attack on Iraq Sueidan July 9, 1948. He was reinterred in the cemetery at Nahalat Yitshak January 23, 1951.

William Bernstein—Born in Passaic, New Jersey, January 27, 1923. He went to public school in Passaic and moved to San Francisco with his family when he was twelve years old. Graduated from Galileo High School in San Francisco, attended Ohio State University, and during World War II entered the U.S. Merchant Marine Academy at Kings Point, graduating in 1944. Bill Bernstein served in the U.S. Navy as a Lieutenant, J.G., and after World War II, was recommended to the U.S. Naval Academy at Annapolis. Instead, he was drawn by Jewish principles to serve as second mate aboard the *Exodus 1947*.

The *Exodus* was by far the best known of the "illegal" immigrant vessels. Originally the *President Warfield,* it was a domestic American steamer of venerable age when it was purchased by Zev (Danny) Shind. It was public knowledge that UNSCOP (United Nations Special Committee on Palestine) would be investigating the Palestine situation on the spot early in the summer of 1947. Thus, from the public relations point of view, it was most desirable that the British be confronted with the attempted landing of a large number of refugees while UNSCOP was there—and its representatives could directly witness exactly how the British handled the stateless survivors of the Holocaust. Thus, the ship was rushed to Sete on the French Riviera. At the same time, 4,553 Jews were brought there from displaced person camps in Germany, with the French co-operating in spite of a transport workers strike and the doubtful validity of the refugees' documentation. July 10, the passengers embarked. The chief officer was Bernard Marks of Cincinatti, Ohio; William Bernstein was second in the operational hierarchy (in effect, chief mate). As usual with the refugee ships, political decisions and thus, ultimate command rested with Israelis (that is, Palestinian Jews).

The British discovered the ship even before it left the harbor and pressed the French to detain it. It quickly set out to sea without a pilot. On route, a British flotilla consisting of the cruiser HMS Ajax, plus destroyers, acted as unwelcome escort. Early in the morning of July 18, close to the Palestinian coast, the British attacked, and boarded the *Exodus 1947*.

In the battle, with no firearms being used by either side, three men were clubbed to death: Two Polish refugees and William Bernstein. The next day, members of UNSCOP witnessed the forcible transfer of the refugees to three British transports which were to take them back to Europe. Except for 130 people who left the vessel for medical reasons in France, all the rest were returned to camps in Germany—whence they again began smuggling themselves south.. Many managed to reach Palestine or Cyprus by early 1948, with the last of the former Exodus passengers arriving Sept. 7, 1948.

Although a number of the American volunteers did have particular political viewpoints, it is noteworthy that Bill Bernstein was not among them: He disclaimed all interest in the political arguments which were an ongoing feature of life aboard ship—he often stated that he was only there to help the remnant of Europe's Jewry reach Palestine. The night before the encounter with the British flotilla he seemed to have a premonition of his impending death and spoke of it to fellow crew members. Bill Bernstein was buried in the Martyrs Row, with the others killed aboard the Exodus, in the cemetery in Haifa.

Spencer Andrew Boyd—Born August 16, 1923 in St. Louis, Missouri. At the outbreak of World War II, enlisted in the RCAF (Royal Canadian Air Force). Trained as a navigator; became an instructor. In 1942 returned to the United States. After a brief period as instructor for the U.S. Navy, transferred to the U.S. Air Force. Served as photographer on a B29. After the war earned a civilian pilot license. Served as administrator of an airfield in New Jersey in 1946; enrolled in the University in Chicago in 1947, majoring in mathematics. In the Spring of 1948, volunteered to serve in the Israel Air Force. Arrived in Israel at the end of June. Spence Boyd was killed in mid-July at the end of the Ten Days when his planeload of wounded from Sodom landed on the sands near the sea west of Rehovot, because of mechanical trouble. The plane was a small Aerovan, piloted by Murray Weissberg of Brooklyn, N. Y. The landing itself was without mishap—but, lacking adequate side arms, all on board were butchered by a passing band of Arabs. Weissberg and Boyd had tossed a coin to determine which would remain with the plane, and which would seek help. Weissberg won the toss, and elected the more dangerous mission of going for help. He left with Spence Boyd's pistol and one of the wounded who was ambulatory. When they returned a few hours later, all had been cut to pieces. Buried with full military honors in the Christian Cemetery at Jaffa. April 6, 1951 his body was transferred to the Christian Cemetery in Haifa.

George (Buzz) Beurling—Born December 16, 1921 in Canada; grew up in Montreal, in a seriously religious Christian home where he acquired the habit of reading the Bible, a habit which accompanied him into adult life. Interested in flying from an early age; also loved music and sports, especially swimming. Served in the RCAF in World War II. Particularly active in the defense of the isolated island of Malta in the Mediterranean. Was an ace fighter pilot, credited with downing numerous enemy war planes; received considerable public recognition for his prowess. Volunteered to serve in the Israel Air Force after turning down lucrative offers from a number of other countries. Seeing this as unfinished post-World War II business, together with his serious approach to the Bible, were likely significant factors in his decision. Killed in an accident over Urbe airfield near Rome, together with Leonard Cohen (Englishman) May 20, 1948. Initially buried in a Catholic Cemetery near Rome with the Jews of Rome closing their shops to attend the funeral. Buzz Beurling's remains were transferred to the Christian Cemetery in Haifa Nov. 9, 1950.

Wilfred (Zev) Cantor—Born February 7, 1921, in Kiev, Russia. When he was 5 years old, his family moved to Toronto, Canada, and established itself there. Joined the RCAF at the age of 18. Posted to England. Member of a bomber crew whose plane was hit over Stuttgart. Avoided capture with underground aid, and eventually made his way back to England. A year later a similar occurrence resulted in his capture and internment in Germany. After returning to Canada in 1945, had some difficulty adjusting to civilian life. Was among the first to volunteer for service with the Israel Air Force, with which he saw considerable activity. Oct. 24, 1948 the DC-3 (Dakota) aircraft he was piloting exploded and crashed on takeoff from the Ekron airfield, killing all on board. The others were Fred Stevenson (Canadian), flight engineer; William Fisher (Canadian), navigator; and Jerome Littman (Englishman), wireless operator. Wilfred Cantor was buried in Rehovot.

William Edmondson—Born in 1927 in the United States, the son of Irish immigrants. Leftist in ideological orientation, opposing class and political repression. Worked as a social worker; viewed World War II in ideological terms and enlisted to fight the Nazis. After the war he went to France to work as a sculptor. Had friends from Israel (Palestine). Served in Aliya Bet, and moved to Israel to participate more fully in the struggle. Although he saw Israel's struggle as primarily one against Arab fascism, he made it a point to say (rather tongue in cheek) that it was particularly appropriate for himself, as an Irishman, to be engaged in fighting against the British. After participating in a number of actions, killed July 9, 1948 by a bullet to the head on the road to Jerusalem. Initially buried in the Christian Cemetery in Jaffa; April 16, 1951, reinterred in the Christian Cemetery in Haifa. Left a young wife in France, whom he had hoped to bring to Israel after the war.

William (Willy) Fisher—Born in Podolia, Russia, August 28, 1923, two months after the death of his father. In 1924 the family moved to Canada, establishing itself in Winnipeg. Enlisted in the RCAF in 1942; served overseas as a navigator until the end of the war when he returned to Canada. Left for Israel by way of England at the end of July 1948, arriving at the end of August. Willy Fisher served as a navigator in the IAF until he was killed with Wilfred Cantor, Fred Stevenson and Jerome Littman in the crash of a Dakota at Ekron Oct. 24, 1948. Buried in Rehovot.

Leonard (Len) Fitchett—Born September 10, 1923, in Moose Horn, Canada; grew up in Victoria, British Columbia. In World War II served as a pilot with the RCAF in the European Theater. On one flight, made a forced landing in France where the Maquis (French underground) found him and returned him safely to his base. Earned a number of commendations for his achievements in the air; credited with shooting down the last German plane before Germany's surrender. Upon discharge, returned to his University studies, where his major interests were classical poetry and philosophy (a volume of Byron had accompanied him in flight). He was drawn to the downtrodden—whether an individual or a people. He felt that Israel's battle for freedom was his own battle, although he was not a Jew. Left the University secretly to enlist in the IAF, telling no one but his sister of his intended destination; his parents were informed only after he reached Israel. His affinity for Israel was such that he planned to remain in Israel after the war, and settle on a kibbutz. Killed in the Beaufighter shot down by ground fire over Iraq Sueidan, Oct. 20, 1948, together with Stanley Andrews and Dov Sugarman. In the course of his service he was reported as having shot down 3 Egyptian Spitfires and having driven off an Egyptian warship.

Moshe Geberer—Born in New York, September 29, 1920. His service in the American Army in World War II included two years in Alaska; attained the rank of Sergeant. Was active in a number of Zionist youth organizations, including Hashomer Hatzair, Habonim, Hechalutz, and Poale Zion. He spent considerable time on an agricultural training farm. In the winter of 1946–47 participated in a special Haganah training course in secret communication, in the United States. Left on Aliyah to Israel at the first opportunity, arriving in Haifa July 24, 1947. Had intended to become a member of kibbutz Kfar Blum, a Habonim kibbutz; for personal reasons went to Jerusalem instead, where he worked in the Youth Department of the Jewish Agency, writing, and translating material from Hebrew into English. In the Jerusalem fighting, did guard duty and general service. Assigned to a unit in southern Jerusalem in the fighting for Katamon. Killed by a sniper's bullet May 17, 1948, while scouting, preliminary to the capture of the Jerusalem railroad station. Initially buried in Sheikh Badr A; Sept. 10, 1950, reinterred on Mt. Herzl in Jerusalem.

William Gerson—Pilot of a C46 (Commando) transport plane, one of several flown from the United States to Mexico just ahead of the April 15, 1948, embargo deadline. This plane apparently was too heavily loaded, especially for the high altitude of Mexico City. It crashed on takeoff from the airport there, April 15, 1948, killing its two-man crew: William Gerson, apparently a dedicated zionist, and Glen King, non-Jewish American mechanic.

Aaron Hanovice—Born in Houston, Texas, in 1922. During World War II Aaron, whose parents had earlier moved the family to Palestine, joined the British forces there and served in a naval unit in Haifa for two years. He then asked for transfer to the U.S. Army in Palestine, and served two years in the American Army in the Middle East, based in Egypt. Aaron Hanovice was honorably discharged from the U.S. Army in Tel-Aviv, in 1945, after V.J. Day. He then took up residence in Tel Aviv, and together with a group of other U.S. Army veterans who were separated from service at the same time, organized a trucking corporation in Palestine (one of their members was Carmi Rabinowitz). In August 1947, Aaron Hanovice was killed from ambush by Arabs as he was returning in a truck convoy from Jerusalem. (His brother Samuel, also born in Houston, Texas, was one of the legendary "Twenty-Three": A British-led commando group which aimed a sea borne raid at Syria before the 1941 invasion of that country. All were lost—whether at sea, or by capture and stealthy execution, has never been determined. There is a memorial to the "23" in the Nautical Officers and Cadet training school in Acre, and in Yad-Vashem in Jerusalem.) Aaron Hanovice was 25 years old when he was killed, and was survived by his widow and a son who was born about a month after his death.

Oliver Garfield Holton—Born in Lakewood, Ohio, August 30, 1914. Drawn to flying from childhood—went to air shows, collected books on planes and built model airplanes. At the age of 20 became part of a group of professional sport pilots. At the start of World War II went to Canada and enlisted in the RCAF. In 1940 shifted to the Eagle Squadron of American volunteers in England. As a fighter pilot participated in the defense of England during the blitz, shooting down several German planes. After being wounded, became a test pilot. In Oct. 1941, returned to the United States to serve as instructor for student pilots. Sent to Africa in 1944; returned ill. Upon discharge, engaged in civilian flying. Volunteered to serve in the IAF in Sept. 1948. Dec. 2, 1948, in the course of testing a Widgeon aircraft, crashed into Lake Kinneret (Sea of Galilee); all on board were killed. The others were Ralph Moster (Canadian) and Alvin Levine (American). (One source gives the date of the fatal accident as Dec. 7.) Initially buried in the cemetery in Jaffa; reinterred in the Christian cemetery in Haifa April 16, 1951.

Joseph (Joe) Kahn—Born August 21, 1908, Philadelphia, Penn. Grew up in Los Angeles and went into business. Drafted into the American Army in 1941; served in the information section of the 26th Infantry Division. Participated in many actions in the Far East, attaining the rank of Staff Sergeant. After the war, returned to his business affairs in Los Angeles. The destruction of European Jewry and the blocking of the road to liberation for its few survivors touched him deeply; in July 1947 he appeared at the office of the "American League for a Free Palestine" ("Hebrew Committee for National Liberation"?) in Washington saying, "I am a soldier; I have fought in the wars of other nations, I now want to fight for my own people; I am at your service." Assisted in the guarding and outfitting of the "Altalena" when it was purchased. In Jan. 1948 transferred to IZL (Irgun) service in Paris. Made contact with former Maquis (French underground during World War II) people and participated in the purchase and packing of arms and forwarding them to Israel. For this, he was arrested briefly. Released in time to meet the "Altalena" at its berth in southern France prior to its sailing for Israel. Served as military police officer on the ship, although on principle he refused to accept any rank designation. After the mini-civil war over the "Altalena" which began at Kfar Vitkin and ended with the destruction of the Altalena on the beach of Tel Aviv (an experience which deeply shocked him), enlisted with the IZL (Irgun) forces in Jerusalem. Participated in the Irgun/Stern breakthrough into the Old City the last night of the Ten Days. Killed in this action two hours before the start of the truce. Buried in Sheikh Badr A. Sept. 19, 1950, reinterred in Mt. Herzl, Jerusalem.

Jerome (Jerry) Kaplan—Born in Bayonne, New Jersey. Served as a Pharmacist's Mate in the U. S. Navy in World War II. After discharge began a course of study preparatory to University work. Upon hearing that Israel urgently needed young people to assist in its struggle, left his studies and volunteered through a Haganah channel. Sailed from New York March 29, 1948, with Mandel Math and other volunteers, arriving in Haifa April 14. From there made his way to Tel Aviv and Haganah military service. Fell, with Mandel Math, in the battle for Latrun of May 13, 1948—the day before proclamation of the State. His body was never recovered.

Ernest (Glen) King—American aircraft mechanic, non-Jewish. Second member of the two man crew killed April 15, 1948 in the takeoff crash of an overloaded C46 (Commando) at Mexico City, Mexico. The pilot was William Gerson.

Jack Klein—Born June 2, 1916 in New York City. Had Hebrew school education which included Zionist orientation. Became active in the Hashomer Hatzair youth organization, occupying a key position such that it was organizationally important for him to remain while many others proceeded to Palestine (pre-Israel). With the coming of World War II, entered the U.S. Army where he became corporal and an expert mechanic. After the war, succeeded in moving his mother, wife and son to Palestine (as tourists) although he himself could not enter because of technical difficulties. Finally succeeded in 1947 via a refugee ship. Became a member of the Hashomer Hatzair kibbutz "Hatsor," in the south. A major defensive tactic in the face of the expected Egyptian invasion was the laying of mine fields. This became a specialty for Jack Klein. Killed May 30, 1948, in the course of setting mines in the fields of Kfar Menahem, when a mine blew up in his hands. Buried in the cemetery at Kibbutz Hatsor.

Ari Lashner—Born April 8, 1915 in New York City. Graduated CCNY (College of the City of New York) where he majored in the social sciences with particular emphasis on education and teaching. Had received Zionist orientation under the auspices of Poale Zion both in afternoon school and in summer camp. Joined Poale Zion in 1932 as a young adult and quickly became an organizer and the central figure in the youth group "Habonim." From 1936 on was active in its summer camps all over the country (Los Angeles, Chicago, St. Louis, etc.). Went to Hachshara (model farm preparation for Aliyah) in Cream Ridge, New Jersey, but was persuaded to return to organizational work, as a truly indispensable individual. Drafted into the American Navy in 1942, where he served as a wireless officer. Discharged in 1945; returned briefly to general organizational work until Jan. 1946. From then on, focused on recruiting people to man the ships, and participate generally, in the "illegal" movement of refugees from Europe to Palestine. Was himself among the first volunteers. In Aug. 1946, Ari Lashner reached Israel on the refugee ship *Haganah* and became a member of the Habonim Kibbutz Kfar Blum, where his wife was already residing. In the kibbutz he came to specialize in electrical work. Killed by a sniper from the east bank of the Jordan March 15, 1948 when he climbed a pole to do some electrical repair work. Buried in the cemetery at Kfar Blum. Left his wife and a daughter.

Sidney Leizerowitz—From Toronto, Canada. Joined Co. B of the 72nd Battalion, 7th Brigade (the "English-speaking Battalion") August 1948. Killed in the Galilee, at Tamra, in the course of Operation Hiram. This operation in the final days of October thoroughly defeated the irregular forces of Fawzi Kaukji's Arab Liberation Army and drove them out of the

Galilee. Sidney Leizerowitz was about 19 years old; he had enlisted just two months earlier. He is buried in the military cemetery in Nahariya.

Alvin Levine—Born in Long Beach, New York, July 30, 1918; grew up there. In World War II served as an Air Force mechanic based in England. With the onset of Israel's War of Independence, left his home, his wife and daughter and came to offer his skills and experience to the Air Force of the homeland of his people. Served faithfully and well. Was one of three men aboard Oliver Holton's Widgeon, killed when it crashed into Lake Kinneret (Sea of Galilee) early in Dec. 1948. Initially buried in Tiberias; remains later transferred to Nahalat Yitzhak.

Baruch Linsky—Born in Chicago May 1, 1921. Moved to California with his family when he was about 10 years old. At the University in Los Angeles he majored in psychology, receiving his BA in 1943. Continued his studies in Berkeley, receiving his MA in 1945. Moved to New York in Dec. 1945 where he began to explore Zionism, Jewish history and the meaning of Judaism. Became active in Ailya Bet work, eventually making for Israel on a refugee ship. The ship was caught by the British Navy near Haifa and all those on it were interned on Cyprus. Early in 1947 Linsky was permitted to enter the land of Israel. Spent several months on a kibbutz in the north and then enrolled at the Hebrew University in Jerusalem. In the Spring of 1948 volunteered for Haganah service. Wrote glowing letters home about events in Israel and its anticipated future. Killed at Hulda May 26, 1948. Initially buried at Hulda. Oct. 26, 1950, reinterred in a Haifa cemetery.

David (Mickey) Marcus—Born February 22, 1901 to parents who were rather distant from traditional Judaism. His grandmother, however, did her best to teach him prayers, familiarize him with the custom of placing a few coins in the Jewish National Fund blue box Friday evenings before the start of the Sabbath—and emphasized that she wanted to end her days in Jerusalem. Upon completing high school, Marcus entered the United States Military Academy at West Point—the regular army's training school for career officers. He graduated in 1924, but did not remain in the army for long. Completed law training in Brooklyn, New York in 1927. Earned the title Doctor of Jurisprudence. Worked in the legal field for the City of New York. In 1940 entered active service in the U.S. Army, rising to the rank of colonel as a headquarters staff officer with the

European expeditionary forces. He had served in the Pacific theater in 1942-1943. Reassigned to Europe, he jumped into Normandy with a group of paratroopers early in the invasion of the European continent. As an American soldier, saw the Jewish survivors of the concentration camps as well as the evidence of those who did not survive. Served to some extent as legal military advisor in connection· with a number of historic events, including the Yalta conference and the surrender of Italy and Germany. Received numerous decorations including Britain's highest award to a noncitizen. Marcus was presented with this exceedingly high honorary decoration, Commander of the British Empire, at a special ceremony at the British Embassy in Washington, April 20, 1948. Most ironically, Marcus at this point was between trips to Israel, where a major foe was the British Empire! Marcus had been sought out and recruited by a representative of Israel's incipient government early in 1948. He traveled widely in the country as military consultant to the Haganah and Palmach. Ten years earlier, Orde Wingate, the Christian British career officer, had given the direction which brought the Palmach into being. Now, the American Jewish Colonel, Mickey Marcus, was guiding the next step: Transition from an underground guerrilla force to the nucleus of a functioning army. He did most important work in logistics and in producing and preparing to implement various kinds of training manuals. Shortly after his return, he was made commander of the Jerusalem sector, with the task of breaking the siege of Jerusalem. He did not succeed in reopening the single blocked road. Under his command, work on a bypass road (variously called Burma Road or Marcus Road) was begun. Accidentally killed by one of his own sentries the night of June 10, 1948, at Abu Gosh, immediately before the First Truce. Survived by his wife. Interred with full military honors at the military cemetery at West Point, New York. (For several years the American Veterans of Israel have been marking Marcus's yahrzeit, symbolic of the death of all Americans killed in the War of Independence, at a simple ceremony in West Point.)

Mandel Math—Born August 22, 1926, in Brooklyn, New York. Given a strongly religious upbringing at home and in school. His elementary education was at a day school (Yeshiva), continuing at Herzliah Hebrew High School in New York. His attendance at Brooklyn College was interrupted by World War II. He served in the U.S. Army, participating in the liberation of the survivors of the death camps of Dachau and Buchenwald. Was courtmartialed—and vindicated—for his religious convictions:

As a "Kohen" (a descendant of the priestly class in the days of the Temple in Jerusalem), strict Jewish Law forbids any unnecessary contact with the dead (other than one's immediate family). Mandel understood this to apply to the ashes and the other remains in the death camps, and therefore refused to participate directly in their burial, since this could be done by others—and there was other work he could do. At his court-martial his position was understood and he was released. Returned to Brooklyn College, but the memory of the European survivors was very much with him. He was particularly agitated by the lack of positive action on the part of the American Government to open the gates of Palestine. Organized a general group to help the Haganah; tried to organize a group of young volunteers within his own organization ("Mizrahi") to serve in the growing war in Israel. Left for Israel March 29, 1948, and promptly enlisted in the Haganah. Killed in the battle for Latrun of May 13, 1948, together with Jerome Kaplan—the day before the State was declared. His body was never recovered.

Harold (Zvi) Monash—Born January 1, 1924, in Berlin, Germany. Was assisted to emigrate to the U.S. in 1936, where he was helped by relatives until his parents succeeded in reaching this country in 1940. Trained as an electrician, receiving his certificate in 1943 at which time he entered the U.S. Army. Shipped to Europe in July. Attained the rank of corporal. His unit took heavy casualties; volunteered for service in a paratroop unit. Captured three German soldiers in Anzio, Italy. Seriously wounded in the fighting for Rome, Monash was sent to the United States for re-cuperation. His final duty was as officer in charge of a group of German prisoners of war. Upon discharge, planned to go on Aliyah and complete his education at the Technion in Haifa. Studied Hebrew by way of preparation. Made his way to Israel, as a student with a youth group on a refugee ship which arrived in Aug. 1946. Studied for a year at the Technion, planning to become a civil engineer. Attached himself to a kibbutz as a means of getting to know the country and its conditions better. Joined the Palmach and was sent to the Jerusalem sector. Killed in action April 25, 1948. Buried in Kiriat Anavim.

Ralph Moster—Born August 29, 1924 in Hamilton, Ontario, Canada. Studied in Vancouver. In World War II, served in the RCAF where he gained broad flying experience. When the Arabs began to invade Israel he felt a strong desire to participate with Israel. Arrived in the country in the spring of 1948 and promptly joined the Palmach. Was assigned to a so-called armored group. He increased its fire power substantially by taking the machine gun from a downed enemy aircraft and properly mounting it on one of the vehicles in his unit. Showed exemplary bravery in a number of actions. Ralph Moster transferred to the IAF as it began taking shape, serving as a light-plane pilot. Appointed head of a Negev flight squadron and later of an air base. Had deep love for the land; felt that the Negev in particular would flourish in the future. Ralph Moster had planned to visit his parents in October, but decided to wait until both a proper replacement could be found for him, and until the Negev was cleared of the enemy. Was one of the three men on the fatal test flight of the Widgeon aircraft over Lake Kinneret (Sea of Galilee) Dec. 2 (or Dec. 7) 1948. His companions were Oliver Holton and Alvin Levine. Buried at Nahalat Yitzhak.

Moshe (Mosie) Perlstein—Born November 24, 1925 in Jersey City, New Jersey. The family moved to Borough Park, Brooklyn where he attended Yeshivat Etz Chaim, a religious elementary day school. He continued his studies at the Rabbi Itzhak Elhanan Yeshiva in New York where he joined and was a leader in the Torah V'avoda youth group. Upon graduation in 1944 he went to the agricultural farm of Hashomer Hadati in Cranberry, New Jersey. In late 1946 or early 1947, went to Palestine where he spent some time at Ein Hanetziv after which he enrolled at the Hebrew University in Jerusalem for advanced studies in Judaica and agriculture, in order to be able to return to work as a more highly trained and thus a more useful individual. With the outbreak of the Arab attacks that marked the beginning of the War of Independence, Moshe Perlstein felt that personal participation in the defense of the Yishuv was right and proper for him. He volunteered his services, and was active in the Jerusalem area. He joined the squad posthumously known as "The 35." As early as Dec. 1947, vehicles attempting to bring supplies to the Etzion group of four kibbutzim far to the south of Jerusalem had been turned back with significant losses. In mid-January this group of 35 youths was to carry relief supplies on their backs for the beseiged Etzion settlements. Jan. 16, 1948 the group was caught and completely wiped out near the valley of Elah. The bodies were first interred at Kfar Etzion, in a common grave. All the Etzion casualties were reinterred on Mount Herzl Nov. 17, 1949. At the time of his death, Moshe Perlstein was 22 years old, his family's only son.

Sam Pomerantz—Born September 23, 1910 in New York City. During the years of the Great Depression, he lived in Newark, N. J., with an uncle who owned a commercial garage. Sam Pomerantz worked there as an automobile mechanic; he had a great love for motors. Graduated the aircraft engineering department of New York University. Worked as a supervisor in aircraft factories and maintenance facilities. In March 1948 left the United States to serve as chief mechanic and roving supervisor for operations in and from Czechoslovakia. This included both the airlift from Zatec of desperately needed small arms, ammunition and Messerschmitt fighter planes in American transport planes (the Air Transport Command), and the later preparations of two flights of Spitfires (Operations Velveta 1 and Velveta 2) for direct flight under their own power to Israel. Perhaps a truly indispensable man: It is most doubtful that these operations could have succeeded as they did without Sam Pomerantz. Killed piloting one of the planes of Velveta 2 when it crashed in the mountains in Yugoslavia in a snowstorm Dec. 18, 1948. His body was brought to Israel and buried at Nahalat Yitzhak Jan. 9, 1949. Survived by his wife.

Carmi Rabinowitz—Born August 11, 1924 in New York City. Reared in an atmosphere which was Zionist, religious and highly aware of the Hebrew language. He attended Yeshivat Etz Chaim (the same day school which included Moshe Perlstein among its students), and only Hebrew was spoken at home. When Carmi was still quite young (in 1932) the family moved to Tel Aviv. There he studied in the Bilu Elementary School and the Montefiore High School, learning the trade of radio technician. At the age of 15 joined the Haganah and later the Palmach. In World War II volunteered to serve in the American Army where he fought in the western desert in Africa and, together with Palestinian friends in the British Army, was able to do a bit (presumably, arms acquisition) for the Haganah. At the end of the war it was suggested to him that he complete his technical training in the United States at government expense (under the GI Bill). He felt that the local situation was far too urgent to permit any such luxury, and immediately reenrolled in the Haganah where he participated in many actions, ranging from small guerrilla battles against Arabs to bringing "illegal" immigrants into shore. With the increased activity that followed the voting of the Partition Plan, Carmi Rabinowitz was assigned to aggressive patrol on the outskirts of the city as a company commander. A basic Haganah tactic was the blowing up of those houses from which hostile activity originated. Dec. 25, 1947 it was decided to eliminate such a three-story building in the Arab village of Tel-a-rish, from which snipers controlled the road to Holon. Carmi served as a sapper, and was killed in the action. He was buried in Nahalat Yitzhak. "Bet Carmi" is named for him.

Moshe Aaron (Moe) Rosenbaum—Born March 30, 1920 in Poland. When he was just 11 months old, his parents emigrated to the United States, the family settling in Brooklyn, New York. The family had a strong zionist orientation, with Moe's father being active in Poale Zion (the Labor Zionist group). American and Zionist idealism were supplemented and reinforced each other. Upon the outbreak of World War II, left college to join the U.S. Air Force. Trained as a navigator, with the rank of 2nd Lieut. Sent overseas to the Mediterranean Theater. Upon being based in Italy, came in contact with soldiers of the Jewish Brigade (Jewish Palestine's special force in the British Army), was very much drawn to them, and decided to go to live in the land of Israel when the time should be right. His plane was shot down on his 13th mission, a bombing run over the Rumanian oil fields. Taken prisoner, he spent the balance of the war in a POW camp in Germany until liberation by the Allied Forces in May 1945. On returning to the United States, enrolled in mechanical engineering, on the premise that this would be a most useful specialty in Israel. Because of the urgency of the situation, he left school in the Spring of 1948, just a month shy of graduation. His extra-curricular interests had been broad, including activity in Hillel (the B'nai B'rith campus organization), in Habonim (the Labor Zionist youth organization), in sports and in the arts, particularly painting. His service for Israel was brief. On May 21, 1948, on one of the early flights of the Czech airlift, the C46 on which he was navigator was caught by ground fog on its way into the airfield in Israel. The plane crashed into a low hill with just one casualty: Moe Rosenbaum, who was crushed by the shifting of the crated half-Messerschmitt in the plane's interior. Buried in Rehovot.

Jacob Rothman—Born January 29, 1911 in Brooklyn, New York. Lived in Newark, N. J., where he graduated from South Side High School. Enrolled in Upsala College in New Jersey where he experienced blatant anti-Semitism, finding that fraternity resident facilities were closed to Jews. He established the first Jewish facility. During World War II, served in the U.S. Merchant Marine as chief radio officer on ammunition ships. Was discharged in Sept. 1945. Worked as chief draftsman for the Congoleum Nairn company and lectured in mechanics at Columbia Univer sity. Was very much moved by the struggle in Israel; said that when he read that 40,000,000 Arabs were fighting against 400,000 Jews, he decided to become the 400,001. Contacted the Haganah people engaged in the clandestine acquisition of arms for Israel and worked actively with them. In the summer of 1948 sailed for Israel as first radio operator on the ship *Kefalos,* which was carrying arms and aviation fuel to Israel from Tampico, Mexico. The voyage was long and difficult but ultimately successful. Jack Rothman was influenced further by Arieh Kesselman, the only Israeli on the ship (Kesselman, too, was killed in the war). Rothman was very much taken with what he saw of the land and the people, and thought seriously about settling there. He enlisted in the Israel Air Force, and was sent on a mission to Italy en route home. Killed in a plane crash on an island off the Italian coast, together with eight Israelis, Dec. 31, 1948. The Jews of Rome, en mass, attended their funeral. Jack Rothman's body was transferred to Israel and buried in Nahalat Yitshak March 6, 1949. He left a wife and daughter in the United States.

Sidney Rubinoff—Born February 20, 1926, in Toronto, Canada. He was the youngest of a family of three brothers and two sisters. Had Technical School education. Sid Rubinoff joined the Canadian Army in 1944, at the age of 18, and served overseas until his discharge at the end of 1945. Went to Israel and joined the Palmach. Killed in action July 17, 1948.

Reuben (Red) Schiff—Born in 1924 in Toronto. He was an only son, with three sisters. Grew up in a hard-working family of very modest circum- stances. At the age of 17, Reuben Schiff joined the Canadian Army; served for five years, most of the time overseas. He was wounded in Germany and was discharged in 1945. Went to Israel late in 1947. He was part of the crew of the Aliya Bet ship *Paducah (Geula).* Red Schiff was in- terned on Cyprus along with the other passengers and crew of his ship as well as those of other ships caught by the British. A group of the sailors of the *Paducah* and *Northland* escaped from a bus convoy taking them to the detention camp at Athlit upon their arrival from Cyprus Nov. 19, 1947; Schiff was among them. Red then went to kibbutz Maayan Baruch. From there, he and Louis (Lou) Ball, among others, joined the Palmach. In the course of extensive fighting in the Negev, Red Schiff (like Lou Ball) was killed. His name appears on the Memorial in Maayan Baruch.

Jack Shulman—Born January 14, 1928 in Paris. As a youth came with his family to New York, where he went to high school. After serving as an instructor in the American Army for 18 months, returned to France and volunteered to serve in the Haganah Camp near Marseilles. From there traveled to Israel with other Mahal people and served in the ground forces. Killed in the course of the capture of Beersheva Oct. 21, 1948. Reinterred at Nahalat Yitshak Aug. 11, 1949.

Avraham David Stavsky—Born the 5th of Styzinia (Polish month) 1906 in Brest-Litovsk, Poland. He immigrated to Palestine in 1932 and was active in 'illegal' immigration. The night of June 16, 1933, Ḥaim Arlosoroff, a leading member of the Palestine Labor Party (Mapai), was murdered on the north Tel Aviv beach. Stavsky and two other Revisionists (the major right wing political party, then in bitter opposition to the Labor Party) were arrested and charged with the crime, which was assumed to have been a political assassination. The other two were acquitted, but Stavsky, protesting his innocence, was found guilty. Of the three judges, one dissented vigorously stating that, in his opinion, Avraham Stavsky was equally innocent and the crime was not political at all. (Many years later, it was reported that an Arab had confessed to the killing, but that his confession had been hushed up.) The death sentence was protested by many prominent voices and July 19, 1934 the verdict was overruled by the Court of Appeals. Stavsky was released and exiled, moving to the United States, where he applied for citizenship. In the U.S., he worked hard and continuously for the 'illegal' immigration of Jews to Palestine. Stavsky served with the War Refugee Board which saved numerous lives from the Nazi Holocaust and was involved in refugee work in Ankara and Switzerland. He held much of the responsibility for the ships "Ben Hecht" and "Altalena". Avraham Stavsky was fatally wounded aboard the "Altalena" June 22, 1948 off northern Tel Aviv—quite close to the spot where Arlosoroff had been killed in the very same month 15 years earlier. He died the following day and was buried in Nahalat Yitzhak Cemetery in Tel Aviv.

Fred Stevenson—Canadian, born in 1919. Pilot or flight engineer. One of four members of the crew of the DC3 (Dakota) which blew up on takeoff from Ekron airfield October 24, 1948. The others were Wilfred Cantor, pilot (Canadian); William Fisher (Canadian) navigator; Jerome Littman

(Englishman) wireless operator. Buried in Jaffa Oct. 27; reinterred in the Protestant Cemetery in Haifa April 16, 1951.

Edward Leonard Troyen—Born in New York City October 22, 1926. Grew up as a totally assimilated American, with a handful of Yiddish phrases his sole remembrance of his Jewish heritage. After high school, entered the field of civil aviation. In the Second World War, served in the U.S. Air Force in the European Theater. Was deeply moved by what he saw of the aftermath of the Holocaust, and in particular by the plight of the stateless survivors who had no government that cared about them. Upon discharge Troyen signed a nine-month contract to serve as civilian instructor in mechanics and flight engineering with the American forces occupying Japan. Made deep friendships there; in particular, the family of one Japanese dentist came to cherish him so much that they continue to mark the anniversary of his death as though he had been a member of the family. Upon his return, he resumed higher education in the United States. When he became aware of the situation in Israel and in particular of the critical lack of trained airforce personnel, he sought out a proper underground channel and offered his services to the Israel Air Force. In spite of his mother's concern and warnings of danger, he promptly left with a group of volunteers for Israel. Their plane had the misfortune to land on the Island of Rhodes where they were sent back via Italy. In Rome, they were lectured by American Embassy representatives; the lecture included a warning not to participate in Israel's war since this would make them liable to punishment for violating the embargo, and to the loss of their American citizenship. Exactly one member of the group was persuaded by this exaggerated warning, and left for home. All the others went to Czechoslovakia, and were taken to Israel via the Czech airlift. Troyen served in the assembling of airplanes, in their maintenance, and in directing and instructing others in technical work. His efforts were most important in getting Israel's planes flying, and keeping them airworthy. In the meantime his mother's health took a negative turn, and he was urged to return home. With difficulty a phone conversation was arranged with his father July 4th. When the senior Mr. Troyen understood how urgent and important was his son's work, he agreed that it was proper for him to remain in Israel under the circumstances. Very close to the Second Truce, with his work completed and himself free to enjoy a brief respite in Tel Aviv, Troyen volunteered to participate in an attack mission. Very severely wounded by enemy fire, he was rushed to Haifa hospital where he lingered for a day, dying July 19, 1948, the day the Second Truce began. He was buried in Haifa cemetery. In a letter to his parents found in his pocket ready for mailing, he had written that as soon as the truce was reestablished he would immediately return home.

Robert Lester Weeckman—Born November 21, 1921 in Los Angeles, California. From childhood, showed unusual talent in the arts—drawing, painting, sculpture, engraving; also, in sports and in photography. In the summer of 1939, made a bicycle trip through Europe with friends. After further schooling, in 1943 joined the U.S. Air Force. He was posted to the Asiatic Pacific Theater as a pilot in an aerial reconnaissance unit. Was awarded decorations after 65 missions, including some 200 hours in battle. Upon discharge, returned to the university; after completing his academic studies he continued in art school. A few months short of finishing, decided to offer his services as a fighter pilot to Israel. This decision came after much soul searching and sensitive discussion with, among others, Jewish war veterans organizations in Los Angeles. In April 1948 he left for New York to be sent on his way to the Haganah recruiting channel for Air Force personnel. July 9, 1948, piloting a Messerschmitt, he set out on a mission from which he did not return. It is conjectured that his plane went down in the vicinity of Gaza. His body was never found. (Shahan gives the date as June 8, the area as El Arish, and adds that he was probably shot down by anti-aircraft fire.)

Chapter 9

UNDERGROUND AMERICAN PROCUREMENT

The two campaigns against the Egyptians which brought the war to a close were made possible by the flow of supplies from abroad and their proper distribution and use. Leadership was, of course, crucial; but leadership is helpless without at least a minimally viable level of supply. Thus the summer and autumn supplies supported the autumn and winter defeats of the Egyptians; the earlier spring supplies made feasible the July victory in the center and the north, and the holding actions elsewhere, then and in June.

In the beginning arms shipments were few and far between. The vital Czech airlift did not begin until the middle of May; before then, shipments were relatively small and scattered. We are able to identify positively only one prior instance of a vessel sufficiently loaded with arms that it merited the designation "arms ship": the *Nora,* early in April, contained 200 machine guns and 4,300 Czech rifles; the *Borea,* arriving May 14, was the next ship to arrive with arms.

Although the preairlift arms shipments, and the airlift itself, focused on rifles and machine guns, these continued to be in seriously short supply through the summer of 1948. And they were so critically short in the spring that the arrival of a plane carrying just 200 rifles and 4 machine guns was apparently decisive in preventing the cancellation of Operation Nahshon. Yet, all historical accounts take for granted the availability of fulsome supplies of explosives in all of the fighting—not only in early 1948, but going back to 1947.

For example, at Deir Yassin (April 9), explosives were plentiful for house-by-house dynamiting—a major factor in the Arab civilian casualties.[1] The explosives were used either raw or in the form of hand grenades, land mines, mortar ammunition, or PIAT ammunition.[2]

It is no exaggeration to state that the availability of explosives in these various forms was vital to Israel's having remained alive until mid-1948—both in terms of defense, and of the various successful offenses (i.e., Operation Nahshon). The explosive devices (grenades, mines, etc.) often

72

were of home manufacture using raw explosives—but where did raw explosives in such fulsome quantities come from?

A major source of explosives was the United States.

In mid-1945, a wealthy American, Rudolf G. Sonneborn, called a special meeting at his home at the request of David Ben Gurion, then chairman of the Jewish Agency Executive. Invited to attend were eighteen Americans; two other Palestinians were also present: Eliezer Kaplan and Reuven Zaslani.[3] The purpose of this meeting was to initiate an informal nationwide network of men sympathetic to the Jewish community of Palestine in its struggle to become autonomous, and to serve, in fact, as a homeland for Europe's surviving Jewish displaced persons. These were not abstract political or sentimental sympathizers; their commitment was of a special kind—it involved cash.

The funds that paid for the Czech airlift, the funds that paid Air Transport Command salaries, the funds that bought and outfitted ships for the "illegal" immigration, the funds that paid for surplus arms and ammunition in Europe and the United States, the funds that ran the warehousing, packing, and shipping operations, licit and otherwise, in the United States—these funds essentially came from periodic parlor meetings and luncheon meetings which grew out of this initial gathering. The most regular was to be a weekly luncheon at the Hotel McAlpin in New York.

This was extra fund-raising, outside the regular, publicized channels for relief and rehabilitation. It may—and should be—asked, "Why a new channel? Would it not have been simpler to go directly to the already existing Zionist organizations?" Ben Gurion states flatly, "But when I asked American Zionists for money to buy machine tools for the Haganah weapons industry, I drew a blank."[4]

And so this loose network was established and grew, essentially on a word of mouth basis: People would involve friends and business acquaintances (including competitors) whom they thought would be sympathetic. For many of the participants it was a completely new experience to be involved in making meaningful contributions to their fellow Jews overseas. Both in their own interest, and in the interest of the security of the various operations, donors were shielded from specific knowledge of how the funds were to be used.

The cooperative contacts that were made in this way had additional constructive results: When technically qualified people were needed for specific projects, word of mouth generally helped to find them; thus, when people were wanted to purchase surplus explosives or small arms from sporting goods stores, enthusiastic, discreet shoppers could readily be found to volunteer.

For a variety of reasons the United States was the natural place for Ben Gurion to come: Physically undamaged by World War II, America's level of affluence was relatively quite high; it had the world's largest Jewish community many of whose members were not at all conspicuous as Jews; it had traditions of freedom and openness, which meant that one could quietly do a great many things without being questioned—and without prior formal official permission; it was a big country, making it easier to be unobtrusive; it had a tradition of popular and governmental support for the Jewish homeland in Palestine, and apparent sympathy for the plight of Europe's surviving displaced persons. And, as the arsenal of democracy, America might well have all kinds of surplus material readily available—and available at low cost.

In all this, the desirability of concealment is implicit. It should be emphasized that such concealment was needed, not because anything illegal under the American law was contemplated, but for protection against the British. Thus, some funds would be used to purchase ships which, from 1945 on, would be used to defy the British ban on Jewish immigration to Palestine. And legally purchased explosives, small arms, munitions-making machinery, etc., would certainly be liable to seizure by the British government upon delivery to Palestine if not before. Within the United States, technical legality was scrupulously observed until the December 1947 arms embargo. Thereafter, every effort was made to remain within the letter of the law—but this was not always possible.

Once the initial impetus had been given to a self-sustaining fund-raising apparatus, work on specific projects could proceed.[5] Thus, late in 1945, Haim Slavin (also known as "Auerbach" and "Millman"), a Palestinian engineer who was a Haganah expert on secret arms production, came to New York City. His task: To put together the machinery and materials for a small-arms industry in Palestine. Among Slavin's immediate war-surplus acquisitions was machinery for making .303 ammunition, and machinery for making gun barrels in various diameters.[6]

The next requirement was for a private warehouse that would be controlled entirely by those involved. Such a place was located in an industrial section of the Bronx, New York, at 4366 Park Avenue (in mid-Manhattan, Park Avenue is New York's most fashionable street; a few miles north, its neighborhood is very different). This warehousing operation initially called itself "Machinery Processing and Converting Co." Its job was camouflage crating; everything shipped had to look innocent—generally, like used industrial machinery. (This was sometimes self-defeating: Some elaborate weapon-making machinery was so thoroughly dismantled that it was not practical to reassemble it in Israel until after the war. In any event, the level of metallurgical skill needed to operate such equipment may well have been lacking in Israel in 1947 and 1948.) Slavin had earlier recruited an American assistant, Phil Alper. Much of their effort went into research on explosives, and into development of a special submachine gun.

The research was done in the most efficient way possible: By reading the available technical literature. An improved procedure for manufacturing smokeless powder (the Olson process) was discovered in this way; but in seeking a shortcut to actual experience via a consultant, a most unfortunate contact was made. A chemical engineer named Abraham Brothman, who claimed to be an expert in the field, charged $20,000 and delivered no information of any value. Although another source did provide the needed information without charge—Israel would not acquire all the necessary equipment to make its own smokeless powder by this process until 1949.

The full, negative effect of the chance contact with Brothman did not surface until 1950 when Brothman and his associates were arrested as members of the pro-Soviet "atom spy" ring, which included Ethel and Julius Rosenberg, Klaus Fuchs, and Harry Gold—a chemist who had worked for Brothman from 1946 to 1948.[7] Although none of our sources suggest it, it appears not very unreasonable to consider that American hostility to Israel—at least, on the FBI-State Department level—was reinforced by finding an apparent link between underground activities for Israel and spying for the Soviet Union. This might possibly have been a factor in the ongoing prosecution (into mid-1950) of those Americans accused of smuggling planes and arms to Israel.

Although Julius Rosenberg was not arrested until July 17 (*New York Times,* July 18, 1950), and the last trial of pro-Israel "conspirators" was concluded July 10, Harry Gold and others had been arrested earlier, and surely had been under suspicion for some time before their arrest. It appears that Brothman bluffed the Communists much as he had bluffed Slavin in delivering to him widely known, readily available information. For swindling his fellow Jews, he was rewarded. For deceiving the Communists, he was jailed by the United States government.

The special submachine gun in question was to be lightweight, accurate, fast firing, and easily maintained. In reliability, accuracy, and simplicity it would be an improvement over the Johnson gun used by American forces in the Pacific in the early 1940s. Carl Ekdahl, a master mechanic who had helped design the Johnson gun and had retired (to Providence, R.I.), was contacted, and agreed to work on the gun. He did the necessary design work and tooling preparation, but adequate field testing in the United States was not possible. Since design details cannot be finalized without component field testing, the machine tools shipped over were not used to produce a field weapon of this kind for the War of Independence. Subsequently, other modifications were adopted and the gun first became the "Dror" light submachine gun, with the ultimate modified postwar product called the "Uzi." At this writing, the Uzi is generally conceded to be the best weapon of its type in the world: Not only is it standard throughout the army of Israel, but it has been adopted by the armies of West Germany and Holland (among others), and rumors persist it was favored by the personal bodyguards of numerous public figures—specifically including Charles De Gaulle when he was president of France.

The American procurement operation was essentially an American operation. One Palestinian was generally at the very top, with a small handful of Palestinians and Americans in key fulltime positions, often doing considerable traveling. The far larger number of fulltime and parttime participants were all Americans. Haim Slavin was the first "top" Palestinian. When he returned home via Switzerland in December 1946, he was replaced by Jacob Dostrovsky, who had come to New York as a representative of the Jewish Agency and had been living in the city since early 1946. As Yaacov Dori he would later become the first chief of staff of the army of Israel. In the spring of 1947, Dostrovsky returned to Palestine, and was replaced by Shlomo Rabinovich (Shlomo Shamir). When, very early in 1948, Rabinovich was called back to Palestine, he was replaced by Teddy Kollek (who, despite his name, is a Viennese-born Palestinian) and is best known today as Jerusalem's dynamic mayor.

Elie Schalit, a Palestinian, was in charge of the paperwork—the tricky language of export declarations and the mechanics of smoothly shepherding shipments through the port of export—and of receiving shipments and temporarily storing them, if their camouflaging had been done other than at 4366 Park Avenue. The consignee in Palestine would always be a legitimate commercial firm which could have some conceivable use for "used industrial machinery." It is natural that only the barest minimum of Palestinians were involved: The manpower shortage in Palestine was so severe that even volunteers who had had no previous military training were welcomed.

We have no quantitative information on the explosives and small arms collected in the United States in the three years beginning with mid-1945. However, we do have interesting samples. There was a Denver operation in which purchases were made in sporting-goods stores from locations up to 1,000 miles away. The material (gunpowder, cartridge caps, and small arms) was packed into oil drums with lead ballast to make the proper weight for a drum of oil, covered by tar paper and plaster of Paris—and six inches of oil was poured over the plaster of Paris. Americans from all walks of life—Jewish and non-Jewish—eagerly did what they could to help. Thus, the proprietor of an amusement park in Asbury Park, N. J., claimed that he collected upwards of 10,000 souvenir rifles and pistols from all over the state; and in Connecticut, State Police helped volunteers collect World War II souvenir weapons.

There was one near disaster: January 3, 1948, one of seventy-seven cases being loaded aboard the SS *Executor* for shipment to Palestine broke open. It was found to contain TNT—for which longshoremen would normally receive hazard pay. Further, the export of TNT to the Middle East was illegal without a special license following the United States proclamation of an arms embargo on December 5, 1947. This, in turn, led to the discovery and seizure of an additional lot of 200 tons of TNT in the form of war surplus demolition blocks. Five and a half tons of Mexican smokeless powder, packed as refractory clay in metal drums, on the very same ship was not affected and reached its destination safely.[8]

Although these are the only specific shipments of American explosives on which we have data, it seems incontrovertible that many, many times these quantities of explosives would have been shipped before December 5, 1947, when it was completely legal to do so without special license of any kind, and some afterwards in the new "black goods" warehouse on Metropolitan Avenue in Brooklyn.[9]

Another unfortunate result of the loading accident was that it led the FBI to Al Schwimmer's airplane operation, which will be described in detail in the next chapter. That is, in investigating the companies from which the seized shipments on the *Executor* were listed as originating, one such company—Foundry Associates—had ordered explosives from the War Assets Administration and had made out a check for $20,000 to Schwimmer. The result was a visit to Schwimmer by an FBI agent on January 14—and continuing FBI surveillance thereafter.

In all other respects, the pieces were quickly picked up. By the end of January, the following companies (some of which had been in operation long before January) were functioning: Materials for Palestine, Inc.— an open collection agency for all kinds of non-embargoed, non-contraband goods requested by the Yishuv. This apparently could include such war-related material as jeeps, ambulances, and parachutes as well as clothing and cigarettes. Inland Machinery and Metals Company now did the crating at 4366 Park Avenue. Radio Communications Engineering Co. lived up to its name; its task was to procure radios, walkie-talkies, and radar. The Eastern Development Co. was working on an improved anti-tank weapon of the type designated "Piat" by the British, "bazooka" by the Americans. Land and Labor for Palestine was busy prerecruiting. Although it might be illegal to recruit people specifically for a foreign army, it was not illegal to give information about how to make contacts.[10] Thus, if a man were started on his way to do civilian work in Palestine and, once there or somewhere en route, changed his mind and decided to join the army, how could Land and Labor be blamed? Recruiting was done to some extent through Land and Labor, to some extent by word of mouth bypassing Land and Labor, and through other channels. A fortuitous contact, for example, permitted the writer to skip Land and Labor and directly use the Steve Schwartz/Hyman Scheckman (Shamir) channel whose function was direct recruiting of an air crew and other rare specialists. Land and Labor had office space in Manhattan's Breslin Hotel at Broadway and 29th Street; nearby, hotels of similar quality (Wellington, Le Marquis, Empire) were used for the next level, interviewing of specialists.

The best-known other channel was the American League for a Free Palestine which saw itself as the American agency of the Irgun (IZL). The latter conducted a very public campaign for recruits to form a "George Washington Legion." Thus the *New York Times* of March 30, 1948 carried a report by a Major Weiser that recruiting for this "legion" was progressing; the next day there was a report that "300 more" had enlisted. Early in May, Major Weiser officially (and publicly) registered as a recruiting agent for the George Washington Legion—and indicated that its services would be offered to the UN.

The result of all this publicity about massive recruiting was minimal indeed. In mid-July, Israel denied the very existence of such a body: "The George Washington brigade is not in action in this country, and has not been heard of here."[11] One American, Harold (Zvi) Kraushar, who had come to Israel on the *Altalena,* said that about twenty of those aboard that ship had indeed been recruited by the George Washington Brigade in the United States, but fought in the regular army in Israel. He told the writer that the number of volunteers that could honestly be credited to this flamboyant recruiting effort, was less than ten: More than half of the twenty actually came from "Betar," the Revisionist Zionist youth movement. The "American League for a Free Palestine" paid the passage of this group of about twenty to France, where they joined the *Altalena* passengers near Marseilles. The crew of the *Altalena* were mostly Americans. Actually it must be said that some air crew members did make themselves available because of this channel. Although there was some initial debate among the fliers as to whether it was better to fly for Haganah or IZL, there were no IZL planes, with the result that the ATC flight crews were augmented by these men.

Thus, the highly publicized recruiting efforts of the free-wheeling "American League" produced a few fliers and a handful of others. Since the numbers of flying personnel remained critically short, it may have been a contribution of some significance—although it is entirely possible that these fliers would have been recruited anyway.

The American underground sent an enormous variety of material—some of it absolutely vital. In this category there were explosives and the tools for making bullets and simple weapons. (Indeed, the machine tools for making more advanced weapons became the nucleus of Israel's post-war armaments industry.) Also in the vital category were the 13 aircraft (ten transports, three heavy bombers) flown to Israel (and described in the following chapters); in the important, but not vital, category would be the additional 48 aircraft crated and shipped to Israel before the end of 1948. These include four P-51s, 17 Harvards, 20 Stearmans, 2 Hudsons, 2 Piper Cubs, 1 Piper, and 2 BT-13 trainers (the BT-13s were flown out in the transports).[12]

Another facet of procurement which apparently was a necessary aspect of the West European arms purchases beginning with the spring of 1948 (and, on occasion, many years earlier), was providing an acceptable, neutral country as the official customer. With the failure of attempts to procure machine guns, artillery, and fighter planes in the United States,[13] the Israeli Yehuda Arazi went to Europe, where he had some contacts going back a dozen years. There, he promptly made a small purchase in Switzerland including five moderately ancient multipurpose Hispano Suiza guns; these reached Israel on the *Resurrection* on April 23. By then, he was involved in the load of French munitions (including a lot of machine guns) which came on the *Santa Ciarra*. But these and subsequent transactions required bona-fide signed receipts for their completion. In 1939 Yehuda Arazi had made such an arrangement with General Anastasias Somoza, dictator of Nicaragua in Central America. Now, in 1948, the American Irving Strauss (brother-in-law of Al Schwimmer's brother-in-law) was prevailed upon to go to Nicaragua, and renew the arrangement. Somoza was most understanding, and readily agreed—since there was a business aspect as well: Deposits would regularly be made to his private bank account in New York City. Over the ensuing months, Strauss made eight trips to Nicaragua, each time with papers to be signed. In the same period of time, upwards of $200,000 was deposited to Somoza's New York account.[14]

And, of course, the funding for the above and for most of Israel's procurement wherever it took place, came from concerned individuals in the United States.

One cannot help but reflect not only on the enormous difference in type and amount of equipment, between the scrap-and-surplus war of 1948, and the super-sophisticated level of post-1967, but also on the parallel escalation in fund raising which has made it possible for Israel to survive in the face of this tremendous escalation of military equipment.

The legitimate, aboveground Materials for Palestine operation shipped an average of roughly one million dollars worth of materials per *month*. Although funds, of course, also went through channels other than Materials for Palestine, 1972's level of American Jewish community support of close to two million dollars per *day* (roughly half through gifts, and half through low-interest loans) was absolutely inconceivable in 1948 when, more than once, the vital Czech operation was totally stymied by the lack of a few hundred thousand dollars. Then there was slow progress even in normally elementary areas. For example, it was more than a year after statehood before the army as a whole was even issued uniforms! A major "bargain" purchase of Polish Boy Scout coats intended to keep Israeli soldiers warm in the winter of 1948/49 had one slight flaw: The sizes were too small for men. And so many male field soldiers had to shift for themselves that winter, while the women—most of whom did office work—had a bonanza of blue-gray coats which buttoned on the wrong side. A felicitous inspiration took the acronym "Chen" (literally "Charm") as the designation for the women's corps. It is made up of the first letters of the words of Soldiery of Women: Chayl Nashim.

We now return to overseas volunteers, with our first emphasis on the air.

Chapter 10

VOLUNTEERS IN THE AIR I: AN OVERVIEW

The airplane was of overwhelming importance to the survival of Israel. For some isolated settlements it was the only reliable means of communication, of evacuating wounded, of meager replenishment of meager supplies—and the very appearance of a plane could sometimes discourage a band of Arab marauders. Furthermore, as the British faded from the scene to be replaced by the invading Arab armies, the speed with which supplies and skilled personnel could be brought in would be a major survival factor—and air was many times faster than the sea. In military terms, it was most important to have a proper air force—for battlefield support, to protect civilian centers, to attack enemy troop concentrations and to neutralize the existing enemy air forces.

The first of the above needs—maintaining contact with isolated settlements—had been met from the beginning by the "primus" air force,[1] named after the widely used portable kersosene stoves, originally patented by a man named Primus. The "putt-putt" of the engines was reminiscent of the noise of these stoves and there may well have been a sense of kinship in the rudimentary functionalism of both. The primus air force consisted of an assortment of light planes piloted by Israelis, some of whom had been trained for such light planes since the 30's. The problem was to produce a fleet of Israeli-controlled transports, fighters, and bombers together with experienced air crews.

Providentially, it was post-World War II: Surplus planes were readily available at a tiny fraction of their original cost, as were a goodly number of trained war veterans.

Well before the UN partition decision in 1947, an American named Al Schwimmer (who currently heads Israel Aircraft Industries, formerly Bedeq, Israel's major aircraft overhaul and development company) formed a Haganah-approved enterprise whose function was the acquisition and reconditioning of transports, perhaps initially intended to be used for smuggling Jewish immigrants from Europe to Palestine. With the partition decision, the work was given added urgency as well as a shift in direction.

The base of the Schwimmer Aviation Company was established in Burbank, California. While ten C-46's and three Constellations were being reconditioned, intensive recruiting of experienced air crews and retraining of pilots was under way. In addition, thirteen young Israelis were given a crash course in flying light planes at the private airport near Los Angeles belonging to a concerned American, Eleanor Rudnick.

A shipment including engine spares and a large quantity of aerial machine guns had been made available in Honolulu. Yehuda Arazi, the Haganah contact, decided in favor of acquisition, in spite of the risk of detection. Arazi was the kind of man of whom legends are made. The fictionalized, melodramatic incident in the book *Exodus*—in which a shipload of refugees in a Cyprus harbor force the British to permit them to emigrate to Palestine under threat of mass suicide—actually took place in the spring of 1946, in the Italian harbor of Spezia. The ship was the *Fede;* Yehuda Arazi was in command (at that time, he headed all Mossad activities in Italy). As early as 1936 he was smuggling arms from Europe to Palestine.[2] The cargo from Honolulu was quickly brought to California, with the engine spares openly going to Burbank, and the machine guns concealed and taken to Mexico. The FBI followed the shipment. Although the FBI did not find anything actually improper in Burbank (it was aware that some cases were missing), this experience made it obvious that a base outside the United States was most desirable. Panama provided the solution: It had an expensive, unused airport (Tocumen), no planes, and urgently wanted the void filled. Lineas Aereas de Panama, Sociedad Anonima (LAPSA) had been brought into being, but it had no business. Its franchise holder met the president of the domestic, nonfunctioning Service Airways, who was already involved, leading to the quick completion of a three-organization front (Schwimmer Aviation, Service Airways, LAPSA); this enabled the hiring of personnel and the transfer of aircraft from American to foreign registration, as needed.[3]

The East-West cold war added significantly to the complexity of events. While American public opinion was very much pro-Israel, and thus anti-British as regarded Palestine, Britain and the United States were at the same time military partners in the shooting war in Greece.

It will be recalled that in 1948, the Greek civil war was under way and the countryside was being recaptured from Soviet-oriented forces. In a coup, communist forces seized control of the Czech government in early 1948. The Marshall Plan was being launched in Europe by the United States, to bolster the economy and spirit of the West European nations.

Thus, it was a time of serious confrontation on the European continent. Historically, the United States had shied away from deep involvement in the intricacies of European politics; now that it was necessarily involved because of the world power redistribution following World War II, it naturally tended to rely for guidance on its senior English-speaking European ally, Great Britain. Furthermore, in the pre-Vietnam period, there remained a naive desire to do the "correct" thing—especially where basic American interests did not appear to be directly involved. Thus, the United States zealously followed Britain's lead in enforcing the UN-recommended embargo on arms for both sides in the Middle East, although it was obvious that the effects of this embargo were completely one-sided—since the Arabs were already well armed (and continued to receive British arms because of "preexistent contracts"), while Israel was pitifully underarmed. And when Israel—having no other choice—procured arms from behind the Iron Curtain, this became a justification for even more thorough American attempts to enforce the arms embargo.[4] In its approach, Britain was not simply blindly malicious: It hoped that by making it impossible for an independent Jewish state to come into being, the Jews would be forced to invite Britain back as their protector and thus establish a permanent British presence, on British terms.

The West European countries, which had suffered under German occupation, could be described as benevolently neutral towards Israel: They were cooperative as long as there was no publicity. But when specific instances of assistance were uncovered by the British or American self-appointed policemen, those channels were closed off: American protection and aid were too important at this juncture. And, of course, the United States, Britain, and the Commonwealth nations were zealous about maintaining the embargo within their own borders, making subterfuge and evasion necessary for procurement and recruitment. Although the Soviet Union had ideologically always been anti-Zionist, in late 1947 it reconsidered. On the ancient premise that "the enemy of my enemy is my friend," it appeared logical that Israel's reaction to British hostility should turn it towards Russia (and, much of Israel did have an ideologically socialist orientation).[5] Thus, the Soviet Union actively supported the creation of Israel in the United Nations and while it furnished no direct material assistance, it was content for Czechoslovakia to do so, at least for a while. In most of Eastern Europe (as in Russia), anti-Semitism was sufficiently traditional to be called indigenous. Two exceptions were Czechoslovakia and Yugoslavia, in part, perhaps, because of their visceral opposition to the Nazis (they, unlike Poland, Rumania, and Hungary, had not been fascist between the two world wars); in part, perhaps, because the very creation of these two countries as fruits of World War I, had been significantly assisted by Jewish lobbying at the peace talks.

Czechoslovakia, particularly, had a long tradition of religious freedom (the Reformer, Jan Hus, had preceded Martin Luther by a century); its attitude towards its long-established Jewish community was a healthy one; and Masaryk was known as a friend of the Jews. The Czechs may also have been extra-sympathetic, since they had suffered under the Nazis longer than the other European countries—since 1938.

And so it was that the Czechs were quite cooperative, on a reasonable cash basis. The first step, at the turn of the year 1947/48, was a contract signed with a Czech arms-manufacturing firm for machine guns, rifles, and ammunition, to be paid for in dollars at current market prices. Delivery was the next problem. A suggestion that shipment be made north across Poland through the port of Gdynia, thence through the North Sea, down the Atlantic, and across the entire Mediterranean, came to naught. Instead, a more direct southern route was worked out—down the Danube, from Bratislava to Vukovar, then by train to the Yugoslav port of Sibenik (near Split), and by ship down the Adriatic, through the Mediterranean, to Israel. There were two major drawbacks even to this fairly direct routing: (1) It was slow relative to the immediate, desperate need; (2) It was uncertain—before May 15, interception by the British Navy was very likely, and after May 15, there would be the hazard of interception by the Arab navies (one could not be certain of their total ineffectuality, in advance). And continued availability of the Yugoslav port was uncertain. The first shipload of Czech arms did get through, entering Tel Aviv harbor April 3, but by this time another arrangement had been made.

The solution arrived at was an airlift. With no planes of their own available, Israel's people in Europe made what Kagan calls an "exorbitant" deal with a private American company (U.S. Overseas Airlines) in Geneva, and hired a Skymaster DC-4 and crew, all but two of whom were non-Jewish Americans, to fly a load of arms from Prague Airport to Palestine.[6] This was the flight known both as Hassida (stork) and Balak 1—the crucially important flight of March 31/April 1 to Beit Darass airfield. It appears that because of this flight, the plans for Operation Nahshon were confirmed.

On their return to Prague, the crew of the DC 4 was met by envoys of the American Embassy, and an immediate end was put to the service-ability of this channel.[7]

How could the airlift be continued?

The answer was at hand in the transports being acquired by Schwimmer and collected under the LAPSA (RX) registration. It was necessary for LAPSA to set up an operational base in Europe. Castiglione del Lago, in Italy, was the initial choice. When the first C46 arrived on March 9, it turned out that this airfield was inadequate; the plane proceeded to Perugia, and waited. While waiting, it was ordered to bomb a Syrian arms ship then in the Adriatic. Syria had preceded Israel in purchasing a large quantity of Czech arms which were being moved slowly and secretively, anticipating Israeli awareness of its existence. The crew of the C-46 protested this order, pointing out that it was highly unlikely that rough and ready bombs thrown out the door of a transport would sink (or even hit) a ship, but that the resultant publicity could destroy the entire air-transport operation which was in the process of being launched. Nevertheless, the order was firm. The plane took off, searched—and solved the dilemma by reporting that it could not locate the arms ship.[8]

Additional transports were being readied for flight to Europe. One Constellation reached Panama in mid-March. April 10, four C-46s went by way of Millville, New Jersey to Kingston, Jamaica, and thence to Tocumen, Panama. April 14, five C-46s flew from Los Angeles to Tijuana, Mexico, thence to Mexico City (where one crashed, killing its crew) and on to Tocumen. Thus, 8 LAPSA C-46s and one Constellation were ready in Panama, in addition to the single C-46 in Italy.[9]

With the Egyptians possessing 40 fighter planes, 4 bombers and 4 transports, and the Syrians 10 fighter bombers and 4 transports—it was obvious that Israel would need its own military air force. Thus, on April 23, a contract was signed with the Czechs calling for ten ME-109 fighter planes, plus pilot training in Czechoslovakia and Czech assistance in reassembling the planes in Israel. The ME-109 was a German plane that had been manufactured in occupied Czechoslovakia—and thus was available. The designation "ME" came from "Messerschmitt"; they were promptly dubbed "Sakinim"—Hebrew for "knives," since "messer" is German (and Yiddish) for "knife."

The pressure of time ruled out surface shipment as a practical means of transport. The Messerschmitts, disassembled and crated, could go in the bellies of two-engine transports such as DC-3s and C-46s. The Czechs spoke of making some of their DC-3s available, but only for the transport of plane parts and spares—not for arms. Since the flights were hazardous, and their number would be limited by shortage of air-crew personnel, and the arms shortage in Israel remained critical, the Czech offer was turned down: Transport flights had to include combination cargos of fighter planes and infantry arms. For this, the LAPSA transports were ideal. The distance being too great for nonstop flight, an intermediate base was necessary: This was to be Catania in Sicily, to serve officially for LAPSA and Service Airways.

May 8, the transports left Tocumen. The basic route was via Natal (Brazil), Dakar (West Africa), and Casablanca, but several of the planes were delayed en route for mechanical reasons. In order to avoid interference by the American and British consulates, the Czech base was away from Prague—at Zatec in the Sudetenland, close to Germany, where the Germans had built an airfield during the war. Zatec was designated "Zebra" in English and "Etzion" in Hebrew. The air-lift terminus in Israel was the airport called Ekron (Aqir): Its code name was "Oklahoma."

May 20, Balak 5 left Zatec[10] (Balak 2 had flown May 12, followed by Balak 3 and 4). Balak 5 was a four-engine DC-4 Skymaster (in addition to the C-46s and the Constellation, a DC-4 had been rented: The same U.S. Overseas Airline plane and crew that had flown Balak 1). Its cargo included the first ME-109, small arms, and two Israeli fighter pilots, Modi Alon and Ezer Weizman.

The same day, May 20, a contract was signed for another 15 ME-109s. The airlift now continued on a regular basis. All flights carried ME-109 parts, arms, and munitions (ammunition and/or explosives). Only the DC-4 and the Constellation could carry a complete fighter plane; the C-46s could hold just half a fighter, plus small arms).[11] In the first month—by June 11—30 Balak flights had delivered 107 tons of cargo. The airlift continued throughout the first truce, reaching a peak of 50 tons in a single week early in July and a similar peak early in August, just prior to the closing of Zatec.[12]

In the meantime, the stopdown had been shifted from Catania to Ajaccio, on the French island of Corsica (the birthplace of Napoleon). There were unavoidable mishaps: A C-46 with one dead engine made a forced landing at Treviso, Italy, where its cargo was seized and held for several months. Another C-46 made a forced landing on the island of Rhodes, an event of which the resident American diplomatic representative was quickly made aware; investigation uncovered Ajaccio as the link in the airlift and American pressure forced France to advise Israel, on June 11, that it could no longer be used, at least during the truce (the first truce came into being that very day). Nevertheless, it was later possible to utilize Ajaccio[13] again, but not for the Czech-Israel air lift.

Feverishly, an alternate stopdown base was sought—and found. On June 15, Yugoslavia made one of its airfields available. This change presented an important advantage: The total route now involved much less of a detour, reducing the mileage from 2500 to 1800 miles. Thus, the airlift was able to continue throughout the truce period.

Yugoslavia was then asserting its independence of Soviet domination, introducing a level of political complexity vis-à-vis Israel. The USSR was in the process of shifting to an anti-Israel position—yet, Yugoslavia did not want to oppose automatically every position of the Soviet Union. On the other hand, this might be a safe area in which to be deliberately different. And, as discussed earlier, there was a level of basic sympathy with Israel. Thus, there were uncertainties in Yugoslav cooperation, but the Yugoslav air strip was to prove most helpful. (On the one hand, a substantial minority of Yugoslavia's population was Moslem—but the operations were kept secret. On the other hand, during World War II, a Yugoslav Moslem unit had voluntarily fought on the side of the Nazis; thus, President Tito, as former leader of the anti-Nazi Yugoslav Partisans, may have felt there was a score to be evened.)

The ME-109s were put into service as quickly as possible; their first action took place May 29, when four ME-109s, each carrying four 150-pound bombs, were sent against the main body of the Egyptian army advancing up the coast toward Tel Aviv. The Egyptians had taken Isdud (Ashdod), and were proceeding north, when the planes struck. Although the actual damage was not great, the Egyptians were disheartened at this most unexpected development—there were not supposed to be any Israeli fighter planes—and stopped. They were further discouraged by minor ground counterattacks, and never advanced further, although it has since been reported that the Israeli army had a pitifully small force between Ashdod and Tel Aviv. Arab caution on the offensive, then and since, has proved to be a most important factor in Israel's survival. Of the four planes participating, one Messerschimtt was shot down, and one severely damaged on landing. A few days later, June 3, an ME-109 piloted by Modi Alon shot down two Egyptian bombers over Tel Aviv (actually,

DC-3 transports being used as bombers, one of which crashed at once and the other crash-landed in Arab territory). The skies no longer belonged to the Arabs; thereafter, the bombing of Israeli cities was rare.

Fighter planes were most important defensively. However, in order to reverse the enemy's offensive posture, it would be necessary to carry the attack forcefully to him. For this, bombers were necessary; with bombers, supply depots could be damaged or even destroyed, and by bombing the enemy's cities civilian morale could be seriously undermined. While heavy transports could function as makeshift bombers, true bombing planes would be many times more effective and far more accurate.

Anticipating this, Al Schwimmer and Leo Gardner had located four B-17s (the workhorse bomber of World War II) and four A-20s in the United States. On June 12, they succeeded in getting three of the B-17s safely out of the country (via Miami–Puerto Rico–Azores–Ajaccio–Zatec). The B-17s were called "Flying Fortresses" because of their heavy defensive armament—twin machine guns in the waist, tail, etc., covering every attack approach. The planes left the United States unarmed; part of the work at Zatec was arming them. Preparation took some time—and then there was a brief delay because Israel was not ready to receive them; they were not cleared to leave until July 14 (toward the end of the Ten Days).

It was decided to reap a bonus from their flight to Israel by having them bomb targets en route. The targets selected were Cairo, Gaza, and El Arish—each to be bombed by one of the three planes. Thus Cairo was bombed the night of July 14; the bombs fell near King Farouk's palace causing great consternation in Egypt's capital which tasted bombing for the first time.[14] Gaza was hit twice: once by the plane assigned to it, and again by the El Arish plane which did not locate El Arish, but dropped its bombs near Gaza instead. Thus, beginning July 15, three B-17s were available in Israel. That day, and in the remaining days and nights of the Ten Days, they were used heavily. They were quickly dubbed the "Hammers" and were widely used in all the remaining campaigns, each sometimes flying as many as five missions a day. They were also employed in operations during the truce periods, as for example, Operation Shoter ("Policeman"), clearing the hostile villages east of the northern third of the main Tel Aviv-Haifa road; Operation Hiram (named for Hiram, King of Lebanon in the time of King Solomon, 3000 years earlier) in the Galilee, and against the Faluja Pocket.

Through the ruse of making a movie, four Beaufighters (fighter-bombers) were gotten out of Great Britain and flown to Israel via Ajaccio. Although they arrived prior to the Ten Days, they could not be used immediately because they were unarmed. Armament, and spares, were later smuggled out, so that three of these planes were ready for Operation Yoav.

Attrition of the ME-109s was high. It may have been an intrinsically difficult model to fly; or, lack of prior experience with this specific aircraft (apart from the Czech cram course) may have been responsible; it is likely that both were major factors. In any event, procurement of an American or British fighter was most desirable. Strenuous efforts resulted in the discovery of a quantity of British Spitfires in Czechoslovakia. These planes had been acquired by the Free Czech Air Force during World War II—and the Czech government was willing to sell them to Israel. The planes were crated; but shipment as surface freight would be much too slow.

As we saw earlier, the closing of Ajaccio had led to arrangements to use a Yugoslav airfield—Podgorica (Titograd)—with rather primitive physical facilities in southwestern Yugoslavia, quite close to the Albanian border. (Proximity to the Albanian border was a nuisance, since Albania's reflex custom was to fire at all aircraft in its skies.) The code name of this airfield was "Alabama." Sam Pomerantz, the American aircraft engineer in charge of technical operations in Czechoslovakia, proposed that the planes be assembled where they were (in Kunovice), then be flown to Israel. What was revolutionary about this proposal was that the maximum range of the Spitfire was 600 miles—and the distance from Podgorica to Israel was 1400 miles! The unheard-of feat[15] of delivery was to be accomplished by installing auxiliary fuel tanks following the removal of all equipment not absolutely necessary to keep the planes in the air. The planes had to fly unarmed, in any case, since the Czechs insisted on this as a precondition, although they said that they had no objection to the necessary armament being flown separately from Kunovice by a transport plane. Since the Spitfires would be flying without any navigation equipment of their own, they would fly as a group, shepherded by a DC-4 (four-engine transport) in the lead. In the Mediterranean, Israeli ships and planes would be deployed along the route for possible air-sea rescue operations.

September 24, six Spitfires left Kunovice for Podgorica. One was damaged on landing; the five remaining planes left for Israel September 27. Three arrived safely; the other two landed on the island of Rhodes, because they ran out of fuel—and were impounded by the Greeks. While additional Spitfires were being readied, Yugoslavia withdrew permission to use Titograd. Not to be daunted, Sam Pomerantz proceeded with design modifications that would give the planes a good chance to go all the way from Kunovice to Israel—nonstop. By November 15 a new lot of Spitfires was ready; there were delays, political and technical, and Podogorica was again made available. With the uncertainties of winter weather, the shorter nonstop leg from Podgorica was safer than a direct Kunovice-Israel flight. There were further delays, now due principally to the weather. By December 18 all was technically and politically clear, but it was snowing. Vexed by the accumulated delays, Sam Pomerantz gave the order for six Spitfires to leave for Podgorica and piloted one himself. The snowstorm was too heavy—4 returned, 2 crashed, and one flier was killed: Sam Pomerantz.

The next day, December 19, twelve Spitfires flew to Podgorica safely —with landing mishaps to two. December 22, ten Spitfires, in two flights, each led by a C-46 mother ship, left for Israel and arrived safely. Thus ended Operation Velveta. One of our sources suggests that the origin of this term is in the brand name of the sunburn cream included in the survival kits issued to all participating pilots. A more interesting possibility is that it derives from "velvet" in its technical sense as a gambler's word: "On velvet" one is speculating not with one's own money, but with money won from the opponent. Since the Spitfires were British planes which had been given to Czechoslovakia, and Britain could readily be considered the opponent—the connection is clear.

December 22 was also the start of "Operation Horev," the final campaign against the Egyptians. The Spits could not be used immediately, because they were still unarmed. At that point Czechoslovakia would not permit any Israeli planes to land on Czech soil to pick up the armament. Fortunately, two idle Dakotas were located at the Bata Shoe Factory in Zlin, Czechoslovakia. Under the peculiar rules imposed by the Czechs at the point, it was all right for Czech planes with ATC crews to fly the Spitfire armament to Yugoslavia where an Israeli C-46 promptly ferried them to Israel. The armament arrived in time for the Spitfires to take part in the last phase of Operation Horev, which ended January 7, 1949.

As the summer of 1948 progressed, the activities of the ATC had become less and less secret. Information leaks developed through occasional forced landings, through British and American investigations, through the indiscretion of some ATC crewmen who insisted on going to

Prague for periodic recreation, and through the stories of occasional disgruntled participants.

On September 18 the Panamanian government canceled LAPSA's registration of the planes that were being used in the airlift; the reason given was information obtained from the American ambassador. Five weeks earlier, on August 12, the Czechoslovak government, under Soviet pressure, ordered all operations out of Zatec to cease.

Nevertheless, although the air bridge from Zatec was terminated, the Czechs continued to cooperate in supplying greatly needed Spitfires, as we have seen above. Furthermore, the loss of Zatec was not an unmixed disaster. Its critical function in supplying surface arms and fighter planes to Israel when these were so desperately needed had been accomplished. Arms which had simultaneously been procured elsewhere, were now securely "in the pipeline" for delivery by conventional surface means.

While it would have been desirable to keep Zatec active in order to airlift the Spitfires to Israel quickly as had been done with the Messerschmitts, we have seen that an alternative solution was worked out. In any event, Zatec operations would have had to be reduced radically soon after August 12: Israel had greater need for the limited number of transports and crews elsewhere, for Operation Dust in Israel. This operation—as we shall see in Chapter 15—was to make it possible to break the back of the Egyptian invasion, in Operation Yoav.

The weight of bombs dropped by the air force in major operations is listed below:

Last part of the Ten Days (beginning July 15, with the arrival of the Flying Fortresses): 11 tons
Yoav (First Negev Campaign, October 17–22): 239 missions, 151 tons
Hiram (North/Central Galilee, October 29–31): 34 missions, 27 tons
Horev (Final Negev Campaign, December 22–January 7): 243 missions, 226 tons

In brief, from the moment its first warplanes took to the air at the end of May, the air force played an increasingly aggressive role: Its support of the ground forces was substantial; it struck behind the enemy lines almost at will, held back by its own physical limitations rather than by enemy strength;[16] it created sufficient respect in the enemy so that the enemy greatly underutilized its numerically and qualitatively superior aircraft. For example, the Egyptians had acquired nine Sterling bombers which they hardly used. The skies primarily belonged to the Israeli Air Force. And the Czech air bridge brought weapons for the ground forces that were vital in May and June, and most important in July.

As we shall see subsequently, hardly any of the accomplishments described in this chapter could have been effected without overseas volunteers.

Chapter 11

VOLUNTEERS IN THE AIR II: AMERICAN TRANSPORTS

To what extent were volunteers involved in the events just described?

The Air Transport Command, which was invaluable in effecting the delivery of arms and planes to Israel, had its inception in the autumn of 1947 in a meeting between three Americans—Leo Gardner, Sam Lewis, and Al Schwimmer—friends who served together in the U.S. Air Force in World War II.

It was the Air Transport Command that effectuated the airlift of Czech arms and munitions in the critical spring and early summer of 1948; it was the Air Transport Command that made available the transports which served as makeshift bombers; it was the ATC that procured and delivered the true bombers (three B-17s); it was the ATC that made it possible for Israel to have fighter planes (Messerschmitts and Spitfires, ferried from Czechoslovakia).

The problem of bringing planes, men, and armaments to Israel did not lie in a shortage of airplanes. War surplus planes were readily available after the war, and at bargain prices. What was needed first was an overhaul and repair facility together with an organizational framework for recruiting mechanics and aircrew—initially, to recondition the planes in the United States, subsequently to transport, fly, and maintain them overseas. Al Schwimmer had earlier been in touch with Shlomo Rabinovich (Shamir), Haganah chief in the United States. Now, with Yehuda Arazi approving the air transport idea, the Schwimmer Aviation Company of Burbank, California, was launched.

The first hazardous task was ferrying the initial lot of planes, in uncertain condition, from the Lockheed terminal at Ontario, California, to Burbank. We would expect that the nationality of all those involved in this early phase, as well as those recruited later, were all Americans,[1] and the majority were probably Jewish. The Haganah liaison man—the man who made policy decisions in late 1947 and early 1948—was Yehuda Arazi ("Albert Miller"), an Israeli with no aircraft background, but with wide experience in the clandestine procurement and smuggling of arms.

93

Thus, when Al Schwimmer received word that a Jewish war-surplus dealer in Oahu,[2] the second largest of the Hawaiian Islands, had access to a lot of aircraft-engine spares and other military equipment, it was Yehuda Arazi who decided that the other equipment was to be inspected and acquired—even though the *Executor* explosives shipment (chapter nine) had just been seized by the FBI in New York, adding to the general uneasiness over the risk of direct arms smuggling. This opportunity was one result of the information and fund-raising network, broadly called the Sonneborn Institute, which had grown out of the mid-1945 meeting in the home of Rudolf Sonneborn (chapter nine).

Following World War II, many Jews had gone into the war-surplus business. At a convention of dealers, Nathan Liff let it be known that his 500-acre yard had a huge amount of navy surplus materiel, including the potentially useful engine spares and perhaps usable arms as well.

In order not to endanger the Schwimmer operation needlessly, an outsider who knew something about arms had to be found. Hank Greenspun, former major in the U.S. Eighth Army, and a cousin of Reynold Selk who was already working with Schwimmer, volunteered as soon as he was approached, although this activity interfered with the launching of a new business venture.

Greenspun readily located crated aircraft engines and parts—and used 0.30 and 0.50 caliber aircraft machine guns. Perhaps fifty feet beyond the limits of Liff's yard, there were stacks of new, factory-fresh machine guns plus boxes of gun mounts and spare barrels. The heat of firing warps gun barrels, requiring spares for ready replacement. Fifty feet of open space was all that separated Liff's yard from the U.S. Naval Depot. The depot was patroled by Marine guards, whose patrol pattern left eight minutes clear in every two-hour period. Hank Greenspun felt that the spare gun barrels were absolutely necessary auxiliaries to the surplus machine guns, and so he added stealing the gun barrels to what was the intended technical crime of violating the arms embargo by smuggling the surplus machine guns to Israel.

Aided by Willie Sosnow, who had come from the mainland to assist him, Greenspun went into the depot with a forklift in the eight-minute unguarded intervals, taking out a case of gun barrels at a time. This, of course, was done at night—the only "fair" time to work, since it was necessary for Liff's protection that he be shielded from the knowledge of anything improper that was taking place, including the packing of his own surplus machine guns.[3]

And so, over a period of several weeks, 42 cases of aircraft engines and 16 of machine guns and extra gun barrels were put together (the latter, with special additional markings). But funds for shipment were lacking. At Greenspun's urging, a small parlor meeting was called by Nathan Liff, and the needed $6,700 was raised in short order.

Fifty-eight crates were consigned to Service Airways, Burbank, (a small New York Airline working with Schwimmer), via the port of Wilmington, California. In Wilmington, the sixteen contraband crates were quickly separated and stored in a warehouse several miles away. The U.S. Customs Bureau came looking for them—without success. But this, together with the FBI curiosity in Burbank (chapter ten), made it imperative that the guns be taken out of the country quickly.

Over a week's time, the cases were unpacked and the guns oiled and wrapped by a large group of part-time volunteers, ranging from movie-studio workers to businessmen, dentists, and lawyers. With difficulty, a yacht, the *Idalia,* was located which appeared to be large enough to hold the 15 tons of guns on a voyage to Acapulco, Mexico. Almost everything went wrong: At loading time, the *Idalia* had to go across the bay to re-charge its batteries and an intermediate craft had to be "borrowed," without its owner's knowledge, to carry the load from the warehouse to the *Idalia;* the tide was low, multiplying the backbreaking work of handling the 200-pound canvas gun sacks; the surface and interior of the yacht were damaged in loading; the ship was so overloaded that its portholes were at the waterline.

The *Idalia's* owner-captain demurred, finally agreeing to go as far as Catalina Island—for a large fee—on the understanding that another ship was waiting at Catalina. When they approached Catalina, instead of a second ship Greenspun produced a pistol, giving the captain the choice of taking the yacht to Acapulco or being shot. They went to Acapulco— the two-week voyage including periodic engine trouble and a major storm.

In Acapulco the yacht's captain reported to the American consul, who advised that he was quite powerless in Mexican waters. The guns were shipped to Mexico City, to become part of the cargo of the Schwim-mer planes that were scheduled to stop there on their way to Panama. But New York announced a change of plan: The Schwimmer aircraft were already fully loaded. Instead, a ship, the freighter *Kefalos,*[4] was on its way to Tampico Bay on Mexico's east coast. It would carry these guns, plus whatever additional munitions Greenspun was able to obtain in Mexico, Nicaragua, Guatemala, and the Dominican Republic.

Greenspun spent a considerable amount of time traveling and inspecting available arms (and he did not like to travel second class). His largest purchase by far was a little over a million dollars in Mexican armaments, including machine guns, aerial bombs, and French 75 mm howitzers.[5] In Mexico, all transactions were accompanied by "mordida"— a cash gift (generally between 5 percent and 15 percent) which is as much a part of the Mexican way of life, as is the business lunch in the United States.

Although Mexican authorities—up to and including President Miguel Aleman—were helpful and sympathetic, Mexico's Arab community (Miguel Abed in particular) made things a bit difficult—and public. For a cover, Greenspun invented the story that he was a purchasing agent for the Nationalist Chinese government.

All of the above activities were time-consuming: The weeks since the original machine guns arrived in California were stretching into months; but the *Kefalos,* now truly an arms ship with a camouflage covering cargo of sugar for fear of possible interception by the British navy, was not released from Tampico. The Mexican government insisted that it needed bona-fide Chinese documents in order to permit the ship to sail.

Fortuitously, on a Sunday, Hank Greenspun and Willie Sosnow found the Nationalist Chinese embassy open, with only a single consul in attendance. They represented themselves as being interested in making heavy capital investments in Formosa (Taiwan). The consul was most helpful and, accompanied by Sosnow, went to another room to find more literature. Greenspun quickly went down the corridor, found an open room, and seized bundles of stationery, envelopes, two metal stamps and stamp pads. The stationery was used to type out bills of material, the stamps to authenticate them. The *Kefalos* sailed a week later, narrowly avoiding the date it was rumored an order to seize and unload the ship would have gone into effect.[6]

A most important element in the cargo was a quantity of aviation gasoline which was to prove vital in keeping the air force flying for the completion of Operation Dust and in Operation Yoav—the rate of flights in Operation Dust (chapter fifteen) having virtually consumed Israel's earlier stock of high-octane fuel.[7]

There is some confusion as to when the *Kefalos* reached Israel. Greenspun speaks of the "United Nations first 'truce period' "[8]—that is, prior to July 9. But the *New York Times* of July 19 has an unclear story concerning an arms shipment, believed intended for Palestine, that was than being loaded on the "Kealos" (*sic*). And Israel's official history of the war describes what must have been this ship as arriving in Israel in September[9]—that is, during the second truce, prior to Operation Yoav. The latter must be the correct date, since this is the only dating that correlates with the importance of its cargo of aviation fuel to the end of Operation Dust, and to Operation Yoav (mid-October).

As noted earlier, the FBI was interested both in the basic Schwimmer operation and in the Oahu shipment. Although sixteen cases were missing, the forty-two delivered to Burbank were thoroughly inspectable, containing proper aircraft engines. While nothing unlawful was found, the fact that the operation was suspect made it mandatory that a foreign base, and foreign cover, be found.

Providentially, Panama had recently spent $9,000,000 building an airport which no one wanted to use. Panama had no planes of its own, and foreign airlines considered the nearby All Brook Air Field, in the U.S.-administered Canal Zone, a safer place in which to invest in facilities. Thus, Panama urgently needed some private company to activate its airport. The void was filled through the New York airline called Service Airways, Inc. An already existent enterprise headed by Irwin Schindler ("Swifty"), its proprietor had readily agreed to join the Schwimmer plan: Schwimmer Aviation would acquire and repair the aircraft, and Service Airways would transport them out of the country. Now, for maximum international credibility, Service Airways would become the contract operator of a new Panamanian airline, whose base of operations would be Tocumen. The official, public name of the airline: Lineas Aereas de Panama, S.A. (LAPSA); its registration: RX.

The above was an American volunteer operation which would be utilized to implement an arrangement being made half a world away.

Clearly, survival of the as yet unborn state of Israel would depend on the delivery of substantial quantities of infantry armament—rifles, machine guns, ammunition, grenades, explosives—preferably, standardized as to type.

It would have been most desirable to purchase the products of major West European and American sources—either as war surplus or as fresh manufacture—but the arms embargo enforced zealously by the United States, Britain, and the Commonwealth nations, within their own borders and through zealous policing by the United States and Britain in the friendly countries of Western Europe, made it impossible to obtain significant quantities with any reasonable prospect of delivery during the critical period. As we have seen, dedicated efforts were made by volunteers in the Western countries to accumulate idle weapons, such as souvenir weapons of World War II veterans; but the Oahu experience and seizures on the East Coast of the United States as well as in other parts of the world made their attempts extremely risky to the participants (which the participants probably discounted), and limited the likelihood of success. Few of these weapons could be expected to evade the embargo, and those that did might well include many that were unserviceable, since they were widely assorted as to type, so that lack of proper ammunition and of replacement parts would render them useless.

The solution was found in Eastern Europe, in Czechoslovakia. Late 1947 and early 1948 saw a behind-the-scenes power struggle between the Liberals, who held power by virtue of the ballot, and the Communists. The struggle surfaced, and was decided by a Communist coup the last week of February 1948. On the twenty-fourth of that month, Czechoslovakia's minister of the interior (and war minister) ordered the Czech police to take over the Liberal party headquarters and arrest its leaders. The following day, Premier Eduard Benes permitted Klement Gottwald to form a new, Communist-dominated cabinet, claiming, "I had to, to prevent chaos." Two weeks later, Jan Masaryk was dead, officially a suicide, but quite possibly, a murder victim. Benes remained a figurehead premier until early June, when he resigned. He died at the beginning of September.[10]

This was the period of paradox in the attitudes of the great powers, when real American concern for the welfare of the incipient Jewish state was coupled with a severe, worldwide enforcement of the arms embargo against Israel—whereas, the Soviet Union, with no genuine concern for the Jewish state, was its major and most consistent public supporter.[11] During this period of its own agonizing transition, Czechoslovakia was particularly subject to pressure from both sides.

The result: Czechoslovakia initially took a strictly commercial, nonpolitical position. She first contracted—and shipped—a large arms order to the Syrians (a shipment that was eventually delivered to Israel, not Syria—see Operation Pirate in our chapter 14). In view of this, the Czechs could hardly refuse an initial large order from Israel for rifles, machine guns and ammunition—at a fair market price—with payment to be made in very welcome dollars. Subsequently, relations became more friendly, and the Czechs agreed not to sell arms to the Arabs, at least temporarily; sold fighter planes to Israel; made available an airfield that would become the air lifeline to Israel; and established a training school or pilots.

While arrangements were being made to transport the first lot of arms by sea from Sibenik, Yugoslavia, after involved European transit by river and rail, the desirability of using the LAPSA air transports became obvious—and urgent. Yehuda Arazi, now back in Europe, having been replaced in New York by Teddy Kollek, first arranged with Angelo Ambrosini, a man of importance in the Italian aircraft industry under Mussolini who had hated the Nazis, to use a private airfield at Castiglione del Lago. Ambrosini was not at all distressed at the thought that a major part of the purpose was transporting arms to Palestine, and he was cheered at the prospect that it might provide employment for unemployed Italian aircraft workers.

The first two Schwimmer planes were now ready to leave the United States. Service Airways applied to the State Department for the necessary license for a C-46 destined for Italy, and LAPSA, for a Constellation going to Panama. The C-46, piloted by Leo Gardner, left Teterboro, New Jersey, with proper legal clearance on March 6. After stops at Goose Bay, Labrador, a U.S. Army Base in Greenland, Iceland, Shannon, Ireland, and Geneva—it reached Castiglione del Lago on the ninth. Unfortunately, it developed that the ground was not firm enough and the runways not long enough for loaded C-46s or Constellations. Another base would have to be found.

In the meantime, this single plane now waiting at Perugia, Italy, could have been well utilized in Czechoslovakia—but it was feared that the entire operation was under FBI surveillance, and that transfer of the plane to Communist Prague airport would trigger these suspicions, and lead to closing everything down, with most of the planes still in Burbank. Yet, this security consideration did not prevent a Haganah authority from ordering the plane to assume another kind of risk of detection: A bombing raid. The cargo of munitions purchased by the Syrians in Czechoslovakia was then supposed to be somewhere in the Adriatic Sea. The C-46 was to find it, and sink it by means of makeshift explosives thrown out the door, although the chances for practical success were virtually nil, and the risk of detection, extremely high. The problem was solved by the C-46 going out on the mission, and reporting failure to locate the arms ship. The arms ship was later located in port, and blown up April 10.[12]

March 13, shortly after the first C-46 had departed, the single Constellation left for Panama piloted by Sam Lewis; its arrival at Tocumen was a major event to the local Panamanians. Unfortunately, it turned out that an engine was in need of repair. Obtaining the parts and making the repairs took three months, so that this Constellation (RX 121) did not arrive in Zatec until June 25. Although by then two additional Constellations were almost ready, it was decided not to delay, since it was thought that the publicity which resulted from the flight of the three B-17s in mid-June (see next chapter) would intensify American efforts to enforce the embargo. This supposition was correct: On June 27, seven Norseman light transports at French airfields, and others at Belgian and Dutch airfields, were temporarily held by the respective governments "because of American pressure." And July 9, the two Constellations were seized "on suspicion" at the Millville, New Jersey, airport just before take-off. (Earlier, the special export license required under the original arms embargo for planes of this weight, had been denied.) The latter were not freed until after the war, when all three became part of the fleet of El Al, Israel's civilian airline. July 27, 1955, one of these Constellations, piloted by Pinia Ben Porat, an Israeli hero of the light-plane "primus" air arm in 1947 and 1948, strayed into Bulgarian airspace, and was shot down. The other two Constellations were retired in 1959.[13]

Early in April, a flight of four C-46s was ready to leave; in charge was former U.S. Navy Lieutenant Commander Hal Auerbach. The planes were to clear U.S. Customs in Millville, New Jersey, for Kingston, Jamaica. There were difficulties with Customs which had apparently been told not to release the planes. After a day and a half of arguing, with Auerbach threatening legal proceedings against Customs for arbitrary abuse of authority, the planes were permitted to leave on April 10 in the evening. Three reached Kingston without incident. The fourth, piloted by Auerbach, had to make a refueling stop at West Palm Beach, Florida; although difficulties were feared, none materialized. These four planes then proceeded to Tocumen.

Presidential proclamation 2776, prohibiting the export of all commercial aircraft regardless of size, would take effect April 15, 1948. Work on the remaining five C-46s proceeded feverishly. At the last minute, April 14, heavily loaded, they cleared Customs at Mines Field, Los Angeles, and made for Tijuana, Mexico, just below the American border. From Tijuana they proceeded to Mexico City. There one of the overloaded planes crashed on take-off, killing the two-man crew: pilot William

Gerson and mechanic Glen King. The four remaining C-46s joined the first four and the Constellation in Panama.

The balance of the C-46s were held in Panama until arrangements had been made to use Catania, Sicily, as a stopping and refueling point for what would become the Czech airlift. With this arranged, on May 8 five of the C-46s left Panama, the others being delayed primarily by a shortage of crew. Included in their cargo were two Vultee BT-13 training planes, at least one of which would later be used as a utility plane in Czechoslovakia. Of the five planes that left Panama for Catania, Sicily, three were delayed en route by mechanical difficulties. The first two planes arrived in Catania May 15. They wanted to leave promptly for Israel, but the military commander of the Catania airfield was quite difficult. He felt that it was his duty to enforce the embargo against any supplies being flown to Israel. He was overridden by higher authorities, and the planes took off for Israel at midday on May 16. Thus, the airlift included one lot of supplies direct to Israel from the West.[14]

The experience at Catania led to a hurried search for a more hospitable stopover point: Ajaccio, on the French island of Corsica.

Somewhat earlier, on April 23, a new kind of contract had been signed with the Czechs: Ten Messerschmitt ME-109 fighter planes would be provided, together with pilot training in Czechoslovakia and the use of Czech technicians to reassemble the planes in Israel, since they would have to be transported, disassembled, in crates.[15] In the event, only three Israelis of eight were able to pass the brief brush-up course aimed at familiarizing trained pilots with this particular aircraft; the other fighter pilots were experienced overseas volunteers. Similarly, the rapid, secure assembly of the Messerschmitts in Israel depended primarily on volunteer Mahal mechanics rather than on the very few Czech technicians who actually reached Israel. This contract had been signed following a basic procurement decision by Shaul Avigur: Fighter plane leads in the rest of the world were unproductive, and it was desperately important to ferry the Czech planes and arms by air.

Although Israel had been able to hold the Arab irregular forces, the regular Arab armies would invade on May 15, when the State of Israel officially was to come into being. Airlifting the Czech supplies was vital—but the Czechs would lease their own transports (DC-3s) for carrying spare parts only—not for arms. The only possible solution was the volunteer-manned LAPSA planes.

Prague airport was a fine, functioning facility, but it was much too accessible to the British and American embassies in Prague. The Czechs made available a former German airfield which had not been used since World War II. Location: Zatec, in the former German Sudetenland. Its code names were Zebra, in English, Etzion, in Hebrew.

Sam Pomerantz, an American engineer, was in charge of all technical operations at Zatec. The aircrews and mechanics were virtually all volunteers—mostly from the United States and Canada, with some English and South Africans. The men were all billeted in Zatec. The Hotel Stalingrad (facing the town square) became an English-speaking enclave. It was completely taken over by the volunteers except for a couple of tables in the dining room, which the "locals" continued to patronize. The kitchen of this hotel benefited directly from the travels of the new tenants. Although postwar austerity that limited the native diet left it monotonous, the fliers were able to bring in oranges and grapefruit from Israel, things like instant coffee, cocoa, and canned milk from Ajaccio, and, once, even a quantity of American cigarettes. Additional volunteers were housed in the nearby Zlaty Lev (Golden Lion), which included a night club.[16]

The first flight, Balak 1, had taken place the night of March 31/ April 1 from Prague airport to the Bet Darrass airstrip using a DC-4 and crew, both hired from an American company (U.S. Overseas Airways) based in Geneva. On their return on April 1, the American crew members were warned by American embassy officials that they were jeopardizing their citizenship by such activity (this was actually not true, but it was an impressive threat), with the result that no further flights of this kind were made from Prague.

By early May, however, the Zatec airfield was available, together with dedicated volunteer crews, men who weighed the risks and alternatives for themselves and decided that they could do no other than to serve Israel at this junction. As noted earlier, the U.S. Overseas Airways Skymaster (DC-4, C-54) would also be provided, on a rental basis, for some of the flights.

The true airlift was begun with the initial flight from Zatec (Balak 2) on May 12; the cargo was arms and ammunition. This flight was most likely made by a C-46. The Israel terminus was a large, former British airfield south of Rehovot, variously known as Aqir, Ekron, and Tel Nof. Its code name: Oklahoma. This airfield, too, was effectively run by Mahal personnel. Most of the auxiliary staff was Israeli—but the base's aircraft mechanics, as well as those in key operational positions, were primarily overseas volunteers. Balak 3 left May 14; this was a two-engine

DC-3 rented from the Bata Shoe factory in Zlin. This plane did not participate further in the airlift since the Czechs had stipulated strongly that their planes might not be used to carry munitions in any form. Balak 4 (probably a C-46) followed a few days later.

Balak 5 took place May 20. It was definitely made by the DC-4, and included the first of the Messerschmitt fighter planes, crated, as cargo. In addition, it brought five Czech technicians and the two Israeli fighter pilots, Modi Alon and Ezer Weizman.

The pace of work and of flights went on feverishly. From then on, almost every Balak included at least half a Messerschmitt together with some combination of light and heavy machine guns, rifles, grenades, mortars, explosives, and ammunition. The additional C-46s were by then arriving in Zatec and from then on did the bulk of the airlift ferrying.

Only nine days after the arrival of the first crated Messerschmitt, a flight of four assembled Messerschmitts was able to take to the air. As noted earlier, they immediately went into action against the head of the main Egyptian column making for Tel Aviv. Two of these planes were lost in that action.

These were incredibly tense and busy days: After all, May 15th was the date on which the official invasion by the regular Arab armies had begun.

The two C-46s which had come from Panama to Catania, Sicily, and thence headed directly for Ekron, landed there in the predawn hours of May 17th. They—and the supplies they carried—were welcome indeed. Their return trip was to Zatec, via Catania and Brno. These planes immediately became part of the air shuttle, assisted now by those additional C-46s which had reached Zatec.

The rate of trips was such that on May 23, Balak 10 and Balak 11 set out. These two C-46s encountered an unexpected hazard at Ekron— fog. A huge bonfire was lit, and every available vehicle was lined up alongside the runway with its lights on. With this assistance, one plane managed to land safely. Before the second plane could land, the fog suddenly thickened to such an extent that the pilot lost his sense of contact with the airfield. The pilot was told to go out to sea and try a fresh approach. Nothing further was heard from the plane. At dawn, three of the crew members (all Americans) limped onto the airfield. They had crashed into a low hill nearby. The navigator, Moe Rosenbaum, also an American, was dead. He had been crushed by the cargo's shifting under the impact of the crash landing.[17]

There was other attrition: One C-46 encountered severe icing conditions crossing the Alps from Zatec towards Ajaccio. It had to make an
emergency landing at the military airfield in Treviso, Italy. Although in
keeping with standard procedure the arms crates were labeled "Glass,"
inspection revealed the true nature of the cargo. The entire American
volunteer crew was imprisoned for the three days it took Danny Agronsky
(the multicultural Israeli responsible for all Italian operations) to arrange
their personal release; and they remained for a considerably longer period
on enforced leave, based at the Hotel Baglioni while he tried to free
the cargo. But the Italians were adamant. Crew and plane finally left,
but the cargo was not released until many months later.[18]

Shortly thereafter, another C-46 made a forced landing on the island
of Rhodes, where it was held by Greek authorities. Worse—its physical
reality spurred agents of the American government to greater efforts to
locate, and interfere with the key stopover point.

Mid-May to mid-June was a truly frantic period. The isolated Balak
1 flight had taken place March 31/April 1. Balak 2 took place May 12,
followed by 3 and 4 at intervals of a few days. From May 20 through
June 10, 26 Balak flights took place. The total tonnage of supplies delivered in these 30 airfreight flights was upwards of 107 tons, including
11 ME-109s with spares, thousands of rifles, machine guns, mortars (or
mortar tubing), and ammunition. The Czech rifles, although new, were not
all in first-class condition. For example, the honor guard at the funeral
of pilot Spence Boyd (chapter twelve), were equipped with very new,
previously unused Czech rifles in order to fire the proper military salute
over the grave. Out of a total of six, two failed to fire. (The writer was
a member of this honor guard, equipped with one of the faulty rifles).

C-46 volunteer pilot Ray Kurtz kept fairly detailed written records.
He wrote that he and his plane (#RX-135) totaled 240 flying hours in
the period between May 8 and June 8, including air transit from Panama
and seven Zatec-to-Ekron round trips. Commercial jet pilots are supposed to fly a maximum of 80 hours per month.

During this intense period, several of Tel Aviv's best hotels as well
as some that were not quite first-class, were taken over by the Air Force
for dormitory and office use. Thus, the Park Hotel was the ATC center;
the Yarkon Hotel was converted entirely to office space, becoming Air
Force Headquarters; and adjacent hotels became dormitory and office
space. Because of the importance of the Yarkon Hotel, an air warden was
stationed permanently on its roof. His task was to record details of all

planes, friendly and enemy, which flew within sight of the building as far as was possible. This work, however, was top secret—and so, at the end of each day, the sheet with this carefully gathered information was burned!

The pace of the airlift and the number of available personnel was such that often aircrews could do little between missions but sleep. Similarly, pressure on the maintenance crews, on whom the safety of air crew and air craft depended, was great.

The DC-4 was grounded for part of this peak period, with the result that 26 of the 30 Balak flights were made by C-46s. According to Shahan, the burden fell most heavily on just three of the C-46 airplanes. The others were accounted for as follows: Of the original ten, one had crashed in Mexico, another near Ekron. Two had not yet left Panama; the most likely reason—shortage of air crew. Of the others, one was held at Rhodes following its forced landing there; one was at least temporarily disabled as a result of enemy fire in its functioning as a bomber near Kibbutz Yehiam in Western Galilee, and another was grounded for five days with motor trouble.

The airlift continued through June, July, and early August—until the Czechs ordered the Zatec operation closed, effective August 12. In a week of intense activity, 50 tons of supplies were flown in 11 flights.[19] In three months (May 12–August 12), the Czech airlift had totaled 95 trips, transferring to Israel 25 ME-109 fighter planes plus spares and some fighter pilots, and 350 tons of munitions. Estimated cost: twelve million dollars.[20]

In a letter dated August 12 from Yehuda Breger, the Israeli officially in charge at Zatec, to Munya Mardor, the Israeli officially in charge of the ATC, pressure by the American ambassador is blamed. The American ambassador apparently threatened to expose the Czechs before an international forum, with using American planes and American citizens on Czech soil for illegal work. The way to avoid this embarrassment would be to end the operation promptly and totally, removing planes and pilots from Czechoslovakia.

Nevertheless, the charge became public in November. Early in that month, Czechoslovakia rejected an American government protest against alleged arms shipments to Israel. A *New York Times* story a day earlier revealed that the State Department had disclosed on September 9 that it had earlier asked the Czechs to halt this arms movement, saying it had received reports that U.S. citizens were involved. The United States said that supplies were going from Czechoslovakia to Israel via ship and secret airfields and, although it would not make public the official Czech reply, it was learned that the Czech government had said that this was none of the affair of the United States. The United States had requested the halt, the *Times* said, because such shipments violated a UN ban; the U.S. government had itself embargoed shipments of American arms to the entire Middle East in an effort to bring an end to hostilities there.[21] It subsequently became clear that the abrupt halt to the airlift the second week in August was the result of a Soviet decision.

To summarize, the planes reaching Israel from the United States in 1948 were:

(1) Those flown out— 9 C-46 medium transports; 1 Constellation heavy transport; 3 B-17 heavy bombers. All left the United States in the Spring, with the C-46s arriving (in several flights) first; the Constellation, towards the end of June; and the B-17s reaching Israel in mid-July (see chapter thirteen for details on the B-17s).

(2) Forty-eight additional planes left the United States (all as crated spare parts) during the second half of 1948. Although the shipping of complete airplanes to Israel was illegal after April 15, there apparently was no serious concern about spare parts. Recognizing that—if *all* of its parts are included—an airplane is simply the sum of all its separate parts plus labor and time, much American effort went into shipping complete planes as crated spare parts. Thus, the ship *Enterprise* left New York Harbor late in the summer carrying—crated in small pieces— two P-51 Mustangs and two Piper Cubs. (Those two Mustangs, assembled as rapidly as possible in Israel, would, in late November, shoot down a British spy plane.) Several weeks later, two Hudsons arrived by the same route, and on October 24, 17 Harvards arrived similarly. Some of these Harvards saw action in Operation Horev, the final campaign against the Egyptians (December 22–January 7, 1949). These were followed by two more P-51 Mustangs, 20 Stearmans and 1 Piper (the latter, light planes). All arrived by sea, safely. Most were light planes; of them all, the Harvards, which were basically trainers, were used as dive bombers in the last Egyptian campaign; and, of the four true fighter planes (P-51 Mustangs), at least two were ready for that final campaign.

Chapter 12

VOLUNTEERS IN THE AIR III: ENGLAND, WESTERN EUROPE, SOUTH AFRICA

Early in 1948, three men were delegated to procure airplanes in three parts of the world: Heyman Shamir (Israeli) to the United States where, as we have seen, he worked closely with the Schwimmer operation; Boris Senior (South African) to South Africa; Harry "Freddy" Fredkens (Englishman) to England and Europe.

England and Western Europe

As a pilot in the Middle East based in Cairo in 1945, "Freddy" had become acquainted and worked with some of the Haganah leadership. Once, he flew Yehuda Arazi to Italy. After the war, Fredkens became a businessman in the Congo. Following the UN partition decision, he quickly made his way to Israel, putting himself at the disposal of the Air Service (pre-Israel's light-plane air arm).

Freddy Fredkens first went to England, where he renewed acquaintanceship with a number of former companions in the RAF. He also acquired a number of light planes: Four Ansons and several Tiger Moths. He began with the Ansons. Getting these planes out of England was no problem (their official destination was shown as Singapore). Unfortunately, one Anson crashed on take-off from Brindisi, and, at their scheduled stop on the island of Rhodes, the other three were seized. The British apparently were on to the destination of these planes—and convinced the Greek government at Rhodes that they were intended for a Communist country (this was the time of the Greek civil war).[1]

Fredkens very quickly abandoned his English efforts; continental Europe became his focus from then on. His major acquisition was a lot of 20 Norseman one-ton transports. The Norseman was a single-engine plane, with relatively short landing field requirements, able to transport a single ton of material. Its capacity was too small for normal commercial uses, but for supply purposes within Israel (particularly to isolated kibbutzim) it was ideal. The American Air Force in Germany had declared

50 of these planes surplus, and refused to sell any to Israel at any price. A reliable buyer, acceptable to the American Air Force, was located; with his cooperation, a fictitious paper airline company was created—and 20 of the surplus Norsemen were successfully purchased.[2] They were first refitted with long-range fuel tanks for the flight to Israel from Italy; most of this work was done in Amsterdam. These planes were later parked at various French, Dutch, Belgian, and Italian airfields. By the end of 1948, 17 of the 20 had been filtered into Israel by volunteer pilots—mostly Americans.[3]

They dribbled in slowly; the first two arrived at the beginning of May, and, by May 10, one of these had experienced its first fatality in service: Under Israel's desperate circumstances, planes like this were considered good rough-and-ready bombers. That is, with a two-man crew, one man could throw out explosives. On such a mission (bombing the Bet Mahsir/ Shaar Hagai (Bab el Wad) area, on the road to Jerusalem), the plane was downed, and its two-man crew killed.

Another Norseman double fatality was very well publicized:

On May 20, George (Buzz) Beurling, Canadian, and Leonard Cohen, Englishman, had taken up a Norseman light transport. Buzz was at the controls, and, according to a witness, was stunt-flying at tree-top level. Coming in for what appeared to be a landing approach at low speed, Buzz apparently changed his mind at the last minute and suddenly opened the throttle fully. Instead of the engine's roaring to life, it stalled and back-fired, throwing a tongue of flame onto the fabric of the plane. The plane crashed, and burned fiercely: Both men died in their seats.

This took place at the small airstrip of Urbe, near Rome. The Jewish community of Rome, including many refugees more or less in transit, turned out en masse for the funerals of both men. Originally, the Canadian embassy had wanted an anonymous, dawn funeral for Beurling. In spite of the undesirability of publicity, the Israeli liaison representatives insisted that such a procedure would be ungracious, that Buzz should be buried with all possible dignity and honor. The dispute was settled by a wire from Buzz Beurling's father who felt it consistent with his son's joining the forces of Israel for funeral arrangements to be made by the representatives of Israel. November 9, 1950, the bodies of both men were transferred to their final resting places: Buzz Beurling to the Christian Cemetery in Haifa; Leonard Cohen (whose parents had moved to Palestine when he was a child, but who as a young man had permanently emigrated to England) to a nearby Jewish cemetery.

That which is public, is publicized: The newspapers made much of this fatal accident, involving two men "believed bound for Israel." [4]

Earlier, we pointed out that 17 of the original 20 Norsemen did reach Israel. The other 3 were part of a single ill-fated lot in Italy. Above, we described the tragic accident that destroyed one of these planes, taking the life of pilot and co-pilot. The two remaining planes were to make the 1400-mile flight from Brindisi to Israel nonstop. Although this was about their maximum design range, the planes had no difficulty covering the distance—but there was a slight (40 mile) navigational error: Instead of reaching the coast of Israel just south of Tel Aviv, they arrived just south of Egyptian-held Gaza. It was night, with a blackout supposedly in effect, and so there was no clue that anything was amiss. The fact that the control tower did not answer their call was not unusual (radios did not always work as they should—and tower personnel were, in those days, not as alert as they should have been). Thus, when the runway lights were turned on, the crews of the two planes landed, happy to be at their destination and the long flight over—and were shocked to find themselves prisoners of war! The Egyptians had not been overwhelmingly clever—they had simply assumed that these planes were theirs. [5]

The Norsemen became part of Squadron 35 where they were used for transports and bombing. As bombers they served primarily in Operation Yoav. As transports, they kept isolated points supplied—most especially Sodom—during the many months of cut-off; also, in Operation Dust, these planes played an auxiliary role (their cargo capacity was several times less than that of the C-46s and DC-3s).

Although the operations of Freddy himself in England were necessarily short-lived, they did suggest that there were practical possibilities of airplane acquisition in that country. And so, in May 1948, Emmanuel Zur, an RAF veteran Israeli pilot with a somewhat British air, was sent to England. He had no trouble purchasing a Rapide and getting it safely to Israel. He promptly returned, and acquired two more Rapides and a Gemini and an Aerovan—all ostensibly for the French lobster trade. All of these light planes made it safely to Israel.

The Aerovan was a peculiar-looking plane—with a short tail and a very high body; it was quickly nicknamed the "pregnant duck." Its major advantage was that it required only a very short field for take-off and landing; on the other hand, it became difficult to handle with a load of much over 700 lbs. This is the plane that made a forced landing July 18 on the sand west of Rehovoth and south of Bat Yam. The co-pilot,

Spence Boyd, was a non-Jewish American volunteer from New Jersey. The cargo: 6 wounded passengers being brought back from Sodom. Two who were able to walk (the pilot, Murray Weissberg, and one of the wounded) were given the only arms on the plane—Boyd's personal pistol—and sent for help. Spence Boyd and the other wounded were found by a band of Arabs, and were butchered before help could arrive.

An ironic footnote: Less than a month earlier, enroute to Israel my wife and I had met Spence Boyd in Rome, and we spent a little time together. He was anxious to learn the Hebrew for "I am one of your pilots" (*Ani tayass mishelachem*). He was concerned that he might, perhaps, sometime make a forced landing near a kibbutz—and he wanted to be sure to be able to identify himself quickly. We suggested that that was only half the problem—what would happen if the forced landing was near an Arab settlement? He answered, "In that case, it's all over."

Zur's most important accomplishment appears to have been the enlistment of the veteran non-Jewish pilot, John Harvey. It was John Harvey who now located and successfully flew one Mosquito fighter-bomber from England to Israel. Harvey then returned to England, located and acquired a second Mosquito, and found a volunteer pilot to fly it to Israel. En route—actually, in the course of take-off from Ajaccio—the plane cracked up. Fortunately, the pilot escaped.

Zur was quite successful in delivering four Beaufighters (fighter-bombers) from England to Israel. Here, the cover was a motion-picture production. A company was formed to produce a film on New Zealand's participation in World War II. One sequence would be a formation flight by the Beaufighters—which would disappear, promptly followed by the disappearance of the company and its personnel. (The Beaufighters would land at Ajaccio, Corsica, which had replaced Catania as the airlift stopover point: At Ajaccio, no questions were asked of airlift planes, nor were documents of any kind required.) The inspiration for this imaginative plan had been the sincere desire of a New Zealand actress (a friend of one of Zur's pilots) to make just such a film on New Zealand.

Seven Beaufighters were originally acquired. Five were ready for flight by moving picture time. One of these crashed, killing its English pilot, the day before the filming; and the other four successfully made it to Israel. The two remaining in England were later seized by British authorities.[6]

Although the four[7] Beaufighters succeeded in reaching Israel they were of no use, because they were not armed. Zur next managed to locate the necessary armament, and some spares as well, but had no means of smuggling them out of England. The volunteer pilot, John Harvey, solved the problem: He knew the owner of a Halifax four-engine bomber, and arranged for its charter. All went smoothly until the landing in Israel. It was the middle of the night, and Oklahoma (Ekron) airbase refused to turn on its runway lights. Despite the plane's calling in code repeatedly, despite its continuing circling of the field with its landing lights—Ekron remained dead. As fuel ran low, the radio operator decided to send out distress signals over all standard frequencies, while the pilot circled Tel Aviv in the hope of initiating some action. Finally, out of fuel and patience, the plane crash-landed in Tel Aviv at Dov Airport, which was relatively easy to locate in the dark, since its runway leads to the sea.

While the plane was a total loss, most of the cargo was saved—but the English operation was brought to a painful termination. Although the Halifax's distress signals had apparently not been listened to in Israel, they had been heard elsewhere; London did a thorough tracing job, and most of those who had assisted Zur were arrested.[8]

The English non-Jew, John Harvey, served and identified with Israel to an extraordinary degree. Not only did he obtain and pilot this Halifax; earlier, he had successfully spirited the Mosquito fighter-bomber out of England to Israel (via Ajaccio). There had been plans to use the Mosquito as a radar-directed night fighter, but since there was no armament for the Mosquito, it was initially converted to photo-reconnaissance use instead. (In any event, Israel's radar technology was not then up to designing the necessary equipment, anyway.)[9] John Harvey also was the leading pilot in the movie ruse which got the four Beaufighters out of England. Thus, Emmanuel Zur's many successes in England apparently depended for their execution on the volunteer John Harvey. Harvey died in Israel's service: In 1950, he was Israel's chief test pilot in the acquisition of several dozen surplus Mosquitoes from the French government. During routine flight-testing there was a malfunction, and the plane crashed into a low hill. John Harvey lies in Chateaudun Cemetery in France, alongside five RAF pilots killed in World War II; the six stones are identical—except that the emblem of the IAF adorns that of John Harvey.[10]

The sum of Emmanuel Zur's English acquisitions, then, were five light planes (three Rapides, a Gemini, an Aerovan), and five proper fighter-bombers (one Mosquito and four Beaufighters). Successful delivery of the five war planes and their armament apparently could not have been accomplished without the full cooperation of the English volunteer John Harvey.

South Africa

Boris Senior, a South African World War II pilot, had come to pre-Israel as a tourist to visit his parents in 1947. With the developing political and military situation, he offered his services to the light-plane Air Service. For a brief time, he was designated commander of its Squadron A.

In February 1948 he was asked to return to South Africa in order to purchase planes, and recruit aircrews.

A lot of fifty P-40 Kittyhawk American fighter planes was just then being auctioned as scrap metal and purchased by Jewish scrap-metal dealers. For service in Israel, those that were usable would be available virtually as a gift. What an answer to Israel's desperate need for fighter planes! But this magnificent windfall could not be utilized at all—South Africa had a stringent law against taking any warplanes out of the country. The decision apparently was that it would be neither politic nor possible to evade this regulation.

Instead, a variety of civilian planes was acquired: 2 Rapides, 2 Bonanzas, one Anson, 3 Fairchilds, and 2 Dakotas. And some 40 fliers were recruited. An attempt was made to fly the 2 Bonanzas the length of Africa to Israel. In bad weather, both were damaged in Rhodesia (one on landing, one on take-off). Both pilots (one of whom was Boris) returned to South Africa.

Next, "Westair Co." was created as a vehicle for exporting the Anson and the 2 Dakotas. In addition, an arrangement was made to lease two more Dakotas from a local company, on the responsibility of the South African Zionist Federation (in South Africa, the Zionist Federation was truly representative of the Jewish community and was a serious and financially responsible entity). The Rapide was put under the umbrella of Pan African Airways, a charter airline, and the three Fairchilds were flown out by three volunteers; the first of these arrived in Israel May 15. Before sending the Fairchilds out, Boris successfully flew a new Bonanza to Israel. Following the earlier mishap, it would have been imprudent for him to fly any plane directly out of South Africa. He simply had some one else fly the first leg, himself taking over in Khartoum. His penultimate stop was at Luxor, in upper Egypt. There, he was assumed to be a playboy on the way to Beirut, and was treated very well indeed. His next stop was the airfield at Nirim, Israel. At Nirim, the initial reaction was hostile: It took a little time to convince the Israelis that he was indeed a volunteer from South Africa and not a lost Egyptian pilot.

In addition to the Beechcraft Bonanza flown to Israel by Boris Senior, another Bonanza came, crated, by sea via Italy. A Rapide, routed via Cairo, ended up in Egyptian hands. The Anson crashed on its way to Israel.

The above were all light planes. The truly important South African acquisition was the four Dakotas (DC-3 medium transports, slightly smaller than the C-46 airlift transports). We do not have precise information on their arrival but it appears to have been early in the large-scale war—that is, late May or early June.[11]

These Dakotas were not added to the Czech airlift, but were kept in Israel where they were used for local transport and for bombing. They were probably also used for general communication with Europe. For the latter, a commercial cover would have been desirable. Thus, the writer flew from Rome to Israel on a Dakota carrying the label of Pan African Airways in late June with a planeload of specialists. It is not unlikely that the plane used was one of these four South African Dakotas.[12]

A fifth Dakota had been acquired in Israel. May 15, when the Egyptians strafed the Tel Aviv airport (Sde Dov), they hit and somewhat damaged a Dakota belonging to Air France. Air France, the only regular international commercial airline to attempt to maintain service with Israel during the war, was persuaded that the plane ought to be written off as a total loss, and insurance compensation was paid. Thus, this plane became available to Israel—which immediately went to work to restore it to flying condition.

There were other acquisitions:

In the pre-state period, the Haganah had set up the light-plane Air Service, whose major acquisition consisted of a quantity of Austers, purchased as surplus from the British at Ekron through the agency of an apparently commercial company, the Aviron Company. According to one report, in April a Palmach unit was able to seize an Egyptian Fairchild on the ground, in the Negev. This plane had been observed making regular stops at a particular point—its pilot was an entrepreneur, acting as a middleman in the drug trade. This light plane was put into service in the Galilee.

Several Egyptian Spitfires had been shot down or crash-landed on Israeli soil; it was possible to put together two serviceable planes from them. Two of these were obligingly downed by the British, due to faulty Egyptian intelligence: Not realizing how seriously and to what extremes the British were pursuing their goal of keeping all warplanes out of Israeli hands (even light planes; London had been most upset over the Auster transaction) Egyptian Spitfires heavily strafed the RAF Spitfires on the ground at Ramat David airfield, May 15. Somehow, they must have assumed that this airfield had already been evacuated by the British and been taken over by Israel. The British pilots were furious; when the Egyptians compounded their error by returning later in the day, the local RAF was ready for them and hit them hard. Four Egyptian Spitfires were probably hit, and two definitely downed.

A gift: A wealthy Dutch Jew, whose wife had done social relief work in Jerusalem before and while it was beseiged, and who refused to leave until well after the siege was lifted, lent a Dakota and two Widgeons during the summer "for the duration."

In August, a DC-5 (a high wing, slightly smaller version of the Dakota DC-3) was landed at Sde Dov by its owner. This man said he had heard that there was a shortage of such aircraft in Israel, and he would be happy to sell this one. It was purchased. It is possible that this is simply a different version of the Dakota story immediately above.

During the summer, two Nord planes came as donations from French Jews. These small planes were used as flying ambulances.

On October 8, a Lockheed Lodestar arrived from Australia.[13]

At its inception (following a meeting November 10, 1947), Air Service had ten light planes. May 15, the day of the invasion by the regular Arab armies, Israel did not possess a single warplane. On that first day of formal invasion, its air force (still called "Air Service" until May 28, when the air force officially came into being), could have put into the air (if it had enough pilots) a grand total of 28 planes. All were light planes, 19 of them being single-engine Austers.[14]

This picture would be totally transformed by the limited number of acquisitions described above and in the following chapter. Hardly any of these acquisitions could have succeeded without volunteers.

Chapter 13

VOLUNTEERS IN THE AIR IV: BOMBERS AND FIGHTER PLANES

The acquisition and delivery of the B-17s which became Israel's heavy bomber squadron, and of the relatively large number of Spitfire fighter planes, deserve elaboration.

Air transport had clearly been the first priority, closely followed by fighter planes. Transports could be and were used as rudimentary bombers by chucking bombs out the door and, in some cases, attempting to rig bombs under the wings or fuselage of the lighter transports. At best, such makeshift arrangements were unsatisfactory. They were dangerous to the fliers and relatively unhazardous with respect to their targets—accuracy was poor, and bombloads would necessarily be small.

Under any conditions, true bombers would be most important—for use against enemy supply dumps, against enemy armor in the field, against enemy strongpoints. But to forces virtually without artillery, the importance of bombers is multiplied many times over. True bombers—bombers that can hit the targets—become the artillery. They are the only means to hammer enemy strongpoints, and effectively to strike enemy formations on the ground. Without them, a turn-around would hardly appear possible.

And so, quite early, four B-17s (heavy bombers), and four A-20s (medium bombers) were located. One B-17 and the four A-20s were idle in Oklahoma as war surplus; the cost for the former was $15,000, and for the latter, $6,000 each. All needed considerable work to put them into flying condition. The other three B-17s, stripped of their military equipment, were in current use: One in California, two in Miami as commercial transports.[1] Charles T. Winters, a non-Jew, was principal partner in the company that owned the Miami B-17s; not only did he willingly sell them—he acted as a volunteer pilot for one. For his participation, he was later arrested, convicted, and sentenced to 18 months in prison and a fine of $5,000.[2]

The original plan was that the four B-17s would leave together, from

Miami for Puerto Rico (Winters' usual commercial run, for which no official permission was required); thence to the Azores, and on to Ajaccio. And from Ajaccio, the planes would, of course, proceed to Zatec, where they would be armed and prepared for Israel. However, with three planes ready and their full crews each assembled, it was decided that waiting for the fourth ship was too risky—some crewmen might be indiscreet. Thus, three B-17s left at midnight June 12.

The departure was quiet, and apparently smooth. A day later, the newspapers trumpeted the news: Three B-17s enroute to Europe had disappeared off the Azores; some wreckage had been spotted on the ocean. Actually nothing had happened—one can always find flotsam in the Atlantic—except that Ajaccio had failed to notify the Azores airport of the safe arrival of the planes. The Azores airport, in turn, had spread the alarm. In the meantime the three bombers had left Ajaccio and were safe at Zatec. But the extra publicity stepped up the level of FBI surveillance, defeating subsequent efforts to release the remaining B-17 and the four A-20s.[3]

Knowing full well just what the level of risk was, the attempt was nevertheless made to retrieve the fourth B-17. Since Miami was now suspect, a very different location was selected as the point of departure: Westchester Airport, in southern New York State. A "Mr. Edmunds" paid cash in advance for sufficient gasoline and lubricating oil to fuel the B-17 fully and the four A-20s which would follow if the B-17 made good its escape.

Very early on the morning of July 11, the B-17 arrived. By afternoon, it was fully fueled, and boarded by its crew of nine men. The Captain, Irwin (Swifty) Schindler, gave the purpose of the flight as flight training. Stated destination: West Coast and eventual return. The true initial destination was to have been St. John's, Newfoundland. Because of bad weather, the plane landed in Dartmouth, Canada, instead. Schindler's cover story was that this plane, part of the Overseas Air Training Corps, had been on a training flight when bad weather forced it to land at Dartmouth.

One customs official became suspicious and checked with his superiors in Ottawa who, in turn, checked with the United States State Department. The State Department ordered the plane returned to the United States at once. This had now become a newspaper matter, with allegations that Israel was the plane's intended destination. Schindler denied this, demanding that he be permitted to return to the States—

intending, of course, to make for the Azores and from there to Zatec and Israel. This would deliver the plane, and also avoid the unpleasantness of arrest and the risk of interrogation. On July 17, the plane was released, supposedly with just enough fuel to make Boston safely. Instead, a very lengthy nonstop flight brought the B-17 to the Azores.

How was this miracle accomplished? By starting with full fuel tanks. Canadian airfield personnel had disregarded their explicit orders to limit the fuel—perhaps, in sympathetic reaction to the aircrew's absolute determination to try for the Azores, no matter how low the fuel in their tanks. Now, with success within reach, defeat was snatched from the jaws of victory. Instead of immediately refueling and taking off, the tired men decided to get some sleep. These extra few hours gave the State Department enough time to pressure the Portuguese officials in the Azores to hold the B-17 and arrest its crew. Captain and crew were returned to the States via Pan American July 25. They were thoroughly interrogated, and Irwin Schindler was later tried before a federal court. The abandoned B-17 eventually became scrap metal.[4]

What of the first three B-17s which had so audaciously been flown to Zatec, at the risk of flagrant violation of the arms embargo, because of the presumed urgent need for them in Israel? For three weeks they sat at Zatec idle and forlorn! On his second Constellation flight to Israel, ATC pilot Ray Kurtz was given charge of the B-17s. This would have been perhaps at the end of the first week in July, since the B-17s had landed at Zatec in mid-June. Kurtz was the natural choice: Not only was he a deeply dedicated, hard-working volunteer, but he had been a B-17 squadron leader in World War II. Between wars, Ray Kurtz was a member of the New York City Police Department.

Kurtz returned to Zatec, bringing a few additional aircrew members, overseas volunteers who had been in Israel, serving in the ground forces. There followed five days of most intensive work, made more difficult by the fact that a Czech three-day holiday occurred at the same time. On the morning of the sixth day, planes and crews were ready—only to be greeted by an urgent message from Israel canceling flight plans.

A scant few days later the operation was reinstated, each B-17 bombing a major target on its way in to Israel. The Cairo and Gaza planes hit their targets, with the El Arish plane probably hitting Gaza (or possibly Rafa) instead. From then on (July 15, towards the end of the Ten Days) the Hammers—as the three B-17s making up the Heavy Bomber Squadron were called—were widely used in all the formal fighting periods, and, on occasion, in fighting during the truce intervals as well.

When the B-17s did reach Israel, the cause of the delay became apparent: Their base was not quite ready. To expand or build an air force without sufficient personnel experienced and competent in even the auxiliary skills of setting up and maintaining an airbase, makes for most uneven functioning.[5] To do so rapidly is even more difficult.

The summer and early autumn of 1948 saw significant additions to the air strength of both sides. The Egyptians obtained two squadrons of Italian Fiat G-55 fighters, plus nine British 4-engine Sterling bombers (capacity: 5 tons of bombs), in addition to 35 serviceable Spitfires; the Iraqis added five Furies; and the Syrians, ten Harvards. Israel had 15 Messerschmitts, two Spitfires (put together from scraps, including downed Egyptian Spitfires), two P-51 Mustangs, and the three B-17s, a single Mosquito, and the three Beaufighters described earlier. Also on hand or in transit were five Dakotas; a DC-5 (whose owner delivered it to Israel); two P-51s and two Piper Cubs crated as "spare parts" on the *Enterprise* out of New York harbor; two Hudsons; a Lockheed Lodestar from Australia. Towards the end of October, Haifa harbor would receive 17 Harvards, well cased, in small pieces; and 20 Stearmans (light planes) and two P-51 Mustangs would arrive in November.

At best, this was a most miscellaneous assortment. And the midsummer picture was bleak, particularly with regard to fighter planes, especially when we recall that the Messerschmitt was found to be most unsatisfactory. Whether this was a basically difficult model or whether limited experience with the plane was responsible, the fact is that its rate of attrition and the level of pilot dissatisfaction were high. Thus, early in August Israel contracted to buy 50 Spitfires which Britain had left with the Free Czech squadron at the end of World War II, at a cost of $23,000 each. They would be overhauled, repaired, and tested at the aircraft facility in Kunovice, some 250 miles from Prague. (Acquiring needed parts from locations all over Czechoslovakia, in itself became a major source of frustration.)

As usual, time was of the essence. Some of these planes, crated, would go via the slow land and sea-freight route. But, with every prospect that only a sound Egyptian defeat could reopen the road to the Negev, and the possibility that such fighting could break out quite soon, delivery by air was highly desirable.

However, effective August 12, the airlift proper had been abruptly closed out. All that remained at Zatec was Israel's lone Constellation which had been crippled in landing on a return airlift flight in July; the American mechanic Ernie Stehlik remained alone, and the repairwork was going slowly. Thus, it was not possible for crated Spitfires to be flown to Israel in the bellies of C-46 transports, as had been done with the Messerschmitts. Sam Pomerantz, the American engineer in charge of Czech technical operations, proposed another kind of airlift: The planes would be piloted individually directly to Israel. Auxiliary fuel tanks would have to be designed and installed, and the planes would be stripped of everything possible, including their navigating equipment, and a transport "mother ship" would lead them.

The direct flight from Kunovice to Israel was vetoed as too risky, although the basic idea was approved. The planes would fly from Kunovice to Titograd, once Podgorica, in Yugoslavia, and thence direct to Israel. Although this distance was well beyond the original design range of this model, there was now a slight margin of safety: It was calculated that Ramat David (a military airport near Haifa) was 6½ hours distant for the modified planes, and their tanks held fuel for 7 hours. Titograd ("Alabama," "Yoram") had come into use as the refueling point for the Czech airlift after it was discovered and American pressure forced the closing of Ajaccio in mid-June. Since the total ending of the airlift in mid-August, the five mechanics living in isolation at Titograd had little to do other than grow beards. The prospect of activity was indeed welcome.[6]

Early in the morning on September 24, the DC-4 Skymaster landed at Alabama (Titograd) from Oklahoma (Israel). Its crew were all volunteers: Four Americans (including one Canadian), one South African, and one Englishman. The cargo, in addition to housekeeping supplies, consisted of six pilots, all provided with Israeli identification papers. Two would pilot a Norseman, then in Titograd, to Kunovice, with the other four as passengers. The Norseman crew would fly the Spitfire armament back to Titograd, while these four pilots, plus two from Kunovice (where there was a Spitfire brush-up course) would each fly one of the six Spitfires to Titograd. One of the two pilots was Sam Pomerantz.

Among the Czech rules was one that the Spitfires had to leave Kunovice unarmed. Armament had to go separately (via Norseman, a fine, utility light transport) to Alabama. There, it would be transferred to the Skymaster, which, in addition to escorting the Spitfires, would simultaneously deliver their armament to Israel. An air-sea rescue team would be on hand in the eastern Mediteranean: Two C-46s to locate any pilots who might have to ditch their planes and to drop life rafts to them, and two corvettes on standby, to pick them up.

The same morning (September 24), the Norseman with its pilot passengers left for Kunovice. Before dark, the six Spitfires were in Titograd; one was damaged on landing, and could not continue. September 27, the Skymaster took off, followed by its five "Fish" (their code designation). All went well until, a little beyond the island of Rhodes, two of the planes (Fish Two and Fish Four) found their auxiliary fuel tanks dry. Since they apparently would not be able to make Israel, the flight captain on the mother ship agreed that the most sensible course was to land on Rhodes. There the pilots were held for close to two weeks—and the planes permanently impounded.[7]

Thus, Velveta I brought three Spitfires to Israel, together with armament for them and for the two rebuilt Spits already on hand well before Operation Yoav, which began October 15. This was a significant addition to the IAF, particularly in view of the fact that much of its apparent strength was then grounded. Planes not airworthy October 15 included 7 of the 15 Messerschmitts, all of the Mustangs, both Hudsons, the lone Mosquito, and 1 of the 3 Beaufighters.

The Norseman ferrying Spitfire arms to Podgorica had been involved in an unfortunate incident. Slowed by unexpectedly strong headwinds, it found itself some 150 miles from Titograd with darkness approaching. Its two-man crew decided it had no choice but to land in the nearest open field. The landing was without mishap—but the local farmers assumed that they must be spies. Turned over to the nearest army post, phone calls to higher authority established that the men were not spies, to the satisfaction of their hosts. But it was decided that it would be best for the local populace to continue to believe that they were indeed spies, and that the army had summarily dispatched them. And so the two-man crew was asked to put on Yugoslav army uniforms before leaving, which they did.[8]

Yugoslavia was then in a most delicate political position. Establishing its independence from Soviet hegemony, it certainly could not appear to be going over to the United States—such an appearance could seriously threaten the very stability of Marshal Tito's regime. Already, there were local rumors that Yugoslavia was being armed by the United States, rumors which had been started by the presence of a number of Americans at Titograd airfield, and the use of the field by strange planes with strange markings. Now these rumors were given fresh substance by the incident of the Norseman and the forced landing of two of Velveta 1's Spitfires on Rhodes. Result: Yugoslavia withdrew the use of the Titograd airfield.

Relations with Yugoslavia had been on again, off again. Following departure of the vitally needed arms ship *Nora* from a Yugoslav port at the end of March, use of the port had been withdrawn. This had been a significant factor in the decision to mount the airlift. Then, when the airlift was threatened with indefinite suspension because of French withdrawal of Ajaccio (Corsica)—only the four-engine aircraft (Skymaster, Constellation) could fly to Israel nonstop from Zatec—Yugoslavia made the Titograd airfield available. Titograd was vitally important from mid-June on (for the balance of the airlift, and for Velveta 1). Now, its use was again denied.

The man in overall charge of Yugoslav operations was Geda Shoḥat, one of the very few Israelis with deep piloting experience including experience with multi-engine planes. Such technically skilled Israelis were so rare that in spite of the critical shortage of flying personnel, it was deemed more important for Shoḥat to function in technical administration (i.e., airfield negotiations, selection of planes to purchase) than to be part of the flying air force. Although use of Titograd was denied, work proceeded at full steam in Kunovice. By November 15, fifteen more Spitfires were airworthy, seven of which were complete with the long-range modifications —one auxiliary fuel tank under each wing, and a third under the belly behind the engine. Shoḥat worked steadily to persuade the Yugoslavs to reconsider, and permit the use of Titograd once more.

On December 7 the Yugoslavs relented; Titograd could once again be used—under rigid conditions: The base personnel now could not go to town at all; although there were no proper facilities for cooking or washing, the men would have to do all of their own cooking on the field, and get by with minimal washing. Even though the weather was already unusually harsh, they would be totally restricted to the primitive airfield, living in the old German underground earthen bunkers (like Zatec, Titograd, too, had been a World War II German airfield). Also, no more Norsemen would be permitted to fly between Yugoslavia and Czechoslovakia; and, there would be a maximum of six planes per flight.

On December 9 Geda Shoḥat was able to advise Israel that all was arranged. Spitfire pilots should now be sent from Israel, each man with his own sleeping and eating gear; they were to come in two planes with Yugoslav markings. Israel argued that the Yugoslav markings would create more problems than they would solve. On reconsideration, the Yugoslavs agreed that it would be best for the transports to have Israeli markings.[9]

Suddenly, a new problem arose: The Czechs would not permit the Spitfires to leave until all Israel's debts were paid. On a war footing, with substantial immigration and relatively massive arms purchases proceeding simultaneously, Israel's cash position was very tight. It was one thing to authorize a contract in the expectation that payments would be made in the indefinite future; it was something else to be faced with an immediate demand for cash. The problem was put to Pinhas Sapir, who somehow came up with an adequate sum. Payment was made in two installments to cover the 6 Spitfires of Velveta 1, 10 Spitfires crated for land and sea shipment, 15 being prepared for flight, and some payment "on account" for the balance. The first installment, covering 16 planes, was made immediately. On December 13, the 10 crated Spitfires, now paid for, were released; it was expected that they would reach the Yugoslav port of embarkation in 8 to 10 days.

Velveta 2 would parallel Velveta 1, but would include double the number of planes, with two mother ships—one for each flight of six Spitfires. The Czechs insisted that there be no evidence whatever of the origin of the planes. Pilots were to wear Israel Air Force uniforms, including rank insignia; there was to be no paper of any kind, including personal letters, that might point to Czechoslovakia—or Yugoslavia, for that matter. In the event of a forced landing, pilots were to give name, rank, and serial number only; to ask for additional fuel; and, if hard pressed, to say that they were testing the long-range possibilities of fighter planes. All maps were to be destroyed before landing; if asked about missing maps, the answer was to be that the route was a military secret. All planes would carry IAF markings. For a possible forced landing, the preferred point was Heraklion, Crete, rather than Rhodes.

On December 15 the second payment was made to Czechoslovakia. The Czechs were so delighted at this evidence of good faith that they gave permission for a transport with IAF markings to land in Prague and pick up a load of spares and crucially important armament for the Spitfires. Officially, this plane was to be delivering a load of oranges for the Christmas holidays, and Benjamin Kagan, the author of two of our source books, who was the chief Israeli negotiator in Czechoslovakia, urged that at least fifty cases of oranges indeed be included, as a goodwill offering.[10]

The Israeli DC-4 arrived December 16, in the evening. The news it brought was that a major renewal of fighting with the Egyptians was not far off—and every possible addition to the IAF would be needed. Although permission for the Spitfires to leave had been granted on the fifteenth, immediately on receipt of payment, a snowstorm prevented take-off. The storm lasted, on and off, for several days; on the eighteenth it appeared to lift. Sam Pomerantz contacted Geda Shoḥat in Titograd via the Israeli embassy radio in Prague, and was informed that the local weather was good. Although the general weather picture was still uncertain, Sam, impatient at the delays already experienced, authorized a flight of 6 Spitfires to take off for Titograd. He flew the lead plane himself. The 6 planes took to the air, and ran into heavy snow. Four returned to Kunovice safely; one crash-landed and its pilot suffered minor injuries only. The sixth plane crashed into mountains in Yugoslovia, killing the pilot. His name was Sam Pomerantz.[11]

The following day, December 19, the weather cleared. Since 15 Spitfires had been prepared for flight, the loss of two still permitted two groups of 6 planes each to leave. In 3 hours 45 minutes, they landed at Titograd. The six pilots in each of these flights were 5 volunteers and 1 Israeli. The Israelis were new, inexperienced pilots; both had just completed their training in Czechoslovakia. Each had a total of only 140 flying hours of which 7 were in a Spitfire. That men so lacking in experience were used in so important a mission is a strong indication indeed of the shortage of pilots. December 22, the planes took off from Titograd for Israel. Of the 12, one did not start out due to mechanical difficulties; a second plane returned, with engine trouble. The remaining 10 planes, in 2 flights, each led by a C-46 transport, made it to Israel in an uneventful flight of 6¾ hours.[12]

The DC-4 was still on the ground, in Prague. From the time it had landed, there was an indication of trouble with one engine. The Czechs—who had initially anticipated that this plane would land, turn around, with some rest for the crew, and be gone—were increasingly uncomfortable at the continuing presence of this clearly marked Israeli plane in Prague airport. Out of regard for this feeling, the plane took off December 19, without attempting to replace the engine. The malfunction continued, and the plane returned. Clearly, replacement was necessary; replacement could only come from Israel; yet, the Czechs did not want a second Israeli transport landing in Prague.

In Israel, Operation Horev—fullscale warfare against the Egyptians—had been launched December 22, the day the Velveta 2 Spitfires arrived.

But these precious planes could not be used without armament, and armament could come quickly only via the DC-4 which was grounded in Prague! In refusing permission for a second Israeli transport to rescue the first, the Czechs showed great interest in acquiring the Constellation which was undergoing slow repair at Zatec. When the Israelis (and Schwimmer) were adamant about the Constellation (indicating an obligation to return it to the United States), another kind of solution was permitted.

The Bata Shoe Factory in the town of Zlin, owned a number of DC-3s one of which had once been utilized in connection with the Spring/Summer airlift. These planes were idle, and might be rented. The proper individuals were approached; the asking price for renting one DC-3 was accepted, with the stipulation that cash was to be paid in advance. The money was wired from Geneva, the overall headquarters for European acquisitions; the Czech markings were obliterated—the plane would fly unmarked—but under no circumstances would a Czech crew be permitted to fly to Yugoslavia. Solution: The volunteer crew of the idle DC-4 was persuaded to fly this DC-3. They took it from Zlin to Kunovice, where it was loaded with Spitfire armament; thence to Titograd, where this cargo was transferred to an Israeli C-46 for immediate delivery to Israel. En route, the DC-3 had the unpleasant experience of tasting Albanian anti-aircraft fire—Titograd is close to the Albanian border. No damage was done, and two more such trips were made. On the second flight the DC-3 delivered to Prague the parts needed for the DC-4; these had been brought to Titograd by an Israeli C-46. The third flight included a full complement of reserve Spitfire arms. With this delivery, its function over, Alabama (Podgorica, Titograd) was closed. Its Israeli base crew had consisted of one Israeli officer in charge, plus two American mechanics and two American radio operators. The Velveta 2 Spitfires were able to participate in the last phase of Operation Horev.[13]

All that remained to be done in Czechoslovakia was to pull the DC-4 out of Prague; finish repairing the Constellation at Zatec, and take it out; crate the remaining Spitfires and spares—and pay the remaining bills. The needed parts were at last being obtained for the Constellation; with the DC-4 engine delivered, the DC-4 was rapidly prepared for take off. The Czechs were most anxious for it to leave Prague, so much so that they worked on it in below-zero weather. The plane took off at 8:00 P.M., but the flight was dogged by communications failures. When the information of the takeoff was received at the Israeli mission in Prague, the communications officer was not present; the novice on duty did not know where to locate him, and put the message under his door. Close to midnight, Kagan, uneasy, called the embassy—only to discover that the message had not been sent, that the night communication with Tel Aviv had already taken place, and that no new contact was scheduled until 4:00 A.M. They would try to raise Tel Aviv before then, but chances of success were dim. The Israeli radio operator in Prague actually did reach Israel—but his efforts were useless. Although the message was delivered to Air Force HQ in time, it was never passed on to the Tel Aviv airport, Sde Dov, which was to receive the plane.

The flight was smooth until, over Greece, the troublesome engine acted up. The pilot decided to risk continuing with just three engines operating and reached the skies of Israel safely. Then, the first frustration: The DC-4 tried to raise the control tower in Tel Aviv—no answer; he tried Ekron, the major heavy-plane base south of Tel Aviv—no answer. He repeatedly circled Sde Dov with his landing lights on, with all of Tel Aviv, including high-ranking air force officials, now aware of his presence—no landing lights were lit. Down to Ekron, back to Tel Aviv—nothing. With fuel now running low, a second engine stopped. In the faint predawn light, Sde Dov—whose runway extends to the sea—could be vaguely discerned. The pilot, a highly skilled overseas volunteer, brought the plane down safely in shallow water beyond the end of the runway. Although the plane was damaged, crew and cargo, including Spitfire parts, were safe.[14]

The justification for failing to turn on the ground landing lights while a plane with its own lights on continuously circled overhead was laid at the door of the fear of an enemy plane whose very particular mission it was to bomb the Tel Aviv airfield. No one could take this lame excuse seriously, since the very few enemy air raids on civilian centers after early June had all been instantaneous hit-and-run affairs, with no concern as to where the bombs fell just so they were dropped and the plane able to get away.

It is far more likely that the gaffe was rather due to lack of experience in a period of transition. Increasingly, Israelis were being placed in critical, decision-making positions. Yet, without a reasonable amount of experience, they lacked the self-confidence without which one cannot act sensibly and flexibly in unexpected situations. And so, a precious plane, important cargo, and the lives of a dedicated crew, were inexcusably hazarded.

Although this appears to have been the last such blunder in the War of Independence, it was not the first. Many months earlier, in July, a Halifax had suffered a virtually identical experience. And during that same month, the pilot and passengers of a crash-landed small transport (Aerovan) were butchered by passing Arabs because of a rigidly enforced policy of refusal to issue side arms for such flights—although the shortage of small arms was then no longer critical (chapter twelve); the resulting outrage caused a reversal in this policy.

The DC-4 fiasco was not totally negative: It is not at all unlikely that it was a major factor in the decision to spend relatively large sums bringing in many new foreign instructors and thoroughly restructuring and professionalizing the entire Mahal relationship.

Chapter 14

THE WAR AT SEA: OPERATION PIRATE

The all-important reinforcements of men and materials could come to Israel only by sea or by air.

Volunteers—Mahal and Gahal—with very few exceptions, came by sea. One way or another, individuals and groups made their way to French or Italian ports of embarkation, where they joined the survivors of the European death camps of all ages for the sea voyage to Israel. Upon arrival in Israel, sorting out took place: Refugees needing care were taken care of; men and willing women of military age were assigned for apparent maximum effectiveness. A small number—those with the good fortune to both be considered top-priority specialists and to strike upon the proper recruiting channel—made the journey much more quickly by air.

For example, the group to which the writer was attached in Rome flew by charter airline from there to Haifa airport. Haifa airport had no night-landing facilities, and so a midday take off forced us to land at Athens. Although we had been warned to expect to be restricted to the Athens airfield, we were actually taken by special bus to a second-class hotel for the night. Our announced destination, of course, was Cyprus—not Israel.

Ships were obtained wherever they were available, and sailed by volunteer and/or hired crews. This was simply an extension of the methods used to transport "illegal" refugees to Palestine since the end of World War II. Lapide makes the interesting statement that ten of these ships, which carried 40 percent of the grand total of 56,468 refugees transported in this manner, "were manned by American crews." [1]

A plaque alongside a model of the ship *Exodus* in the Smithsonian Institution in Washington, D.C. lists the ships by name. (A description of the voyage of the *Exodus* will be found in the biography of William Bernstein, chapter eight).

Until mid-May 1948, the hazards were weather and the British fleet. The seaworthiness of some of those old vessels was questionable. The ratio of successes to failures leaned heavily in the direction of the latter. Only a small proportion of the refugees successfully evaded capture and internment by the British, and successful delivery of people depended on evasion of the British. Supplies were also best delivered by evasion, deception, sometimes, perhaps, assisted by bribery—although our sources generally shy away from this aspect. Thus, Lorch relates that a ship carrying a vital cargo of field guns and machine guns concealed under a thick layer of onions was boarded by the British on May 13—and released the night of May 14. Apparently the pungent smell of the onions discouraged probing too deeply into the hold.[2]

Arms ships, as such, were rare and precious indeed. This ship, originally the *Santa Ciara* now relabeled the *Borea,* included five 65 mm field guns (not very impressive artillery—unless one has no other), 211 French Chatellerault machine guns and 3 million rounds of ammunition—buried beneath several hundred tons of potatoes and onions. This was part of Yehuda Arazi's emergency European substitute for a far more grandiose plan, which was to sail a surplus American escort aircraft carrier, loaded with American surplus planes, tanks, and guns, to arrive in Israel by May 15. To this end, steps had been taken to acquire the *Attu,* moored near Norfolk, Virginia. But the American arms embargo, given added impetus by the accidental exposure of a shipment of explosives in loading the *Executor* January 3, 1948, made such a scheme totally impossible. And so, Arazi had flown to Western Europe, and was at least able to arrange this much more modest—and extremely important—delivery.[3]

We are aware of just one earlier arms ship, the *Nora,* whose cargo of 4,300 Czech rifles and 200 machine guns was delivered at the start of Operation Nahshon and was vital to its success. This was the first purchase of Czech arms, which had taken the slow overland route to a Yugoslav port. There the *Nora,* which had been chartered in Venice with a load of potatoes, crossed the Adriatic, unloaded its potatoes, loaded the munitions, and covered them with the potatoes. The ship left in the middle of March, and arrived in Tel Aviv on April 3.[4]

Of course, shipments of souvenir weapons, explosives, and machinery for manufacturing weapons had been coming regularly from the United States. But these shipments, camouflaged as "used industrial machinery" consigned to a commercial factory in Palestine, were a small part of the mixed cargo of regular freighters that might call at a number of Mediterranean ports. At any rate, by the end of March 1948, general shipments for Palestine were subject to seizure at Arab ports.

The American example was followed in the major pre-1948 European arms shipment. Men of the Jewish Brigade particularly had collected weapons from arms dumps in the immediate post-World War II period. These had been dispersed, in France and Italy, in refugee camps. The exposure of one convoy, in 1947, placed all the French stocks in jeopardy. A direct appeal was made to M. de Pré, director-general of the Ministry of the Interior. It will be recalled that, beyond possible sympathy for the Jews, French-British rivalry in the Middle East was both bitter and of long standing, and de Pré gave permission to remove all such arms from French territory. It was decided to use the Magenta farmstead, near Milan ("Alef"), as the place of assembly of arms and of camouflage packaging.

Eliyahu Sacharov who, in Palestine, had been on the receiving end of the camouflaged American shipments, followed the American model, both in deceptive packing, such as use of the hollow spaces in genuine machinery, etc., and in open shipment to textile factories and to firms like Solel Boneh (the building contractors organization). In addition to weapons, some locally purchased TNT and cordite were included. By the end of 1947, Magenta had been cleared out. The total of six shipments included 200 Bren guns and spares; 1,000 British Army rifles; 500 German Army rifles; 400 sub-machine guns and 500 revolvers of various types; 1,500,000 rounds of .303 and 9mm. ammunition.[5]

It is noteworthy that the meager arms with which Israel entered the war, included all the Magenta shipments, all the prior American shipments, and all the arms stolen from the British in Palestine, Egypt, and elsewhere during and after World War II.

Mardor (p. 191) adds that there were three major shipments of explosives from Italy as follows: January, 1948—50 tons; February—165 tons; May—320 tons. There is no reference to this in any other source.

So much for arms shipments by sea while the mandate was in effect.

With the termination of the mandate on May 15, British physical opposition had to cease except in the Haifa port enclave which they held through June 30 and where they forbade the arming of any Israeli vessels. But this was replaced by the likelihood of a blockade of the relatively short coastline by the Arab navies and of hostile action by them on the high seas. For protection, Israel needed an instant navy in addition to an instant air force. As it turned out, Arab (primarily, Egyptian) attempts at blockade and harassment by sea were totally unsuccessful. This failure was due to the same kind of combination that stopped the Arab invasion by land: Israel's making the most of very little, together with Arab hesitancy and irresolution on the offensive.

Israel's striking navy consisted of a few superannuated corvettes which had been rusting in Haifa harbor since their seizure by the British, beginning in 1945, when they had been used to transport illegal immigrants. At best, such ships (called "destroyer escorts" in American terminology) have half the speed and weight of destroyers and substantially less armament. Open reconditioning of these retired vessels could not begin until May 15; their only functioning guns were antiquated 65 mm and 75 mm field pieces bolted to the deck.

On June 2, an unopposed Egyptian warship shelled Caesarea, midway between Tel Aviv and Haifa. There were no casualties; one aluminum shed was slightly damaged.

June 4 saw a more serious engagement. An Egyptian convoy, consisting of a corvette, a transport, and a landing craft, sailed towards Tel Aviv at midday. The Israeli reconditioned corvette *Eilat* challenged them rather futilely; its own shells fell far short, and it took some minor damage from the enemy guns. The Israeli Air Force went into action with three light planes which were neither proper fighters nor bombers (a Bonanza, a Fairchild and a Rapide). Only one bomb hit its target, but the Egyptians turned tail and headed for home. The cost to Israel was serious—the Fairchild was hit by antiaircraft fire, and it was lost with its two-man crew.

For the most part, the navy's function consisted of deterring enemy action by showing itself—patrolling and escort work. Its role in the unhappy *Altalena* affair has already been described in chapter seven; we are not aware of any casualties inflicted by the navy in that affair. During the Ten Days it took the offensive: The night of July 17, two of the reconditioned corvettes, using deck-mounted field guns, shelled Tyre in Lebanon (Es Sur in Arabic, Zor in Hebrew). Neither damage nor casualties are recorded, but this was an important move psychologically. Earlier, the navy's amphibious company had sustained relatively heavy losses in attacking the village of Bet Alfa on the Carmel Coast.[6]

The neatly managed seizure, on the high seas, of a complete shipload of arms and munitions en route to Syria took place in August. For obvious reasons, Israel called this Operation Pirate. This fanciful label is self-denigrating and inaccurate since the wartime seizure of enemy munitions is a normal proper act of war, and was managed with scrupulous concern for the safety of the ship's crew. Genuine piracy involves the violent seizure of peaceful commercial property, usually with serious hazard to the lives of civilians. It is a lovely story indeed.

Late in 1947, before Israel's first contract for Czech arms, Syria completed a massive purchase of its own. Although our sources differ on the quantities, it appears that there were at least 6,000 rifles, probably 8 million rounds of ammunition, perhaps some machine guns, and other explosives and grenades. The Haganah traced the shipment to the *Lino,* which would deliver its cargo to Beirut. What should be done? If there were no practical means of seizing the ship, it should be blown up. How? Not by the normal Haganah way of attaching explosives below the waterline, but by a more modern method: from the air.

At the moment (the end of March), the first of Schwimmer's C-46s was waiting idly in Italy, and so it was decided that the *Lino* should be sunk by bombs to be rolled out through the open door of this plane. Overruled were arguments that chances of hitting the ship were poor, and of sinking it, poorer—whereas the resultant publicity could be devastating. Munya Mardor, the veteran Haganah explosives expert, argued against using the plane as did its crew, but Shaul Avigur's telephone order from Geneva was definite. The problem was solved when the crew reported it could not locate the ship—and the ground people lost it as well. It was relocated with the cooperation of the Italian navy, an assistance elicited by Haganah agent Ada Sereni, the widow of Enzo Sereni, one of a number of Palestinians who were killed as a result of parachuting behind German lines in Europe; Italy had been her base of operations for some time. It was suggested that since Italian elections were approaching, it would be prudent to detain this arms ship for a while, since the Communists might be planning to use its contents in a coup.

The *Lino* was seized in Molfetta and towed to Bari, where it was to be held for forty-eight hours. Mardor immediately gathered a small team, prepared a time device to blow a hole in the ship once they themselves were gone from the area, and succeeded in neatly sinking the ship. (This took two nights; the first night, the ship could not be safely approached.)

The details of such an underwater mine (given by Mardor in *Illegal,* p. 208) may be of interest: The waterproof rubber inner tube of a motorcycle tire was filled with TNT. In order to explode, TNT requires the sharp blow of a detonator. Therefore, detonators were placed inside rubber contraceptives, with potash powder around the outside. A bottle of sulphuric acid was turned upside down over many layers of newspaper. The newspaper was the time fuse: After the acid ate its way through the paper, it contacted the potash. The resultant heat set off the detonators, which set off the TNT, which sank the *Lino*.

Such explosives could sometimes be too successful: In November 1940, the British caught the crowded refugee ship *Patria* and planned to intern its occupants on a Mediterranean island to teach the Jews that this was no way to get to Palestine. With the ship under close guard in Haifa harbor, the Haganah decided to sink it gently, as a token of its determination to continue rescuing Jews and bring them in. Mardor did smuggle an explosive device onto the ship—but it blew a relatively huge hole, causing the ship to sink and turn on its side very rapidly, drowning some 250 Jewish refugees. It was explained that this must have been due to the fact that the ship's metal plates were far more rusty and rotten than anticipated.[7]

The Syrians' Czech arms lay at the bottom of the harbor of Bari from early April until summer. Then Syrian agents made arrangements for salvage, and the major part of the original lot was loaded on the *Argiro,* which set sail for Alexandria on August 19. Not very far at sea, the ship slowed because of apparent engine trouble—caused by two of its Italian crewmen; this enabled a fishing boat to put alongside and transfer two foreign naval people who indicated that they were Syrians onto the *Argiro*. These men made vigorous use of the wireless equipment, speaking in a foreign language—which turned out to be Hebrew, when two Israeli corvettes pulled alongside.

The entire crew and cargo were peacefully transferred to the corvettes, and the *Argiro* was sent to the bottom of the sea. The contents were a most welcome addition to Israel's arsenal, arriving in plenty of time for Operation Yoav, also called Ten Plagues, in mid-October.[8]

How serious a loss this was for the Syrians may be questioned. Their army was relatively well equipped from the beginning; perhaps the original intention was to equip more "irregulars" with part of the purchase, using the balance as reserve replacement equipment.

Again, during Operation Yoav (October 15–22), the Israeli navy seized the initiative, although the Egyptian navy remained far superior in equipment. It saw its task as aggressive patrol, especially against the Egyptian naval centers at Gaza and Ashkelon. On October 19 there was an inconclusive duel with an Egyptian corvette near Gaza. Beginning the following morning, those Egyptian forces retreating from Ashkelon along the beach were shelled.

The most tangible achievement of this period was the sinking of the *Emir Farouk*—the flagship of the Egyptian navy—in the sea off Gaza, with heavy damage to an Egyptian minesweeper in the same action. An interesting sidelight is that neither side publicized this significant engagement—the Egyptians, out of embarrassment at suffering such a defeat; the Israelis, because it took place the night after the truce ending Operation Yoav came into effect.

What emerged was recognition that the seas were safer for Israel than for Egypt. Thus, the Egyptians ceased supplying their forces in the Gaza strip by sea, and American and British insurance companies shortly reduced the high surcharges they had placed on shipping to Israel at the beginning of the war.

In the last operation of the war against the Egyptians (Horev, December 22, 1948–January 7, 1949) the Israeli navy continued to dominate the sea-lanes off Gaza and northeastern Sinai. The Gaza Strip remained cut off by sea, with the navy shelling the Rafah–El Arish–Gaza coastal communications route. In addition to direct damage, the threat from the sea forced the Egyptians to transfer significant defensive strength away from other areas.[9]

Egypt's sole attempt to assert naval aggressiveness during this final campaign—the shelling of Tel Aviv—was distinguished largely by its comic aspects. A report was received that two Egyptians vessels were stopping and searching ships supposedly bound for Israel. While Israeli ships went to look for them, the Egyptian vessels stationed themselves off Tel Aviv on the night of January 1, 1949, and calmly proceeded to shell the city. But—every one of the shells was short and fell harmlessly into the sea! Furthermore, the ships' geography was a little off: all the shells were aimed at the sparsely settled northern outskirts instead of the heart of the city. And when Israeli ships did catch up with these Egyptian ships the next morning, both sides fired at each other without effect before breaking off the engagement. What was perhaps the crowning touch was supplied earlier by Israeli identification: When Israeli radar (in one of its very few tangible achievements) sighted the hostile vessels well ahead of their arrival, and notified the X Room (evaluation center), the Egyptian vessels were identified as "ours."

In summary, through the standard Israeli combination of daring and bluff, the navy succeeded in neutralizing the substantially larger and more powerful Arab sea forces and in keeping the shipping lanes open and thoroughly secure.

Volunteers were very much in evidence in the above operations at sea. The navy was headed by an American volunteer, Paul Shulman, and its skilled positions were laced with volunteers. Thus, one who served as an engineering officer on the corvettes and frigates, Israel's "battle ships," from May 1948 to May 1950, participating in patrolling and in the bombardment of installations from Tyre to El-Arish, relates that in toto, crews were about half Israeli and half volunteer. He adds that "Israelis probably could have operated the ships alone, but much less rapidly." [10] We cannot rationally go beyond this qualitative statement (Operation Pirate involved volunteers on the corvettes, but would likely have succeeded without them.) Generally, without volunteers, there would have been a less functioning navy.

The ships of Aliya Bet delivered volunteers and refugees (too often via British internment on Cyprus). Those refugees of military age and in good health, became immediate manpower assets to the army; some had been given rudimentary military training in Europe (and in Cyprus). We noted earlier, that about 22,000 such passengers were delivered primarily by volunteer crews; in addition, volunteers served on the crews of the other ships. For example, the nonvolunteer *Tirat Zvi* (Vivara) had a contract (Italian) crew, plus 4 Israelis and 2 volunteers; the nonvolunteer "Monte Chiarro" included 2 Israelis and 1 volunteer. [11]

Thus, events at sea were very much "volunteer" events.

Chapter 15

THE CRUCIAL NEGEV CAMPAIGN: OPERATION DUST

Operation Yoav radically altered the de facto map of Israel, and was the first of two major blows which conclusively defeated the Egyptian army, bringing the Egyptians (and, subsequently, three of their allies) to the armistice table. Its success hinged on the volunteers.

As we have seen, the Ten Days campaign in July marked a radical change for the better. When the first truce came into effect on June 11, Israel was on the defensive virtually everywhere. Although the Ten Days in July did see a number of Arab attacks with heavy Arab pressure on some southern kibbutzim, with some territory loss to the Egyptians near Negba in the south and to the Jordanians and the Iraqis north of Jenin in the center, these were minor gains compared to Israel's successes.

Israel retook a number of most important areas including a widened corridor to Jerusalem, and significant additional territory extending to Gat in the south; Ramle, Lydda and the Lydda Airport, and Ben Shemen in the center; Nazareth and the central Galilee in the north. When the second truce was imposed July 18, it was clearly the Israelis who held the initiative, and the Arabs who were on the defensive—a complete reversal of the June situation. But the fighting ended with the Negev still cut off from the rest of Israel. There was one crossroad which was of vital importance to both sides, which was to some extent dominated by both. That is, the north-south road—Israel's land route to the Negev—was controlled by the Egyptians from Iraq Sueidan and other strongpoints; the east-west road—which connected the Egyptians at Faluja and further east (as far as the southern approach to Jerusalem) with the main Egyptian forces on the coast—was subject to harassment by Israel. The UN had ruled that both sides were to take turns permitting the other to use the necessary road. As might be expected, this ruling was not adhered to very conscientiously, and both sides prepared for a renewal of hostilities.

While the Egyptians had been overly cautious—perhaps even timid—on the offensive, their defense against frontal assault generally was most

135

effective. Now, with the demonstration of Israel's improved offensive capability during the Ten Days, it was to be expected that the Egyptians would prepare major defenses in depth and so be well able to prevent any major Israeli breakthrough to the Negev. Although Israel's own military supply situation had improved very substantially, this could not directly benefit the Negev which had had only meager supplies to begin with, and which, since before the first truce, remained completely cut off from the rest of the country (except for some light-plane contact with a few kibbutzim).

An indefinite stalemate might now be quite satisfactory to the Arabs, but for Israel it was vital that the way to the Negev be reopened; otherwise, sooner or later, its isolated kibbutzim would fall and the entire Negev would become Egyptian territory—leaving Israel, at best, as a truncated ministate.

A frontal assault against the fortified Egyptian positions would be extremely costly; and realizing the level of training and of equipment of the Israeli forces in mid-1948, it might not succeed at all.

What could be done?

One could dream of an ideal solution: A relatively massive build-up of men and equipment in the northern Negev so that, in place of a very costly and probably hopeless frontal assault on the Egyptian shield, the Egyptians could be smashed from their undefended rear, in what is sometimes called a hammer-and-anvil operation. The tenuous connection between the Egyptians to the east and the main force to the west could quickly be severed, forcing those eastern Egyptian forces to a defensive posture requiring minimum immediate attention, making it possible for them to be finished off later.

Although the layman automatically thinks of the hammer-and-anvil analogy when one force is positioned behind the enemy and another strikes from the front, in actuality, a far more daring, sophisticated and far-reaching approach was used: the wedge. When one attacks a bear with a spear, the unexpected thrust may so confuse him that his natural defenses are disorganized so that a fatal blow may be struck quickly. If, however, this does not happen, if the spear has been aimed carefully at a vital spot, and it is held in place long enough, its continued presence will eventually cause collapse. Whereas the hammer-and-anvil is limited to the destruction of the force directly trapped between rear and frontal forces (which must be quite large, and relatively close to each other), the wedge, which need be strong enough to withstand whatever may be thrown against it, is simply, by its continued presence, intended to produce the collapse of an entire front.

Israel's then chief of operations, Yigal Yadin, discussed this wedge approach in the September 1949 issue of *Bamachaneh,* the magazine of the Army of Israel. He credits B. H. (Captain Sir Basil) Liddel Hart, one of the world's outstanding military strategists, as his effective mentor. In the period between the two world wars, Hart was an outspoken advocate of mobile, mechanized warfare. Although his own countrymen ignored him, the Germans acted along the lines he proposed. This indebtedness was specifically acknowledged by General Heinz Guderian, whose panzer divisions destroyed the French army, and by Marshal Erwin Rommel.[1] Some years later, Hart quoted the Yadin article and explained, "The true aim is not so much to seek battle as to seek a strategic situation so advantageous that if it does not of itself produce a decision, its continuation by battle is sure to achieve this." Thus, if the strategic point is properly selected, and driving an initial wedge does not produce an immediate result—holding that wedge long enough, will do so.[2]

Specifically, the wedge force would break out towards the sea, cutting and holding the main Ashdod-Gaza-Rafa road at a predetermined point, thus isolating all the strong major attacking forces of the Egyptian army from the lifeline to their support elements. This force would be far behind the Egyptian front line; if it succeeded in causing the collapse of all the enemy above it, it would destroy the Egyptian forces in the northern Negev, removing the Egyptian proximity to Israel's more populated areas, and removing the Egyptian threat to the northern Negev kibbutzim; the Negev would be physically reunited with the rest of Israel, and the Egyptians, in turn, would now be totally on the defensive. Further, if this plan succeeded, a second breakthrough to the coast, further south, if succesful, would encircle that much more of the Egyptian army, and liberate additional territory.

Secrecy would be an important factor, not only because the element of surprise would effectively multiply whatever actual strength could be mustered, but because of the peculiar standards of the United Nations. From the very beginning, the United Nations piously opposed all violence, deliberately overlooking the fact that the purpose of the invasion by the Arab states was to destroy Israel, which had come into being through United Nations action!

Not only did the United Nations deplore violence per se, but it sent observers whose assigned function was to see to it that the military status quo was not changed during periods of nonfighting. Thus, military supplies and military personnel were not supposed to be augmented or shifted about; this would keep the strength of the two sides relative to each other, as it had been. What was completely outside this frame of reference was recognition of how unbalanced the two sides were initially in personnel and in equipment. And the ultimate absurdity was that since it was not practical for the limited number of United Nations observes to attempt to control supplies coming into the Arab states or to even observe the reinforcements of men and material which each Arab country sent towards the front, they focused entirely on limiting Israel in this regard. And so Israel had the added handicap of the presence of UN observers, creating a very special need for home-front secrecy.

Whereas lack of secercy would blunt the plan, the presence of secrecy would not be able to get the plan off the ground. Assuming that the minimal number of men and equipment necessary were available, they would have to be gotten into position. As we noted earlier, significant surface movement was impossible although an occasional jeep might sometimes sneak through; the only road was under the eyes and guns of the Egyptians.

The only possible route was by air.

In order to mount an airlift, airplanes of significant cargo capacity, aircrew to fly them, and an adequate Negev landing strip were the obvious necessities.

At that time, some of the Negev settlements had landing strips adequate for light planes, and some had no landing strips at all; none had runways remotely adequate to handle C-46s, which were the heavy transports of the IAF. On August 14, an air reconnaissance mission was undertaken with a double purpose: to inspect and photograph certain Negev areas in the hope of uncovering a new location suitable for the landing of heavy planes, and to photograph enemy positions around the Dead Sea and Gaza. The Gaza flight was the last portion of the mission; heavy anti-aircraft fire there disabled the plane, forcing a landing behind enemy lines. Fortunately, two Egyptian officers arrived in time to save the pilot and photographer from being massacred by Bedouins who arrived quickly on the scene. Before the plane had been shot down, the basic reconnaissance information had been radioed to headquarters, and it was negative: No area had been seen that appeared suitable for a heavy-plane runway.

The decision was then made to lengthen substantially the landing strip near the settlement of Ruhamma. The entire kibbutz joined in the project which, at the very beginning, was carried out only at night in order not to attract attention. However, time pressure was such that work was shortly undertaken by day as well, apparently without attracting attention. Working conditions were made particularly difficult by the terrible white dust which was the natural surface of the runway area. It was this that suggested the code name for the operation: "Operation Dust." The actual landing field was aptly named "Dustbowl."

On the morning of August 22, HQ was advised that the 4100-foot runway was ready. That night, the first C-46 landed safely on it. Operation Dust was underway.

Actual distances were quite small: from Aqir, which had been the Israeli terminus of the Czech airlift under the code name "Oklahoma," and was also called "Tel Nof" or "Ekron," to Ruhamma was only 25 miles (due south); from Ruhamma to the truce line east of the major Egyptian stronghold of Gaza was only about ten miles. Aqir was Israeli's major military airfield in the south, and it is from there that all Dustbowl flights originated.

To maintain secrecy, all flights were to be made at night. Additional advantages of night flights were that chances of interception by enemy fighter planes were close to zero, since the Egyptians did not like to fly at night, and antiaircraft fire (except that which was radar-controlled) would be much less accurate than by day. Nevertheless, the strain of these flights was great. Not only were they close to enemy concentrations, but they necessarily were over enemy lines, and involved landing on a rudimentary airfield with minimal identification and minimal facilities on a continuing tight schedule.

Planes would take off at 15-minute intervals. Those headed south (from Aqir to Dustbowl) would fly at 5,000 feet and those returning at 6,000 feet, to minimize the hazard of collision. Because of the time needed to load and unload each plane, plus the separation intervals for flights, three flights per night was generally the maximum possible per plane.

The runway at Dustbowl was completely dark, except for a small number of flare pots grouped in the shape of a diamond. Only after proper radio identification in the code of the day (it was a common security technique to vary identification codes on a daily basis) would the runway lights themselves be turned on—and then for as brief an interval as possible. Early in the operation, until a generator and landing lights were available, the landing lights consisted only of each plane's own lights plus a line of flare pots which were lit by hand before each landing, and extinguished promptly thereafter.

The flight itself was short—hardly fifteen minutes of direct flight from Aqir to Dustbowl. However, it took a roughly equal segment of time for the heavily laden planes to climb to proper altitude, and additional time for them to descend.

The fact that the distance was short hardly reduced the tension. As everyone who has flown even once as a passenger is aware, time in the air between destinations tends to be relaxing—strain is caused by takeoff and landing. And, in Operation Dust, about all that the aircrews were doing was taking off and landing. This was being done with planes loaded to their maximum capacity, from poorly lit airstrips over territory from which, from time to time, random antiaircraft fire would be directed towards them. The sandy soil at Dustbowl did help the planes to stop relatively quickly, but the dust raised by the propellers was a nuisance to the men, and a menace to the engines.[3]

However, for all the primitive conditions at Dustbowl, the real limiting factor on the number of flights appears to have been fatigue: Fatigue of the aircrews, and fatigue of the aircraft. Added to the obvious fatigue factors was a continuing conflict between the aircrews and the Israeli loading crews over the matter of loading and weight control. Anxious to maximize the effectiveness of each flight, the Israelis wanted to fill every available cubic foot of cargo space, regardless of weight considerations. This, of course was quite understandable; equally understandable was the concern of the aircrews that the aircraft not be overloaded. One might almost class this as a cultural conflict. The result necessarily was to promote bad feeling and frayed nerves on both sides.

Human fatigue, compounded by the shortage of aircrews, must have contributed to the mishaps that are regarded as inevitable in operations of this kind; this was compounded by aircraft fatigue. When an airplane crashed, there was no replacement for it. And the fine dust and sand in Dustbowl tremendously increased the wear and tear on all moving parts, seriously shortening the usual life expectancy of the engines. For obvious reasons, replacement engines and proper spare parts were in critically short supply. Thus, the most dedicated and ingenious efforts of the maintenance men could not prevent the number of aircraft available—and thus, the number of flights—from decreasing as time went on. By mid-September, the pace of the operations slowed, with several aircraft grounded for heavy maintenance; there were some nights when only two planes were fit for work.

During this enforced lull, a second runway was built in the Negev, near Dorot, and the exhausted crews had an opportunity to recuperate. By October 10, operations resumed in full tempo and lasted until October 20,[4] when they were no longer necessary. Operation Yoav had begun on the 15th day of October, and by the 20th, the Egyptian forces in the northern Negev had been routed. The way to the Negev was broad and secure. The Egyptians would stabilize their forces in the central Negev, and in a narrow coastal strip whose northernmost point was Gaza. A substantial Egyptian force was permanently cut off in the Faluja area from which, after a long period of tenacious and effective defensive fighting, they would eventually depart honorably, with all their arms and equipment under a UN-arranged evacuation. Beersheba was to fall to the forces of Israel the next day (October 21).

In a period of sixty nights, Operation Dust had totaled 417 flights, moving 2200 tons of equipment and 1700 men into the Negev, and returning many wounded and exhausted men to central Israel.[5] The operation had involved six Norsemen, five DC-3s (Dakotas), six C-46s (Commandos), and one C-54 (Skymaster, DC-4).

The 2200 tons of equipment flown to the Negev in Operation Dust was not all direct military equipment; much food for the beleaguered kibbutzim was included as well. Nevertheless, the formidable force of 1700 men was well equipped by then prevailing standards. For this operation, artillery, heavy mortars, jeeps, and subsidiary equipment were available to the forces of Israel on a hitherto unprecedented scale. An original Israeli tactic, for instance, was the jeep cavalry: Jeeps with machine guns mounted fore and aft swiftly striking deep into the Arab rear (often at night since the Arabs intensely disliked night fighting). During the Ten Days, for example, a strike of this kind into Lydda village paved the way for its fall and that of Lydda Airport.

The official army history describes the opening of Operation Yoav: When all was in readiness a probing force was sent to try to pass the crossroads to the Negev, as was its right under the cease-fire terms, with notification to the UN that this was taking place. Not unexpectedly, the Egyptians opened fire, damaging one vehicle. This was the trigger; Israel struck heavily. At 6:00 that evening, the Egyptian airfield at El Arish was heavily bombed by the Israeli Air Force, with air attacks also on Gaza, Majdal, and Bet Hanun. It is pointed out that this was the first time an Israeli attack opened with strikes by the IAF. As a feint and a harassment, one light Israeli ground force cut the railroad and mined the road on the international Egyptian border very far to the south, between Rafa and Khan Yunis (one might call this a miniwedge). And that same first night (the night of October 15/16), the men who had been positioned by Operation Dust made their major strike in the vicinity of Bet Hanun, which is just north of Gaza, on the main north/south road.[6] This strike from far behind the Egyptian advance lines, appears to have been the determining factor in the large-scale success of Operation Yoav. It cut off all Egyptian forces to the north and east, throwing them on the defensive and rendering all the Egyptian coastal forces to the north vulnerable.

Specifically, with the start of operations, repeated costly frontal attacks from the north against Iraq el Manshiya to the east of Faluja, and the police fortress at Iraq Sueidan, west of Faluja, were outright failures. It was then decided to attack and take the north-south road from Julis to Huleikat. This was a major gateway to the Negev, and included the crossroads, or junction, of north-south and east-west roads which should have been accessible to both sides under cease-fire terms, and the blocking of which by the Egyptians had been the "trigger" for Operation Yoav.

The junction attack succeeded on October 20 because the wedge of Bet Hanun had held for five days—and did its intended job. We noted that this wedge was driven—that is, strong defensive positions were seized in the Bet Hanun area—the night of October 15. Beginning October 16, it came under attack by considerable Egyptian artillery, by an armored force which twice tried to erase the wedge, and infantry forces placed so as to attempt to protect the coastal road from the wedge. Without the wedge, not only would these forces have been free to intervene in the junction sector, but there would not have existed the continuing threat to the Egyptian lines of communication combined with the danger of isolating and destroying the substantial forces north and east of the wedge, which led the Egyptian High Command to decide on a complete withdrawal of all coastal forces to the north in favor of concentration in the Rafa-Gaza sector. In the retreat, some 5,000 Egyptian soldiers were left behind.[7] The entire Egyptian front had collapsed. That is, except for the Iraq Sueidan-Faluja enclave. While theoretically this should have been part of the general collapse, the preponderant local Egyptian ground strength, combined with the superb leadership of the Sudanese Colonel Sayid Taha, formed and held a pocket which was to be fully dissolved only as a result of the armistice agreement many months later.

Thus, the wedge of Bet Hanun clearly is the hinge on which the success of Operation Yoav turned. And the wedge was made possible only through Operation Dust—a volunteer operation.

Two factors were necessary for its success: Yadin's conceiving the strategy in the first place, and the volunteer aircrews making it physically possible via the Operation Dust airlift. Had either factor been lacking, there could have been no wedge at Bet Hanun, and Yigal Alon's crucial attack on Huleikat on October 20 which tore open the road south to the Negev—leading directly to the substantial Egyptian collapse and Israel's retaking of much of the Negev—would have had little chance of success. Operation Ten Plagues would have failed, with the Egyptian lines somewhat dented but the Negev still cut off. The extent to which this totally escapes most of our sources is quite remarkable. Among others, military historian O'Ballance, General Glubb, and professional historian-journalists Kimche, Kurzman, and Slater apparently are totally unaware of the significance of the "Wedge at Bet Hanun." Lorch's reference (quoted above) first alerted us to it, and Bell's later work (cited in a footnote in this chapter) made it explicit. It remained for us to tie together the wedge and Operation Dust.

Lorch details ground operations: Kagan makes no specific reference to ground operations, but, at the conclusion of his description of Operation Dust, he states very succinctly: "The Negev was saved." [8]

On October 22, the situation in the south was radically different than it had been on October 15. For the first time Egypt had been decisively defeated. Instead of a hand strangling the Negev, with fingers probing to less than 20 miles from Tel Aviv in the north and to the outskirts of Jerusalem to the east, the northern Negev was now solidly linked to central Israel; Beersheba and considerable northern Negev territory east and west were now part of Israel; and Egypt's occupation of Palestinian territory was reduced to a strip along the coast from Gaza south; a continuing strip adjacent to the border of Sinai; and the isolated pocket in the Faluja area.

There were to be serious diplomatic difficulties, however. The UN was outraged at Israel's smashing military success in this limited campaign, and ordered a return to the pre-October lines. Israel, in turn, was incensed at such a stance and—quite understandably—flatly refused to budge. After all, even if one did not accept Egyptian responsibility for starting the fighting (since Egyptian forces had fired at an Israeli vehicle which should have been permitted to drive south), and even if this entire campaign was therefore somehow illegal—surely it was far more improper for the Egyptian army to be in the Negev altogether. Egypt claimed to have been protecting the Negev Arabs, particularly those in Beersheba. Ralph S. Bunche, chief UN mediator following the death of Count Folke Bernadotte, produced a brilliant solution: There should be no armies in the retaken area, but policing—to preserve order and protect *all* people —was necessary, and would be done *by Israel.* This would be a theoretical (and very temporary) demilitarization, with the de facto *post*-October borders intact.

Contemporary post-script: In October 1973, a variation of the audacious "wedge" tactic was again used against a most powerful Egyptian force— again, with signal success: Two huge, well supplied armies were rendered ineffective by this bold move. This time, the *wedge* was driven on to the west bank of the Suez Canal, beginning Monday evening, October 15: Precisely on the 25th anniversary of the original "wedge" at Bet Hanun (October 15, 1948). By the end of the week, the wedge was so firm and threatening that the massive Egyptian armies on the east bank (reported as totaling 70,000 men plus massive numbers of tanks, armored vehicles and artillery) were themselves close to collapse—where, earlier, they had posed a real threat to break into the broad Sinai expanse, from their newly established base along the east bank of the Suez Canal. At that point (October 20), Moscow felt it imperative to press for prompt cease-fire. By the time fighting stopped, the southern Egyptian army was entirely cut off from its supplies by expanded wedge forces on the west bank, and virtually at the point of surrender. And the northern Egyptian army was in real danger of shortly seeing its supply lines cut the very same way, with retreat across the Canal the only certain way to prevent this likelihood. The sudden, forceful UN cease-fire action in the third week of the Yom Kippur War destroyed Israel's momentum and saved both Egyptian armies.

Chapter 16

THE AIR FORCE IN ISRAEL: RAF VS. IAF

The sea and the air highways outside the physical land of Israel were major areas in which the volunteers functioned. We have seen that ten of the ships of post-World War II Aliya Bet, carrying 40 percent of the total number of passengers, were sailed by volunteers, and the balance primarily by hired contract crews with a sprinkling of volunteers and Israelis. The navy's few military ships were sailed as well by crews that appear to have been manned significantly by volunteers, and many of the navy "specialist" slots, at sea and on land, were filled by volunteers.

We have seen that volunteers were responsible for locating, acquiring, repairing, and flying out those transports and bombers that came from the United States in the first half of 1948—and stay-at-home volunteers must have been involved in those crated planes that came by ship later in the year. Volunteers were very much involved in the Czechoslovak airlifts—of arms and Messerschmitt fighters as cargo in those American transports (the "Balak" flights), and of Spitfires flown direct (Velveta 1 and 2)—and the fighter bombers that were successfully flown out of England were flown out by volunteers. Similarly, the European and South African planes were acquired via volunteers and flown to Israel by volunteers. In all likelihood, a small number of "contract" individuals also participated in these operations. Thus Julian Swing, a volunteer flier whose service was largely in the ATC, stated: "As to contract personnel, I recall they made up less than 10 percent of total personnel." [1]

What of the air situation *in* Israel? To what extent was this a volunteer operation? During the latter half of 1948, the air force in Israel was divided into squadrons as follows:

No. 1 (or 100) Communications Flight. Successor to Squadron A, which was the natural continuation of the prestate Air Service. This was the very light plane squadron, whose main base was Sde Dov (Tel Aviv). A branch of this squadron continue to function in Galilee, at an airfield in Yavniel, as it had since very early in the war. The airstrip at Dorot, in the Negev, often held as many as three of this squadron's planes—Austers, Pipers, Fairchilds, Rapides, and a Norseman. When the number of Norsemen grew, these planes became the nucleus of another squadron, 35 Flight. Only in this squadron were most of the pilots Israeli.

35 Flight. This squadron was made up of moderately light planes, initially the Norseman 1-ton transports, to which were added the Harvard (AT-6) trainers when they were received in the autumn. This squadron was steadily occupied supplying isolated settlements in the Negev, the Galilee, Sodom, etc. Because of its greater capacity, the Norseman was an improvement over the lighter planes as a rough-and-ready bomber and was used accordingly, until it, in turn, was overshadowed by Israel's heavy transports (technically, they were just medium transports), the DC-3 Dakotas and C-46 Commandos. The continuing shortage of fighter bombers was such that the Harvards, designed as training planes, were used as dive bombers in battle. The complement of pilots totaled nine— all overseas volunteers.[2]

The squadron was commanded by the late Theodore H. Gibson, Jr. Ted Gibson was a non-Jew—the son of a minister in Miami, Florida— described by one who served with him as "probably the bravest man I know." A leader of the "follow-me" school, he is described as flying supply missions to isolated Sodom when others turned back, and as leading the attacks with bombs attached to the wings of the Harvard trainers. At the same time, his maturity and stability were most important in calming his men and others of the flying volunteers. During idle periods, there was a tendency for some of the men, particularly Americans, to get rather out of hand. After the war, when this squadron was disbanded, Ted Gibson continued to serve Israel in El Al, the national civilian airline; he was killed in the crash of an El Al freight plane near Zurich, Switzerland, November 21, 1951.

ATC. The Air Transport Command. Its function was the Czech airlift; the airlift was actually underway for many weeks before an administrative reorganization produced the official "Air Transport Command" label. As detailed earlier, the principal aircraft used were the Commandos (C-46) which had been obtained from the United States via Panama. These two-engine transports called for a crew of five. Almost everyone involved was a volunteer.[3] One of these volunteers states that the crews on the ATC *and* communications flights he was involved in between June and December, included perhaps a grand total of four Israelis; all the others were overseas volunteers. Another, who dates his ATC service from May to September, indicates that all his flights were made with five-man volunteer crews—no Israelis at all. He also states that the air raid on Damascus was made by a five-man, all volunteer crew. The third, whose ATC service extended from May to August, suggests that perhaps 20 Israelis and 100 volunteers participated. At the same time, he, like the others, states that the airlift could not have succeeded without the volunteers. Recognizing that under "Israelis" must have been included ATC administration (those who made the political and financial arrangements), those who saw to communications (via Israel's Prague Embassy), and whatever limited number of mechanics were not volunteers—it is clear that the ATC flight crews must have been virtually all volunteers.[4]

106 Transport Squadron. Made up primarily of the C-46 aircraft, this squadron was an outgrowth of, and successor to, the ATC. It will be recalled that the main thrust of the European airlift was halted with the closing of Zatec on August 12. Although there were undoubtedly occasional subsequent transport flights between various European airports and Israel (for example, those earlier detailed in connection with Velveta 2), this could hardly justify continuing a separate ATC structure indefinitely. In any event, reorganization would have had to come. Once a situation is no longer desperate, the military mind—understandably—becomes most unhappy with a structure that is not totally formal. The volunteer who can leave at whim, or refuse a specific assignment for reasons of his own, however valid, becomes a negative rather than a positive factor, particularly in the situation of 1948, when entire operations could well hinge on the presumed participation of a very few key individuals. Thus, phasing out the ATC and replacing it with a formal IAF Squadron was a step forward, although it did not really solve the problem. As it turned out, this was also a problem within the IAF proper. Some volunteers were most unhappy, and vocal, over conditions and orders. This was a conflict of cultures, and of confidence. Most of the flying personnel were non-Israeli, and even included a number of Swedes. This squadron was later integrated into the 103.

103 Squadron. Dakota (DC-3 or C-47) fairly heavy two-engine transport and bombing squadron. These planes, somewhat smaller and lighter than the C-46s, took a four-man crew. With the airlift already under way using C-46s (some still enroute) and the Skymaster, the Dakotas (three arriving by the end of May, two more a little later) were immediately put into service as a separate squadron, based at Ramat

David in the north. An immediate major function was bombing. For technical reasons, it was also easier to adapt the Dakotas for semiautomatic bomb release than the C-46 Commandos. Thus, the Dakotas were the IAF heavy bombers until the arrival of the B-17s in mid-July. Thereafter they were also used in part for bombing missions, as were the C-46s. They also served an important function in transport and communication. Initially, all of this squadron's air crews were non-Israelis. In the autumn of 1948, Israelis began to come in.

101 Fighter Squadron. The squadron of true fighter planes and fighter-bombers: Messerschmitts, Spitfires, etc. The terms "fighter" and "fighter bomber" can often be used interchangeably, since most World War II fighter planes had provision for being fitted with bombs (frequently, under the wings), depending on tactical considerations. Thus, if the plane were to attack enemy fighters or defend against them, one would not want to be encumbered with bombs, since speed and mobility would be paramount. On the other hand, for attacking enemy forces in the field, bombing in some instances would be far more effective than strafing. This squadron was variously based at Ekron, Herzlia, and Qastina/Hatsor (Hatsor in the south; it should not be confused with the ancient fortress city of Hatsor commanding the Via Maris near Ayelet Hashachar and Mishmar Hayarden in Galilee). All its original pilots were volunteers (many Canadians), with 3 exceptions: Mordecai (Modi) Alon, its first CO who was killed in a Messerschmitt October 16 (during Operation Yoav); Ezer Weizman, who succeeded him as squadron CO and eventually became Officer Commanding the IAF; and the South African, Eddie Cohen, who may technically be considered an Israeli since he settled in pre-Israel in 1947 (Cohen was killed in the very first Messerschmitt mission, May 29). There is a likelihood that by January 1949, a growing minority of Israeli pilots was attached to this squadron, although we know of only two who flew combat missions even then.

69 Heavy Bomber Squadron. This, the Hammer Squadron, was made up of the three B-17 heavy bombers successfully taken out of the United States in June. The normal crew size for each of these planes was nine men. With the exception of one Israeli former RAF pilot, all were volunteers, chiefly from the U.S.A. This squadron has since been disbanded.[5]

Squadron 505: The non-flying squadron. Squadron 505 was the administrative designation for Israel's early warning radar network, which was completely under the control of the air force.[6] Unlike aircraft, which require a high level of skill and experience on the part of the operators as well as on the part of mechanics and ground technicians, successful operation of a radar under normal conditions requires a relatively low level of training for the operator.[7] The airplane requires skilled technicians to bring it to the point of usability, and then skilled operators to use it properly. But radar can far more aptly be compared to complex telephone equipment: in order for the equipment to be used successfully, experienced technicians and a very few experienced supervisors are indispensable—but local people, with no prior experience, can quickly be turned into passable operators. Volunteers were the backbone of the technical staff and were the key supervisors in all areas. Without the volunteers, there could have been no functioning radar network in 1948.

In detailed discussion of the vital supply role of the air force, we did not intend to deemphasize its direct battlefield function. We suggested earlier that all the Arab attacks were essentially probing actions in strength. That is to say, no Arab army was willing to sustain major damage to itself as the price for making a major advance into Israel—for it could then fall prey to its brother Arab nations. Each Arab army did its best to advance so long as the cost of advance did not appear too high. There were two major deterrents to Arab advance into Israel:

(1) The tenacious kibbutz-by-kibbutz defense on the ground. Resident villagers, with little army support, held out long after ordinary military calculations declared them defeated. Thus, each lightly armed, seemingly indefensible kibbutz, became effectively a major strongpoint.

(2) The Air Force. Frequent bombing, particularly in the Galilee and to some extent in the Center, served to put those Arab forces psychologically on the defensive. For example, there is one report that an Arab concentration at Tulkarm, preparing to cut Israel in half by a break-through to the sea which at that point is less than 10 miles distant, was discouraged by a bombing attack.

It is interesting to note that the slightly smaller Dakotas were favored as bombers over the C-46s for two reasons:

(1) The happenstance that the C-46s were involved in the Czech airlift;

(2) For mechanical reasons, it was relatively easy to adapt the Dakota doorway to automatically fuse the explosives as they

were pushed out. A more cumbersome procedure was needed with the other planes. Initially those few Israelis who served as part of air crew on these planes, served as bomb pushers.

These deterrents were to be of paramount importance in two kinds of situation: (1) Late in the spring when the regular Arab armies invaded and Israel's defenders were still pitifully underarmed, and (2) during the Ten Days and later during the Egyptian campaigns when it was extremely important to discourage those Arab armies not in the immediate battle zone, from attacking in their own areas.

By the autumn of 1948, the reorganized air force no longer was a sort of cork to be thrown into the breach in an emergency. Rather, it was a legitimate, separate command with both separate and support functions. Thus, each major campaign (Yoav, October 15; Hiram, October 28; Horev, December 22) began with air strikes at preselected targets. The weight of bombs dropped remains impressive in terms of that war: 151 tons in operation Yoav; 27 tons in the brief operation Hiram; 226 tons in the final Operation Horev.[8]

Air force casualties continued during this latter period. Earlier, we mentioned the death of Modi Alon in a Messerschmitt on October 16, and the loss of a Beaufighter and its three-man crew on October 20. On October 24, a Dakota exploded shortly after take-off from Ekron; its four-man crew all were killed. December 2, a Widgeon crashed into the Sea of Galilee killing its three man crew. Earlier, we described the death of Sam Pomerantz in a Spitfire in Yugoslavia December 18. The final flying casualty of the war was Zvi Zepel whose light plane[9] was shot down by enemy fighters on his return from a sortie. Of this final group of air-force casualties, all were volunteers except for the Israeli fighter pilot Modi Alon and the light-plane pilot Zvi Zepel.

The precise value of bombing may well be argued endlessly by military experts. Here, we have examples of its limitations: A significant part of the total tonnage of bombs dropped in Operation Hiram was the opening strike by the B-17s aimed at Tarsheha. But debriefing indicated that they had actually hit a point somewhat to the east of the intended target.[10] Yet, this did not prevent the swift success of Israel's ground forces in clearing the north-central Galilee. Again, some 90 tons of bombs were dropped on the Faluja area during Operation Yoav[11]—more than one-third of the total tonnage used in the entire operation, yet Israel's ground forces did not succeed in taking this objective. Similarly, an unfortunate strafing blunder had no decisive negative effect (apart from the two specific casualties caused, and the pilot's feeling of heartsickness): On December 28, a long Israeli column on the Auja-Abu Ageila road was hit by the IAF, with one soldier killed and one badly wounded, and some vehicle damage. A major source of this error—in addition to inadequate communication—was the fact that the column included a number of recently captured Egyptian vehicles still bearing Egyptian markings.

Still, the fact that the bombing cannot do the entire job by itself certainly should not be taken to mean that it is worthless. At the very least, it puts the enemy psychologically on the defensive. In the case of Operation Hiram, bombing at least made the task of the ground forces a bit less difficult; with reference to the Faluja pocket, the Egyptian forces were kept bottled up, preventing the development of what might otherwise have become a moderately serious threat to Israel's rear.

Bombing also means interference with the enemy's supplies and communications, certainly factors which contribute to success or failure in battle. And, fighters (or fighter bombers) provide important tactical support on the field of battle and behind the battlefield.[12]

Perhaps most important of all, an effective air force denies air dominance to the enemy. And I am aware of no serious modern battle outside jungle conditions which was won with the other side effectively dominating the skies. Even those who denigrate the positive role of air power, must concede that the IAF, by clearing the skies, made it possible for the ground forces to achieve what they did. This, perhaps, is the most apt summary of the function of an air force in modern warfare: It makes it possible for the ground forces to win. This was precisely the role of the IAF in June 1967, much romantic exaggeration notwithstanding. In late 1969 and early 1970, the obverse was emphasized: The IAF was used to make it clearly inconceivable that the Egyptian ground forces might win.

We do not mean to imply that the Egyptian air force was *totally* grounded. It appears that one of their Sterling bombers flew at least one mission, attacking a column heading for El Arish six times, without causing any casualties;[13] and their fighters flew a number of sorties during Operation Horev. However, whenever they were sighted by Israeli fighters, and stayed to give battle, they were defeated. Thus, for example, December 28 two Egyptian Fiat G-55s were downed by Israeli Spitfires. The Egyptians achieved their lone triumph that day when their Spitfires shot down Zepel's light plane (Auster or Piper) which was on a scouting mission. A week later (January 5) a patrol consisting of one Israeli Spitfire and one Mustang sighted a flight of three Fiats. One Fiat was shot down, and one damaged. This campaign was marked by numerous such encounters.[14]

The following day, January 6, with its ground forces in disarray and the road to the Suez Canal apparently open to Israel, Cairo agreed to discuss a cease-fire with Israel. The major aim of Operation Horev had been precisely this: To force Egypt, by far the largest and most powerful of the Arab forces to agree to direct armistice talks with Israel; and this apparently would not happen until the Egyptian army was substantially destroyed.

However, military activity did not cease the instant Cairo agreed to talk about talking about a cease-fire. In this fluid situation, events took a bizarre turn.

Great Britain's opposition to the Jewish state was expressed in a number of practical manifestations. There had been the long history first, of "legal," and then physical, opposition to Jewish immigration to Palestine. Concurrent with this the periodic seizure of Jewish arms had taken place. With the ending of the mandate, Britain zealously enforced the embargo on arms to Israel from its territory, and did its best to police this embargo worldwide. At the same time, Britain did make substantial shipments of war material to the already well-armed Arab states, on the premise that it was merely meeting its obligations under preexisting contracts. In the field, Britain operated directly against Israel through Transjordan's Arab Legion which continued to be laced with British officers and whose commander was an Englishman, Sir John Bagot Glubb (Glubb Pasha). And, until its spy plane was shot down by two Israeli P-51s in late November,[15] the RAF had flown a number of high-altitude reconnaissance flights over Israel, presumably for the benefit of the Egyptians, whose army had been equipped and trained by Britain.

With all this involvement, the initial Arab failure to win culminating in the total defeat of the Egyptian army was also felt by elements in the leadership of Britain as a British defeat. The likelihood of Israel's taking the east bank of the Suez Canal (the canal was then legally under British control) was viewed by British policy makers as an insupportable affront. Thus, when Israel was about to take El Arish in the northeastern Sinai, Great Britain invoked the British-Egyptian Mutual Assistance Treaty of 1936, causing Ben Gurion to order the army to pull back from virtually captured El Arish, and make for the strongly defended border town of Rafa instead.[16]

With the treaty invoked, an incursion into Egyptian territory (Sinai) could be regarded as involving Britain. It was decided that the first step was to find out where the Israeli army really was. And so, on the morning of January 7 an RAF flight consisting of four Spitfires of Tactical Squadron 208, based at Faid near the Suez Canal, took off on an armed photo-reconnaissance mission. Its purpose: to determine just where the Israelis were, and bring back as much information as possible on the situation. Israel was not notified of this action; presumably, the British would have considered it demeaning to do so.

It appears that one of the planes was equipped for photography and the other three were escorts; this is normal procedure on reconnaissance missions. On the escorting planes, all cannons were loaded. At 11:35, two Israeli Spitfires from Squadron 101, piloted by volunteers, saw three Spitfires firing on Israeli vehicles on the Rafa-Auja road. One of the planes engaged the enemy; the second Israeli pilot saw the plane hit and the enemy pilot eject while the plane crashed. A second enemy Spitfire climbed into the sun and began firing, at a height of about 7,000 feet. The Israeli pilot then saw its RAF markings, fired back, and downed this plane, whose pilot also parachuted; the two Israeli planes returned to their base at 12:27. Their report of downing RAF planes was greeted with skepticism until, at 12:45, the ground forces reported to headquarters that three RAF planes had been downed—two by air action and one by ground fire—and two of the pilots taken prisoner.

At 15:30 hours (3:30 P.M.) a patrol of four Israeli Spitfires from Squadron 101 encountered a flight of five planes with RAF markings, carrying explosives under their wings. Actually, this flight consisted of one Mosquito modified for photo-reconnaissance and four Tempests flying escort. The two squadrons promptly engaged each other, with the result that one British plane—a Tempest—was downed, and its pilot killed.[17] This plane crashed near Kibbutz Nirim, about nine miles from the Egyptian border. The point of crash is a rather strong indication that this plane was indeed flying over Israel. We mention this because, in the British parliamentary inquiry which followed, much was made of a British claim that its planes very carefully refrained from crossing into Israel's air space. Actually, such a consideration is irrelevant. Surely Israeli incursion into Egyptian Sinai was in no sense less proper than the earlier Egyptian invasion of Israel itself. And third parties who suddenly appear in a battle zone without prior announcement and prior acceptance of their special status by all concerned, can hardly expect to escape being bloodied. Nevertheless, these engagements were most disquieting. The English-speaking

"Israeli" flyers were hardly happy over the prospect of fighting British airmen in RAF uniforms with whom they had served together in World War II, and there was the possibility that Britain might now openly enter the war on the side of the Arabs. And so, since the objective of the campaign was not the conquest of buffer territory but simply to bring the Egyptians to direct armistice talks, and since this was indeed an immediate prospect, the order went out to all ground forces to turn back from the open road to the Suez Canal. There was much grumbling over the order; Yitzhak Sadeh, grand old man of the Palmach, was particularly unhappy. There was a feeling that going to Suez would indeed give Britain the come-uppance she deserved—but the order was obeyed.

The situation was complex. On the one hand, Israel may have been spent at that point. For one thing, this campaign was already relatively lengthy (more than two weeks long at that point); and the Faluja pocket and the Gaza-Rafa strip still held strong Egyptian forces which Israel apparently did not have the power to take. With the British threat added, the risk of a cease-fire not being accepted became grave indeed. On the other hand, with the Egyptian army substantially in ruins (apart from the two by-passed enclaves), if the British were bluffing and, more important, if the Egyptians did not go promptly to the armistice table, there was little to prevent the Army of Israel from driving to the Canal a little later on.

What actually happened was that British reinforcements were immediately dispatched to the Transjordanian port of Akaba and, on January 12, armistice talks between Israel and Egypt began on the island of Rhodes.

The air force also played an important role in Operation Fact: Establishing an Israeli presence at Eilat on the Gulf of Aqaba which was of the greatest importance in persuading the Jordanian armistice negotiators (and the UN) of the validity of Israel's title to the Negev. Even more important than the territorial area, was the fact that this gave Israel an outlet by sea to East Africa and the Indian Ocean.

Operation Fact was considered top secret. It was feared that if word leaked out ahead of time, there might be an international uproar, even though the original UN partition plan had awarded all of the Negev to Israel, and even though none of its neighbors had an official presence there.

This operation apparently hinged on the air force. The first step was to send a small scouting party south from Beersheba. This group was to cross the Negev wilderness, a series of rocky, forbidding mountains and valleys, much of it quite trackless, terribly hot by day and intensely cold at night, arriving as quickly as possible at a flat area some thirty air miles north of the Gulf of Aqaba, which air reconnaissance had indicated was suitable for a landing field. Air reconnaissance was, on occasion, to be most helpful to the ground columns in finding the least difficult paths. The scouting party consisted of engineers from the Negev Brigade who were to force some kind of path for the party's four-wheeled vehicles, and air force ground personnel who would prepare the intended air field for immediate use. They started southwestward on the Beersheba-Auja road, then southward toward the central Negev on a dusty path, and thence further southward making their own path as they went.

Having started before dawn on March 5, and pushing as quickly as possible, the destination—the flat area some thirty air miles north of the gulf—was reached the afternoon of March 6. This natural air field, called Sde Avraham, immediately became the focus of a major airlift of supplies and of personnel from the Negev Brigade. The principal planes used were the two-engine transports: C-46s and DC-3s. To avoid detection, most of the flights were made at night. Initially lacking electric generators and lights, metal boxes were used filled with sand over which gasoline was poured and lit. The next day, men of the Negev Brigade began the extremely difficult land journey south, from Sde Avraham to the Gulf of Aqaba. Simultaneously, elements of the Golani and Alexandroni Brigades traveled southeastward from Beersheba to the large oasis at Ain-Hussub (Hatzeva). At this point, Golani turned south, and Alexandroni north to Sodom. From Sodom, on the dark, rainy night of March 8, elements of Alexandroni went by boat halfway up the Dead Sea, whence they climbed and occupied the heights of Ein-Gedi.

Golani would go south to the Gulf of Aqaba, staying just inside the international border with Transjordan. The actual border was simply the lowest point, for its entire length, of the valley connecting the Gulf of Aqaba with the Dead Sea. This valley, called the Arava, is one of the hottest places on the face of the earth. This route, however, would be physically easier to traverse than the central Negev, apart from the murderous heat, since it was primarily flat and open (although sandy in spots, making tracked vehicles highly desirable). But the border was unmarked and quite open. It was expected that Transjordan's Arab Legion might well have occupied a number of points on Israel's side of the border, from which they might have to be forcefully evicted, since possession of the Negev was important to Britain's plans for Transjordan.

Golani moved, prepared for trouble, and there were several minor clashes with Arab Legion elements. Generally, these were broken off rather quickly by the Legion's retiring to its side of the border (in at least one instance, as a result of an Israeli flanking movement). And there is evidence that several places were evacuated just ahead of the Israeli advance, including Um Rash Rash, which today is Eilat.

Actually, the military forces on both sides were under orders to avoid a major clash—Israel, because of political fear that an "invasion" of what should have been its own territory would lead to a strongly negative world reaction; Transjordan, because the Jordanian command felt that its Negev units were isolated, so that if Israeli strength on the spot appeared to be overwhelming, the only practical course was to retire before being destroyed and before pointlessly losing men and possibly giving Israel an excuse for widening the war.

The key confrontation took place at a point below Sde Avraham, where a Jordanian force was well dug in, blocking what in that area was the only path south.

The relatively strong appearance of the Israeli force as radioed to Glubb by the local Jordanian commander, brought authorization for immediate total withdrawal. Without the airlift to Sde Avraham, the Negev Brigade could not possibly have mustered more than a minute fraction of the strength it showed in men or equipment. Without the presence of such physical force, the blocking Arab Legion would have held.[18] Then, regardless of whether Israel backed down or fought, there would have been an international political uproar with Jordanian possession of the southern Negev a publicly established fact. The effect of Golani's race down the Aravah would have been negated, the units at Um Rash Rash would, in all likelihood, have fought instead of evacuating—and all but the northern Negev would, in *fact,* very likely have been Jordanian.

It is noteworthy that even at this late point (March 6 to 10, 1949), the air force orders for Operation Fact were cut in English.[19] The official policy of using Hebrew only had long been established, but, apparently, English was still the necessary, practical means of communication inside the air force. For quite some time after the ground forces reached Eilat and established and built an airstrip there, the air was its principal supply route. Only much later, with the building of a reasonably good road and the simultaneous growth of Eilat as a city, could the importance of supply via the air shrink.

Thus, from its beginnings through the very important acquisition of assigned territory called Operation Fact in March 1949, the Israel Air Force was functionally a volunteer service. We have seen in detail that every single squadron's planes (except for the lightest plane Squadron, most of whose pilots were Israeli) were manned almost entirely by volunteers, and even in March 1949, when the volunteer fliers were being phased out, it was still necessary for English to be the functioning language for communication. Throughout the fighting war the majority of experienced mechanics, too, were volunteers. The achievements of the IAF in the War of Independence—in fact, its very existence as a serious factor—could not have taken place without the volunteers.

Chapter 17

OVERSEAS VOLUNTEERS IN OTHER AREAS

We have seen that Israel was quite short of individuals with specialized military skills. Early in 1948, particularly, was she desperately short even of totally untrained individuals. Thus, overseas students at Hebrew University in Jerusalem, even those with no previous military training whatever, were a precious commodity. Overseas students, who were willing to stand watch after being shown which end of a weapon is pointed at the enemy, must be said to have made a distinct contribution, particularly in the Jerusalem area. And those who joined Haganah or Irgun squads and participated in clearing actions, all the more so.

Thus it was that the squad of thirty-five men wiped out in the Valley of Elah in mid-January while attempting to bring supplies on their backs to the already beleaguered Etzion group of kibbutzim, included a young American Hebrew University student quite innocent of military experience.

Moshe Perlstein, the youngest child and only son of a devout family, long-time residents of the Borough Park section of Brooklyn, New York, had come to Palestine shortly after World War II via a religious youth movement following completion of fairly advanced Hebrew studies at Rabbi Itzhak Elhanan Yeshiva in New York. After a sojourn at Ein Hanetziv, he enrolled in the Hebrew University, majoring in Judaica and agriculture as further preparation for life as a religious farmer. He was twenty-two years old when he was killed.[1]

In retrospect, the expedition of "The 35" seems to have been doomed by a decision made by its own, brave squad leader. A night earlier, the squad had been lost, and had to return to its base. This night, preparing to set out from a point farther west, orientation took so long that it was clear to all concerned that the group could not reach its destination before daylight. It was the squad leader who decided to set out, then, anyway, rather than lose another day by starting early the next evening. Under the circumstances, such impatience is understandable, as is a bit of self-delusion: "We will surely be able to hide successfully all day in that sparsely settled area." As it happened, they were discovered in the morning; armed Arabs by the hundreds from nearby villages poured out, and by late afternoon it was over: There were no survivors.[2] Similarly, two

158

other natives of Brooklyn, New York (a young poet, Carmi Charney—now known as T. Carmi—and a young rabbi, Ezra Spicehandler) are credited with stopping one Arab Legion probe into New Jerusalem a number of months later.

Even those meager weapons with which Israel first faced the Arab onslaught, were present to some extent because of volunteer cooperation. That is, in the immediate post-World War II period volunteers in the allied armies succeeded in "liberating" some quantities of surplus weapons, and starting them on their way to Jewish Palestine, generally via the Jewish Brigade, whose people did their own "liberating" as well.

It will be recalled that large-scale modern warfare involves the on-going consumption of huge quantities of material, including small arms and ammunition. In order to effect continuous replacement of material, the supply lines, including several stages of warehousing between factory and field, must be fairly full. But when war suddenly comes to a halt, the warehouses and their normal outlets block and overflow, and what had been vital replacement weapons of destruction, instantly become dead items which it is a nuisance to store and which soon will be ordered scrapped; furthermore, these weapons have always been "expendable" items which should flow out of the warehouse—as distinguished from permanent base equipment which, of course, should remain. Thus, individual volunteers in Europe and North Africa with a little money or a little dedication (or both) could—and did—procure weapons and arms for Jewish Palestine.

Further, particularly in 1947 and 1948, there were quiet collections of souvenir weapons which had been brought back home by demobilized American servicemen. Probably this particular effort was not highly productive. Of the weapons collected, some would have been useless because of inherent deterioration, some, for lack of proper ammunition, and some shipments of such arms were apparently caught by the FBI. Nevertheless, it is not unlikely that some quantities did get through and were used.

Arms obtained from supply dumps in Egypt were promptly smuggled into Palestine, where they were disbursed and hidden, largely among the agricultural settlements. (Some of these arms had been liberated from British supply dumps in Palestine itself during World War II.)

As a matter of prudence, because of the continuing danger of the confiscation of Jewish weapons by the British, at least some of the arms obtained in Europe were temporarily secluded there, as detailed in an earlier chapter. Although obtaining excess arms in the immediate post-war period in Europe was often done on an individual volunteer basis, a major organized channel for delivery was the Jewish Brigade. This all-Palestinian force was only permitted to come into being by the British as late as 1944. The delay was, of course, political: In the early days of the war, Britain was most reluctant to permit Palestinian Jews to volunteer as individuals, even to serve in general units, except to the extent that an equal number of Arabs volunteered. But the ongoing lack of Arab volunteers and the pressing need for military manpower finally forced a practical decision. The Brigade served primarily in Italy, with later postings further west and north, and so was in an excellent position to funnel arms and DPs to Palestine in the postwar period. Some, in fact, returned to Europe for this purpose after their discharge.

There are, of course, no statistics on the proportion of usable weapons and explosives obtained with volunteer cooperation. From the United States large quantities of explosives were successfully shipped, as were the raw materials for making bullets; stainless-steel tubing for mortars and PIATS,[3] and machine tools for the manufacturing of bullets, rockets and small arms, as well as assorted rifles and a large number of planes as spare parts.

In Israel itself, the volunteers were ubiquitous. In its only article on the subject, the illustrated weekly *Davar Hashavua* writes that the men of Mahal (volunteers from the west) were to be found mostly in the air service, navy, and artillery; also, some in the infantry. The article focuses on a selection of acts of heroism performed by men of Mahal in the infantry.

Harry Krivitsky, American, reached Israel in April. He was a company commander in an action September 16 [the article is mistaken as to date— October 16 would be correct for this action, which was part of Operation Yoav] whose purpose was to capture a Negev crossroads near Iraq Sueidan. Krivitsky's company was to take the right-hand fortified trench while a companion company took the left-hand trench. However, the other company was pinned down. Virtually single-handedly, Krivitsky cleared out the three Egyptian bunkers making up the trench fortification. And he led the subsequent holding action in the face of a prompt, heavy Egyptian counterattack. Due to this success, it was possible to conquer the fortified trench on the other side of the road a few hours later.

Lawrence Feinman, a 20-year-old South African corpsman who reached Israel in July 1948, worked under fire. David Zusman, a 23-year-old South African who also arrived in July, although wounded, insisted on walking all the way to the hospital, so that others could be taken in the limited transportation available.

Dr. Stanley Levin, a surgeon who arrived in May from Johannesburg, was the only surgeon in the hospital in Gedera during the Ten Days. July 18, he was on his feet for 36 continuous hours, performing 28 operations.

Fernand Bibelezer was a resident of Paris who came in July; he had World War II experience with the French underground. October 21 he was commander of the leading half-track in the taking of Beersheba. His half-track fell into an anti-tank ditch; although wounded in the face and neck he refused first aid and continued fighting for six hours until the Beersheba police station was taken. Only then did he consent to enter an ambulance.

Mordecai Alimi was a machine-gunner, born in Algiers in 1926. In the battle for Beersheba, the attackers at one point were held up at the railroad station. With the attackers stalled, the Egyptians prepared to counterattack. The Israelis, now low on ammunition, were ordered to retire to the first row of houses. All except Alimi did retreat. Instead he ran forward 60 yards with his Bren gun, then set it up on the ground and very slowly fired the bullets in his three magazines. This caused many Egyptian casualties and stopped their counterattack. With his own ammunition completely gone, Alimi then zig-zagged his way back to the first row of houses—a distance of some 300 yards.

October 11, a small group patrolling near the Egyptian lines came under the fire of an Egyptian Bren-gun carrier equipped with both Vickers and Bren machine guns. The ground was open and there was no place to flee. The men went flat on the ground as the carrier kept coming closer (from 300 to 200 yards), firing heavily. At this point, Fernand Lishterz, a 24-year-old citizen of Mainz, France, who had served in the Maquis and had come to Israel in June, picked himself up and ran towards the enemy vehicle, zig-zagging as he ran. From a distance of perhaps 40 yards he threw two grenades, both of which fell rather close to the carrier. The Egyptians were astounded at the bravery of this man and concerned lest the next grenade fall into their vehicle. And so, the heavily armed gun carrier turned tail, and the squad was saved.[4]

Driving forward into the heart of enemy fire particularly when the situation looks hopeless, has become Israeli's standard operating procedure. It works—often resulting in far fewer casualties than would otherwise be the case.

Stories like the more or less random incidents related in the article which involve a handful of volunteers, can be multiplied many times over throughout Zahal (the Army of Israel). (While they are not exclusively restricted to winning armies—they are characteristic of them.)

For the ground forces, then, it appears that men of Mahal were widely scattered. The areas of greatest concentration were the Medical Corps, the 7th (New) Brigade (where it is estimated that some 300 Mahal served), the Armored Corps (8th Brigade) and, to some extent, the Givati Brigade. And wherever one looked—if one looked hard enough—

a scattering of volunteers was likely to be found. For example, our Appendix E includes the statement of one participant who served in the all-Israeli Carmeli Brigade recalling that there were about five Americans, all volunteers serving in that brigade. The 7th Brigade had an "Anglo-Saxon" Battalion, and several units in the Armored Corps were referred to as "Anglo-Saxon." Similarly, one unit was called the "French Commando."

"Anglo-Saxon" was the universal Israeli designation for those who came from English-speaking countries. In the words of more than one slightly puzzled volunteer, "Throughout my life I've been called a dirty Jew, and now, in Israel, suddenly I'm an Anglo-Saxon!" ("Anglo-Saxon" was definitely a positive status term, quite analogous to the view of British ancestry in the United States during the same time period.)

The Tank Corps, which was part of the 8th Brigade, is of particular interest especially since the tank battles won so stunningly by Israel in the Sinai in 1967 were reported to have involved a larger number of tanks than participated in any previous battle in world history, including World War II.

Initially, the Armored Corps was divided into six companies, two of which were tank companies. Of course, one was called "Russian" and one "English," based on the language spoken in each. The Russian company was made up of 10 French Hotchkiss tanks, vintage 1935. These vehicles were operated by those who claimed to have had experience in East European armored forces.

The English company's equipment consisted of the three World War II tanks—two Cromwells and one Sherman—which the Haganah had "acquired" from the British army on the eve of its departure. These three modern tanks had been obtained with the cooperation of British army men: The Sherman was an expensive purchase, and the Cromwells were delivered by their drivers, who stayed to help operate them.[5]

Both of these tank companies were placed under the direct command of Felix Beatus who had come to Israel from Stettin, Poland, in May, 1947. A citizen of Poland, he found himself in Russia as a result of the 1939 Molotov-Ribbentrop Pact which divided Poland between the USSR and Germany. Drafted into the Red Army in 1941, he was first trained as a tank driver. In 1943 he was transferred to the Free Polish Forces then being set up by the USSR, where he ended the war as a major in charge of a unit of tanks. Upon demobilization, Beatus joined the westward flow of East European Jews, reaching Israel in 1947.

The command communication problem was formidable. Beatus spoke only Russian and Polish—no Yiddish, no Hebrew, no English. The Brigade Commander, Itzhak Sadeh, spoke Russian—but the Operations Officer, Shaul Yoffe, understood only Yiddish and Hebrew. Thus, the tank company commander could communicate with his commander of operations only through an interpreter. Similarly, an interpreter was needed for him to communicate with the English-speaking tank company. Actually, two interpreters were needed, since no one could be found who was fluent in both English and Russian; therefore, two men were used—one to translate from Russian to Yiddish and one from Yiddish to English. What this did to operating efficiency is best left to the imagination.

The tanks' first accomplishment was the successful attack on Lydda Airport during the Ten Days, but it does appear that the fall of the airport was predetermined by a deep jeep "cavalry" strike into Lydda village the preceeding day.

An important role was assigned to tanks with the opening of Yoav. They were to spearhead the attack on Iraq el Manshiya. The Irish ex-British soldier who had originally delivered one Cromwell to Zahal, and had remained with it ever since, was supposed to be restricted to base for some military infraction. Learning of the planned attack the day before, he came before the Brigade Commander cleanly shaven in pressed uniform (as is proper in the British Army) to beg temporary release from restriction in order to drive "his" tank in the battle. Immediately after, he would re-restrict himself. Permission was granted. Nonetheless, the tanks' performance there was extremely poor; the Russian company never even reached the battle site, because of technical and communications difficulties. The two English Cromwells did reach the battlefield, but the cannon of one was quickly put out of action, and the other experienced difficulty with its tank treads. Both managed to retire without further damage.

As a result of this miserable performance, Felix Beatus was relieved of his command. The failure in the field was the climax to other evidence of unsuitability to the realities of Israeli military life. For one thing, his was a rather Russian approach to officer's privileges: The barber shaved him in his office every morning; he instituted a separate officer's dining room long before this was done anywhere else in the army; he and his immediate subordinates installed themselves in rather ostentatious quarters in the vicinity of the Lydda Airfield. Then, his notion of maintenance ("conservation") was to have the outside of the tanks brightly polished (genuine mechanical maintenance apparently was an undignified area of concern). And the Russian terrain, and Russian use of tanks in massive numbers, were indeed vastly different. And so, the vast tank experience that Major Felix Beatus brought was neutral (at best) in Israel's tank corps in the real situation of 1948.

The problem of inflated or inappropriate credentials was a very real one. Almost every branch of the service had its share of bluffers, who tended to be believed because of the desperate need for the experience they claimed to embody. The writer recalls one South African who came to us (Radar Squadron 505—see chapter eighteen) in 1949 with quite impressive credentials, but left us feeling a little uneasy. We told him that we would start him as a technician on the line, in the main radar workshop—this being an excellent way to test an individual's technical qualifications. He promptly disappeared, and returned a few weeks later as a high-ranking officer in the Israeli Navy. He had a number of grandiose and (impractical) plans for naval radar-sonar projects and was now coming to us for "a little technical advice." This "little advice" actually would have meant doing the projects: Generating and feeding him with technical information that was his claimed field of competence. After a couple of months of high-level projects-in-the-sky, with nothing produced, the Navy fired this fine acquisition.

Major Beatus was the highest-ranking "Russian volunteer" in Israel— and he was neither Russian nor a volunteer. As an individual Polish Jew, he had come to settle in mid-1947; he has since established himself in the tourist business in Israel.[6] Thus, by the definition we have adopted, he is an Israeli (one who came before the war, intending to settle permanently). There were no Russian volunteers whatever in Israel during, before, or after the War of Independence. The USSR's only practical contribution to Israel at this time was to permit the Czech airlift to take place. But no Russian equipment was supplied, nor were there any Russian or East European "volunteers" or "advisers" in Israel. The sole exception is the tiny number of Czech technicians who came to Israel to help assemble the first Messerschmitts. They worked with volunteer mechanics, and did not remain very long. And, as we have noted elsewhere, there obviously was Czech cooperation in Czechoslovakia.

Thus, any and all East Europeans in Zahal were individual Jewish refugees who had come to settle.[7]

What, then, of Zeev Cantor, pilot of the Dakota which exploded at Ekron October 24, whose country of origin Shahan identifies as Russia?[8] Investigation verifies that Cantor was indeed born in Russia—but his famly moved to Canada when he was five years old! His first name was Wilfred (Zeev is the Hebrew equivalent), hardly a Russian name, and his World War II service was in the Royal Canadian Air Force, as befits a citizen of Canada.[9]

The three true tanks were by no means all of Israel's armor. Apart from the half-tracks, which are multipurpose personnel and machine-gun carriers open at the top, there were the "sondveechim," of which there may have been several hundred. These were home-made armored cars, each consisting of a truck-body whose walls and roof were made of a sandwich of two metal plates with cement filler. There was a fixed turret at the top, with two medium machine guns, one pointing fore and one aft. "Sondveech" is the Hebraization of "sandwich." The sondveechim were largely manned by Israelis.

Finally, a shipment of 30 Sherman tanks, which had been acquired as surplus in Italy, reached Israel in mid-autumn. Some of these were ready for Operation Horev at the end of the year. It is likely that these were manned largely by Mahal volunteers.

The Armored Brigade (also called the 8th Brigade) did not function as the regular Zahal brigade did. Rather, it would be divided, with specific units assigned to work with specific other brigades in particular actions. In one sense, this could be considered somewhat parallel to the way in which some Air Force planes would be assigned to cooperation with ground units in the taking of particular objectives. Considering Israel's masterful tactical use of tanks in 1956, and especially in 1967, the poor use made of tanks in 1948 is noteworthy. Thus, although some of the 30 Shermans which had been acquired in Europe and delivered in the last quarter of 1948 undoubtedly were used in Operation Horev together with the two Cromwells and the single Sherman acquired much earlier, they are not credited with any spectacular or even major battlefield successes. In 1948, it appears that the tank was not a weapon that had been mastered and integrated; it was rather like an elephant: an impressive monster which it was good to have because the other side had more of them, but one whose real usefulness was at that time severely limited by a combination of unfamiliarity, unreliability, and its need for special care.

In any event, the real contributions of the units of the Armored Brigade—their effective punch—was by means of weapons whose characteristics had already been digested.

The limited "Operation Assaf," December 5 through 7, whose purpose was to take a specific number of Egyptian-held strongpoints in the western Negev (some of which had been occupied by the Egyptians after the truce) in preparation for Operation Horev, was primarily an armored brigade action in cooperation with the Golani Brigade. At that point, Unit 9 of the Armored Brigade had equipment which included 11 half-tracks with heavy machine guns and antitank guns; two jeep squads each consisting of 10 jeeps, each jeep armed with 2 machine guns, and each squad further equipped with 3 antitank weapons; an armored squad consisting of 2 armored cars armed with Browning machine guns, one armored car with a 37 mm cannon, one armored car with a 6 liter cannon, and 2 half-tracks armed with light antitank cannon.

Highly mobile armor of this kind was able to take the designated objectives and hold them in the face of a number of Egyptian counterattacks, some spearheaded by Locust tanks. In one such attack, 5 out of 12 Egyptian tanks were disabled. The PIAT, a lightweight rocket-firing pipe, was a most effective antitank weapon.[10]

In summary, the armored units as a whole had a relatively high proportion of Mahal, but there is no hard evidence that they could not have functioned without the volunteers, nor that the success of any specific military operation turned on the participation of the volunteers. This is certainly not to say that volunteers' participation was not significant; it is simply to emphasize that the direct contribution of Mahal volunteers in the armored corps was not the kind of tangible thing that can be weighed so specifically that a particular military success can be said to have depended directly on it.

Israel's experience with tanks in the War of Independence was not good. The tanks were a total failure in Operation Yoav, with the result that we find no reference to tanks playing any major role in Operation Horev, the final Egyptian campaign. This, even though the enormous total, for that war, of 30 war-surplus Sherman tanks had been delivered to Israel in the autumn of 1948, and it must have been possible to put some of them into serviceable condition by the latter part of December. The reasoning must have been that the tanks could be used as a kind of mobile artillery, but it was too dangerous to place one's self in the position of depending on them, since they were unreliable, and thus could cause the collapse of any action dependent on their proper functioning.

Following the war, Training Course A was instituted in which tank gunnery was taught according to antitank principles. This was followed by Course B which was the real start of Israel's armored corps. It lasted a year and was an open-minded study of the tank's characteristics. But this was just a beginning. When Major Felix Beatus was fired following the tank debacle early in Operation Yoav, he was replaced by Shaul Yoffe, formerly of the Palmach, as new commander. One result was that the corps retained what can best be called a Palmach poverty approach; that is, that this very costly tool—the tank—should not be unduly hazarded. Tactically, it might be best to plan for infantry to precede the tanks on the battlefield.

Then the war games of 1952 and 1953 took place, with the "Blue" armor under the command of Uri ben Ari, who had studied German blitzkrieg tactics in World War II. In 1952, a deep penetration of 80 miles behind the Red front lines by the Blue Armor astounded everyone—and roused the anger of the top brass of the Israeli army: This was an unconventional, improper, and unfair use of armor. Tanks would continue to be used as armored artillery, to reduce each strongpoint totally before moving on to the next.

In spite of this, in the next year's war games the tanks were again used in substantially the same fashion—and this time, at Tel Kuneitra near the Faluja road, the totally unexpected appearance of the tanks caused the Israeli infantry to panic and flee. The panic was so thorough that the soldiers actually threw their arms away while they ran, even though they knew that it was just an exercise. This was no longer an internal army matter. It had been witnessed by Prime Minister and Minister of Defense, David Ben Gurion. From then on, the priority of armored corps procurement moved to the top. Tank development, mechanically and strategically, had the green light.[11]

There was one major handicap: The question of mechanical reliability. This was solved by raising a generation of engineers, technicians, and mechanics who came totally to dominate the tank and all of its elements. The tank was no longer a mysterious wonder, purchased from abroad, with an instruction manual that had to be followed blindly to make repairs. Rather, it was a complicated device whose operating characteristics one knew, so that one could control, modify, and improve it either in one's own workshop, or through specifications given to the manufacturer. (This conquest and total control of the complex, sophisticated tank, paralleled a similar development in the Air Force. Both these arms—the tanks and the air—also very strongly emphasized another fundamental: gunnery—accurate shooting.)

The result, then, was that tanks could now be relied on for something quite new in warfare tactics: Taking the lead in deep penetration, destroying the enemy's rear rather than his front—in a sense, an extension of the jeep cavalry tactics first used in 1948.

Thus, in 1956 the Sinai campaign was marked by deep tank penetration via flanking movements, and the 1967 Six Day War saw a further development in the Sinai: Tanks used to smash very rapidly through extremely strong, broad enemy defenses in depth, then to continue without pause far to the enemy's rear, engaging and destroying his reserves.

No discussion of volunteers and Israel's land forces in 1948 would be complete without an analysis of the activities of the volunteer who became the subject of a widely-read biography and a motion picture: the man popularly known as Mickey Marcus.

By far the most prominent of the overseas volunteers, the American Colonel David Marcus, whose official nom di guerre in Israel was Mickey Stone, was a man who had served on General Eisenhower's staff in the European Theater of Operations in World War II, a man of great personal dynamism, who brought a commodity which apparently was missing in Israel: intensive staff experience. That is, experience in all aspects of military logistics—clothing, feeding, and moving large or moderate groups of men; employing such groups in imaginative offensive sweeps, while keeping necessary supplies and replacements flowing efficiently. In short, the basics of making the transition from strongpoint defense and local attack to the coordinated maneuvering of an army. Berkman writes of this extensively, as well as of Marcus's important participation in the writing of army training manuals, in the field, and in advising on training in several sectors.[12]

Unfortunately, with the enthusiasm of an authorized biographer, Berkman tends to romanticize and exaggerate—therefore, we dare not rely on his statements alone to establish Marcus' indispensability. Thus, in translating the simple directive stating, "Colonel Stone (Aloof Stone) is appointed commander of the Jerusalem battle sector, . . ." he writes, "Brigadier General Stone is . . ." and further, "Mickey Marcus was a general in the Armies of Israel—the first in two thousand years." This is inaccurate reporting. At that time, even the Chief of Staff (Yaacov Dori) did not formally hold the title "General"; and, as for "first"—Stone (Marcus) was given this command of the three brigades fighting to open the road to Jerusalem at a time when other brigade and section commanders were also functioning. In fact, reading the text of the appointment carefully (Berkman provides a photostat), we find that the title "aloof" is simply used as identification (as one might refer to "Mr. Smith" or "Capt.

Cohen"), since "Colonel" is the title Stone (Marcus) brought with him from the American Army.[13] (Today's Israeli army does use "aloof" to designate a general officer—but this emphatically was not the case in 1948).

In addition to Marcus's earlier ubiquity, Berkman states that Marcus was "pivotal"[14] to the saving of Jerusalem, in that he was irreplaceably responsible for the fact that the new emergency road ("Burma Road") which bypassed Latrun and thus broke the siege of Jerusalem, was safely completed and functioning before the start of the first truce. (Actually, it was very far from being a proper road at that time.)

Of course, as commander, Marcus was technically responsible for all successes and failures from May 28 to June 11. The failures include two major attacks on Latrun, the "cork" blocking the regular main road to Jerusalem. While we do not ascribe these failures to any personal lack on the commander's part, we likewise do not see evidence that his participation in the building of the by-pass road was such that it would not otherwise have been completed. In tribute to Marcus, and in view of his tragic death, a marker was actually put up, labeling it the "Marcus Road." Marcus had served in Israel from early 1948 (interrupted by an April visit to the U.S.) until his death: He was shot by one of his own sentries early in the morning of June 11 (3:50 A.M.), becoming the last official casualty before the first truce. Both the method and timing of Marcus's death would be called unbelievable melodrama—if not for the fact that it actually happened in just that way. The designation that has stuck, however, is the "Burma Road."

Yet, the fact that our standard Israeli sources do not acknowledge Marcus's contributions as being of major importance, does not prove conclusively that they were not; there was a tendency on the part of Israeli sources to minimize the importance of the role of overseas volunteers.

For a contemporary view of Marcus's real contribution, we turn to periodicals. *Haganah Speaks,* reporting on Marcus's death, states that Marcus reorganized the Haganah, setting up its training program and developing its fighting tactics.[15]

Maarachot, a Hebrew-language monthly for the Israeli soldier, quotes from the eulogy of Israel Galili.[16] Galili had been head of the pre-army Haganah, and remained part of the Army High Command. He listed Marcus's contribution as morale ("that *such* an American should come to us!"), his personality, and the fact that he was an outside expert who would be listened to. Galili related one incident: On his return from an exercise in the Negev, Marcus burst straight into the office of the prime minister saying, "You have excellent foot soldiers—but lacking shoes and heavy equipment. Give them these two and you will have the best soldiers in the world." (Apparently Marcus alone was able to do this kind of thing and be listened to.) Galili added that Marcus had been a "bridge to our brothers in the United States." A number of Marcus' military maxims and principles are then quoted:

> In discussing the function of the commander ("boss") and of general headquarters, he stresses the importance of clear channels of communication. He said that tactics teach the soldier how to stand, strike, move. But much more is needed: Discipline and self-confidence—that is to say, the morale aspect—which support the physical aspect.
>
> On war: The purpose is to destroy the enemy's strength—not simply to persuade him to desist from his blows. Therefore, it is necessary to control foreign territory and to continue advancing until the enemy is silenced by means of penetration of his weak and vital points. For this, the requirements are adequate striking force and reserve. A military operation must not be planned to go directly in accordance with a single plan only. There are many possible solutions. Things do not happen by themselves—they are caused. The implementation of action is not to be left to happenstance.
>
> In wars, the attack leads to victory. The force of the first blow can sometimes meet force adequate enough to hold it. Therefore, the concept of "reserve" is all important. The leader of every military unit, from squad to brigade to army, is to be taught to conduct his battle through use of the reserve.
>
> Only through the highest standards of personal physical fitness will men be able to move without adequate food, water, cover and sleep.
>
> Use must be made of every manpower source in the country.
>
> In the Army, it is never possible to say that there is enough of anything—most especially, of time.

As we look at the way Zahal, the Army of Israel, has functioned in the field in 1948, in 1956 and in 1967, it appears to have been directed by precisely these maxims. What is particularly noteworthy is that these principles were adhered to far more closely in 1956 and 1967 than in 1948. In fact, under Marcus's own command, they were violated. Thus, the battles for Latrun were lost because of poor communications, lack of adequate reserve, insufficient preparation and lack of alternate plans. One might add that the physical conditioning and the training of many of the men were also poor.

Realistically, none of these violations by Mickey Marcus of his own military maxims was avoidable. Troops, arms, and time all were in critically short supply. Without enough men and fire power and reserve, it was not possible to have an adequate reserve or for the opening strike to be devastating. Without enough reliable radios, communications had to be inadequate. And with the likelihood that a cease-fire might be imposed by an outside political force (the UN) at any time, it was necessary to act immediately, and repeatedly. The possibility remained that an inadequately mounted attack might succeed. And, if it did not take its physical objective, at least it would serve to keep the enemy on the defensive. Since the enemy was far more heavily armed, better trained and better supplied, this was no small achievement.

Thus, Marcus laid important groundwork for the kind of army that Zahal was later to become—an army characterized by excellent training and physical conditioning, by prior planning of various alternatives to be implemented in the field on all levels, by the flexible use of strong reserve forces, by well-maintained communications for maximal overall coordination combined with disciplined initiative on the spot. The year 1948 was characterized by see-saw fighting, with some positions changing hands repeatedly, and with specific missions sometimes called off because of a minor mischance. Zahal of 1967 had the strength and direction and morale to take its objectives at will, regardless of the strength or quality of enemy defenses. This was the army that Mickey Marcus envisioned and planned for.

Of course, it would be unrealistic to assert that Zahal could not have become such an army without Marcus. In all likelihood, the very same thrust and direction would have developed sooner or later—probably, a little later, a little less directly, a little less surely.

But there was another immediate service rendered by Marcus: The 1948 Israeli military leadership encompassed an age range of men from a little over 20 to above 60. Their experience, in some cases, was limited to the Palestinian underground and the reading of military manuals; in others there was some World War II field experience, but not at high command levels—Palestinians did not rise very high in the British army. In venturing into new areas (like the building of an army), people with responsibility but without direct experience generally opt for one of two extreme approaches: either "going by the book"—rigidly following the detailed manuals used by others—or, throwing the book away—being guided solely by intuition. Either approach, alone, can be disastrous. The proper blend can be developed most rapidly and at the least cost, when flexible, experienced, respected individuals are present for guidance at the outset. This was a major part of the service rendered by Colonel David (Mickey) Marcus.

We quote from the wire of condolence sent by David Ben Gurion, to Marcus's widow:

> In the short time he had been with us—too short, alas!—he succeeded in making an outstanding contribution to the history of the days in which the State of Israel came into being.
>
> As a man and a commander he endeared himself to all who came in contact with him, and his fame spread throughout all ranks of our armed forces. They all admired his superb courage, his remarkable military intuition, his unlimited devotion, and his natural spontaneous human fellowship.
>
> His name will live forever in the annals of the Jewish people.[17]

The *Palestine Information Bulletin,* the Jewish Agency publication from which the above is taken, adds that Marcus

> had personally visited all fronts and inspected operations. All units of Haganah and Palmach loved him for his brilliant work combined with the utmost personal simplicity to all. He shared the rations and the hardships of the soldiers through the hard Jerusalem seige.

It is in the nature of public relations releases generally, and obituaries particularly, to emphasize the positive. It would be unrealistic if we failed to point out that any outside expert coming into a functioning situation is bound to generate some resentment among some people. This is natural and, within limits, it is good. Thus, all was not sweetness and light, and there were some who were even ready to believe that Marcus's death may not have been entirely an accident. Such rumors were set to rest by an official inquiry which found the shooting to be completely accidental.[18] This conclusion was underlined by the fact that the sentry responsible suffered a temporary mental breakdown shortly thereafter.

What can we conclude? Essentially, Mickey Marcus was a most important factor in the ground war in the critical first half of 1948 in vital areas: Logistics, training, strategy. His fine combination of experience and flexibility probably had long-range as well as short-range effects—but these factors are made up largely of intangibles, so that we are unable to point to any specific aspects of the outcome of the war that would likely have been very different without him. Thus, even for Marcus, we can only establish qualitative importance, not indispensability.

Of course there were also other volunteers whose experience and ability made them most valuable additions to the land forces. Prominent among these was Ben Dunkelman, who was an outstanding Canadian armored corps commander in World War II, rising to the rank of major. In Israel, he initially served very modestly as part of a mortar crew; when his identity was established he was transferred, and shortly became commander of the Seventh Brigade.[19]

The ubiquity of overseas volunteers in the land war is clear. But ubiquity is not indispensability; and we are quite unable to point to a single specific instance of participation by volunteers in the land war that was clearly critical in terms of the outcome of the war. On the other hand, it would be foolhardly to dismiss the accumulated weight of all the volunteer participation: Probably, in toto, it did make a most significant difference, but in the nature of the situation, it is not possible to actually put one's hand on it.

Chapter 18

THE RADAR STORY

An early decision made Israel's as yet nonexistent early warning radar network part of the air force. As the name implies, it is the function of "early warning" equipment to sight aircraft at relatively great distances, quickly identify it as friendly or enemy and, if hostile, warn the populace well in advance. For administrative convenience, and possibly to confuse enemy intelligence, this unit was identified as a squadron: Squadron 505, the nonflying squadron.

The designation 505 appears to have been chosen to match the word "radar" which also reads identically backward and forward—as does the very apt Hebrew equivalent, mkm (pronounced "makam"). "Radar" is the acronym for *r*adio *d*irection finding *a*nd *r*anging; "mkm" is the acronym for *m*oded *k*ivunim u'*m*erchakim—measurer of directions and distances.

Before proceeding, let us describe what radar is and how it works.

A radar is essentially a radio transmitter, a sensitive radio receiver, and one or more visual indicating devices.

Radio energy is radiated in the form of electromagnetic waves. The length of these waves may range in size anywhere from a fraction of a millimeter to several kilometers. Just as a radio operates on a single wavelength (or very narrow band of wave lengths), so does a radar operate in a single wave length or narrow band of wave lengths. Those wave lengths which are generally used for radar operation are between 1½ meters and a few centimeters in length.

At the instant that the radio energy is sent out in a powerful burst, a luminous trace, in the form of a line, starts across the operator's screen. The speed of this trace is proportional to the speed at which the radio energy is traveling. If the radio energy hits no target, the trace is completed as a straight line. If the energy pulse hits a target, some of it is reflected back to the radar where it is amplified in the set's receiver and causes a break, or deflection, in the line which the operator is watching. (In another kind of presentation, the amplification would be a bright spot in the line which the operator is watching.) Since the speed of the radio waves is constant, a target close to the radar will cause the deflection closer

174

to the beginning to the luminous trace, and a target farther away will cause deflection farther from the start of the trace. The screens on which the trace appears can be calibrated in distance units, such as miles or kilometers, and give the distance to the target directly. By having a mechanical or electromechanical indicator showing in which direction the antenna is pointed when the target indication is strongest, we have pinpointed the target.

There is no basic difference between a search radar and other types of radar. There are simply special modifications for special purposes. For example, the fire-control radar has refinements which make its information extremely precise. In addition, this information is sent to automatic computers which automatically aim guns and which can be used to keep the set trained automatically on the target. All this works equally well and equally accurately on a bright sunny day and on a starless, moonless night.

There was one exception to the total air-force control and responsibility for early warning: the Haifa area, which a subsequent military and political decision awarded the navy, whose headquarters was in Haifa. Although two 505 men, a highly competent South African who was in charge of 505's mechanical workshop, and the writer, inspected and approved Stella Maris ("Star of the Sea," the beautifully situated church property on the brow of Mount Carmel) almost on the heels of the departing British,[1] when the political decision was made, we turned our radar site recommendation over to the navy. It actually did not matter at all: In early July, neither navy nor air force had any early warning radar worthy of the name. Although both hoped that purchases and 505 construction "in the pipeline" would shortly remedy the situation, the fact is that no equipment put to use throughout 1948 was suitable for the reliable long-range detection of aircraft. However, even this did not matter, since the second half of 1948 saw no air raids against Israel's population centers worthy of the name.

For example, single Egyptian planes dropped small bombloads near Rehovot killing a few chickens, and at the Ekron airfield ("Oklahoma"), blasting a few holes in the ground. (Even Egypt's unopposed air raids in the period immediately following May 14 were small-scale terror raids, bad for morale and for those hit, but insignificant militarily or economically.)

Of course, one could not know this in advance. The responsibility of military leadership is to prepare for reasonable contingencies, knowing that it is likely that some may not come to pass. Similarly, much effort goes into many avenues of research, recognizing that some must be fruitless—but one never knows in advance which. Thus, Chayl Mada (Science Corps, Zahal's military research branch which included volunteers but does not appear to have been dependent on them), in addition to directly productive projects such as the manufacture of explosives, put considerable effort into developing a remote-control cart loaded with explosives. Such carts could be used to blow holes in the walls of enemy-held Teggart fortresses, obviating the inordinately high risk of the standard method of individual soldiers running to the wall with a heavy load of explosives on their backs, placing the explosives, lighting a fuse, and attempting to avoid destruction by the explosion and enemy fire. And something similar might be used as a rudimentary torpedo against enemy ships. In spite of considerable effort, results were indifferent at best and proper artillery was finally obtained. Also, like the U.S. Army before 1948 and after, there was much playing with the "snooperscope," an intriguing infrared device for night sniping quite unrelated to realistic military needs. One may say that it is virtually an axiom that some dedicated effort must be in vain.

And so coastal radar stations were put up north of Tel Aviv, and later, south of Haifa—both at attractive locations where the British had maintained search radars of a totally different order. Sometime after it was demonstrated that the existing equipment should have a normal, theoretical range of some 20 miles (for picking up single Dakota-type aircraft), the station north of Tel Aviv was closed, and replaced by one immediately south of that city; and another was subsequently opened southeast of Haifa, near the mouth of the Emek (Valley of Jezrael). As had been the case before the first radar station was opened in July, the air-raid sirens would still sound only after the now very rare appearance of an enemy plane. Thus, to be coldly realistic after the fact, the radar network was not needed, nor was it capable of serving an early warning function. Still, the framework of an early warning organization was established and important lessons of realistic limitation were learned.

There were minor successes: First, the successful establishment of a temporary radar station just above Gaza in the Bet Hanun area, in the wake of the Egyptian retreat, towards the end of Operation Yoav. This station was to track the Egyptian ships in the Gaza roads,[2] radioing their location to vessels of the Israeli Navy which were coming down to sink them. The station did its job well, and the *Emir Farouk* (then the flagship of Egypt's navy) was indeed sunk, but it turned out that none of the radar station's transmissions had been heard by the ships! (The crucial item of communication was controlled by a navy liaison team). Then, late in November, the radar network apparently did pick up a British spy plane, which was promptly shot down by two P-51 Mustangs. And on the night of January 1, two Egyptian ships enroute to shell Tel Aviv were sighted by radar—but identified by the Evaluation Center as "ours" (chapter fourteen).

Whatever its limitations, the radar unit could not have come into being at all in 1948 without Mahal volunteers, although in terms of the total roster, the volunteers probably did not exceed 15 percent.

Commanding officer of the unit was an American of broad Jewish background and appropriate technical experience; the only one whose qualifications and experience truly fitted him for the original development work that was necessary—but, as top administrator, his technical talents were essentially lost to the unit. Second in command was a man who was born in Palestine, but grew up in South Africa, and engaged in military research in Britain during World War II. In charge of station location was a South African trained as a town planner. The mechanical workshop was headed by an immensely capable South African, who did wonders for the morale of his men with green paint. This identified "their" property. Thus, anything small that was not nailed down sooner or later received its green-paint baptism and was condescendingly lent to others—this, at a time of such acute shortage that even the simplest tools were priceless. The chief machinist was also a South African; the few additional mechanics included one South African and two or three Israelis. In charge of the radar operators (those who look at the screen) was an Englishwoman; her male chief assistant was a South African. In charge of the Filter Room, where tracking of planes and ships—which may be reported by more than one station —is consolidated, was a South African woman. There was a scattering of other volunteers—American, British, South African—as station chiefs, operating supervisors, and in administration. The paymaster was Israeli, as were the storekeeper, drivers, and most of the operators.

What of the close to two dozen radar technicians—the irreplaceable heart of every radar operation?

In total numbers, they were about evenly divided between Mahal volunteers and Israelis.[3] In terms of immediate competence, none of the Israelis had had any experience with any radar equipment; in effect, they were radio technicians, ready to move ahead to radar. In the American armed forces, the radar training period was about six months, with competent instructors. Thus, with time very much a factor, anything that would actually be accomplished depended totally on the already experienced volunteers, while the Israelis, in effect, simultaneously received on-the-job training. Among the Israelis were a few graduates of the Haifa Technion, which then was not a true engineering school but simply a technical college, and technicians with miscellaneous backgrounds, including two brothers. These two young men had been born in the Greek port city of Salonika, once famous for its Jewish community, and with their parents and the balance of the city's Jewish population, were rounded up following the Nazi occupation. All apparently faced certain doom in the Bergen-Belsen concentration camp. American pressure on Spain is credited with saving a number of these Greek families. Under Spanish law, citizenship passes on to all succeeding generations regardless of geography or other allegiance. Since these families were able to be traced back to the Spanish expulsion of 1492, Spain was able to save these technically legal Spanish citizens whose remote ancestors had been forced to flee Spain some 450 years earlier.

It does not appear that Spain was terribly anxious to do this good deed. Although formally neutral, Franco reciprocated the German assistance he had received in the Spanish Civil War, by officially sending a "volunteer" force to the Russian front. It is suggested that American pressure, made potent by severely limiting Spain's oil supply, inspired the Spanish to insist on protecting these long-lost Spanish citizens. Spain's demand on Germany, of course, was that these beloved citizens be returned to it; at the same time, it made it clear to the United States that under no circumstances were they to settle in Spain. And so, via North Africa, they came to Israel (Palestine) as quickly as practical. Both brothers were fine natural technicians, and in a few months had caught up to the average volunteer and, in time, one surpassed even the best of the Mahal technicians.

In July, the Mahal technicians included three men from New York, one of whom was the writer, whose radar training and experience had been with the U.S. Navy in World War II; several South Africans and Englishmen, whose radar experience was varied; and two more Americans whose radar experience was quite limited. One of these Americans continued to profess amazement at finding himself in Israel's armed forces: He said that he had believed "Land and Labor" in New York, when they said that they were recruiting men to relieve Israelis of farming chores so that the Israelis could serve in the army.

The first makeshift radar workshop was in Sarona, a former Teutonic

Knights Templar settlement near Tel Aviv. It was next shifted briefly to an unused basement room in the newly completed Weizmann Institute of Science building in Rehovoth (now filled by a computer, commonly referred to as the "golem"). At about the same time as the first radar station was opened in July, decently roomy facilities were made available at Sarafand, which had been a major British Army base, near Rishon le Zion. From then on, Sarafand was the working headquarters of the radar unit, including workshop, machine shop, storeroom, billets, etc. Its tasks would include checking out, reconditioning, repairing, patching together whatever equipment and bits of equipment could be obtained from all possible sources, so as to be able to open stations as quickly as possible.

Not only was full and partial equipment lacking, but even taken-for-granted necessities like connectors and cable were almost nonexistent. Thus, the rumor that there was a graveyard of British planes at the Ekron airbase brought most of the radar technicians down one bright summer day to investigate. The junked planes were there, and they did contain all kinds of electronic odds and ends, some of which undoubtedly would prove useful. While our people were scavenging, a short distance away, across a wire fence separating this junked airplane area from a billeting area, two men were burning dry grass near their Quonset huts. The burners did not realize that the open fence was no barrier at all to their controlled fire—and it was not long before the fire was on our side, rapidly making its way through the waist-high dry growth toward the planes most of which had fabric skins. Such a fire, aided by a bit of breeze, moves somewhat faster than the average radar technician; only a fortuitous shift in wind direction prevented our being fried—an occurrence that would have left Israel substantially bereft of radar technicians. A piece of fire apparatus quickly appeared—and was carried back and forth heplessly, on the wrong side of the fence. The planes—and most of their insides—were destroyed. We came away with whole skins, with very little in the way of parts, and with the loss of a cold chisel which to us, then, was irreplaceable.

When the main workshop was moved to Sarafand, the Weizmann Institute facility was retained for special projects. Several technicians remained, and the writer was put in charge of what may with equal accuracy be designated the I.A.F. Radar Development Laboratory, or Three Men in a Basement. Selection of the writer was based on the fact that, in addition to experience as a radar technician, he alone held an Electrical Engineering degree (B.S., Columbia University, 1948); my wife and I left for Israel immediately upon my graduation early in June; she served as a sergeant in the IAF codes and ciphers section.

After completing the building of a radar transmitter from scratch which, although it was neither stable nor reliable, actually worked, having been copied from a much smaller British airborne model, the next major assignment was to design and build a night-fighter fire-control apparatus. That is, a system which would simultaneously send out two sets of slightly separated, highly directional signals of equal strength—one set for vertical direction, one for horizontal. To the extent that the plane was not precisely lined up on its target, the signals echoing back from the target would be unequal. A visual device was needed that would show this to the pilot in such a way that he could instantly take effective corrective action, with the two combatant planes maneuvering at speeds of several miles per minute (one visual device would be needed for vertical, one for horizontal direction; a third should indicate distance). This was to be designed and built by one raw engineer and two technicians, with limited literature and tools so rare that each had to wait his turn to use a screwdriver! Still, this was the land of miracles: Although those involved spoke more than once of increasing their usefulness by deserting to the front, work went on most seriously, with a great sense of urgency. The temptation to leave for the front was particularly strong early in Operation Ten Plagues, when every ambulatory male in Rehovot was temporarily drafted. When the army co-opted even the fiftyish laundryman who had been crippled by his concentration-camp experience, and the even older Yemenite felafel vendor, it was difficult indeed to continue esoteric radar-development work wholeheartedly. For a long time, no one took even a Shabbat (Sabbath) as a day off, until, one day, we were quietly informed that the plane for which our work was intended—the Mosquito whose acquisition is described in chapter twelve—had already been converted instead for photo reconnaissance. Armament for it was not likely to arrive soon, and so it could not function as any kind of fighter. Besides, the flying air force was not enthusiastic at the prospect of cluttering up the cockpit with our experiments, and in any event, those enemy fighter planes that showed, came up only during the day!

With this, the separate radar facility on the Weizmann Institute premises was closed and the remaining technicians transferred to the main workshop. The writer was assigned to an important—and practical—problem. For quite some time, the fliers had been complaining of extremely accurate enemy antiaircraft fire, by night as well as by day. Conclusion: Enemy searchlights, and enemy antiaircraft guns, must be radar-controlled. In all of Israel, there was only one individual with experience in radar countermeasures (what to do about the other fellow's radar): The writer.[4]

Thus, I spent the winter of 1949 adapting locally available material (e.g., chocolate-bar wrappers)[5] to the very different function of confusing enemy radar, as well as devising tactics which fit the local situation, and recommending a long-range program dependent on certain additional equipment. Although the recommendations were sound, they were of no current value since the fighting war was over. With the completion of this assignment, I was put in charge of the main radar workshop, which by now was receiving more equipment than it could comfortably digest, unfortunately much of it still quite unsuitable for aircraft early warning—the likely result of an "anything is better than nothing" approach to purchasing. Still, the situation was many, many times better than it had been a year earlier, with some decent equipment now already in hand. One particularly impressive set was rushed to usability in preparation for an impending Syrian campaign, a campaign which was forestalled by the Syrian armistice agreement of July 20.

And so, in mid-1949, the radar "squadron" followed the earlier pattern of the flying air force, now taking on Israeli leadership. Remaining volunteers (and some new Mahal) were very clearly transitory: They served to condition new equipment and to instruct those who would succeed them.

Part Three:

EVALUATION

Chapter 19

WHAT IF THERE HAD BEEN NO OVERSEAS VOLUNTEERS?

Clearly, the volunteers served in every theater of the war, from before its beginning (in Aliya Bet) to beyond the end (in remaining for training purposes, and/or becoming Israelis). No one would deny that their physical presence alone was a positive morale factor, combating the sense of total isolation and abandonment that was then very real.

Morale, however, is an intangible; the task we have set ourselves is to investigate and locate tangible instances in which there is very high probability that the participation of Mahal volunteers actually affected the outcome of the war.

Aliya Bet was largely pre-1948. In many cases those volunteers who sailed the ships of Aliya Bet suffered greater privation, ran greater physical risks, and served for longer periods of time than those in Israel's armed forces. They brought upwards of 20,000 immigrants many of whom were of military age and were designated "Gahal"; 40 percent of the more than 55,000 European refugees came on ships sailed by volunteer crews. Some were brought directly; more often they arrived via capture and internment on Cyprus. They certainly made an important contribution to the army's manpower, as well as supporting the political climate that earlier led to the UN partition decision. However, this, too, is in the realm of the intangible; in searching for specifics, we might point to the shipload of Gahal personnel which was immediately trucked to the first of the major battles for Latrun, except that that battle—like all battles for Latrun until 1967—was lost; and while the early arms ships were of overwhelming importance (e.g., the *Nora*, which arrived at the beginning of April, 1948, with arms which apparently were vital to the success of Operation Nahshon), indications are that they were not sailed by volunteer crews.

As for those ships that were sailed primarily by volunteer (American) crews, who received no meaningful pay, theoretically those volunteers could have been replaced by hired crews, but with two disadvantages: 1) the substantially increased cost would have necessitated running fewer ships or cutting down elsewhere, perhaps in buying fewer planes; 2) risk of cupidity, incompetence and unreliability increases with the number of hired crews engaged under marginal conditions. In addition, the fact that volunteers had come from safe, comfortable America, was a positive morale factor for the refugee passengers.[1]

Specifically, we can say that the volunteers of Aliya Bet were an important part of the general enterprise; we cannot say that their absence would clearly and directly have negatively altered the war.

When we look at the first half-year of the land war (December, 1947–May, 1948) then we recognize that every individual was indeed important: had more volunteers been in Israel, it is likely that local results would have been more positive, and vice-versa. While we realize that the country's holding together or collapsing during this period was the sum of the results of a very large number of local engagements, we cannot say that it depended on the success of each of those that succeeded. Thus, while Ramat Rahel at the southwestern tip of New Jerusalem continued to be held, at one critical point, because of the leadership of a particular American, it would be foolish to suggest that if Ramat Rahel had fallen that day, it would not have been recaptured, or if it had fallen permanently, that the fate of Jerusalem would surely have been substantially different. (In effect, it did briefly change hands several times.) We are stating the paradox that the valor of each soldier—most especially in Israel at this period—is of the greatest importance. Yet the outcome of a war, or even a large battle, can rarely be seriously ascribed to any single individual. Individual acts tend to be like individual strands in a rope— their sum makes up the rope that does the job; several single strands might have been eliminated, and the rope still have held. But, particularly if the rope appeared to be under severe strain, it is most doubtful that more than a very few strands could safely have been omitted.

With reference to the navy, it appears clear that without Mahal participation, there certainly would have been a navy, but the navy would not have been able to do as much as it did in so short a time. And if the navy had functioned less well, would the tangible results of the war have been different? We cannot say "Yes," in any direct area; our best answer is that both the contribution of the navy to the war, and of Mahal to the navy, are qualitative: real and important, but beyond specific measurement.[2]

With reference to the army (land forces), we drew the same conclusion (chapter seventeen): Volunteer participation was surely significant, but is beyond specific measurement.

How about the air?

Operation Nahshon clearly is the first major hinge on which the fate of Israel turned. Both the Army history and Lorch state that Balak 1 (Hassida)—the first planeload of arms from Czechoslovakia—was, so to speak, the lubricant which permitted this hinge to turn. Without this critical event, at this crucial point, the entire operation would have been delayed or cancelled.[3]

It appears that we have, indeed, found a pivotal point that depended on volunteers—but I felt that deeper investigation was called for. In attempting to document the crucial importance of this single flight at the Army archives at Givatayim near Tel Aviv, the writer was informed that this statement could be neither verified nor contradicted from the existing records. I then questioned Colonel Lorch as to the basis for his statement, and he emphasized that it was a subjective conclusion. The arrival of the single planeload of arms the night before the High Command meeting had been a weighty factor in the decision to proceed with the operation, keeping the assembled men in readiness. However, one could not state with absolute certainty that the operation would have been cancelled had that plane not landed when it did—this is a perilous, "iffy" question. However, Lorch added, the cargo was so critically needed that the guns were actually cleaned in trucks en route to their dispersal points. Thus, it is by no means beyond question that Nahshon would have been cancelled or even delayed without Balak 1.

Further, in our correspondence with Remez (Appendix E), we are given the names of five Israelis who, he says, were capable of flying the plane, and one of whom actually accompanied it. However, on reflection, we presume that the function of the one Israeli who was on that flight was liaison, not flightcrew—to identify the Beit Darras airstrip at night, and to communicate with the Palmach people on the ground to facilitate unloading, refueling, and take-off.

Further, we could argue that Remez is not realistic in suggesting that the five "qualified"[4] Israelis he mentions were sufficiently experienced on this kind of four-engine transport, which normally takes a crew of six, to have successfully made this rather difficult flight, and, therefore, overseas volunteers were nevertheless necessary. (We are specifically aware of one —Gedda Shohat—who was truly qualified.) But there is no point arguing this, because it develops that Balak 1, under *our* definition of mercenary, was a mercenary flight! That is, plane and crew were hired to do this one job. Concerning this operation, Kagan writes, "Thus an exorbitant deal was made in Geneva with U.S. Overseas Airlines, a private American company. And, on March 31st, a Skymaster DC-4 carrying a cargo of arms left Czechoslovakia. The crew, with the exception of two men, was made up of non-Jewish Americans." [5]

Thus the result of our exploration of the suggestion that Nahshon depended on overseas volunteers through its dependence on Balak 1, is completely negative. The decision to proceed, taken April 1, might well have been made even without Balak 1, and this flight itself was made by a *contract* plane and crew, from Prague airport: It was *not* a "volunteer" project.

Setting this one event aside, then—what of the totality of the Air Force/Air Transport Command: To what extent were air operations truly dependent on overseas volunteers?

Broadly speaking, available aircrew personnel could be divided into three categories: 1) a pool of trained light-plane Israeli pilots (some of whom might be ready for more advanced training, and some of whom would likely be occupied with other duties); 2) a modest number of Israelis who had graduated from flying courses in the RAF or other allied air forces (as noted earlier, Shahan lists a total of 26); of this limited number, it appears that few indeed had deep experience; 3) overseas volunteers, with World War II training and experience.

Thus, although eight Israelis started the brief two-week Messerschmitt brushup course given by the Czechs in Czechoslovakia, only three completed it, the others being replaced by overseas volunteers.[6] Of the three, two, Eddie Cohen and Modi Alon, were killed in action—Ezer Weizman alone surviving, eventually to become head of the Air Force. Of the two, Eddie Cohen is considered by some to be South African rather than Israeli.[7] A native South African, veteran of the South African Air Force, he immigrated to kibbutz Maayan Baruch in 1947, apparently intending to settle permanently.

Clearly, a deeper level of training was needed for the "trained" Israelis, and more Israelis needed training. An intensive course was begun in Hdrace-Kralove at the end of June 1948. A parallel course, in Italy, was found to be proceeding at too leisurely a pace, and its members joined the Czech course. To minimize costs, three American volunteers were added to the staff of this training school. By September, the Israelis had advanced beyond training planes, and were ready to begin on the Messerschmitts, but the Czech instructors refused to take them up. There was skepticism as to their true readiness, probably combined with an official "go slow" policy; Zatec had been closed down a month earlier, and relationships were much cooler. Another American volunteer was sent from Israel to conduct this phase of the training.

Two of the Israelis who completed this course remained for Operation Velveta, this, in itself, being an indication of the continuing critical shortage of pilots. The others reached Israel in mid-November, where they were assigned to light-plane work. The first two, and two from the second group, were specially selected for further training in Harvard and Spitfire aircraft, at Hatzor airfield. These four men were graduated at a "wings parade"—the Air Force's first—March 14, 1949.

Mention should be made of another group of Israelis sent to flying school in Holomec, Czechoslovakia, in August 1948. After three months, they were returned to Israel to continue training at Ekron. Their course was completed even later: May 9, 1949—after which they were assigned to light planes. A group of Czech Jews, planning to emigrate to Israel, also went to the flying school at Holomec at the same time as this group of Israelis.

Although, as noted above, the first group at the Alika flying school near Rome quickly joined those at Hdrace-Kralove, a second class was started in Alika for Israelis later in 1948. Their training, too, suited them only for light-plane work. After their return to Israel in mid-February they joined the graduates of the similar Czech school.[8]

The higher level of training that followed was done in Israel, primarily by volunteers, and some overseas contract personnel.

It appears, then, that the first new Israeli fighter pilots, in whose training Mahal men played an important part, were not ready until mid-March, 1949—after the fighting war was over. The direct products of the European schools at that point were trained only for light planes.

Thus, it does seem that during all the fighting, the fighter-plane pilots were almost all Mahal. We have been able specifically to identify only three Israelis, of whom one, Eddie Cohen, was killed in the very first fighter-plane action on May 29, and the second, Modi Alon, was killed October 16. There must have been at least one more by the beginning of 1949, since Doyle (Appendix E) states that two Israelis participated in the January 7 actions.

In the balance of the Air Force, the story was the same: virtually no Israelis were qualified to fly the heavy transports or the bombers as pilots or air crew; the few[9] who might have been were assigned to what were regarded as even more important tasks—procurement, recruiting, administration. This was unavoidable: Proper recruiting of airmen, intelligent purchasing of planes, practical arrangements for use of European airfields, etc., could only be effected by Israelis with air experience. And there were not nearly enough volunteers; Kagan, referring to the tail end of the Czech airlift, writes of "planes being flown by men half dead with fatigue";[10] the same was true of Operation Dust—air crews worked far beyond normal limits of endurance.

Furthermore, even light-plane pilots were in extremely short supply. For example, Spence Boyd, an American Christian volunteer, lost his way while flying a load of wounded from Sodom, crash-landed in a sandy area a few miles west of Rehovoth, elected to remain with those who were not mobile—and was cut to pieces, with his passengers, by a marauding band of Arabs. The accident was ascribed to *pilot fatigue;* the plane was a single-engine Aerovan. This occurred July 18, 1948. Half a year later, an American rabbi, Samuel Burstein, who had made his own way to Israel "was welcomed and recruited . . . although I had only a private pilot's license and 60 hours flight experience" [11] all in light, single-engine planes.

Clearly, then, without Mahal aircrews, most of the transports which made up the Czech airlift and Operation Dust, as well as the B-17 heavy bombers, would never have left the United States; without Mahal mechanics at the Czech and Yugoslav airfields and in Israel, these planes could not have remained airworthy; without Mahal pilots and crews, only a fraction of the airlifted Czech arms and fighter planes could have reached Israel—and there would have been almost no one to fly the fighters and bombers and transports when they did arrive. Without Mahal pilots, even the scale of light-plane operations would have been substantially reduced. Without Mahal, Operation Dust could not have been mounted; a trivial fraction of the weight of material could have been delivered by light planes: A trickle of troops and small arms—no jeeps, nothing heavy, no significant part of what was required to establish and hold the wedge of Bet Hanun—which was the fulcrum on which Operation Yoav (Ten Plagues) actually turned. Of Operation Dust, Kagan wrote succinctly, "The Negev was saved."

In addition to the above analysis and the testimony of the participants (Appendix E), further evidence of the preponderance of Mahal in the Air Force is to be found in the casualties. Shahan lists a total of thirty-one flying personnel killed.[12] Except for the two Messerschmitt pilots discussed earlier, every one of the eight additional Israelis was killed in a light plane.

Of the remaining twenty-one, all were Mahal volunteers from English-speaking countries.[13]

In concluding that without Mahal there would have been neither an ATC nor an air force nor an Operation Dust, we go beyond any of our published sources. These sources, and the correspondence at the end of Appendix E, say only that the volunteers made a major contribution to the air force—not that they were indispensable. Why?

Perhaps, until now, no one was interested in this specific question. What is more likely, however, is that the kind of tendentious thinking we discussed at length in the Introduction, is at work here. Thus, Rivlin's letter to us (Appendix E) quotes an Air Force spokesman as saying that those involved in Operation Dust and in Operation Ayin (Horev) were about half Mahal and half Israeli.

This is not false, but it is highly misleading. The Mahal half were pilots, flight engineers, navigators, and the Israeli half were base personnel! One of our questionnaire replies (Appendix E, Swing) says the same thing—adding, however, that the Mahal half was indispensable to the functioning of the operation. Aharon Remez, in 1948 official Israeli head of the Air Force (Appendix E), encourages the fiction that it was a substantially Israeli air force all along; that the "assistance" of "Mahal volunteers and hired pilots" was needed only to "maintain the intensity" of air operations. But the testimony of direct participants (Appendix E), supplemented by our study of the pilot training schools, seems to us to be incontrovertible. With the assistance of Mahal instructors, Israeli airmen in reasonable numbers did not begin to be ready to really handle multi-engine planes and fighters until 1949—there were virtually no qualified Israelis available in 1948. Only with several hundred volunteers as aircrew, mechanics, and in charge of actual activities (Air Force Operations, for example, was run by South Africans; Codes and Ciphers, by an American; Meterology, by an American) was the Air Force able to function.

We reiterate: Mahal volunteers did not *help* the Air Force—they *were* the Air Force in 1948.

If there had been no air force Mahal, what would the likely consequences have been?

First, we saw that Mahal pilots were needed even for some of the light-plane flights to remote areas (e.g., Sodom, Negev); without Mahal, the number of these flights would have been distinctly reduced; but let us assume that the only consequence would have been added hardship to those areas. Next, there is the question of delivery of aircraft: With an airlift limited to contract flights, even if unlimited funds were available (actually, funds were very tight), flights would have been few and far between: We have seen that the contract crew and plane that flew Balak 1 incurred the displeasure of the American State Department, with the result that even though they had been paid an "exorbitant" fee the next Czech-Israel flight took place only a month and half later, with initiation of the volunteer airlift proper from secluded Zatec. Let us suppose that the Messerschmitts, therefore, had to be shipped by sea with, somehow, one or two coming through by air. It is hardly conceivable that any could have been flying prior to the First Truce (early June). It is even unlikely that any would have been ready for the Ten Days (mid-July); in fact, without experienced Mahal aircraft mechanics in Israel, preparation time would surely have been far longer, and airworthiness and maintenance highly questionable. On the other hand, the American sea deliveries would not have been affected. The crated Harvards and lighter planes, as well as the P51 Mustangs would have arrived over the later half of 1948, as they did. One or two Spitfires might have been patched together from enemy salvage, as they were. Perhaps some of the single-engine and a couple of the multiengine transports would have been gotten through (in addition to the light planes which were already on hand). That would have been the total, in 1948: No Beaufighters, no Czech Spitfires, no B-17s, almost no multi-engine transports which also served as bombers.

To fly this substantially reduced assortment of planes, there would have been the three Israeli fighter pilots mentioned earlier, plus a few dozen men with basic training on other planes and little experience. They would have done their best, and the attrition rate for planes and pilots would have been frightening: Instead of 1948 being (as it was) a year of positive apprenticeship for the air force, it would have been a year of terrible attrition, giving a negative "set" from which it would have been difficult to recover.

How might the land war have been affected by such an attenuated air force?

We saw that the first mission of the IAF was psychologically important in halting the Egyptian advance toward Tel Aviv (at Ashdod, May 29). However, it is quite possible that the Egyptians would have halted there anyway. It had taken them two weeks to advance to this point through territory that was primarily Arab-settled; now they were at the outskirts of territory that was largely Jewish, and their advance was characterized by timidity in contrast to their defense, which was formidable.

The next result would have been Israeli failure to control the air. We saw the tide shift in the air with the shooting down of two Egyptian Dakotas over Tel Aviv at the beginning of June, by the Israeli pilot, Modi Alon. Control of the air was maintained, not by a single incident, but by the ability to put a significant number of fighter planes into the air regularly, operated with sufficient skill to beat the enemy regularly. If the skies were hostile rather than friendly, Israel would have continued to hold out. Biafra is an example of a technically underequipped people being able to survive for an extended period under attacks by superior forces who also control the skies. *But the turnaround would have been impossible.*

With neutral skies, an inferior force can sometimes defeat one that has superiority in numbers and equipment in the field; but we are aware of no instance where this has been done, in non-jungle terrain, when the technically superior force also firmly ruled the skies. Thus, without an air force able to control, or at least neutralize, the skies, it appears most unlikely that the Ten Days would have been anything more than a continued stalemate—leaving Israel without the broadened Tel Aviv/Jerusalem corridor hinterland, without central Galilee, and without the sense of elation that comes from advancing against the enemy when, in the past, one could only hang on. (As Nahshon marked the turnaround against the Arab irregulars, so the Ten Days marked the turnaround against the Arab regular armies.) But there is an even more basic reason that the Ten Days could not have succeeded. As discussed above, without Mahal, Israel could have realized, at best, only a small fraction of the rifles, machine guns, and munitions of all kinds which streamed in on the Czech airlift from mid-May on. And without these tools, Israel's ability even to maintain a stalemate would have been doubtful indeed.[14] Furthermore, in such a situation the loss of the *Altalena* would, indeed, have been disastrous. (As we noted early in chapter six, precise detailed data on the specific flow of supplies by sea and by air is not available. But, making full allowance for momentum, we cannot believe that the airlift would have continued into August if it were not felt to be absolutely vital at least through June.)

It is unlikely that, without a successful Ten Days, the first Negev campaign (Operation Yoav) could have been launched at all. But let us suspend our sense of the probable, and consider this campaign by itself, but without Operation Dust, whose dependence on Mahal we have established.

Without Operation Dust, the October Negev campaign could only have been a frontal attack—an attack which, as we have seen, must have foundered, with the Negev still cut off. While the Egyptian link to southern Jerusalem would likely have been cut, the map of August 1948 would have been virtually unchanged. With the major campaign against the primary Arab army a standoff rather than an audacious success, with the field for maneuver much more limited from the narrow southern border of August 1948 than in the broad reaches of the actual post-October border, it is hardly likely that a second or third Egyptian campaign would have been much more successful. Thus, the aura of invincibility which has surely been a factor in Israeli success ever since, would have been lost. In terms of hard geography, the bulk of the Negev would have been as Egyptian as the Gaza Strip; the cut off kibbutzim would have continued to exist, by Egyptian sufferance, in an inspected, truly demilitarized enclave. Sodom, isolated, would in all likelihood have been surrendered in exchange for transit rights to these Negev kibbutzim. Israel's southern border would be Jerusalem corridor, Gat—Isdud. This radically truncated Israel would have been far different in outlook, in development, in real strength, and in prospects for survival, than the real Israel we see.

Thus, we can—we must—credit the volunteers with being a most vital link in the chain of events that determined the outcome of the War of Independence.

Among those with whom the writer spoke, some insisted virtually as an article of faith that although the volunteers undoubtedly helped, the same results would have been achieved without them: The price, in lives, might have been much higher, but whatever results were necessary would somehow have been achieved. This conviction is expressed in an apt Hebrew phrase: "V'off ol pi kane" ("in spite of the objective realities"). It is interesting to note that the post-1948 generation is rather skeptical of this kind of approach, referring to it derisively as "v'off ol pi kane-*iut*" ("in spite of the objective realities-*ism*"). Thus, for example, it is an objective fact that Latrun had to be taken, to break the siege of Jerusalem; yet three (some count five) major attacks in late May and early June utterly failed. The building of the by-pass "Burma" road was not in preference to taking Latrun: It was done out of desperation, since Latrun appeared impregnable. Even while the road was being built it was recognized that this desperate effort might be in vain, since there was a very real threat of UN action to inhibit its use unless it could be "proven" that it had been completed before the start of the First Truce—whereas, if Latrun were taken, there could be no possible question. It is true that

Israel was stronger later—but Latrun was never taken—not until the 1967 war. It is an objective fact that Israel had to take and hold Jenin, the northern anchor of the central Arab triangle. Yet, for lack of strength Israel abandoned Jenin after having taken it for a day in early June, after several days of severe fighting in the area; Jenin remained in Arab possession. It is an objective fact that Israel had to take Tulkarm, the central anchor of the central Arab triangle. A scant ten miles from the sea, midway along Israel's narrow waist, Tulkarm stood like a drawn bow threatening to cut the country in half—yet Tulkarm was not taken. Israel also failed to retake Mishmar Hayarden from the Syrians, although repeated counterattacks were mounted. And the Egyptians held most of the Faluja pocket in the face of strong Israeli attacks in the autumn and winter of 1948, and they held the Gaza Strip throughout the relatively long (15 days) final Egyptian campaign. Since at its peak strength Israel could not crack these Egyptian defensive enclaves in spite of its general record of success, even with the assistance of air power, one must express the gravest doubts over the possibility of Israeli success against the Egyptians without the Air Force and Operation Dust.

Thus, objective analysis is quite persuasive that Operation Dust was quite indispensable to the success of Operation Yoav and all that followed. It is not absolutely inconceivable that a groundpath to the Negev could have been smashed open by prolonged direct frontal attack; but a lengthy head-to-head battle with both sides focusing on a narrow sector, would be far more likely to have broken both armies—encouraging the other Arab armies to attack (they remained aloof while the Egyptians were being defeated: they must have wanted to be certain of their opponent's doom before first leaping in for the kill) with results frightening to contemplate. Perhaps the grim picture of a truncated Israel drawn above, is actually optimistic.

What was the participation of overseas volunteers in Israel's War of Independence?

Careful analysis of all sources (our Appendix F) led us to the conclusion that the grand total of all overseas volunteers from Western countries was in all likelihood a bit over 5,000, give or take a few hundred. Of these, the median estimates by country of origin are: 1,300 Americans (including Canadians), 1,350 British, 900 South Africans, 1,000 from Continental Western Europe, and 600 Latin Americans.

What is immediately striking, is the extremely low proportionate participation by American Jews—particularly when the total of 1,300 is broken down (to a maximum of about 1,000) to eliminate Canadians and the relatively high proportion of non-Jews who were present among the Americans. In round numbers, the proportionate participation of Jewish Americans as overseas volunteers was approximately one-fiftieth that of South African Jews!

We analyze the reasons for this meager American participation in Appendix G, including the question as to whether this may be a reflection on the American Zionist movement in 1948. Our focus here, however, is not on why there was not more Americans participation—it is rather, what did the actual American volunteer participation accomplish? Since we know that there does not exist any overall precise breakdown of the participation of overseas volunteers in the War of Independence, there certainly does not exist a further delineation of specific volunteer participation in terms of country of origin. Nevertheless, we do not hesitate to state that just as the flying air force, in effect, was totally dependent on overseas volunteers, the proportion of Americans (Jews and Christians) was such that neither the Air Force nor the ATC could have functioned without the Americans. (The greatest concentration of Americans was in the air.)

To summarize: Since the total number of volunteers from Western countries was something over 5,000, with a fair amount coming and going during the period in question, it is reasonable to suggest that the number actually serving at any given time was probably not more than 4,000 at its peak (presumably late Spring/early Summer 1948).

They served in all areas, with concentration primarily in Aliya Bet, in the Navy, in Jerusalem early in the war, in the Seventh (New) Brigade, in the armored corps (8th Brigade), to some extent in Givati Brigade, in the medical corps, in radar, and in the Air Force.

What was the military significance of this participation?

There was the intangible boost to morale in knowing that others cared enough to come from across the seas to fight as volunteers. The ships of Aliya Bet brought some supplies and a number of recruits (some Mahal and many Gahal, who had generally been given rudimentary military training in the Cyprus detention camps or in Europe). The Navy made the seas safe for Israel and helped carry the fight to the enemy. Jerusalem was held through long and difficult days, with meager arms, few defenders, and a shortage of food and water. The brigades in which Mahal was concentrated fought in the Galilee, in the center, and in the south. The medical corps went wherever it was most needed. In all the above areas, the direct participation of overseas volunteers was most important to the levels of success achieved, although tangible measure of the "worth" of this participation is not possible.

The overseas volunteers were indispensable to the functioning of radar and of the Air Force. Although we could not credit radar with any significant contribution to the outcome of the war, we found the air forces to be of the highest importance: in flying in the small arms and munitions of which the ground forces were desperately short; in clearing the domestic skies of enemy planes; in "morale" bombing of enemy capitals; in direct support of ground troops by heavy bombing (by the standards of that war) and strafing attacks on enemy troops, armor, transport, and supplies—and by frightening the enemy into non-use of his heavy bombers, and minimal use of his fighters; and, most directly and tangibly, by carrying out the operation without which defeat of the Egyptians and occupation of the Negev would not have been possible: Operation Dust.

One may suggest further that the men of Mahal also gave basic direction to the subsequent development of elements of the ground forces, to the Navy, to the Air Force, to radar, and perhaps, even antiradar. (This is not to deny that, as with the tanks and helicopters, where current tactics are indigenously Israeli—the very same decisions and directions might not have been arrived at all the same.)

Did Mahal matter?

The Mahal volunteers did, indeed, matter.

Chapter 20

AFTERWORD: PARTNERSHIP

Israel's reaction to world Jewry in the aftermath of the Six Day War was striking. Again and again the same note was struck: "For the first time, we sensed that the Jews of the world were with us, as one community."

What created this feeling in 1967 "for the first time"?

On the one hand, Israel's enemies were clearly, openly, blatantly preparing to annihilate her and, simultaneously, young Jewish volunteers (and some non-Jewish) from all over the world did their best to get to Israel and help in whatever way they could. There was also the outpouring of cash, the public meetings, and the public statements; but the willingness of numbers of young people to risk their own lives by coming *physically,* seems to be the element of transcending significance in establishing the sense of such deep commitment that, for the first time, Israelis felt an overwhelming bond of community from, and therefore with, overseas Jews.

To the average Israeli, this did, indeed, appear to be the first time. But, was this truly the first time? What of the Sinai Campaign in 1956? What of the War of Independence in 1948?

In 1956, there was no such outpouring of volunteers. The basic reason probably is that, then, Israel struck relatively sooner. The sense of impending doom was in its very early stages. The timing of Israel's strike against Egypt in 1956 appears to the writer to be comparable, in terms of the crystallization of world public opinion, to late April 1967. And, in April 1967, there was as yet no outpouring of volunteers, nor was there as yet a general conviction that all of Israel's neighbors were bent on its immediate extermination.

Recognizing that 1956 was different—was not 1948 essentially like 1967, only more critical? In 1948, the war went on much longer; Israel's preparedness both on an absolute basis and relative to its Arab neighbors was far, far, lower; and its need for overseas volunteers was truly desperate —whereas in 1967, except for certain medical specialists, the volunteers brought no important, usable skills. And, although more volunteers should have come in 1948—the absolute number that did come, and serve, was substantially larger than those who came in 1967.[1]

198

Why was this not realized by the average Israeli—so that the "new" sense of community could have been enjoyed for all the lonely years between 1948 and 1967?

Our Introduction suggested several possible reasons for consciously and subconsciously minimizing the role that overseas volunteers had played in 1948. Since the Independence Day celebration following the Six Day War for the first time genuinely publicized Mahal—perhaps the basic reason had been a problem of inner security (essentially on the part of the older generation). When one is completely sure of one's self, when one's strength had been tested most successfully, then one can afford to be open. Until then, so long as some insecurity remains, there is a tendency to insist that not only is one now totally self-reliant, but that this has always been the case.

Happily, this period is now past. Israel—whose daily greeting, whose highest hope, whose deepest prayer, is "Shalom" (peace/wholeness)—has proven that it has the world's most effective fighting force (per capita); and so, that sense of insecurity is no more.

For many, there must also have been the gnawing self-doubt that comes with rejection. The vast majority of 1948 volunteers returned to their native lands. It appeared that Israel was worth dying for, but not good enough to live in. There was resultant feverish secular[2] insistence that it was the duty of every Jew to live on the soil of Israel, in spite of its apparent drawbacks. Today, with Israel transformed over the past two decades into a country in the first rank of Western science and technology, and sociologically distinctly healthier than any of the "advanced" countries, it is recognized that, from every point of view, it is truly a *privilege* to live and raise one's children in Israel.

With the visceral realization of these realities, it should now be possible for all concerned to appraise the earlier contribution of overseas volunteers truly objectively. From the beginning, when pre-Israel said, "Give us the tools and we will do the job"—"us" were not Israelis as opposed to Jews elsewhere: "us"—the users of the tools—were representatives of Jewish communities all over the world, in the fullest possible partnership with those living in Israel.

The action of the 1948 volunteers in forging this implicitly covenanted partnership with all their hearts, with all their souls, and with all their might, may even transcend in importance their very real contributions to the physical well being of the then infant state of Israel.

APPENDICES

Appendix A

GLOSSARY

Aliyah Bet: In the American press this designation was commonly used to refer to the underground transport of refugees to Palestine after World War II. However, as used by Israelis, it is a broader term also including the underground acquisition and transport of military personnel and of military equipment. Actually, the "Mossad le Aliyah Bet" (Committee for Illegal Immigration) had been established as early as 1937 (one source insists on 1938) for the purpose of promoting and implementing immigration of Jews to Palestine outside the severe limitations imposed by the British mandatory administration. It was natural for recruitment and procurement to be added to the duties of this already-existing network of contacts, both before and after World War II. The entire organization is sometimes referred to as the "Mossad" with special names for its two major categories of activity: "Bricha" (Escape) applied particularly to the transport of people inside Europe following World War II, and "Rehesh" (Acquisition) applied to procurement of supplies. Lines of authority and responsibility tended to be informal. In addition to the Haganah Mossad, the IZL maintained its own somewhat similar, though smaller, organization. We use the term "Aliyah Bet" in its broader sense.

In our definition, non-Israelis, away from their home countries, who participated in Aliyah Bet activities directly related to the war, are also considered overseas volunteers. Thus, for example, Americans at the airfield in Zatec, Czechoslovakia, participating in the airlift of planes and arms to Israel, we consider overseas volunteers, although they may not have served in the Israeli armed forces, or even on Israeli soil. The official designation for this airlift was ATC—Air Transport Command.

Gahal: An acronym for "Giyus hutz la 'aretz," which literally means "draft from outside the country." These people came from overseas, and went straight into the armed forces. However, their circumstances were quite different from those of the Mahal (see definition below). Many came from the postwar refugee camps, and considered the land of Israel their true homeland. Jews from North Africa were also included in this category, on the presumption that their basic goal was permanent emigration to Israel. This was not universally true; for example, some of the urban Jews from Algiers might more accurately have been classed with the

203

volunteers from France and England. On the other hand, a few of the Mahal volunteers regarded themselves as on the way to becoming permanent residents of Israel. But without detailed case history studies of each individual, it would be impossible to attempt to make corrections of this kind. Therefore, our practical approach must be to consider all of Mahal as overseas volunteers, and to exclude all Gahal from this category.

Haganah: (Originally called Irgun Haganah Ha'ivrit B'Eretz Israel, the identical opening word led to occasional confusion by the uninitiated with Irgun Z'vai Leumi.) Literally, self-reliance or self-defense; the defense organization favored by the majority of the Jews of Palestine. Under the discipline of the Jewish Agency, its general policy was one of restraint (*havlaga*) towards Arabs and British on the soil of Palestine; force was to be used minimally and defensively. It graduated from the concept of static, "stockade" defense in the late thirties, concurrent with the Irgun breakaway (see "Irgun" below) and the appearance of Captain Charles Orde Wingate (see "Palmach" below). For the decade preceding 1948, its major activist focus was the Mossad. Worked with the dissident undergrounds, IZL and LHI, from October 1945 to the summer of 1946. Following wholesale British arrest and detention of the Jewish Agency leadership and hundreds of Haganah and Palmach people, and seizure of a major arms cache at Yagur on the same day (Black Sabbath—June 29, 1946), the Haganah broke with the dissidents. Earlier—December 1944– April 1945—the Palmach, often described as the striking arm of the Haganah, had moved against the dissidents on several occasions. The Haganah was increasingly active in response to mounting Arab attacks from the end of 1947; with the establishment of the state, it became the core of the Army of Israel.

Irgun Z'vai Leumi (IZL or Irgun): Literally, National Military Organization; broke away from Haganah in 1937. Made up of militants dissatisfied with the extent of Haganah restraint in the face of Arab attack at that time. Insisted that every Arab killing of Jews be balanced by an equal number of Arab bodies, among other things, as a means of pressuring the Arab communities to police themselves. Shifted to anti-British emphasis shortly before World War II. Declared truce with the British from the start of World War II. Disillusioned by British negativism towards Jewish refugees during the war, IZL proclaimed revolt against British rule in Palestine in 1944. Partially disbanded June 1948; finally disbanded September 1948.

Jewish Agency: The enlarged Jewish Agency came into being in

1929 as a partnership between Zionist and non-Zionist Jews for the up-building of Palestine. It was to be a service agency to, and political representative of, the Jewish community in Palestine. The term had appeared earlier, in Article Four of the League of Nations Mandate for Palestine, which specified, "an appropriate Jewish agency shall be recognized as a public body for the purpose of advising and cooperating with the administration of Palestine in such economic, social and other matters as may affect the establishment of the Jewish National Home and the interests of the Jewish population in Palestine." This was effective with the inception of the Mandate in 1922.

The same article recognized the Zionist Organization as such an agency. The 1929 reorganization resulted from years of negotiation between Zionists and non-Zionists—the latter, Jews who were interested in developing Palestine as a viable refuge but not as a future Jewish state. However, the revised Jewish Agency, functioning in Palestine on behalf of Palestine's Jewish residents and immigrants, tempered by difficulties with the mandatory power, inevitably became increasingly Zionist. Officially and factually the Jewish Agency was the representative of the Jewish people in Palestine. This extended beyond the political, to the military: Together with the Vaad Leumi (National Council of the Jews in Palestine), it was involved in supervising the Haganah, which was the Establishment underground defense force. Prior to the establishment of the State, it appointed a council of 37 and a committee of 13, the latter to serve as a directorate ("Minhalat Ha'am"), with David Ben Gurion as Chairman. With the establishment of the State, the "13" became the Provisional Government, serving until the first election (January 1949). The Agency has continued its existence, performing extra-governmental functions. These focus on immigration, absorption of immigrants, land settlement, and promoting world support of the state. This arrangement was confirmed by the Zionist Congress in 1951, by the Knesset in 1952 and by formal written agreement in 1954.

Knesset: Parliament of the State of Israel.

Lohamei Herut Israel (LHI): Literally, "fighters for the freedom of Israel"; often called the "Stern Gang" outside Israel. A splinter of IZL, founded in 1940 by IZL leader Avraham Stern, who denounced the IZL-proclaimed truce with Britain. Stern, who was so anti-British that he tried to make a deal with Hitler that would create difficulties for Britain,[1] was killed by British police February 1942. Partially disbanded June 1948, LHI remained in existence until late September 1948.

Mahal: An acronym for *mitnadvey hutz la'aretz* (literally, "volunteers from outside the country"). This designation applied essentially to overseas volunteers from the free countries of the West, primarily, those from English-speaking countries (who, interestingly, were referred to in Israel as "Anglo-Saxons"). They were regarded as coming entirely of their own free will, with the likelihood that they would return to their countries of origin after the war.

In order to help protect the citizenship of the Mahal Americans, a limited oath of allegiance was administered, so that it could be said that they were serving "with" rather than "in" the armed forces of Israel. This small difference in oath resulted in no practical difference whatever in service (rank, discipline, action, etc.). Under then current American law, taking an abstract oath of allegiance to a foreign government (or voting in a foreign election) was clearly a cardinal offense, whereas actually risking one's life in the service of a foreign government could be presumed to be less reprehensible. The fact that some Mahal were permitted to opt out of the army at their own initiative was a practical accommodation on the part of the army—not the result of a special form of oath.

Mossad: See "Aliyah Bet."

Palmach: Acronym for *plugot mahatz* ("striking forces"). Set up by the Haganah in 1941 as the core of a permanent, underground, guerilla "army," its members were drawn primarily from kibbutzim (communal farming settlements). Virtually coincident with its creation by the Jews, Palmach was officially recognized by the British as a potential anti-German guerilla force when British defeat in Egypt appeared imminent (1941).[2] Its effective roots were in the Night Squads organized by Orde Wingate, a magnificent maverick British officer, in 1937 to combat Arab anti-Jewish attacks, which apparently were condoned by the British. The official justification for Wingate's work was that the Night Squad patrols protected the pipeline conveying oil from Iraq's Mosul fields to the British refineries in Haifa. The rash of such attacks, begun in 1936 and extending into 1939, is referred to as the Arab Revolt. During World War II, Arab sympathies and actions were predominantly against the Allies. The basic tactic of Palmach before 1948 was to strike guilty Arabs only, often deep in Arab territory, generally under cover of night.

Palmach units were the shock troops of the Haganah. As companies, and under-strength brigades, they bore the brunt of the front-line fighting up to and beyond mid-1948. Superseded by the expanded, reorganized Army of Israel. Although the Army of Israel came into being in May

1948, with the IZL and LHI undergrounds quickly absorbed (except in Jerusalem), Palmach was permitted to retain separate identity and administration until November of that year.

Yishuv: The Jewish community in Palestine; literally, "settlement."

Zahal: Acronym for Zva Haganah leIsrael, generally rendered as "Israel defense forces." Established by order of the Provisional Government May 28, 1948, it immediately relabeled the underground Haganah as Israel's regular army. June 2, the IZL agreed to merge with Zahal, shedding its separate identity, except for the Jerusalem area; a similar step had already been taken by LHI. Zahal includes all branches of Israel's armed forces—sea and air as well as land.

Appendix B

AN INDEPENDENT ARAB STATE;
JERUSALEM INTERNATIONALIZED

In general, the long-term and consistent approach of Palestinian Arab spokesmen had been to reject, out of hand, any proposal that included an independent Jewish state in Palestine no matter how small.

Thus, the fate of every proposal for partition, beginning with the British Peel Commission report in mid-1937, was to be rejected by both sides; by the Jews as unfair, inadequate, and contrary to the terms of the mandate; by the Arabs, as unacceptable because it provided, in principle, for a Jewish state. This was a fundamental departure from the accepting approach of the Emir Feisal, who, correctly or not, was the accepted spokesman for the Arab world in 1918 and in the years immediately following. Expecting that a number of Arab territories would be started on the road to independent nationhood, putting a relatively small Jewish territory on the same road was not objectionable, and should insure Jewish support at the Peace Conference, and, perhaps, promote the flow of Jewish funds as well.[1]

Under the stressful conditions of late 1947, the Jews accepted the UN partition plan out of dire necessity. The Arabs continued to reject the very principle of partition. Thus they would certainly not take any steps to set up a new Arab state in part of Palestine, not so long as they felt that a little fighting would quickly permit them to set up such a state in all of Palestine.

The *New York Times,* March 21, 1948, reports that the Arab League initially welcomed the U.S. plan for trusteeship for Palestine, to replace partition on the understanding that this was a plan for an all-Arab Palestine government which might include some special recognition for its Jews. When it became clear less than a week later that President Truman's idea was for a temporary trusteeship whose purpose was eventual peaceful partition, Haj Amin el Husseini, the Grand Mufti of Jerusalem, and the Arab League immediately rejected the trusteeship proposal.

The aim of the Arab League and some Palestinian Arabs to bring into being an independent Arab state, was opposed by Abdullah, king of Transjordan. Golda Meir, then Myerson, later to become Prime Minister of Israel, met twice with Abdullah secretly accompanied by Ezra Danin. The first meeting, in November 1947, was at Naharayim, in the northern Jordan valley. She returned from this meeting encouraged. Abdullah would never attack the Jews; he would annex only the Arab parts of Palestine, and would gladly accept partition. The second secret meeting, in Transjordan's capital in Amman, on May 10, 1948, was quite different. Now, Abdullah said, "I'm no longer alone, I am one of five; I must come into the war." He offered an alternative: if the Jews would cooperate in his annexing all of Palestine, he would give the Jews special status—and there would be no war. This no-Jewish-state proposition could hardly be taken seriously—although, in its immediate aftermath, weighty consideration was given by the Yishuv's governing council to postponing the promulgation of the state of Israel and thus the invasion by the regular Arab armies, because of the critical military-supply situation.

Well aware of Abdullah's ambition and of the natural accessibility of western Palestine to physical control by Transjordan's Arab Legion, Azzam Pasha, secretary general of the Arab League, declared on May 19 that the Arab armies would each establish an administration in the area under its control, until such time as an independent Arab state could be established. Earlier, the *New York Times* of April 13 had stated that a committee of the Arab League was reported considering the establishment of a provisional Arab government under the Mufti; and the *New York Times* of April 27 quoted the Mufti to the effect that the Arabs would set up their own state after May 15 unless trusteeship were approved.

These moves appeared to have been equally well suited to establishing an Arab state in all of Palestine or, if areas of Jewish sovereignty should somehow survive, in the remainder of Palestine. This would clearly forestall the expansionist ambitions of Palestine's neighboring Arab states; the Arab League itself did not presume that it was merely altruism that brought them to combine forces to drive the Jews into the sea. (Haj Amin el Husseini, the ex-Grand Mufti of Jerusalem, who was mentioned so prominently as the presumed leader of the Palestinian Arab state, was a notorious Jew hater. From the mandate's earliest days, he had been active in promoting physical attacks on Jews, and he had spent most of World War II in Berlin.)

After the fighting had ended, trying for at least half a loaf, the Grand Mufti petitioned the UN Conciliation Commission for recognition as the representative of the "Government of the Gaza Strip." This request was turned down in mid-March 1949, emphasizing the de facto jurisdiction of Egypt, as indicated by the Egyptian-Israeli Armistice Agreement of February 24, 1949.

A fundamental, unanswered—and probably unanswerable—question, was that of authentic representation. What leader or leaders truly represented the Gaza Strip Arabs? The west-bank Arabs? Those Arabs who had fled Jewish Palestine? No one seriously urged an internationally supervised election procedure—such a procedure is of little or no value when the participants have lived all their lives in a semifeudal atmosphere with no previous voting experience—and, in early 1949, probably had no deep interest in high-level politics. The basic deep antagonism between the east-bank Transjordanian and west-bank Palestinian Arabs is worthy of note. Glubb's book, for example, conveys deep contempt on the part of the Arab Legion with its romanticized Bedouin self-image for the Palestinian peasant villagers.

Thus, it was effective control that became the determining factor in recognizing jurisdiction; and effective control was exercised by the occupying armies. Israel's preference had definitely been for a new independent Arab state. For example, Foreign Minister Moshe Sharett (Shertok) said so explicitly in the course of his report to the Knesset on June 15, 1949, but in the practical interest of expediting the armistice agreements, Israel was quite ready to recognize the jurisdiction of the occupying Arab governments.

More, Israel might be said to have cooperated in establishing such jurisdiction; the term "Hashemite Kingdom of Jordan" was used for the very first time in the Armistice Agreement of April 3, 1949. Using this designation rather than "Transjordan" had clear implications for the future. In return, Israel expected Jordanian cooperation in moving the armistice to a genuine peace treaty. This expectation proved false. Over a period of a year, Abdullah digested the west bank, proclaiming the official merger of the west bank, including the Old City of Jerusalem, into the Hashemite Kingdom of Jordan, April 24, 1950. The reaction of the other Arab League countries to this annexation was outrage. They threatened to oust Jordan from the League. Abdullah met this with a counterthreat: If Jordan were ousted, he would immediately sign a peace treaty with Israel! The League then, in mid-June, agreed to recognize Jordan as "co-trustee" until the final unspecified settlement. It is likely that Abdullah did intend eventually, "if conditions permitted," to sign a peace treaty with Israel—many consider the prime cause of his assassination, at El Aksa Mosque in Jerusalem on July 20, 1951, to be his ongoing secret negotiations with Israel.

The UN-sponsored armistice agreements recognized the jurisdiction of its occupying neighbors over the various parts of what the UN partition plan had decreed would come into being as the Palestinian Arab state. Such occupation was viewed as temporary since the UN Conciliation Commission set Lausanne, Switzerland as the site of Arab-Israeli peace talks scheduled to begin April 26, 1949. The meetings took place, on and off, for many months, getting nowhere; the Lausanne Conference was officially adjourned in mid-September. Towards the end of 1949, there were open talks between Israel and Jordan which also bore no fruit.

Thus, the presumed temporary occupation of parts of Palestine by its invading Arab neighbors became an ongoing fact; a fact which was changed in June 1967, when instead, Israel became the de facto occupier of these areas.

The Jerusalem area theoretically was a special problem. When "trusteeship" was not applied to Palestine as a whole, the term and concept were picked up for the Jerusalem area. This seemed the natural thing to do, since, under the original partition plan, the Jerusalem area was to have been internationalized. Although the UN set up a Trusteeship Council for the Jerusalem area, it did not take practical steps for its implementation. Gradually, the two occupiers each incorporated its sector of Jerusalem into itself. Thus February 1, 1949 Israel incorporated the New City of Jerusalem into the state, ending a separate military government status which had officially prevailed since August 2, 1948, under emergency regulations; in addition, Israel announced that the Constituent Assembly would meet in Jerusalem on February 14th. Shortly thereafter, Foreign Minister Sharett urged that if internationization be applied at all, it should be applied only to the Arab-occupied Old City, which contained virtually all the religious shrines of international interest. The UN discussed Israeli administration of the New City, Arab administration of the Old, with an international federal authority of some kind overseeing both. By the end of March, Israel had moved five ministries to the New City. Discussions continued, with Israel urging international control for the religious shrines alone, wherever they might be.

During the succeeding months, the UN actually adopted and pressed its plan for UN control and internationalization of a unified greater Jerusalem area; its pressure included suspending action on Israel's application for UN membership. However, the UN apparently was quite powerless to implement its decision without the consent of Israel and Jordan. And Israel and Jordan were united in absolutely rejecting all suggestions that they yield any of their sovereignty over the parts of Jerusalem they occupied: in legal terms, the UN-supervised bilateral Armistice Agreement between Israel and Jordan (April 3, 1949) was claimed to have superceded all preceding UN plans and decisions.[2]

November 29, S. K. Tsarapkin of the USSR, who three months earlier had held that the task of the UN in Palestine was completed, now urged complete return to the 1947 partition plan in order to maintain UN prestige. This statement, reflecting a significant shift in the Soviet attitude towards Israel, led nowhere. A week later Major General John H. Hildring, a former member of the U.S. delegation to the UN, in a speech in Brooklyn described the UN plan for international control of Jerusalem as both unnecessary and unworkable. Nevertheless, on December 9 the UN General Assembly approved the plan—and by December 13, UN representatives themselves were seeing that it was unworkable. That same day, David Ben Gurion, Israel's Prime Minister and Minister of Defense, announced that all offices of the Israeli Government would soon be transferred to Jerusalem—although he could not yet proclaim it the capital of Israel. In the meantime, the UN had not been successful in its much more limited efforts to promote access to Jewish religious shrines in the Old City, or use of the Hadassah Hospital and Hebrew University facilities on Mt. Scopus—a Jewish enclave in Arab territory—all of which were guaranteed by the Armistice Agreement.

January 23, 1950, the Knesset proclaimed that (New) Jerusalem had been the capital of Israel since the creation of Israel. Earlier, the UN Trusteeship Council had adopted an administrative statute for Jerusalem, at the same time barring all moves to implement it except for pleas to Israel and Jordan to cooperate. In mid-April, USSR Deputy Minister Malik wrote to UN Secretary General Trygve Lie announcing that the USSR was withdrawing its support for the UN Assembly Resolution on Internationalization since it was opposed by both the Jewish and Arab populaces. April 24, 1950, Abdullah officially proclaimed the merger of all occupied areas of Palestine, including the Old City of Jerusalem, with the Hashemite Kingdom of Jordan, after this was approved by Jordanian parliamentary resolution. Three days later Great Britain granted de jure recognition to the merged state as an entity, indicating that its recognition of the specific boundaries and of Jerusalem as part of the merged Jordanian state was de facto, pending a final settlement.

In mid-June the Trusteeship Council voted overwhelmingly (9 to 1) to drop the impractical, unapplicable Jerusalem statute it had earlier drawn up, and to report its failure to the Assembly. The question was taken up by the Assembly again in December and, after several days of discussion, on Dec. 15, 1950 the UN Assembly officially shelved the entire issue.

It is not unrealistic to suggest that the experience of the Palestine issue determined the future course of the UN. Having voted the partition of Palestine into a Jewish and an Arab state as the most practical solution to the Palestine problem, the UN totally failed to take constructive action to bring this solution into being.

When the Jewish state was threatened with destruction by its neighbors (themselves members of the UN), no meaningful action—not even censure or the threat of censure—was taken to deter this most flagrant action. Not only did the UN fail to do anything to protect the Jewish state whose existence it had decreed, but its even-handed approach worked to Israel's detriment in Israel's most critical period—and, thereafter, consisted largely in efforts to roll back the results of those successes which Israel managed to achieve. Israel, taught by the UN that its physical survival depended solely on itself, viewed it as the height of immorality for the UN that failed to protect it when it needed protection, now to attempt to take away the fruits of its success against aggression. And the UN, having been impotent when it was desperately needed, could not later assert an authority which, in effect, it had earlier denied possessing.

The UN status as goodwill advisor instead of as the truly determining factor in specific crises, was further underlined by its failure to bring into being the originally proposed Arab state at all. Instead, it promoted armistice agreements which gave recognition to continued occupation of the Arab-state areas by the invaders, Egypt and Jordan, and by the defender, Israel. Then it watched the peace talks peter out without getting anywhere, leaving the armistice agreements as the ongoing de facto arrangement. The UN did not even insist upon peace treaties as the price of acquiescence in "permanent" occupation of the Gaza area by Egypt, and the West Bank by Jordan.

This failure of the UN to use acquiescence in ongoing occupation of seized territory as means of forcing the occupiers to a contractual peace, may well be faulted as simultaneously:

1) The cause of continuing warfare in the Middle East ever since 1949;

2) The abdication of any real moral leadership.

Since it is that lowest common denominator, the natural urging of selfish national interest on the part of individual member nations, that has brought this about—periodic appeals to morality on the floor of the UN which, of course, requires a sacrifice on someone else's part, succeed only in generating a sense of deep cynicism on the part of those who continue hoping that the tragedies of war would lead to something better.

Appendix C

ARAB MILITARY FAILURE FROM
THE ARAB PERSPECTIVE

To begin with, there was deep distrust among the various Arab armies. Rather than coordinate their efforts under a truly unified command, each operated independently—and each was convinced that the others were holding back. The idea that the others were not doing their share, suggested that one's own army ought not to be overly committed—particularly since it would be necessary to come out of the war as militarily strong as one had gone into it both in terms of internal stability and in terms of strength relative to one's neighbors.

There were claims of incompetence verging on sabotage in the procurement of war material. Thus, the Syrians had difficulty believing that Operation Pirate (discussed in chapter fourteen) could have succeeded without treasonous collusion on the part of the Syrian in charge who was actually quite innocent. And the Egyptians, who were very well equipped indeed—although there likely were logistical problems from time to time—tended to blame equipment malfunction on corruption back home rather than on inadequate maintenance on the part of field soldiers. The Transjordanian situation was compounded by ongoing distrust between the Arabs and the Englishmen who headed the Arab Legion, Transjordan's army. Further, it appears reasonably clear that Abdullah would have been just as happy not to fight at all—that he did not really object to Jewish sovereignty over Jewish areas—but that he very much wanted to annex all the Arab areas, including Jerusalem, and to have special rights of access to the Mediterranean through a major port. But once committed, the Legion fought as hard as any of the others, and—as we noted in connection with the Etzion group of kibbutzim—the Arab Legion actually was the first regular Arab army to enter the war. Further, it is claimed, in *Soldier* by Glubb, that after the Ten Days the Legion was almost completely out of ammunition. Thus, when in early March 1949 the Iraqis stated that they were leaving the Central Front and going home, the Legion was totally defenseless, and hastened to acquiesce in the results of Operation Fact and to sign the armistice agreement with Israel for its own protection. To me, this smacks a bit of a self-serving overstatement—although it is a fact that, early in the war, the Egyptians seized a Transjordanian ammunition ship in the Suez Canal, taking its contents for themselves.

The final Arab argument was that the Arabs were greatly outnumbered by the Israelis who were also far better equipped. Specifically, Glubb states that on May 15, 1948, all the regular armies were a total of only 21,500 going into Palestine to fight against 65,000 Jews (including an estimated 20,000 overseas volunteers, including Poles and Russians). Kimche, in *Destinies,* p. 243, gives the more realistic figure as a total of 35,000 Jews; elsewhere, we conclude that the number of volunteers could never have been more than a few thousand at any given time, and that no volunteers came from behind the Iron Curtain. Similarly, Glubb advises that at the start of October the Arab armies in Palestine totaled 50,700 regulars plus 5,000 irregulars—as opposed to 120,000 Israelis. (Kimche's figure for the Israeli army in early October is 80,000.) Kimche's figures are reasonable for Israel and, assuming the accuracy of Glubb's figures for the Arab armies, we must point out that he is writing essentially of front-line soldiers (those in Palestine), whereas the figures for the Army of Israel are for the entire army, necessarily including a substantial number for rear-echelon work (as well as a very high proportion of new recruits).

Defeat, as such, apparently must not be admitted: Glubb explains his loss of Lydda and Ramle in the Ten Days by stating that it was obvious in advance that these places were strategically indefensible, and if the Jews attacked, they would have to be abandoned: There was no sense making a major fight to hold them.

As for ammunition—no one who fought the Arabs was aware of any shortage. Neither Syrians nor Egyptians nor Jordanians showed any signs of being short of ammunition or equipment. Further, the Jordanians shelled New Jerusalem during the Ten Days as though their supplies were limitless, and they frequently broke the truce with heavy firing for many months thereafter—until the "sincere" cease-fire.

Our conclusions are that the ratio of Arabs to Israelis in the field was much closer to 1:1 or 2:1, than the dramatic 40:1 or 80:1 figures that are sometimes used; that the Arabs' armies began the war with overwhelming superiority in military hardware (tanks, artillery, planes, machine guns, ammunition); that they did not use it well on the offensive, often being stopped by a far lower level of equipment mixed with a far higher level of determination; that, even by the end of the war, Israel's total equipment probably was not superior to that of the Arabs, but that Israel made more effective use of it, and that Israel often achieved local numerical superiority and multiplied its equipments' effectiveness by concentrating forces at particular attack points. In short, what one perceptive writer calls "the cultural and sociological components of military power, as opposed to just hardware,"[1] were indeed most important.

It is not unlikely that Arab procurement of military supplies was somewhat tainted by graft, but this, in effect, was simply an overcharge since there was no apparent significant shortage of supplies in the field. As we have seen, Israeli procurement was dedicated, imaginative, and quite free of any suspicion of corruption—although not free of waste, and of "overhead" payments to others. High living on the part of some may have been an occupational necessity (perhaps coinciding with personal proclivity; there is evidence that the Israeli arms procurer Yehuda Arazi fit into this category as did the American, Hank Greenspun). This is certainly not a new tendency.

Generally (with exceptions both ways), Israeli leadership in the field was broad and effective—and Arab leadership disorganized and timid on the offensive but quite good defensively.

Appendix D

A BRIEF DESCRIPTION OF THE MAJOR AIRCRAFT IN-
VOLVED:

Messerschmitt:
ME-109 (sometimes referred to as BF-109, for Bayerische Flugzeugwerke,
the name of the manufacturing company at the time of its original design).
The ME-109 was the basic fighter plane of the German Air Force in World
War II. Its first prototype was flown in 1935; it was used throughout the
war, with various modifications (we have no information on which specific
model or models went to Israel). Basically it was a single-engine plane,
with one-man crew, carrying one 30-mm cannon and two 13-mm machine
guns.

Spitfire:
This plane was the basic British fighter plane of World War II; it was the
only British fighter in continuous production throughout the war. It was
used as a fighter, fighter bomber, and reconnaissance plane; it was extremely popular with its pilots. More than 20,000 were built, encompass-
ing 40 major versions. For example, the Mark VB had a range of 1,135
miles; the Mark XIV a design range of 850 miles. The 1,400-mile flight
from Yugoslavia to Israel may thus have been somewhat less radical than
some of our sources indicate—although it is absolutely clear that the
Velveta flights far exceeded the design limitations of these particular aircraft. They were modified, with auxiliary fuel tanks added under the wings
and wherever there was space inside. Like the ME-109 the Spitfire was a
single-engine plane with one-man crew; its basic armament consisted of
two 20-mm cannons and four .303 machine guns.

Bristol Beaufighter:
Designed for use as a night fighter and against shipping. It mounted four
20-mm Hispano cannons, six .303 Browning and one .303 Vickers machine
guns. A total of 5,962 were produced; it was a two-engine plane with a
basic two-man crew.

The labeling of the American planes is somewhat confusing, because
of the basically different identification system used by the U.S. Air Force
and the U.S. Navy. Specifically, the Air Force used the letter "A" to designate the light bomber; "B" for medium or heavy bomber; "C" for transport. On the other hand, the Navy used letters to designate manufacturers.

Thus, "C" indicated Curtiss-Wright (or Cessna or Culver); "D" indicated Douglas (or McDonell).

B-17:
> The Air Force designation for a long-range bomber of which more than 12,700 were produced between 1941 and 1945. It carried up to 8 tons of bombs with a crew of 10. It was called the "Flying Fortress" because it did not require fighter-plane escort: It mounted its own multiple sets of twin machine guns in a number of locations, such that it was able to defend itself from every direction of approach.

Dakota:
> Often described as the best all-round aircraft built (in the pre-jet age). Labeled DC-3 (for Douglas Commercial), or C-47 (Air Force Transport) or C-53 (Air Force Troop Carrier). Military production exceeded 10,000. It was a two-engine plane, with a crew of four. Basically a transport, also used in Israel (by both sides) as an auxiliary bomber.

Curtiss Commando (C-46):
> A transport similar to the Dakota, but somewhat large and heavier. Also a two-engine plane, it carried a crew of five. It was in operational use from 1943 to 1945, primarily in the Far East. More than 3,000 were produced for military transport use.

Skymaster (DC-4 or C-54):
> This plane was distinctly larger and heavier than the above. Used for cargo and/or personnel, it was a four-engine plane with a crew of six. In military operational use 1942-45.

Constellation (C-69, built by Lockheed):
> A four-engine aircraft similar to the Skymaster but somewhat larger. Only 20 delivered before the end of World War II; essentially it was a postwar commercial aircraft.

DC-5: modified DC-3, slightly smaller than the original.

P-51 Mustang:
> Built by North American. Long-range fighter escort and ground attack plane; more than 10,000 built between 1942 and 1945. Single engine, with one-man crew. It mounted four to six .50 machine guns and carried up to 2,000 lbs. of bombs or ten 5-inch rockets.

The above is taken primarily from Kenneth G. Munson, *Aircraft of World War II* (Garden City, New York: Doubleday & Co., 1968).

Appendix E

BASIC NEW DATA

I. TESTIMONY OF VOLUNTEERS

Following are texts of the questionnaire and covering letter circulated with the cooperation of the American Veterans of Israel:

Dear Friend,

I would appreciate your help. I am working on a doctoral thesis, the title of which is, "An Attempt to Evaluate the Significance and Participation of Overseas Volunteers in Israel's War of Independence."

The question as to whether we (my Mahal Service was from June '48 to July '49) overseas volunteers really made a significant difference in the War of Independence, is one on which many people have deep convictions (one way or the other)—but very little factual information.

In order to help me develop as much factual information as possible, I will appreciate your filling out the enclosed questionnaire. All additional information—including names and addresses of other Volunteers—will be appreciated. A return envelope is enclosed.

In filling out the questionnaire, please note the following definitions:

Israeli—one who had previously lived in Palestine, and who considered it his home. While this term is technically valid only after May 14th, 1948, it is applied to earlier situations, as a convenience, to avoid a cumbersome phrase like "resident of Jewish Palestine, on our side."

Overseas Volunteer—one who left his home overseas to serve with Aliyah Bet or with the Israeli Armed Forces (regardless of intention of settling in Israel); or one who happened to be in Israel on temporary basis (e.g., a student), and who remained and served. In short, all entitled to Gahal [1] or Mahal or special ATC status, regardless of pay or religious origin.

Aliyah Bet—this designation is meant to include not only the underground transport of "refugees," but also of military personnel, and of arms and planes (by air and by sea).

Scope—1947 to July 1949: Israel, Europe, the Mediterranean, etc.

Your cooperation is very much appreciated.

220

Questionnaire on Israel's War of Independence, 1947-July 1949

	Arms Procurement or Ships or Military Units	Location	Approx. Dates (Mth/yr) From — To
I served with			
	_____	_____	_____
	_____	_____	_____
	_____	_____	_____

Please answer separately for each operation which you consider significant:

Operation and approximate date	Approximate no. Israelis	Approximate no. overseas volunteers	In my opinion, *without* overseas volunteers, this operation		
			could	could not	have succeeded
_____	_____	_____	____	_____	
_____	_____	_____	____	_____	
_____	_____	_____	____	_____	
_____	_____	_____	____	_____	

Name_____Address_____

Zip_____

Comments and/or Names and Addresses of others who may have helpful information:

_____

_____

_____

_____

_____

_____

The Association of Americans and Canadians in Israel circulated approximately the same form, with the same definitions, and with the following introduction:

ASSOCIATION OF AMERICANS AND CANADIANS IN ISRAEL
Dear Member,
An individual who served in the Army of Israel in 1948 and 1949 (and who has been an overseas member of A.A.C.I. for a number of years), is currently working on a doctoral dissertation entitled "An attempt to evaluate the significance and participation of overseas volunteers in Israel's War of Independence." Since documented facts of the type needed are virtually nonexistent, the researcher has turned to the A.A.C.I. as a means of contacting a large number of people with first-hand knowledge. The researcher has assured A.A.C.I. that the results of his work—whether published or not—would be available to A.A.C.I. The following questionnaire is designed for maximum ease in answering; *answers at greater length will, of course, be most welcome, as will suggestions for additional people to contact.* The replies may be sent either to A.A.C.I. office in Tel Aviv, or direct to Rabbi A. Joseph Heckelman, 192 Columbia Boulevard, Waterbury, Conn. 06710, U.S.A.

The AVI mailing produced 33 replies, and the AACI mailing, 10 replies, for a total of 43.[2] Considering the length of time that had elapsed, and the likelihood that not more than a fraction of the volunteers were actually reached, this is an excellent return.

Furthermore, the range of first-hand experiences covered is extremely broad, among other things including IZL, Hagana, Aliya Bet, the Navy, the Air Force, tank and anti-tank units, radar, general army service, and something of the involvment in America and Europe. With the format of our questionnaire dictating succinct replies and eliciting objective evidence as well as subjective conclusions, we feel that we have developed a uniquely valuable collection of new data—subject to the limitations discussed in our Introduction.

Information through other veterans associations: There is no separate Canadian organization; Canadians are welcomed as members of the American Veterans of Israel (several of our replies are from Canadians). There appears never to have been a separate Latin American organization; a lead to a supposed British Mahal group, which the writer attempted to follow in London in the summer of 1965, led nowhere. The one group with whom successful contact was made was the South African Mahal Association in Johannesburg. Because they were circulating their own exceedingly detailed questionnaire, they felt it would be impractical to circulate mine. However, this communication did lead to contact with

Gideon Shimoni, who discussed, in relevant detail, the results of his many months of investigation of the participation of South Africans. We are not aware of any functioning European veterans organization. Thus, our questionnaire could only be circulated through the AVI and AACI. Now, to summarize and quote the returns themselves:

MOSHE BRODETZKY, volunteer who served with the IZL in the Jerusalem area from April 1947 until well after the end of the war, gives the following figures for Israelis and overseas volunteers in a number of actions: Bet Sefer Leshoterim (Police School-Sheikh Jarrah) 120, 2; Pahgi 60, 1; Deir Yassin 120, 10; Malcha 120, 40; Ramat Rahel 60, 20.[3] He points out that in that period of critical shortage of men as well as materials (first half of 1948) "Each individual counted—how can you opine that it could have succeeded without? (The only exception is where one of us overseas volunteers was the prime cause of a defeat—then his *lack of presence* may have let someone else succeed.)"

RABBI MOSES B. SACHS, a Hebrew University volunteer who served in the Jerusalem area 12/47-11/48 writes "I do not think of volunteers in categories of dispensable/indispensable but of making very *significant* contributions. In the beginning many Mahalnik H.U. (Hebrew University) students contributed important skills *as persons;* others were in units (I remember three) which held various points. We had a half Mahal unit *inside* the Jewish Agency Building until just before the explosion. We were sent then as a group to Atarot (just redeemed in June 67). As the struggle developed from atrocities to a major war, our H.U. Mahalniks were gradually dispersed—used as individuals—for their personal skills. In Jerusalem every person who really served was vital to the effort, so short we were of skilled persons and of men and women to do all manner of jobs from making ammunition to listening to British military radio and British officers of Arab Legion conversing over radio, to manning machine guns, to standing guard at posts of varying degrees of personal danger, to participating in major attacks."

ELIEZER WHARTMAN, who served in the Jerusalem area (Moriah Infantry Battalion, May 10, 1948–July 10, 1948; thereafter in the Mahal Resettlement Office) writes that there were roughly 20 volunteers in a total of about 4 Battalions, and that the Jerusalem operations *could* have succeeded without the overseas volunteers.

ABRAHAM KENNY, who served in the Carmeli Brigade (Galilee), 2/48–9/49, recalls a total of five Americans in the Brigade. He cites one instance in which he feels he played a crucial role as "the only available man to operate the armored car in that operation," which he identifies as the battle of Birwa east of Acre, probably in late May or early June. (The only cross-reference to Birwa we find is in *Toledot*, pp. 247-9, where it figures in Operation Dekel in mid-July. Particularly in the Galilee, the same locations figured in actions several times.)

RABBI JEROLD BOBROW, who served in the Carmeli Brigade from mid-April to December 1948, and in arms procurement in the New York City area prior to that, writes: "It is difficult to understand how either Aliya Bet or arms procurement could have succeeded without Mahal help. While it would be difficult to determine the outcome of the war surely there is no question as to the importance of Mahal and Gahal." In specifics, he shows 12 volunteers and 3 Israelis in his arms procurement activity, which could not have succeeded without the volunteers. (Note: People engaged in such activities in their native land are excluded from our definition of *overseas* volunteers.) The one action he refers to is the battle for Central Galilee (Operation Hiram) in the last days of October 1948; his squad (10) included two volunteers, who were not of vital importance.

SHOSHANA (KLIERS) CARMELI advises that she served in a wireless unit (France, Italy) Dec. 1946–Jan. 1948, and on the ship *United Nations* (Italy to Israel) Dec. 25, 1947–Jan. 1, 1948. The crew of this Aliya Bet ship included 2 Israelis and 1 volunteer, who was not crucial to its success.

IRVING CALIC served on the immigrant ship *Mala,* May 1, 1948–June 19, 1948. He gives no information as to the number of Israelis and number of overseas volunteers. The following also omit such information: *Matityahu Harris,* who served in Zahal Nov. 1948–Nov. 1949, and remained to become an Israeli (he also served in the Sinai Campaign and in the Six Day War); *Moses Stambler,* who was in the Navy June 1948–June 1949 at Stella Maris and Bat Galim; *Sidney Rabinovich,* who served in the 51st Battalion of Givati Brigade, from Hatsor to Latrun (May–June '48); in the Artillery around Rosh Pinna (July–Aug.); and in Navy radar at Stella Maris (Aug. '48–Feb. '49).

BENNO KATZ, who served in the 51st Battalion of Givati Brigade (in the south and the Negev) Mar. 1, 1948–May 15, 1948, and thereafter in the Alexandroni Brigade (34th Battalion), in the central sector, mentions one action at Hill 69 (near kibbutz Nitzanim, south of Ashdod) in which 30 Israelis and 6 volunteers were involved.

D. GLASSMAN[4] served in Taas March 1948–Oct. 1948, and at kibbutz Haterim, in a military framework, Nov. 1948–June 1949. "Taas" is taken from the first word of "Taasit Neshek Tzvait"—Manufacture of Military Weapons. He writes, "I was involved in many forms of military production but mainly in the development and production of the Dror light submachine gun, which was the forerunner of the Uzi. . . ."

REUBEN E. GROSS served in the Israeli Air Force (Tel Aviv and Jaffa) from 11/48 to 3/49, and "Supplied radio link between USA and TA from March to Sept. 1947." As a licensed amateur radio operator (generally referred to as a "ham"), his Staten Island home radio was a natural—and most important— direct link with Tel Aviv. Unfortunately, after some time those in charge decided to use a virtually unbreakable OSS-type code, which necessarily advertised itself as a code. This led to FCC-FBI investigation, and to the total loss of this channel of communication, via suspension of Gross's license. (See Slater, *Pledge*, pp. 108–113.)

SHLOMO SOKOL writes: "I left the States in December (1947) and was in the framework of Hagana in France. Camp St. Jerome in Marseilles. Operation: Military training of new immigrants." Involved were one or two Israelis and "several tens" of overseas volunteers. He states that the (training) operation could not have succeeded without the overseas volunteers, and mentions that Israelis were in over-all charge.

JULES DONESON (YOCHANON DANON) states that he served in the 71st Battalion (Galilee) from July 1948 to May 1949, that he was the only volunteer in his unit, and not of vital importance there.

SAMUEL E. ALEXANDER, who served from March 1948 to May 1949, and was in a number of actions from Central Galilee to the Negev, writes: "I was always with Israelis. The various units I was in were Hagana units made into Zahal. Most of my buddies were from kibbutzim . . . In all of my experience with Hagana and Zahal we had no more than 5 Americans around at one time. . . ." Volunteers were not of decisive importance in any of the direct actions in which he participated.

RALPH ANSPACH, who served on a refugee ship, and then in the Anti-Tank Battalion in the Negev from Operation Ten Plagues through the taking of Eilat, writes that his battalion was such a minor part of the total forces involved that the operations could have succeeded without the volunteers, or without an equal number of Israelis.

TOM TUGEND, who also served in the Anti-Tank Battalion in the Negev (4th Anti-Tank Unit) Sept. '48—June '49, writes: "I served in an Anglo-Saxon[5] unit, so there was no Israel-Mahal mix within the unit. The two operations above (Faluja pocket and the taking of Eilat) were many-pronged, and I have no real idea how many other units were involved and their composition. My overall opinion on your basic point: Mahalniks made a major contribution to the Air Force. In the other services, their real contribution was minimal."

MORRIS SWARTZ, who served in the 8th Brigade, 82 Regiment, writes: "I was in the first tank brigade of the Israel Army. We had two Cromwells and one Sherman—we were all 'Anglo-Saxon's[5] a term not of our manufacture. The men in our group were made up in the beginning of four Canadian Jews, two South African Jews, two English Jews, and get this, nine English army deserters of the Christian faith. As to our performance in the 48 war, I would refer you to . . . the part played in it by the 82 regiment led by Colonel (now deceased) Yizhak Lador. . . . We were in every major action from the first day of the fighting, till the last day . . . there were no 'Israelis' at that time in the tanks, except for the top brass."

JOE FELDMAN, who also served in the 8th Brigade (Armored) from Nov. 1948 to May 1949, writes: "A great number of the 8th Brigade was composed of 'Mahal'. The 8th Brigade was in operation about June 1948 onwards." He adds, "The War of Independence in 1948–1949 was a fight against overwhelming numbers of Arab troops. Every man made a difference. . . ."

BEN OCOPNICK, who served in all branches, advises concerning his direct experiences: He served in Aliya Bet November '46–March '47; with reference to one ship, the "Chaim Arlosoroff" (Ulua) he states that its crew included 25 volunteers and 6 Israelis, and could not have functioned without the volunteers. April to June 1948 he served in the Givati Brigade. Referring to the 3 major attacks on Latrun (all of which failed) and the opening of the road to Jerusalem, he indicates participation by 400 Israelis and 35 volunteers; the volunteers were not crucial. He served in the Navy from June to August, participating in the shelling of Tyre (Lebanon) by the Israeli corvette "Wedgewood". 80 Israelis and 15 volunteers were involved; the volunteers were not crucial. From September 1948 to April 1949, he served in the Air Force (flying control); while he does not recall numbers, he states that this could not have succeeded without the volunteers. With reference to the shooting down of an Arab bomber (date not given), he states that this could not have succeeded without the volunteers.

DAVID BAUM, who served on an Aliya Bet ship ("Hagana") from April to August 1946, and in the Israel Navy May 1948–May 1950, writes: "Served as engineering officer on the corvettes and frigates. Participated in patroling and bombardment of installations from Tzor (Tyre) to El-Arish. Crew was about ½ Israelis and ½ overseas members. Israelis probably could have operated the ships alone but much less rapidly."

I. MELTZER, whose service was similiar (Aliyah Bet, June '47–June '48, Israeli Navy, June '48–October '48) writes, with reference to his Aliya Bet experience, that 45 volunteers and 4 Israelis were involved; that it could not have succeeded without the volunteers. He adds: "Was part of a group, under Major Stan Pilzer of Washington, D.C., who tried to establish, organize and train an Israeli Marine Corps."

ISIDOR RABINOVICH, another Aliya Bet veteran (April–November, 1947) writes concerning the "Northland" (Medinat Hayhudim), which transported 2,600 Romanians and was intercepted by the British, with all being transferred to internment on Cyprus, without loss of life. The crew consisted of 4 Israelis and approximately 20 (unpaid) Americans. He states: "Our ship could have been brought to Europe (from Baltimore) by an all-pro crew who might then have been flown back to the States and a second team of paid continental sailors taken on (indeed a half-dozen officers and crew were exchanged in this fashion). But a paid crew would have been less tractable, more devious (one (hired) Second Mate—absconded with a sum of money; (another)—Second Engineer—had bluffed his way and had to be replaced by one of our untrained, but capable, volunteers. And our presence was a tonic to the passengers . . ."

ELIHU BERGMAN, who served in Aliyah Bet from April '47–April '48, including embarkation preparations, time in detention camps, etc., advises concerning the

"Geula" (Paducah), with which he was connected April–November 1947, whose crew consisted of 3 Israelis and 30 volunteers, "A U.S.-originated ship. The volunteer crew was not critical. Could have been manned by a contract crew." Concerning the "Tirat Zvi" (Vivara) which went from Italy to Palestine March–April 1948, whose crew included 4 Israelis and 2 volunteers, he says, "This ship was manned by an Italian contract crew. The Haganah personnel were supervisory."

S. FINARD, who served with the "Headquarters—Organization" of the Navy in Haifa from April '49 to August '50, states that 15–20 volunteers were involved with him, and that the work he was engaged in could not have succeeded without the volunteers.

AARON LEBOW, who served primarily in Aliya Bet from February '47 to Nov. '48, details his service as follows: "Medinat Hayhudim", 3 Israelis, 27 volunteers; 7 months in Italy, 50 Israelis, 2 volunteers; "Monte Chiarro", 2 Israelis, 1 volunteer; "Pan York", 25 Israelis, 5 volunteers; patrol boat, 15 Israelis, 1 volunteer. He says that every one of these operations could have succeeded without the volunteers. He adds, "On the above ships many French and Italian (and Spanish Loyalist-exile) seamen were employed. In Italy many refugees worked with the Palmach. Italians were commonly employed for special jobs. Americans were rare, and usually lasted only a few weeks."

ELI FREUNDLICH, who served with Aliya Bet beginning December 1946, with IZL (Tel Aviv Section) from February to July 1948, and in the Air Force July 1948 to July 1949 (Tel Aviv Airfield), writes concerning each: "Aliya Bet was manned almost exclusively by non-Israelis. Irgun: There were very, very few overseas volunteers actively serving with the Irgun. Air Force— There would not have been one without Mahal."

DAVID MACAROV, who was involved in ship procurement in New York, September 1946–May 1947, with Chim and Chish (Hagana garrison and field forces) Nov. 1947–June 1948, and with the Air Force June 1948–May 1949, writes: "I cannot divide my participation by operations, but if I had not worked in the ship procurement area in New York, some other American would have been found, and not necessarily someone planning on aliyah. On the other hand, the Israeli Air Force was heavily dependent on Mahal, and the section which I headed could not have worked in English, as it did and had to, without me. I was, in fact, practically indispensible, not because of being an American, but because the skill which I possessed was known to be possessed (in English) by only one other person in the country, and he physically could not hold the equivalent job in the Army, Navy, and Air Force simultaneously, as he tried to do."

MILTON SACKIN, who served in the Air Force June '48 to June '49 details two operations[6] (radar station near Gaza—20 Israelis, 5 volunteers; radar station near Gedera—30 Israelis, 3 volunteers) and states that the operations could not have succeeded without the volunteers. He adds, "In the specific areas I observed, the contribution was mainly to morale rather than any significant physical help. From speaking to other people the overall feeling is that except for pilots and airplane maintenance, this was equally true in most places."

The following deal primarily with the Air Force.

HAROLD KATES, who served as an Air Force mechanic at Sarona repair depot (near Tel Aviv), Herzlia (101 Fighter Squadron) and Ekron (Aqir), April–November 1948, writes only "In my view the skill and experience that was available was not fully utilized."

VICTOR PERRY, who served in the Air Force Training Command, July 1948–July 1949, writes that from August to December 1948, there were no Israelis and 8 to 10 volunteers among the instructors. In 1949, when he was director of the ground school for pilots, there were 3 to 4 Israeli instructors and 3 to 4 volunteer instructors (students, of course, were Israelis). He states that this operation could not have succeeded without the volunteers.

LOU LENART, the Flight Commander of the first mission of the IAF Fighter Command, which apparently was decisive in stopping the Egyptians at Isdud, May 29, 1948, writes that this operation (a bright night attack) could not have succeeded without the volunteers. The four ME 109 pilots were 2 volunteers and 2 Israelis. This volunteer served in Europe and Israel from April to November 1948.

SAM KATZ, who served at Ramat David July 1948–July 1949; at Ekron (Aqir) July '49–December '49, and in the training command until April '50, writes: "I served in all air operations during my stay there—my duties included flying supplies to the encircled kibbutzim during the truces, and using and flying our C-47's as bombers during the breaches of the truce. We also trained and checked out Israelis as flying personnel. There were few Israelis as pilot or co-pilot in the beginning—I can only remember Ben Porat (Pinia) who flew as co-pilot in the beginning (now deceased). Toward the end of my stay, we had several pilots and co-pilots who were Israelis. Named Black, Avisar, Yehuda Pupko. I can't remember all of the first names. I remember most of the pilots were from the United States with the rest split between South Africa and Canada. Israelis served with us as Bomb Chuckers, but most of the crew were volunteers."

MURRAY N. WEISBERG, who served 1948–1949 at Sde Dov (Tel Aviv), states that no Israeli participated in any of his missions, which could not have succeeded without volunteers. He adds: "Air Force and Air Transport—over 95% volunteers. I flew a Piper Cub or Beech-craft Bonanza or Aerovan. Continuous flights of our aircraft caused significant damage to the Arabs, and kept them from destroying our cities and military installations."

THEODORE J. STERN, who served at Tel Aviv, Dorot-Ruhamma, Yugoslavia, and Ekron (Aqir) from March '48–March '49, states specifically that perhaps 4 Israelis were involved in the ATC arms flights; most of the crews were volunteers; the operation could not have succeeded without the volunteers. "There just weren't enough trained Israeli flight crews." He adds: "Many of the overseas volunteers talked too much, complained too much and left without accomplishing anything. Their main effectiveness was in areas such as the Air Force, where specific technical skills were required. The Americans made the poorest showing and griped the most. The South Africans served well and willingly in all areas. Overseas volunteers were useful in Aliyah Bet also, mostly because they had passports and could travel fairly freely. Some were technically helpful, but most were not."

SAMUEL Z. KLAUSNER, who served with the Haganah in Jerusalem, March–May 1948, and in the Air Transport Command, May–September 1948, states that a Haganah action (in March) against an Arab village, which involved 80 Israelis and 2 volunteers, did not depend on the volunteers. But the air raid on Damascus, for which the crew was 5 volunteers, and the Czech air transport flights, all of which, in his experience, involved 5 man volunteer crews, could not have been accomplished without the volunteers.

JULIAN SWING, an ATC veteran, who served on the Czech airlift, May to August 1948, and at Aqir until January 1949 (on bombing missions and transport of troops and supplies to the Negev), estimates that perhaps 100 volunteers and 20 Israelis participated in the former, and perhaps 200 volunteers and 200 Israelis in the latter. He states that neither could have succeeded without the volunteers.

B. BRESSLOFF, who served in the 69 Squadron, at Ramat David and Ekron (Aqir) August 1948–October 1949, participating in "20 bombing missions against key Egyptian and (other) Arab targets such as Majdal, Faluja, El Arish, Rafa, Gaza, etc.," states: "As far as Air Operations were concerned, Mahal airmen made a significant contribution to the establishment of the Israel Air Force during the war and also by initiating the training of Israeli airmen."

JACK J. DOYLE, who served as a pilot in the Negev airlift from Aqir (Operation Dust), from September 10 to October 11, 1948, and as a fighter pilot in the 101 Fighter Squadron at Herzlia and Qastina October 14, 1948 to May 18, 1949, details six of his missions. In each of the first five, participants were 2 volunteers and no Israelis. Specific details include: October 21—1 Egyptian Spitfire destroyed, 2 damaged; December 27—trucks, armored cars and heavy guns strafed; December 28—in a fight with 8 Egyptian Fiat G 50s, 1 destroyed and 3 damaged; December 30—2 Egyptian Spits destroyed; January 1—dive-bombed RR and railway junction; cut RR.

The sixth action involved 6 volunteers and 2 Israelis. Details:

January 7, 1949—Air action—Rafah-Khan Yunis—4 Spits destroyed, 3 damaged.[7] He adds: "In the above summary I show that the operations could not have succeeded without overseas volunteers. All but 2 pilots on the Squadron were Jewish and Gentile overseas volunteers. The same held true for supply squadrons (excepting Piper Cubs) and bombing squadrons. 75% of the technical ground personnel were the same, overseas volunteers. This summary deals only with the air war, that I participated in, but it held true when it came to artillery and heavy weapons. In my view, without the experts from overseas, there would have been a much different war. The highly trained pilots, artillerymen, sailors, etc., made the difference. This was shown in the 2 past campaigns."

EUGENE BLUM, who served in the Meteorological Section of the Air Force from August 1948 to November 1949, at Ramat David, Ekron (Aqir), and at Ariel (H. Q.) writes:

"Most of the operations from the bomber and supply bases were by former members of the U.S. Air Force, British Royal Air Force, Canadian Royal Air Force, South African Air Force. There were also some crew members and mechanics from the Australian Royal Air Force and, two pilots from the Indian Royal Air Force. These two Indian pilots, in spite of their names, Abe Nathan and Abe Cohen, were as Indian as Nehru or Gandhi.

"There were very few members of the Bombing or Supply section of the Israeli Air Force who were Israeli at that point. This represents: Pilots, navigators, bombardiers, and mechanics and armament technicians.

"The meterological division if I remember correctly had only two overseas volunteers, myself and Leo Krown (the organizer or head of the Meteorological section). Probably the bravest man I knew was Ted Gibson, pilot, son of a Florida minister. A man who flew supply missions to Sodom when others turned back, and later flew bombing attacks against the enemy while flying trainer planes with bombs attached to the wings. Ray Kurtz, who bombed Cairo, was another brave man. Was later killed transporting planes about 1950 or so."

ED KAPLANSKY, who was with Aliya Bet, on the "Northland" (*Medinat Hayehudim*) March–October 1947, and in the Air Force June 1948 to September 1949, estimates "100 plus" volunteers in the flying components of Air Force and about 25 Israelis. He further advises that 35 Flight, 103 Squadron, 101 Squadron, 106 Squadron, 69 Squadron and A.T.C. were "almost 100% Mahal aircrew (flying personnel)"; No. 1 Communications Flight—"almost 100% Israeli pilots." He adds:

"Israel Air Force in the flying department, consisted mainly of Mahal types. The numbers I cite above are strictly for air crew. Without Mahal Israel would not have had an effective air force in 1948. In all other areas, the contribution by overseas volunteers, although significant, was nowhere near as important or as crucial as in the air force. All other services would have functioned anyhow with or without Mahal types. This opinion is based on my own experiences as an operational I.A.F. pilot, and as a crew member of the Haganah ship Northland."

He continues furnishing details on the various flying units:

"35 Flight. In 1948 commanded by the late Theodore H. Gibson, Jr. of Miami, did both transport work with Norseman aircraft and dive bombing with Harvard (A.T. 6) Trainers. Total complement of pilots during my stay was 9, all foreign volunteers. This outfit disbanded after War of Independence.

"103 Squadron. In 1948—transport squadron using Dakota (DC-3 or C-47) aircraft—until the fall of '48 exclusively foreign aircrew. This outfit still exists.

"101 Fighter Squadron. In '48 had 2 Israelis, Mordecai Alon, its C.O. was killed during the summer of '48, and Ezer Weizman, Chaim's nephew, who was O.C. 101 during 1956 Sinai Campaign and later O.C. I.A.F. and now deputy to the C.I.C. All other pilots were foreigners, many Canadians. 101 still exists.

"106 Transport Squadron. Had C-46 aircraft—outgrowth of Air Transport Command; mostly foreigners, many Swedes. This outfit existed during 1949 only and was later integrated into *103*.

"69 Heavy Bomber Squadron (also called the "Hammer" Squadron). B-17 aircraft. Only 1 Israeli former RAF pilot (Jack Ratushnick who suffered persecution because of his I.Z.L. background); all other aircrew were mostly from the U.S.A. This outfit has been disbanded.

"A.T.C. (Air Transport Command). With C-46s mainly transported equipment from Europe. Mainly from Czechoslovakia—This whole outfit was almost exclusively foreign."

II. Correspondence with Key Israelis

1) A reply (received September 1966) to a series of questions, by Lt. Col. Gershon Rivlin, Editor-in-Chief of "Maarahot," the Israeli army publishing house.

1. Q.: When was the first Israeli checked out for flying transport planes, and when and where was the first operational flight made with an Israeli as the chief pilot (of a transport)?
   A.: No records available.
2. Q.: Could the flights from Zatec have gotten under way at all without non-Israeli personnel?
   A.: Would have been very difficult, but under the compulsion of "sheer necessity even impossible" performances are possible.
3. Q.: Could the training school for Israeli pilots and air crew at Zatec have gotten under way at all without non-Israeli personnel?
   A.: The training schools were not at Zatec but at Olomuc and Hradec-Kralove. The school had been run by Czechs only. Assistant trainers were also Americans.
4. Q.: Without this "school," what is the earliest likely date that an effective school could have functioned to turn out personnel able to operate modern (late World War II vintage) fighters and transports (as opposed to the California school, which apparently produced light-plane pilots only)?
   A.: As a matter of fact the training of aircrew in Israel was continued upon the closing down of the facilities in Czechoslovakia at the end of 1948. This could have been done earlier if need arose. Israeli pilots started to train in the training bases at the end of 1948 or early 1949.

5. Q.: With regard to the Negev airlift (Aqir-Ruhamma, Aug. 17 to mid Oct. 1948), how many of the 417 flights were captained (chief pilot) by Israelis, and how many by non-Israelis?

   A.: No detailed records available. But mixed crews were cooperating Some captains were Israelis.

6. Q.: For the following, information by periods would be appreciated (Periods: Before May 15, 1948; May 15–June 6; June 6– July 9 July 9–18; Oct. 15–22; Dec. 22–Jan. 8, 1949): Also, (July 18–Oct 15); (Oct. 22–Dec. 22).

   The number of Israelis, and the number of non-Israelis as flying personnel in (a) fighter-plane sorties; (b) bombing missions; (c) supply and rescue missions inside Israel; (d) supply missions from outside Israel. Where crews were mixed, how many missions were captained by Israelis? How was the numerical strength of the armed forces divided, at the close of each of the above periods, between Israeli and non-Israelis? (In the latter, I include *all* Gahal and Mahal, regardless of official status.)

   A.: Generally, before the 15 May 1948, Israeli aircrew outnumbered non-Israeli flying personnel. After that date the relative strength changed No data are available as to their relative participation in operations.

7. Q.: Lorch and Ben-Gurion[9] both write that "Nahshon" would have been called off had Balak I (the first transport from Zatec) not landed the night of March 31/April 1. Can this be documented?

   A.: I think this is wrong. The "Nahshon" Brigade was assembled without depending on this transport. Luckily the first Balak arrived a night before the move.

8. Q.: What documentation is there to specifically evaluate the importance of the work of Mickey Marcus (with particular emphasis on staff work, logistics, and planning)?

   A.: Only what people say in their memoirs or tributes.

2) In a later letter (March 13, 1968) Col. Rivlin writes in part:

". . . No. 1 Squadron (light planes) was the main operational formation before the 15/5/48, and the pilots were quite all of them Palestinian (graduated of "Aviron" Co. or the Palmach and ex-RAF men). The arrival of the Mahal in greater numbers was after the 15/5/48 when was possible politically and when fighting and cargo planes were brought, and experienced crews were needed.

"The part of the Mahal crews in "AIN" (Operation Horev, the final Negev campaign) and "AVAK" (Operation Dust) operations are estimated by the Air Force about 50% of the whole force."

3) We quote at length from a letter (21 March 1968) from Ambassador (to Britain) Aharon Remez, who in 1948 was Officer Commanding the Air Force:

". . . For the purpose of historical accuracy, I cannot confirm that no Israeli pilots were capable of flying "Balak I." At the time, there were a number of Israeli pilots in the service of the Air Force with adequate experience. However, they were engaged in several other assignments. The decisions as to who should fly this particular operation were not taken on the grounds of whether or not there were Israelis who could do it, but rather out of consideration for the most efficient operation possible under circumstances where the very few Israelis had to be charged with responsible duties in many other places and operations under way at the same time. I could think, off hand, of at least four or five Israelis who had the necessary experience (Hayman Shamir, Gedda Schochat, Zur, Cooperman, Brier and others). However, as stated before, they were carrying out duties which could not very easily be assigned to Mahal volunteers.

"Nevertheless, it would be perfectly correct to state that there were not enough Israeli pilots, trained in the flying of multi-engine heavy transports, to carry out the almost unceasing runs during that period from European ports to Israel and back, and the operation of flying to Israel of the B-17 bombers and other medium transports (C-46's, etc.). Only with the assistance of the Mahal volunteers and hired pilots could we maintain the intensity of these operations. As a matter of fact, Mr. Ami Cooperman, who was then in charge of operations at the Air Force Headquarters in Israel, was sent to Europe to join the crew that flew in "Balak I" on 31 March."

Our comment, which takes issue with some of the above, will be found in chapter nineteen.

Appendix F

How many volunteers were there?

The number will never be accurately known. One might think that Army records would be most useful. But individual data and army unit data in the Zahal archives, never included identification of overseas volunteers as such! The next place to turn would be the rosters of the various Mahal clubs. Since these clubs supplemented the volunteer's meager Army pay (2 Israeli pounds per month, with the Israeli pound then worth less than $4) on the basis of established volunteer status, it would be a rare volunteer who did not enroll—but no Mahal club records are currently in existence. Thus, we are forced to turn to less direct sources.

One serious investigator states:

> Mahal numbered some 5,300 volunteers, whose largest single contingent was made up of roughly 1,770 Americans. (To arrive at these figures, we were again compelled to reconcile several divergent records which nobody, knowing the circumstances of their compilation in '48, can expect to be precise.) Unlike their predecessors of 1917, American Mahal fought on all fronts in all three arms of Israel's Defense Forces. Several Israel Army units were made up almost entirely of English-speaking volunteers, particularly in the Air Force, where English remained for many years the *lingua franca* of command. One brigade alone suffered seventy-two battle casualties, with the abnormally high rate of 30% of all her officers wounded or killed in action.[1]

The figures in another source are quite different. Quoting those then fixed as minimum figures by "the man in charge of Mahal personnel," the total is given as

> ...approximately 2,400. These include more than 500 from France, more than 500 from England, more than 300 from South Africa, more than 300 from the United States, and the balance from Latin America, Canada, Scandinavia, and the other countries of the world.[2]

These figures are radically different: The first total is more than twice

234

that of the other, with almost six times as many Americans estimated. But the low figures are identified as *minimum* reliable numbers; later, we shall see the current best estimate, not the *minimum* reliable figure, which the official Army history chose to record, given by Akiva Skidell, the very man referred to as its authority by the Army history. Let us first investigate another source.

A thorough study was made by Shahan. Through one channel of interview and estimate, he arrives at a total of 1,500 Americans (including those who served on the refugee ships)—quite close to Lapide's figure. Taking another approach, adding the aircrews (310) and ground personnel (mechanics, etc.) presumed to be Americans, he got a total of 467 which he rounds off to 500, and suggests adding about 250 (for turnover, etc.) making 750. If we assume that an equal number of Americans served in all other units (a rather arbitrary assumption), we have support for his figure of 1,500 Americans.

Shahan also gives us a table which he put together from study of the individual record cards of all Mahal *specialists* in the Military Archives. Actual figures in the table show a total of 661 (247 Americans, 143 South Africans, 109 English, 60 Canadians, 21 Swedes, 18 Frenchmen, 63 others).[3] While this table appears to be complete, we must recognize that it covers only a very limited group: Those whom Zahal wished to retain as specialists, *after* January 1949. With regard to this group, we quote from Akiva Skidell's letter to the writer (April 25, 1968):

> The separation of the volunteers into those who would be discharged from the Army (and repatriated if they so wished) and those who would be retained under special contract began at about the time of the formulation of the Mahal definition, i.e., in February, 1949. As I recall, it took a good few months—perhaps until June or July—to straighten it all out, to complete all negotiations and to sign up those who were to be signed up. In some cases, of course, it was a matter of continuing, or revising, of regularizing, the various and sundry arrangements which had been in effect prior to this date. All this involved primarily the Air Force—there might have been perhaps 10% Navy personnel and just a few Army people. The total number of paid experts (who were nevertheless volunteers in a sense—some, though not all, might have made more money elsewhere, but would probably have had less fun) must have been in the vicinity of 400-500. At a later stage, when some of these boys went home, other experts were brought in from abroad into the Air Force, but that was after my time, and these were strictly professionals.

Since Shahan's tabled total of 661 must include these post-fighting "professionals," whom we exclude from our definition of volunteers, we have effective corroboration for Skidell's remembered figure of 400 to 500 Mahal volunteer *specialists* serving *after* January 1949.

Thus, these figures are of no real value in arriving at a reliable estimate of the total number of skilled, moderately skilled, and unskilled Mahal who served during the war. What these figures do establish, however, is the value that Zahal placed on the skills of these specialists. With the fighting war apparently over (a possibility of resumption of hostilities with Syria remained—this did not materialize until 1967), with funds in seriously short supply (Israel did not own a single jet fighter; its radar equipment was primitive, and generally unsuited to the demands made of it; the Navy was making do with overage, underarmed corvettes as its heavy warships), Zahal gave priority to retention of several hundred Mahal specialists!

Let us return to the question of total numbers. Quoting further from Skidell's letter of April 25, 1968 to the writer:

> I am afraid I can't help you with figures, certainly not by period. I doubt very much if such figures are available. You must remember that things were in a state of chaos—no one kept any count of anything much. I doubt whether there are even figures on the size of the Army—I have never seen any, and perhaps they are not yet made public. As to Mahal, it wasn't very clear who was Mahal and who was not—there was no standard definition until February '49 when some kind of compromise definition was laid down retroactively, in order to get out of the mess of claims upon the Army—not all well-founded—for financing the return home. An attempt at a count of Mahal was made only as late as June, 1949, but clearly the large majority of Mahal had by then returned, or had left the Army and remained in the country, and wasn't included in the count. So figures here are very tricky. I can only give a very rough estimate: 1500 from the U.S. and Canada, 1500 from England, 1000 from South Africa, 500 from France, another 500 from other European countries—Holland, Belgium, Italy, Switzerland, Scandinavia. Denmark alone, I recall, had 40 volunteers of a Jewish population of 7000,[4] the highest relative number, and some 600 from Latin America. (These figures total 5,600.)

In prolonged conversation with Akiva Skidell (at Kfar Blum, summer of 1968), we reviewed the official definition of Mahal,[5] and agreed that for purposes of this work it needed broadening to include such categories as, for example, university students who served with the Haganah or IZL or Aliya Bet after 11/29/47, but never joined the Army, which could not come into existence until after 5/15/48; mechanics who may have served entirely outside of Israel (e.g., some of those at Zatec and Titograd); those few killed in accidents en route to Israel; ATC volunteers who may have insisted on remaining outside the Army framework, and discontinued service prior to February, 1949. The basic definition we adopted in the Introduction does include all such categories.

The problem of total numbers was discussed in depth. Recognizing that the ATC, transport and bomber squadrons and mechanics were largely American, but remembering also the critical shortage of such personnel during the war, we could not justify a total for Americans in the Air Force greater than 500, amply allowing for turnover, with the feeling that a lower figure might be more nearly correct.[6] Although the number of Air Force personnel was a small fraction of the total of ground and sea personnel, and we would therefore generally expect to find many more times the number of volunteers outside the Air Force—it appears that this was uniquely not true in the case of the Americans.

The large size of the American Air Force in World War II, as well as its preponderance of medium and heavy bombers and transports, provided a large pool of men with just the kind of flying and maintenance experience needed so desperately by Israel. In addition, or perhaps, therefore, the recruiting efforts for the Air Force personnel were greatest in the United States. Finally, relatively many American non-Jews volunteered for flying duty from the United States. Thus, while the land-army to air-force ratio of other volunteers might be in the neighborhood of 5:1 or 10:1, it may perhaps be assumed that the ratio of Americans was about 1:1 (these ratio assumptions are arbitrary). Thus, 500 American Air Force volunteers would suggest another 500 American volunteers as those serving elsewhere, for a revised total of 1,000 in Zahal. (May the Canadians forgive us—as we use the word "American," it embraces the Canadians as well. No slight is intended; rather, there is an instinctive sense of identity. See Appendix H for an attempt to separate citizens of Canada from those of the United States, and American Jews from non-Jews.)

Then, as an estimate for all the categories of volunteers who did not serve directly in Zahal, we suggest the number of 300, for a grand total of 1300 Americans. While this is, indeed a "best estimate," properly to indicate its probable imprecision, I suggest plus or minus 100.

We now turn to a final source. Gideon Shimoni is a South African who had been engaged for many months in researching the fully detailed story of the South African volunteers when the writer met him in the summer of 1968 (first, at the Zahal Archives in Givatayim, north of Tel

Aviv; again, in Jerusalem). He estimated the total number of Americans (including Canadians) as 1,000, British as from 1,200 to 1,500, and South Africans between 800 and 1,000.

Shimoni's figures focus on those who served in Zahal, and do not include our "other categories" which must have been almost 100 percent American. For example, the Aliya Bet volunteer crews were American, and the aircraft mechanics in Europe were American. Thus, we add 300 "other category" Americans to his estimate, arriving at 1300, as we did with Skidell's adjusted figure, for which we extracted support from Shahan's data. (Lapide's 1770 seems to be distinctly too high.) The general impression was that the number of Americans, British, and South Africans serving in Zahal was roughly equal, basically corroborating Shimoni's and Skidell's figures. Now, taking the minimum and maximum in Shimoni's figures and Skiddell's figures as adjusted by our discussion above, and adding the "other categories," we total 3200 as a probable low figure for English-speaking volunteers, and 3900[7] as a probable high. To this we add Skidell's 1000 from continental Western Europe and 600 from Latin America, with an arbitrary plus or minus 100 for each—giving a minimum total of 4600, and a maximum total of 5700 (actually, not very far from Lapide's total of 5300).

Our conclusion: There is a high degree of probability that the total number of Mahal-style overseas volunteers was somewhere between 4700 and 5600.

The number of volunteers was not constant: Aliyah Bet, which for our purpose may be considered as beginning in 1946, was phased out of existence during 1948. Following the pattern of 1946 and 1947, many volunteers made one or two trips, and then moved on—to private life in the States (sometimes including fund-raising), to settlement in Israel (Palestine) or, in 1948, to serve in the Navy or some other branch of Zahal.

Early in 1948, new volunteers were a trickle; the influx reached major proportions in the spring, continuing into the early summer. By late summer and autumn, the trend was reversed, with many volunteers leaving. As 1948 drew to a close (and on into 1949 and beyond), the thrust of overseas recruiting shifted from military specialists who would perform in the field, to instructors in military specialties (retaining the Mahal designation), just as, earlier, emphasis had shifted from mass recruiting to military specialists. Throughout this transition period, a core of volunteers remained in Zahal's various branches—some leaving Israel and Zahal later, others remaining for a military or civilian career. Postwar Mahal clearly played an important role as instructors, turning Israelis into specialists,[8] but this is outside the range of our basic investigation of the wartime participation of overseas volunteers.

Since we concluded above that the grand total of *all* volunteers was probably a bit above 5,000 plus or minus several hundred, there is little likelihood that the peak number at any one time could have exceeded 4,000. Zahal numbered 49,000 at the beginning of the First Truce (June 11), and about 60,000 at its end (July 9). It is likely that this is the period of service of the maximum number of volunteers. Thus, we have a strong presumption that the absolute number of volunteers never exceeded 8 percent of the total under arms.

Eight percent or less, uniformly distributed, is hardly quantitatively impressive. But relatively small numbers, concentrated in particular units or particular areas or specialties, may be most important. Thus we saw earlier that it is unlikely that either IZL or Palmach exceeded 3,000 each, yet many impartial observers credit IZL with a major share of responsibility for driving the British out; and the Palmach is universally credited with a fighting effectiveness out of all proportion to its numbers.

Earlier, we saw that a few volunteers were widely scattered, so that virtually no major force was totally without volunteers. At the same time, we did find major concentrations of volunteers, and especially volunteer specialists, in a few specific services: the Air Force, radar, the Navy, the 7th Brigade, the armored corps (8th Brigade—identified by one source as 10th Brigade), and the medical corps. In summation, Lorch writes: "Numerically Mahal's contribution to the Medical Corps was considerable, but here, too their impact transcended their numbers."[9]

The importance of the concentrations of volunteers was discussed earlier.

Appendix G

WHY SO FEW AMERICANS?

As the country with by far the highest Jewish population in the world, America is of special importance and interest.

In Appendix F we concluded that the total number of English-speaking volunteers was probably between 3,200 and 3,900. Of these, perhaps 25 to 30 percent were South Africans; about one-third Americans (and Canadians); about one-third were British, with a small scattering from elsewhere in the British Empire. Thus, the absolute number of American volunteers was on the same order as the number of Englishmen and of South Africans—which means, unavoidably, that the ratio of American Jewish volunteers to the American Jewish population was many times lower than from any other major English-speaking country.

At that time, the world Jewish population was divided approximately as follows:

Europe—3,779,300. This included 2 million in the Soviet Union, with the population of some of the other European countries: Czechoslovakia, 42,000; Yugoslavia, 10,000; France, 235,000; Finland, 1,800; Denmark, 5,500; England, 345,000; Irish Free State, 4,500.

The Jewish population of Asia, excluding Israel, was 280,000 (including 30,000 in India and Pakistan). The total figure for Africa was 745,500 including, among others, Morocco, 286,000; Algeria 130,000; Southern Rhodesia 3,500; Union of South Africa 100,000. For Australia the figure was 37,000, and for New Zealand 3,500.

In the Americas, we have Canada 180,000; U.S. 5,000,000; and all of Latin America 597,800 (including, among others, Argentina 360,000; Brazil 110,750; Cuba 10,000).[1]

From Western Europe, one would expect a high level of participation on the part of those who had had military experience (it has been suggested that the proportion of Jews in the Maquis—the French underground—was as high as 20 percent). However, a mitigating factor might well be a sense of war weariness on the part of many of those who had suffered the years of Nazi occupation. Furthermore, it was already several years after liberation and enough time had gone by so that most of those who were native to Western Europe had put down roots both economically

240

and in terms of families. And some activists would be expected to get involved in semi-underground activities on behalf of Israel. Thus, the estimate of 500[2] French volunteers (presumably including a very few middle-class North Africans—e.g., from Algeria—who had Mahal status as citizens of France) out of a total population of 235,000 is about one-fifth of one percent.

The South African participation was significantly higher: close to 1,000 volunteers out of a population of 100,000—or very close to one percent. It appears that several factors combined to promote this high level of participation. While the European undergrounds had done their fighting in their own countries and often rather close to the participants' actual home areas, for South Africans and the balance of the English-speaking world, it was normal to do one's World War II fighting far from home. In addition, a great many South Africans had served in or near Palestine during and after World War II; thus it was a familiar area which had had a chance to involve them in an emotional and physical contact.

Then there was, and still exists, an extraordinarily strong sense of ethnic difference in South Africa. Not only is it a matter of blacks and coloreds and whites, but within the white community there is very strong awareness of difference in ethnic origin (Dutch as opposed to English), carried forward and reenforced in ideology, politics, and religion. Thus, there is an ongoing awareness of being a member of the Jewish community, of a very different order than is currently the case in the United States, for example. As a result, the South African Jewish community is organized and unified to a greater extent than any other, and the South African Zionist Federation has been a uniquely strong, healthy, unifying, community-wide organization.

Contiguous to the above is a sense of genuine peril; in simplified terms, the ruling majority white community is the Dutch apartheid-oriented group. The Jews stand at the opposite extreme, with the English in between. As a generalization, one may say that the Jewish community as a whole—for valid deep traditional reasons—symbolizes opposition to the degradation of one race by another; it is a small community, and a most visible and exposed community. Many have a feeling that South Africa is a time bomb which may not explode for a generation or two—or, which may go off at any time. Thus a strong thrust to prepare an alternative, i.e., the Jewish state, would be expected.

And then, purely on moral grounds, one would expect those who are young and mobile and hopelessly in the minority to want to leave a country where it is likely that many individual legal safeguards will soon be lost, and where the law of the land confirms and promotes second-class status for its nonwhite citizens. Psychologically and ideologically, Palestine had been close to Jewish South Africans. Thus an extraordinary combination of factors including physical experience, rising peril at home, and psychological and ideological proximity combined to create extraordinarily high participation by South Africans.

Participation of 1,200 to 1,500 Englishmen out of a total population of 345,000 is about one-third to one-half the ratio of South African participation. This is quite impressive when we recognize that some of the elements making for the high South African participation were unique to that country. On the one hand, this might raise a bit of a question in our minds as to the reliability of the indicated extent of British participation. On the other hand, some of the positive factors were the same (i.e., World War II service in or near Palestine), and there were two factors uniquely British that may have spurred participation: 1) The extent of economic difficulty and drabness in post-World War II Britain, as a subconscious factor; 2) a special urge on the part of sensitive young people to feel it their special responsibility to correct the perilous situation in Palestine which *their* government was responsible for creating.

For all of Latin America, the indicated volunteer participation is 600 out of a Jewish population of approximately 600,000. This is about one-tenth the ratio of South African participation, and is quite reasonable: Although there is a strong sense of Jewish community in Latin American countries (parallel in some ways to that of South Africa) and, on the part of some, a sense of impermanence since a substantial proportion were of the generation that fled Europe, by and large, Latin American Jewish communities are not quite as organized as the South African community; the psychological distance to Palestine was much greater; and the experience of having served in the Middle East during the war, in fact, the experience of having served away from one's country in World War II altogether, was almost totally lacking.

The participation from the United States was, in proportionate terms, one-fifth that of Latin America and one-fiftieth that of South Africa. That is, adjusting the total figure of 1300 to eliminate both Canadians and the high percentage of non-Jews in the air force,[3] we are left with perhaps 1,000 on a population base of 5,000,000. This is shocking—particularly in view of the fact a large number of American Jews had had overseas military service during World War II. Furthermore, intensive recruiting was done in the United States, and special financial arrangments were made with many of the aircrew. Thus, the proportion of those who came forward without individual solicitation and persevered to serve in Israel, is even lower.

Let us examine this minute level of participation from another point of view, that of the total number of American Jews with military training. Sixteen million Americans passed through the armed forces during World War II; assuming that Jews were three percent of the population, and served in this proportion, the number with some level of training would have been about 480,000. Or, if 16 million was 10 percent of a total American population of 160 million, about 10 percent of the total population saw some military service. In a Jewish population of five million, this would suggest 500,000 Jews. Actually, the definitive study of participation by American Jews in World War II gives the figure as 550,000.[4]

In the immediate aftermath of World War II, then, there were some 550,000 Jews in the United States with some level of military training. Of course, this potential should be reduced by the same factors that undoubtedly applied in all other countries. These would include those whose training and service had not really been military (e.g., clerks), those who were disabled, those who remained for a military career, those who were older, those who had begun to establish themselves economically and build families, and those who had resumed higher education and were fearful that if they interrupted they would not be able to resume, and so forth.

If all these factors—none of them unique to the United States—reduced the realistic potential manpower pool to perhaps 100,000, to find that only 1,000 actually went remains disturbing. It remains even more disturbing when we realize that a significant number of those who actually went (possibly on the order of 100) were between 17 and 20: that is, they were too young to have served in World War II, and had no military experience whatever. The number is so small that it unavoidably brings into question the efficacy of the Zionist movement. We use "Zionist" in its commonly understood 1948 meaning: one who participates in a Zionist membership organization, agreeing with its aims and exposed to its direct influence.

Let us arbitrarily postulate that one percent of the Jewish population were hard core, ideologically committed Zionists. We would expect that the proportion of these idealists who had served in World War II, would be at least as great as that in the general Jewish population, of whom 550,000 had served. This would mean that 5,500 committed Zionists or young people from committed Zionist families had some level of military training. From such a select group, we would expect a very high proportion of volunteers (and, our postulated figure of one per cent committed Zionists may well be several times too low)—yet, not more than 1,000 served altogether, and the majority of these were without any formal Zionist background.[5]

Some factors that have been suggested to explain the low rate of American participation are: assimilation into the national American mainstream to a distinctly greater extent than in the other Western countries; a lack of serious personal identification with the Holocaust or with Palestine; compounding this, a deep sense of personal security in the U.S.; poor Jewish education; the State Department travel ban. All but the last, to some extent could fall under the heading, "a lack of Zionist orientation."

As for the low rate of Zionist participation among the volunteers, Jessie Zel Lurie's statement that the ratio of Zionist volunteers was the same as the Zionist ratio in the total American Jewish population, appears to us to be reasonable.[6] There may be some mitigation in those youth-movement people who immigrated or served on the Aliya Bet ships in 1946 and 1947, except that we should assume that the former at least was equally true of all other Western countries. It is surprising that Zionist volunteer participation was not disproportionately high, particularly in view of the small total number. We can only conclude that the Zionist movement failed with its own members if it meant to impart a sense of personal involvement.

The exception to the general picture of Zionist nonfunctioning lay with those Zionist organizations which, in predominantly middle-class American Jewry, should have been neglibly small but which, in terms of pragmatic action and personal participation in the War of Independence, were pertinent indeed. While the centrists focused on propaganda and fund raising (and propriety), the orientation of the groups both on the left and the right—particularly the youth groups—had been for the member's personal immigration (Aliyah) to Palestine.

Thus, ever since the end of World War II, small numbers of members of the youth groups of these organizations had been going to Palestine to settle or to serve in Aliya Bet. And so, it ought to have been a natural step for some youth-movement people still in the United States, to volunteer for service in Israel during the War of Independence. (Although no data exists, it is not unlikely that the small total of Zionist volunteers was roughly equally divided among the narrow-based right and left groups and the broad-based center.) And those who did not serve in Israel, took the lead in assuming other kinds of serious risks. Thus, the 1948 foreman of Inland Machinery, whose "business" was the careful crating of embargoed war materials for smuggling to Israel, was Yaakov (Jack) Dorfman, a warm, strong, dedicated American leader of Hashomer Hatzair, a left-wing youth organization. Out of a work force on the order of a dozen men, two or three were also members of Hashomer Hatzair. The others, all deeply dedicated, came without any formal Zionist organization background.[7]

As we saw in chapter nine, the American supply network was quite extensive—and so, a few of those who might have otherwise have served in Mahal may, quite rightly, have felt that what they were doing in the United States actually was a more constructive contribution. In addition, there was one uniquely American deterrent: The passport-citizenship question.

While British citizenship cannot be lost under any circumstances, American citizenship can be lost quite readily. Thus, in the first parliamentary election in Israel early in 1949, Americans were warned not to vote lest they lose their citizenship and, in contrast, English citizens were publicly encouraged to vote with no risk whatever to their English citizenship.

At this time, the wording of the American Neutrality Act was ambiguous, so that there was a distinct possibility that those who served in a foreign army would be risking their American citizenship (to minimize this risk, Israel devised a special oath of allegiance, so that one would be serving "with" rather than "in" the Army of Israel; it later turned out that no one lost his American citizenship as a result of such service).

To add genuine difficulty to this uncertainty, in the spring of 1948 the State Department put a stop on the issuance of passports to individuals of military age who looked as though they might be intending to make their way to Palestine. Thus, the volunteer was required to put forth extra effort and use subterfuge (which may have not always been successful) to obtain a passport. And readiness to go without a passport required an extra level of commitment—there was the implication, which turned out to be untrue, that leaving the country without a passport might threaten one's citizenship. Some individuals who came to Israel with American passports and then surrendered them to Israeli authorities with the thought that they might be able to make good use of them while the individual served in Israel, were unpleasantly surprised when Israeli bureaucrats refused to return the passports when these individuals later applied to return home. They were forced to apply for the same "laissez-passer" issued to individuals who had left the United States without any passport. (The writer was saved from this minor unpleasantness only because one flyer in our planeload of volunteers absolutely refused to surrender his passport: He had served with the Loyalists in Spain, and possession of the "little green book" (American passports were then green) had prevented his being massacred in the final Rebel breakthrough. (This was the only Spanish War veteran in Israel of whom the writer had any knowledge.)

And so, all of these reasons together—plus unreliable propaganda which, sometimes, would indicate that only highly skilled military specialists were wanted, and, at other times, that anyone with one good eye and the ability to pull a trigger was needed—plus American isolation, comfort, and psychological distance—perhaps give a rational explanation for the spectacularly low rate of participation of American volunteers in Israel's War of Independence.

Appendix H

HOW MANY OF THE AMERICANS
WERE JEWISH?

There had been on the order of 500 Americans, including Canadians, in the Air Force. The general impression of those who served was that the proportion of Canadians, and of non-Jews, in the Air Force was quite high. As noted in chapter nineteen, no reliable figures exist; however, an analysis of the Air Force casualties, while not statistically precise, is significant in giving a rough indication of the likely extent of service as aircrew by Canadians and by non-Jews.

Of the 21 volunteer flyers killed in the war,[1] 11 were from the United States, 5 from Canada, 4 from England and 1 from South Africa. These figures suggest that perhaps half of the flyers were from the United States, 25 percent from Canada, 20 percent from England, and five percent from South Africa. While these figures (particularly for the South Africans) may be off by a factor of two or even three—since the number of both Americans and Canadians is relatively high—the indicated ratio of about 4 Canadian flyers to every 10 American flyers should be taken seriously, recognizing that the actual ratio might be anywhere from 3 to 5 Canadians per 10 Americans.

In terms of religious origin, of the 21 fatalities, 7 were not Jews.[2] Of these, 1 was English, 2 Canadian, and 4 citizens of the United States. Thus, of the 11 aircrew fatalities from the United States, 7 were Jewish and 4 were Christian.

In other words, out of a total of 16 American and Canadian fatalities, 5 were Canadian (Jews and non-Jews), and 4 were non-Jews from the United States; that is, 9 of the 16 were not Jewish citizens of the United States. In this small sampling, just under half (7 out of 16) of those whom I classify broadly as Americans, actually were Jewish citizens of the United States! Projecting this directly onto my conclusion that about 500 American volunteers served in the Air Force, this would indicate that there is a high probability that only about half were actually Jewish citizens of the United States. The imprecision in such a small sampling suggests that the likely range was in the neighborhood of 200 to 300—perhaps a maximum of 300 Jews from the United States, and a minimum of 200 non-Jews and Canadians.

In Appendix F it is suggested that there likely were 800 Americans who served in all branches outside the Air Force; it would not appear unreasonable to suggest that on the order of 100 of these were Canadians[3].

Thus, subtracting an indicated minimum of 300 (200 air force plus 100 other branches) from the original American total of 1300, leaves 1000 as an apparent *maximum* for the total number of Jewish volunteers from the United States serving in all branches.

Appendix I

SUMMARY OF THE MAJOR FEDERAL COURT ACTIONS INVOLVING ALLEGED VIOLATIONS OF THE ARMS EMBARGO

Let us begin with four news items covering a little more than two weeks in July 1948. All are from the *New York Times.*

1) July 14: New York. "Watchful Government Officials" seized two Constellations belonging to Service Airways at the airport at Millville, New Jersey. These planes are thought to be linked to a mysterious B17 in Halifax. The officers of Service Airways are listed as Al Schwimmer, president, and Irwin Schindler, vice-president.

2) July 19: Tampico, Mexico. Police sought to trace a large arms shipment (including cannon and machine guns) which was discovered as it was being loaded on a ship. It was reported, without confirmation, that a Jewish group was shipping these arms to Palestine from the United States via Mexico. The ship is the *Kealos* (sic), of Panamanian registry, whose lifeboats carry the name Larranga. (The Marine registry lists the *Larranga* as a 3,804-ton freighter, out of New York, owned by the U.S. Maritime Commission.)

3) July 25: New York. Irwin Schindler was arrested by the F.B.I. on his return from the Azores on the Clipper, *Bold Eagle,* of Pan American World Airways. The warrant charges violation of Section 452, title 22 of U.S. Code, to "unlawfully, wilfully and knowingly export and attempt to export from U.S. to Nova Scotia an airplane, arms ammunition and implements of war listed in proclamation No. 2549, issued by the president of the United States April 9, 1942, and proclamation No. 2776, issued by the president of the United States on March 26, 1948, without having obtained a license therefore." What it specifically involved was a B17 which allegedly was flown from Westchester Airport to Halifax, where nine small arms were found on board (.45 caliber automatics and .38 German lugers). Of the nine men on the plane, two were found to be without passports, and they were transferred to Ellis Island for immigration clearance.

4) July 30: Camden, New Jersey. Federal District Judge Thomas Madden refused to dismiss a court order holding two four-engine Constellations at Millville Airport since July 13. These planes are owned by Service Airways. Assistant United States Attorney Groner Richmond Jr. charged that Service Airways (and Schwimmer, its president) are a "front for a Jewish organization seeking to send arms and airplanes" to Israel: That the plane was being prepared for flight to Prague and from Prague to Palestine in violation of a Presidential order.

Many months later—in mid-November—a federal grand jury in Miami, Florida, issued warrants for nine men, accused of being members of an international ring of smugglers which had been furnishing bombers and guns to the Israeli forces. Twenty-one others were named as co-conspirators, but would not be brought to trial. (It should be noted that "conspiracy" is a rather vague charge, and implies a paucity of direct evidence. It is generally used only when the government has a particular desire to "get" the accused.) The specific charges involved three B17s which had flown out of the country towards Palestine June 11th, 1948; also a Constellation which had crashed abroad after ten missions. In addition, arranging for the transportation of four A20 attack bombers which the Government had seized at Fort Lauderdale, Florida in August. Those for whom warrants were issued were Charles T. Winters, Adolph W. Schwimmer, Irwin R. Schindler, Abraham J. Levin, Leon Gardner, William Sosnow, Michael Kane, Leonard Burns, Irwin L. Johnson.[1]

January 21, Charles T. Winters admitted that he was guilty of conspiracy to export war planes (three B17s, one Constellation) to Palestine. Of the other accused, two (Irwin Schindler and Abe Levin) stated that they would plead in another federal district; three were regarded as being still at large in the United States, and three were presumed to be in Palestine. February 4, Charles Winters was sentenced to 18 months in Federal prison and fined $5,000. Judge Alfred Barksdale denied his petition to change his earlier plea of guilty to innocent. John S. Pratt, special assistant to the United States attorney general, told the court that the action of the defendants (exporting these planes to Zatec in June, in violation of the Munitions Export Control Act), "endangered the security of the United States and jeopardized the relations of this country in a way that is almost frightening."[2]

Irwin Schindler was most fortunate in that he came before an understanding judge in New York City. As reported by the *New York Times* of March 10, 1949, Irwin R. Schindler, 33-year old veteran of the Army

ATC, pleaded guilty to a conspiracy charge lodged against him last summer after he attempted to fly a B-17 bomber to Israel in violation of a presidential proclamation. Federal Judge Simon H. Rifkind suspended sentence, placing Schindler on probation for a year. He had faced a maximum penalty of two years in jail and a $10,000 fine. John S. Pratt, special assistant to the attorney general, had asked an 18-month sentence, since a similar term had been given in Florida to another participant in the incident. Judge Rifkind said that Schindler, who lives in Queens (a residential area of New York City) with his wife and two children, "manifestly" was "not the type of person who was preparing for a life on the wrong side of the law."

It is interesting to note that the government found it desirable to use the very same special prosecutor for the Miami and the New York cases.

During this same period, towards the end of November 1948, the New York and Eastern Trading Co. Ltd. of London and five individuals were fined a *total* of just 1,650 British pounds (about $6,600 then) for attempting to export 35 armored cars in violation of Britain's ban on the export of arms to the Middle East.[3] A British court had fixed a far lighter penalty than the Federal Court in Miami.

Individual judges may—and do—sometimes react very differently to people charged with the same offense. The American judiciary is, and should be, quite independent in this regard.

Thus, a resident of Asbury Park, New Jersey, who was involved in transporting part of a lot of 200 tons of war surplus M3 demolition blocks, had been released with a fine of $500 for "unlawful and improper storage" by Judge John C. Giordano who made it a point to express his sympathy. This took place in June 1948.[4]

As we noted elsewhere, the six men held responsible for the abortive attempt to ship large quantities of explosives on the *Executor,* were let off without even a fine upon their plea of guilty. Federal Judge Sylvester J. Ryan said: "You endeavored to provide means of defense to an otherwise defenseless people. I do not regard you as criminals. . . ."[5]

Government policy surely makes itself felt in the decision to ignore, or to bring to trial, individuals accused of violating certain laws. The effort that goes into investigation and apprehension, the kind of statutes that are invoked, and the intensity of the prosecution itself, are a matter of policy. Thus, although there was ongoing public pressure to overlook the offenses of those technically guilty of violating American law while assisting Israel, government prosecution continued. (For example, towards the end of July, Congressmen Fulton and Smathers offered a bill pardoning all violators of the American arms embargo. Although bills of this kind rarely stand any chance of passage, since what is involved is overt forgiveness for those who have broken the law, the very fact that they are proposed is a strong indication of public opinion. Still, the prosecutions continued.)

Oct. 25, 1949, nine months after the shooting war in Israel had stopped, three months after the last (Syrian) armistice agreement was signed, seven men were brought to trial in federal court in Los Angeles for conspiracy to violate the Neutrality Act, the Export Control Law, and Presidential Proclamation 2276, by unlicensed shipment of aircraft and engines (ten C-46s and one Constellation) to an embargoed Middle Eastern nation (Israel).[6] The defendants were Adolf W. (Al) Schwimmer, president of Service Airways (Service Airways was also charged), Ray Selk, Sam R. Lewis, Abe Levin, Leo Gardner, William Sosnow, Herman M. (Hank) Greenspun. The trial was lengthy, coming to an end in February 1950. The jury found three of the men (Sosnow, Lewis, and Greenspun) not guilty; three of the men (Schwimmer, Gardner, and Selk) were found guilty with a recommendation for leniency. They, and Service Airways, were fined $10,000 each for conspiracy to violate the Neutrality Act by smuggling planes and equipment from Florida to Israel in 1947 and 1948. Judge Peirson M. Hall was quoted by the *Times* as saying that this offense is "probably as serious as can be committed."[7]

We noted previously that the Czechs expressed keen interest in keeping the damaged Constellation at Zatec. Under no circumstances would Schwimmer permit this; the streamlined, triple-rudder Constellation was a most advanced aircraft. Appendix D points out that only 20 of them were delivered before the end of World War II. That is, it was essentially a post-war airplane which had become available through surplus channels only through the accidents of bureaucratic procedure. Had the damaged Constellation been abandoned behind the Iron Curtain, it might have given some vague semblance of support to the idea that the Communists were being technically benefited. Therefore, long after the closing down of Zatec in August 1948 and the final phasing out of all Czech operations following Velveta 2 at the end of 1948, repair work on the Constellation continued. Ernie Stehlik, an American expert mechanic with much specific experience on the Constellation, remained alone (of all the Americans) at Zatec through the winter, spring and summer of 1949. The fact that Stehlik was of Czech descent, and thus could communicate with the

Czech mechanics, made the situation bearable. The *New York Times* of September 19, 1949 reported a September 18th story from Paris to the effect that a Lockheed Constellation had arrived at Schiphol Airport, Amsterdam, a day earlier with only three of its four engines. Its markings were Lineas Aereas Panama, S.A.; its pilot, Sam Lewis, its copilot, Col. Harry Brown. The story went on to relate that this plane was one of four mysteriously acquired from air-force surplus two years earlier; the other three had been impounded by Federal authorities at Millville, New Jersey. Further, the story continued, this plane had lost one engine crash landing at Prague a year earlier; the KLM shops would install a new engine and then the plane would fly back to the United States with its pilot ready to defend himself in the trial described above. Subsequently, (Sept. 22) Sam Lewis denied an earlier *Times* report that he had "sneaked" this Constellation to the Azores. He stated that he had twice flown planes out of the United States, both times with proper clearance. The first was the flight of this Consellation from Newark to Panama March 13, 1948; then, a C46 form Los Angeles to Mexico April 14, 1948. The *Times* of November 2 reported that the federal court in Los Angeles had denied a move to dismiss the charges, and the trial proceeded as described above, with sentence handed down in February 1950.

Nor was this the end. In July 1950, a year after the final armistice agreement, three men were brought to trial before the same Federal Court in Los Angeles on the charge of "conspiracy" to violate the United States Neutrality Act. The substance of the charge this time was that these men had forced a yacht owner to accept a cargo of arms and ammunition in the Los Angeles area and to sail the yacht to Mexican waters where the cargo was transferred to another vessel for shipment to Israel. The three men were Herman M. (Hank) Greenspun, who had been found not guilty on an earlier charge; Lloyd Rosenbloom, and Lawrence C. Ives. At this point (according to Greenspun) Israel's strategists were fearful that another open trial would draw attention to the question of sources of funds for such operations with, possibly, a negative effect on current important fund raising. Therefore, it was urged that all plead guilty, it being understood that Greenspun alone would be sentenced. Greenspun sees the hand of Senator Pat McCarran of Nevada (a major target of Greenspun's Las Vegas newspaper) in this: He suggests that, if not the trial itself, then at least his being singled out for punishment, may have been a result of a personal vendetta by the senator. However, according to Greenspun's own account, he was far more responsible for the

Hawaii—Los Angeles—Mexico—Israel arms-smuggling than anyone else. In any event, when Greenspun pleaded guilty July 10 in the afternoon, so that his morning paper would be first with the story—charges against the others were dismissed. The same judge who had presided at the earlier trial, Judge Peirson M. Hall, assessed a fine of $10,000. This was the final trial.

Thus, in spite of the repeated efforts of the United States attorney general's office to punish those who had assisted Israel, only one man was sentenced to prison in the United States: Charles T. Winters.

We recognize that many were indeed guilty of technical violations of the law.

And so, the question should be asked: How is it that normally loyal, patriotic citizens deliberately break the laws of their country? The usual explanations given for such behavior are either political (deep ideological commitment to another "vastly superior" system) or monetary (succumbing to an irresistible bribe). Clearly, neither of these factors obtained here; furthermore, almost without exception these men had recently fought a war to defend their country, with deep feelings of commitment to their country's cause and of the basic rightness of their country's position.

Let us grant that some of the participants may have been substantially innocent. These men, mercenaries by our definition, performed a limited, interesting job for fair (perhaps, somewhat above normal) pay. They need not have been fully aware of the illegality of the job. Thus, some of the B-17 crew members did consider their job completed with delivery to Zatec.

But what of all the leaders, and a great many of the participants who knowingly and deliberately violated an official policy, the arms embargo, which their government apparently was doing its best to enforce? (The following applies specifically to the United States.)

We suggest that it was ultimate faith in their government that led these men to defy it. Was not a firm, viable Jewish homeland an extension of the humanitarian justification for World War II? Was this not a specific instance of the promotion of those higher purposes which give governments a moral justification? Was the firm support of the United States for a Jewish State not repeatedly on record (beginning with President Wilson's prerelease approval of the Balfour Declaration in 1917, extending through repeated Congressional resolutions and Presidential statements) including immediate de facto recognition of Israel by the United States May 14, 1948?

That the U.S. would try to discourage its citizens from participating in the fighting, could be (at least partially) ascribed to concern for their physical welfare, and one—particularly a Jew—who felt deeply committed, might well insist that risking his life was primarily his own concern, and reject paternalistic government concern for his safety.

But what of the arms embargo? In the general context of concern for survival of the Jewish commonwealth, the embargo could best be regarded as an aberration. On the one hand, there was not only the general record of support—there was also the specific boost via immediate recognition of the new state of Israel within hours of its formal proclamation; on the other hand, Israel clearly could not survive without arms—enforcement of the embargo was equivalent to strangulation. It was not only a matter of one hand not knowing what the other was doing—rather, it was a matter of one hand destroying what the other was building.

These, then were the moral imperatives for breaking this particular law:

(1) Humanitarian. The remnant surviving Hitler's genocide must not now be abandoned to extermination.

(2) Patriotic American. Active support for Israel is basically parallel to American ideals at their finest. Such support is a corrective to the acts of those abusing their positions of power to promote Israel's destruction.

(3) Historical. Recognizing the fundamentally anti-Western thrust of the Arab world, it is very much in the long-range interest of the Western countries to have one reliable, naturally Western country in the area.

(4) Zionist. The multi-millenial, semi-messianic dream of a re-established sovereign Jewish commonwealth was now palpable—and hung in the balance. How could one refrain from doing his utmost to tip the balance affirmatively?

For one moved by the above considerations, it was a *privilege,* beyond comparison or delineation, to fully participate.

Appendix J

USA AND USSR: UNDERSTANDING
THEIR PERPLEXING ACTIONS

Viewed through the lens of the present, past events are often di
torted. Thus, it is a widespread assumption that the United States alwa
was a good friend to Israel, and the USSR, its mortal enemy. Yet, in tern
of concrete actions, most especially during the critical first half of 194
such an assumption is very far indeed from the fact.

In terms of long-established ideological positions, it is true that tl
USSR had, indeed, always been anti-Zionist,[1] and that the United State
favored the promotion of a Jewish homeland in Palestine. The very sul
stance of the Balfour Declaration[2] was approved by President Wilsc
(after consultation with Justice Brandeis) prior to its promulgation.[3] An
occasional congressional resolutions and periodic statements by goverr
ment officials, political leaders, political party platforms, and nonpolitic:
public figures, all put the United States on record as consistently favorir
a Jewish homeland in Palestine, through all the intervening years.

At the same time, powerful counterforces were growing; Arab o
position was becoming more visible. To what extent this was due
natural nationalism, magnified by intra-Arab terror, and to what exter
it may have been artificially promoted and expanded by British and othe
interests wanting to ingratiate themselves with the Arabs and hoping t
this means to extend their welcome in the Arab countries, it is not possib
to state to any degree of accuracy. What, initially, was a minute level
natural Arab nationalism was given anti-Zionist focus, and was give
an apparent reality which increasingly concerned certain elements influer
tial in American foreign policy.

The two elements directly concerned were the military and the o
interests. The military looked at the map of the Middle East, and co
cluded that if a choice had to be made between Arab friendship and
Jewish dream, clearly the Jewish dream would have to go. Similarly, tl
American and international Western companies whose business was th
enormously profitable processing of the oil that happened to lie beneat
the soil of many of the Arab countries, felt that nothing must be dor

to jeopardize their continuing to make this vital product available to the Western countries. And the State Department became the focus and the champion of this view. (It is conceivable that the mix was not untainted by a bit of genteel anti-Jewish feeling coupled with a touch of romantic pro-Arabism.[4])

The either-or view was taken most seriously, although it was deeply flawed. In the first place, a strong Western attitude would have rapidly deflated the dogma of absolute universal Arab hostility to the Jewish homeland. In the second place, the long-range historical current is one of Arab hostility to the West. A major element in European history for roughly 1,000 years (from the founding of Islam in the seventh century almost to the brink of the Industrial Revolution) was the ongoing war between the Moslem East and the Christian West. It is even possible that this antagonism was foreshadowed in the centuries of warfare between the Persians and the Greeks. Thus, while countries of the East and West may use each other to mutual advantage, anything like genuine friendship would seem to be rather out of range.

For recent, hard proof we need only recall Great Britain's fate following its actions during the War of Independence. Before, during, and after the war Britain continued to supply both Transjordan and Egypt with arms, including much heavy equipment. During the war, Transjordan's army, the Arab Legion, was commanded by an Englishman, Sir John Baggot Glubb, or Glubb Pasha, and many of its officers were English. As was noted earlier, the British flew a goodly number of high-level reconnaissance missions over Israel in the autumn of 1948, and January 7, 1949, RAF planes based in Egypt flew low-level reconnaissance missions over the Israeli border and apparently went into action against Israel, with the loss of four RAF planes. Further, Britain had done its utmost to strangle Israel by pressing enforcement of the arms embargo against Israel, all over the world. Yet, less than a decade later the British were unceremoniously thrown out of both those countries. Kimche (*Pillars,* p. 33) relates a most eloquent incident:

In the spring of 1948, passengers arriving at Almoza, airport of Cairo, were greeted by an Egyptian passport official. "Egyptian passports first," he announced. "Foreign passports next; British at the end of the queue." One English traveler protested to the Egyptian official at being kept waiting in this discriminatory manner. "I have been waiting fifty years for this moment," was the Egyptian rejoinder.

As for oil, which indeed is vital to the economy of all industria nations, it is too often overlooked that oil *revenues* are vital to the economies of the oil-producing Arab countries. Thus their selling oil at substantial profits to the West is not an act of charity, it is something which the producing countries must sell; they cannot drink it, and they need the revenue it brings in.

Nevertheless, it was the fearful attitude that dominated the State Department—very likely, under the attractive delusion that this was the essence of realism, tough-mindedness, and sophistication.

The words of Dean Acheson, who was a major maker and implementor of State Department policies from 1941 (when he joined the department as Assistant Secretary of State for economic affairs) until 1953 (when he left office as Secretary of State), are eloquent in this regard:

> I did not share the President's [President Truman's] views on the Palestine solution to the pressing and desperate plight of great numbers of displaced Jews in Eastern Europe, for whom the British and American commanders in Germany were temporarily attempting to provide. The number [of postwar Jewish refugees] that could be absorbed by Arab Palestine [sic] without creating a grave political problem would be inadequate, and to transform the country into a Jewish state capable of receiving a million or more immigrants would vastly exacerbate the political problem and imperil not only American but all Western interests in the Middle East.[5]

The above retrospective statement is clear indeed. In the face of ongoing, widespread, publicly expressed support by the American people for the Jewish homeland in Palestine and for the admission of significant numbers of the survivors of the European holocaust whom no other country was willing to accept, and who had not then displaced a single Arab resident of Palestine, the State Department was obdurate. The State Department saw its duty to America's higher interests in frustrating the thrust of the expressed will of large numbers of Americans. This was done quietly, but extremely effectively.

Prior to and during World War II, American public opinion could be placated by blaming the British. After all, Palestine was a British responsibility; outsiders should do no more than offer occasional advice. Thus if Britain violated the basic concept of its mandate, ultimately that was its own business. The period following the war saw a much more concerned American president at the helm,[6] who found it necessary to become involved directly in making policy.[7] But the execution of policy was necesarily left to the State Department. And the State Department then took practical steps—quietly—of the greatest importance in attempting to destroy the incipient Jewish state.

In Appendix G, we noted the American refusal to issue passports to those suspected of volunteering for military service in Israel, perhaps partially for their own protection. But what would appear to be an enormously cold-blooded act aimed at deliberately destroying the Jewish state, was the embargo on arms to the Middle East put into effect December 5, 1947, underlined by the subsequent extension of the embargo to even commercial aircraft, which went into effect April 15, 1948. It is unfortunate that those State Department records which, if complete, could shed direct light on these decisions, are closed and will remain inaccessible for years to come.[8] In the absence of such direct records, we must fall back on what has been published—but the evidence appears to be thoroughly convincing.

Not only as a matter of elementary common sense, but in view of the following statements there can be no doubt whatever of awareness of the need for a far higher level military strength than then existed to sustain a Jewish state.

There is a 1945 memo from Acting Secretary of State Joseph G. Grew:

> ...We know that Pres. Roosevelt understood this clearly, for as recently as March 3, after his trip to the Near East, he told an officer of the Department that, in his opinion, a Jewish state in Palestine (the ultimate Zionist aim) could be established and maintained *only by military force.*" [9]

In an August press conference (following the Potsdam heads-of-state meeting), Truman said that he had no desire to send 500,000 American soldiers to the Middle East to make peace in Palestine. Then, there is a September memo from the State Department Division of Near Eastern Affairs:

> No government should advocate a policy of mass immigration unless it is prepared to assist in making available the necessary *security forces,* shipping, housing. . . .[10]

In mid-1946, there is the statement that the U.S. was

> neither disposed nor prepared to assume risks and obligations that might require us to use *military force.*

And the Joint Chiefs of Staff urged that no U.S. armed forces be involved.[1]

Truman's aim remained "justice without bloodshed," but blood was being shed on an increasing scale. The Jews, pessimistic over the prospects of international enforcement of the partition plan, wished openly to estab lish a Jewish militia. The British reply was that they would not permit this so long as they were in control. Truman records that it was reported to him on February 13, 1948, by American diplomatic missions in the area that the Arabs were expected to start *full-scale military operations* in late March. Four days later, he appealed to the Arab leaders to "preserve the peace and practice moderation." They rejected it flatly. . . . Again,

> The Joint Chiefs of Staff, on several occasions, submitted memoranda to show that we could not afford to send more than a token force to the area.[12]

Similar evidence of ongoing awareness of the need for military strength is to be found in Acheson:

> At the time of which I am writing, President Truman's views centered exclusively upon two points: first, immediate immigration into Palestine of 100,000 displaced Jews from Eastern Europe; second, the determination to assume no political or *military responsibility* over this decision.

Surely this is an indication of the need for military force. Later, we again have awareness of the need for physical strength:

> By mid-June (1947) he (Secretary of State Marshall) had changed his opinion. "An agreed settlement no longer appears possible," he wrote to Ambassador Warren Austin at the United Nations. Every solution would meet with strong opposition. *"A certain degree of force* may be required (for) any solution."[13]

And when the Arab reaction to the partition decision of November 29 1947, was to declare that they would never permit the Jewish state to come into being, to follow it promptly by the killing of Jews in Palestine as part of this posture, it was obvious to all that military strength was needed if the projected Jewish state and its people were to survive. So obvious was this that during the winter and early spring of 1948, trustee-ship rather than statehood was advocated by the United States at the UN, since no country or group of countries was ready to volunteer the 100,000 soldiers it was felt would be the minimum needed to protect the incipient Jewish state.

In the face of this crystal-clear awareness of Israel's desperate need for arms and men—the State Department deliberately promulgated an ostensibly even-handed arms embargo which was meaningless applied to the already overarmed Arabs[14] whose military supplies were to be further supplemented by "pre-existent" British contracts, while the Jews had been kept pitifully underarmed by the British.

If a serious, "fatherly" UN militia had come into being, it is likely that Israel's history would have been rather different—that the anticipated Arab state would have come into being together with the Jewish state, both following the partition-plan borders, and a strong, serious militia, putting down political violence firmly, might well have led to accommodation and normal relationship between the two Palestinian states—and so, perhaps, between Israel and the balance of the Arab world. At the same time, a paternalistic umbrella would have prevented the independence, dynamism—and military prowess—of the Jewish state. To a great degree, the arms embargo forced the kind of intense, bootstrap development and total self-reliance which formed the Israel of today.

For the arms embargo was vicious indeed: Taken at face value, this restriction effectuated by knowledgable, professional diplomats, must be regarded as realistically intended to destroy the germinating Jewish state; the unavoidable killing and maiming of its people was regarded as a regrettable, necessary part of the process. The most charitable, and probably correct, view is that the embargo was intended to force the Jewish leaders to recognize that their state could not come into being, that they would have to beg the British to return as protectors, completely under British terms. How else explain, simultaneously with the embargo, the steadfast refusal to commit enough American troops to a UN militia to permit that militia to come into being? Reluctance to permit Russian participation in such a militia, is surely not a rational, total explanation.[15]

Nor was this in any sense a "paper" embargo: As we have seen earlier, it was enforced quite vigorously within the United States, and wherever in the world American power could reach. It appears likely that the extension of the embargo to commercial planes (April 15, 1948) was aimed specifically at the Schwimmer operation, which was quite legal under the terms of the original arms embargo.

Nor was there any tendency to forgive alleged violators of the arms embargo after the war. On the contrary, the deliberate policy of the Department of Justice was to prosecute and seek maximum penalties. (The actual penalties for those found guilty varied radically, depending on the judge.) To defend this solely in terms of cold war paranoia will not wash: on the contrary, the Czech airlift was a direct *result* of the American arms embargo, not the cause of it. Israel's natural expectation was that following the UN partition decision, surplus American arms would be readily and openly available. The basic reason for stealth in earlier arms procurement in the United States was simply in terms of getting the material past the British in Palestine.

Now, in place of the natural next step which normally would be expected even of a totally neutral country—permission quietly to purchase commercially the arms needed for survival—the arms embargo was an extremely powerful blow, whose force was multiplied because it came from a friend. It was the American embargo that made the Czech airlift vital and the Russians who permitted this vital airlift to take place.

The time sequence is absolutely clear. The American arms embargo was proclaimed on December 5, 1947. The Communist coup in Czechoslovakia took place at the end of February[16]—and the first flight of the Czech airlift from Zatec, took place May 12. The first Czech arms contract (for the shipload that was delivered on the *Nora* early in April) was negotiated before the coup, but so far as we can see, all other arrangements, for additional arms, fighter planes, use of airfield, etc., were made after the Communist takeover, with the full knowledge of the Communists. Although the Czech airlift was made necessary by the prior American arms embargo, it is nevertheless possible that the existence of the airlift did, in turn, promote suspicion of Israel in some American quarters.

No less an authority than David Ben Gurion recently said:

The State Department, in 1947, was against a Jewish State. Bevin said he was sure the UN would impose Trusteeship and that would be the end of Zionism. I now have the proof, in a recent book on [by?] Moussa Alami. But the Russians were with us. We received arms from Czechoslovakia—with Russian approval, of course. The Americans imposed an embargo on the Middle East—which meant in practice only us. The Arabs did not need their weapons, they already had enough. But without the Soviet arms we would not have been able to survive.[17]

What did the USSR actually do, in order to earn such great praise? Did they send skilled volunteers? Did they send modern Russian planes, tanks, guns? Did they send rifles, grenades, ammunition from Soviet arsenals? Did they send funds?

The answer is that Soviet assistance took none of these forms: Troops, skilled or otherwise, were not sent, nor were volunteers permitted to go; no military equipment whatever—not even a single bullet—was started on its way to Israel from Russia. And certainly no funds were made available. Absolutely nothing was forthcoming either officially or unofficially, from the Soviet Union. All that the Kremlin did was to permit the vital Czech airlift and some surface shipments to take place!

And on the diplomatic front, the USSR was Israel's staunchest and most consistent supporter—beginning with the pre-state period and extending beyond the middle of 1948. It is noteworthy that the American State Department professionals were astounded at this Soviet support for the Jewish State. Being totally committed to the unquestionable correctness of their pro-Arab logic, there could be no doubt in their minds that the same consideration must move the Soviets to act in the very same way—wooing only the Arabs.

But in mid-1947, Andrei Gromyko, Deputy Foreign Minister of the Soviet Union, fought for the right of the Jewish Agency and other Jewish representatives to appear before the UN General Assembly. Gromyko's persistence over the opposition of Great Britain and the United States, at least resulted in the appearance of the Jewish representatives before the UN First (Political) Committee. He also urged that UNSCOP (UN Special Committee on Palestine) should visit both Palestine and the Jewish refugee camps in Europe. The UN partition decision of November 29, 1947, included positive votes both by the United States and the USSR. However (as noted earlier) the US arms embargo was promptly put into effect: December 5, 1947. Shortly thereafter the State Department publicly requested an investigation of the allegation that relief-agency funds were being used to finance illegal immigration to Palestine (the *Pan Crescent* and the *Pan York* were reported to be carrying 12,000 visa-less persons towards Palestine).[18]

Before January was over, the State Department ruled that passports of U.S. citizens volunteering to serve in Israel's ranks would be recalled. And the U.S. consulate in Palestine warned that American citizens fighting in either the Arab or Jewish forces would lose their passports, and that naturalized US citizens would lose their citizenship.[19]

At the same time, American political pressures were mounting. In what, through the years, has become the standard empty Arab threat, Emir Faisal al Saud announced that if the United States continued to support partition, Saudi Arabia would cancel its US oil concessions, and would be joined in this action by all the other Arab states. On the same date, James A. Farley, a lifelong major Democratic political figure, stated that the UN must carry out partition; and two leading labor-union figures CIO President Philip Murray and AFL President William Greene, urged the U.S. to lift its arms embargo.[20]

At the beginning of March, the UN Security Council adopted a US resolution calling for Big Five consultations on the Palestine situation. A few days later, it fell to USSR representative Gromyko to urge continuing support of the partition plan, while US Representative Austin ambiguously indicated that he hoped to confer with Jewish and Arab representatives. Four days later, Austin denied that the US had dropped support for partition and the following day shifted emphasis from partition to economic union of the Jewish and Arab states.[21] Then, a little past mid-March, US representative Warren Austin asked the UN Security Council to halt action on partition and to call a special assembly session to reconsider a solution to the Palestine problem and to set up a temporary trusteeship. In reply Deputy Ministry Gromyko insisted on partition. Secretary of State Marshall stated the trusteeship was the sole possible solution. A few days later Marshall was reported as saying that trusteeship was the only way to keep the troops of the USSR out of the Middle East area.

As the end of March approached, President Truman denied that the partition plan had been abandoned, but urged trusteeship as a necessary temporary measure. The Security Council now sought hard data on the extent of the practical commitment to trusteeship by the United States, that is, how many troops was the United States ready to commit? The Jews had initially rejected trusteeship, and by now the Arabs were rejecting it also. Thus, statements of rejection were made both by the ex-Grand Mufti of Jerusalem and by Dr. Khalidi, Secretary of the Arab Higher Committee.[22]

Gromyko remained the staunch champion of partition in the UN. He now charged the United States with wrecking the partition plan, saying that the United States really wanted Great Britain to return to its mandate in Palestine. He unequivocally opposed trusteeship. Austin, the US representative, then formally moved for a special assembly session on the problem, at the same time deferring a motion on trusteeship since adequate support apparently was lacking. Support for the plan by other UN members, the Western countries in particular, would depend on an advance firm commitment of troops by the United States, a commitment which it was not ready to make. The only Jewish supporters of the trusteeship idea in Palestine were a tiny minority group focused around Dr. Judah Magnes of the Hebrew University. This group, calling itself "Ihud," had strong pacifist leanings and consistently favored a joint Jewish/Arab state.

Throughout March there had been pressure for a truce, generally favored by the Jews and opposed by the Arabs. Nevertheless, Jewish and Arab representatives did meet sporadically under informal UN auspices at Lake Success, in Long Island, N. Y., as late as April 7. By April 8 it was acknowledged that the talks had failed; the fighting continued.

As did the arms embargo. In a letter to representative Emanuel Celler, Under-Secretary of State Lovett rejected the plea of forty-one congressmen to lift the arms embargo; in addition, this letter emphatically barred enlistment by United States citizens in the Jewish armed forces.

On the critical question of American troops to enforce trusteeship, James Reston wrote in the *New York Times* of April 14 that the United States would not enforce either trusteeship or partition. If, and only if, the Jews and Arabs first agreed on a truce would American troops be sent as a peace-keeping force.

At a special session of the General Assembly beginning in the middle of April (which had been called at the earlier instance of Warren Austin), Austin held that an international force and an Arab/Jewish truce were prerequisites to trusteeship. A week later the United States offered a new plan to suspend partition and maintain the status quo until the regular assembly session in September.[23]

On the face of it, the American trusteeship plan was indeed impossible. Not only did those most directly involved not want it, but it could not be implemented without troops and, at this point, no neutral country was willing to contribute troops unless the United States took the lead. And the United States insisted on a precondition for its troops which clearly was not going to be met: a truce. So long as they had the upper hand—which clearly was the situation in March, April, and May—the Arabs would under no circumstances seriously agree to a truce. Thus it appears that Gromyko was essentially correct in pointing out, as we noted above, that the basic purpose of the trusteeship move was to produce reconsideration of partition, with the expectation that this might well lead to an invitation to Great Britain to resume its governorship of Palestine, since it would be the only Western country ready to commit an adequate number of troops. That this presumed plan was never implemented is probably due in large part to Gromyko's exposure of it, and perhaps also to the realization of UN members—in particular those on the UN Palestine Committee—that any reintroduction of British armed forces would simply not be tolerated by the Jewish community in Palestine which felt that much of the level of Arab success against it was due precisely to the activities of British forces of law and order in that country.

The American arms embargo continued. And British efforts continued. In early May, with trusteeship now clearly in disfavor, Sir Arthur Creech Jones proposed an alternative: A neutral administrator to maintain government services until the Jews and Arabs would come to terms. Two days later the French offered a modified version of this plan. Either plan would have required troops, and it might well be expected that its proponents realized that an invitation to Britain to supply the troops would be the ultimate result. The USSR stated quite emphatically that such plans were illegal because of the existence of the partition resolution.

And so, due largely to Russian support, and in the face of serious American opposition, the partition plan—the juridical basis for the creation of the state of Israel—remained in effect. With the mandate due to expire midnight Friday, May 14th, the State of Israel came into legal being by proclamation midday Friday, May 14, in order to anticipate the Sabbath. This proclamation was immediately followed by *de facto* recognition by President Truman—an act that astounded both the USSR and the American delegation at the UN. *De facto* recognition is less than complete recognition; it is official acknowledgment that a particular government exists, to which one is not yet ready to extend full diplomatic recognition.

De jure recognition is full diplomatic recognition. The USSR was the first country to extend *de jure* recognition to the state of Israel—which it did on May 15. The United States did not grant *de jure* recognition until Feb. 1, 1949, after Israel's first general election (January 25).

Towards the end of May, V. A. Tarasenko of the Ukraine charged at the UN that Great Britain was a belligerent because of its aid to the Arab Legion. And at the end of May, in what may be considered an example of Russian humor, as well as a mild attempt to introduce a Russian presence into the Middle East, Andrei Gromyko charged that the Christians, Moslems, and Jews were failing to protect the religious shrines in Palestine, and he suggested that the task be given to atheists.

By mid-November 1948, there appeared to be a definite shift in Russian policy in that S. K. Tsarapkin called for a return to the original partition-plan borders. This could conceivably be seen as the USSR making itself the promoter of the still nonexistent Arab state which, if it came into existence, would then be deeply grateful to the Soviets. By late 1949 it was abundantly clear that the USSR had fully reverted to its traditional anti-Zionism: The Soviet history journal *Vaprosy Istori* purged nine editors as being pro-Zionist. It reported at length the thoughts of one V. E. Lutsky who called for a fight against the very idea of a Jewish state. He said that a Jewish state is a cosmopolite ideology, a weapon of subversive activity of Anglo-American warmongers. This same Lutsky had written a pamphlet in August 1946 describing Palestine as an Arab country and the Jewish National Fund as a capitalistic and monopolistic organization. By the end of November the USSR was publicly charging that Israel had become a tool of Western aggression; and nationalism as exemplified by Israel, was also attacked.[24]

How can we understand this short-lived, radical shift in Soviet policy? Why this glaring inconsistency, precisely at the time when it was vital to the state of Israel?

To suggest "the finger of God" is much too broad. The historian wants a more tangible answer, if possible; an answer that demonstrates an underlying consistency in Soviet policy, an underlying consistency so basic, that it could readily see radical surface shifts in direction, as flexible tactics. Russia had long been interested in advancing to the warm waters to the south. From 1946 on, the immediate purpose was to get Great Britain out of the Middle East. In the wake of British departure there would be, if not a vacuum, at least some turbulence, a possible opportunity to move ahead. Palestine was the natural focus; it was already in some turmoil; it appeared that the emerging Jewish state would by definition be anti-British, and so, in gratitude for Russian support, it might very well become a Russian client.[25] In any event, an independent Jewish state was necessary to guarantee British eviction and to create diplomatic opportunities.

But traditional anti-Zionism, probably reinforced by older and deeper Russian antisemitism, was such that assistance was limited to diplomacy and to not interfering with Israel's arms procurement in Czechoslovakia, at least not until midsummer 1948. Still, this encouragement was enough for Israel initially to see itself as a possible neutralist bridge between East and West even though the basic Jewish orientation is to freedom and the West. In one sense, the fundamental Western concepts of freedom and individualism are the secular equivalent of biblical principles. And when anti-Zionism and antisemitism reasserted themselves (in the Stalinist "doctors' plot" and in the Czech "treason" trials of 1952), all but the most optimistic wishful thinkers realized that the mediating neutralist dream was gone: Israel was formally and irrevocably, by nature, so to speak, part of the West.

Part of Israel's problem is that, whereas its being Western is the cause of its being hated by the opinion molders among its Arab neighbors, there is little natural balancing encouragement on the part of the powerful Western countries. At this writing, the United States has only recently substantially and consistently supported the State of Israel. Although there has been progress, the pattern has been irregular. American support was most important to the initial UN approval of the partition plan, but this was followed by a prolonged attack on partition with the proposed trusteeship plan, along with the arms embargo's undercutting Israel's ability to survive; the United States was the first to recognize Israel *de facto*—but did not extend *de jure* recognition until early 1949; for many years after Jerusalem became Israel's capital, the United States refused to recognize this, maintaining its embassy in Tel Aviv; following the 1956 preemptive war against Egypt, the United States was scathing in its denunciation of Israel, and totally failed to implement the two major guarantees made to Israel as conditions for Israeli withdrawal from Sinai (the right to use the Suez Canal, and keeping the Gulf of Akaba open to Israeli shipping); only in the past half decade has the United States clearly become a supporter of Israel in the UN—and then, until very recently, its voting support was generally limited to abstaining from censure motions rather than vetoing negative votes.

On the directly practical level, we have seen that the American arms embargo, coupled with very strong attempts to prevent American volunteers from serving in Israel, came very close indeed to permitting radical truncation and perhaps destruction of the Jewish state at its inception. It was the arms embargo that made the Czech airlift absolutely vital—but the Czech airlift could not have been possible without violation of the parallel American ban on volunteer participation. Yet, neither then nor subsequently has there been any interference with private fund raising for Israel—although to some extent it was private American fund raising that made defeat of the American arms embargo possible! (It has been facetiously suggested that the dollars that paid for the airlift, made a bit of a Marshall Plan country of 1948 Czechoslovakia.) Although to a great extent American diplomats continued to be bluffed by threats of withholding the oil which the Arabs have to sell (there have generally been more alternate sources than alternate customers, and the Arab countries must import their food) it is the American military thinkers who thoroughly revised their thinking, particularly after 1956, and recognized that the ongoing existence of Israel is most important to the United States if it wishes to remain a superpower. Between Western Europe and Australia, where else can the United States find a totally reliable ally of the West? Thus, it appears that the realists in the Pentagon are most responsible for the increasingly hard support of Israel by the United States.

The inconsistency in America's relationship with Israel can be seen, broadly, as the product of wide public support, undercut and frustrated by career professionals dedicated to what they are convinced is best for the United States regardless of mawkish humanitarian considerations and public opinion.[26]

It is embarrassing and uncomfortable for a President to fight and overrule his own State Department. Truman did it for the partition plan and, half a year later, for immediate *de facto* recognition of Israel. It is perhaps too much to have expected him also to have erased the arms embargo—although to the writer this appears to have been more critical than the diplomatic steps. In the event, America was sufficiently free and large so that dedicated initiative, in violation of the spirit (and sometimes the letter) of the embargo, was able to overcome it (and zealous officials were themselves bound by the limitations of the law).

It is not motivation but acts that are decisive in the outside world. There is much realism in an old Arab proverb:

A hunter went killing sparrows one cold day. As he carried on the slaughter, his eyes were streaming. Said one bird to another: Look at the man crying. Said the other: Never mind his tears, watch his hands.[27]

Thus it was that the acts of Israel's consistent enemy, the USSR, played a crucial role in its birth and early survival. To recapitulate: One aim of Russian foreign policy, at least since the time of Catherine the Great,[28] has been to establish a presence in the Eastern Mediterranean. This thrust—which had some mixed success in the nineteenth and early twentieth centuries—was suspended for a generation following the Bolshevik Revolution, while the Communist regime established and stabilized itself. As World War II drew to a close, this Russian drive to the southwest was resumed.

Thus, the Potsdam Conference included a demand for Soviet trusteeship over one of Italy's former African colonies. As expected, this was rebuffed and was followed, in 1946, by Soviet attempts at subversion of the governments of Iran and Egypt. When these normal approaches failed, and with Britain pushing a somewhat reluctant United States to assume a larger role, at least diplomatically, along Russia's southern tier, Gromyko adopted the unusual temporary tactic of championing the Jewish state, to make sure that the British would be thrown out and the area opened to fresh initiatives.

As we have seen, support for the Jewish state grew through 1947, continuing past mid-1948. Once its objective had been accomplished, with Britain firmly out of Palestine and Arab anti-Westernism given added focus by the assured existence of a hate object, the tactic shifted to denunciation of that same Israel whose coming into being the USSR had promoted. Why? Because Israel, by its nature, was Western, or because it produced a bit of restlessness on the part of some of the Jews of the USSR? Certainly not. The anti-Israel shift was signaled well before either of these had visibly crystalized.

Basic, consistent Russian strategy was to promote conditions which would permit, and expand, Russian presence in the Mediterranean. This meant appearing to the Arabs as their good and true friend, that is, as the enemy of the West in general, and of Israel in particular. To establish credibility with the Arabs, two steps were taken: (1) The "doctors' plot" was invented—i.e., that a group of Jewish doctors had deliberately plotted to kill Stalin—and that its own Jews were thus secret enemies of the Soviet Union. (2) A handful of loyal, devoted (Jewish-born) Communists were publicly sacrificed—in the 1952 Czech "treason" trials. That is, those very agents of Moscow who had scrupulously carried out Moscow's orders not to interfere with the Czech airlift as a basic part of Russia's 1948 tactic, now were accused of treason for having done so. They were convicted and executed. The USSR's pro-Arab credentials were established.

Yet it remains a fact that the Czech airlift did save Israel. And the Czech airlift could not have taken place without Israeli arrangements, the Schwimmer airplanes, overseas volunteers to fly the planes, American dollars—and Russian permission.

In America, the professional diplomats—those amoral patriots who were the counterparts of the Russian strategists—would have seen Israel destroyed. The past twenty years have seen a total reassessment on the part of these same cold American strategists. It appears that they now view Israel as the necessary cornerstone of ongoing American presence in the Eastern Mediterranean. Strictly in military terms, Israel is seen as the strongest, most reliable ally in a vast area of great strategic importance. Israel survived in spite of them, because of American funds (not government funds, of course, but the private contributions of individual sympathizers), and because of American volunteers, whose participation was generally significant, and occasionally vital. Obviously, the dedication of its own people was the *sine qua non,* but would not have been sufficient for Israel's survival.

If the anti-Israel convictions of America's professional diplomats had not prevailed—if there had been no arms embargo—the Czech airlift and Russia's real, positive contribution never would have been; the fund raising situation would have been less critical; and the need for and effectiveness of volunteer participation would have been at least somewhat reduced.

Israel came into existence because, first, a viable nation was formed through half a century of pioneering effort. This nation was tempered by physical hardships and the need to rise against the hostility of neighbors and imposed outside government. Brought to a height of self-awareness by the European holocaust which incinerated ten times as many Jews as lived in the land of Israel in early 1948, this 3400-year-old people said:

> This is the end of the line. Here, where we were first born as a people, we will now be reborn—or die. But we will no longer bow. We thirst for peace. The heavenly and earthly Jerusalem equally are named "City of Peace." But peace means an upright peace, in which none shall make us afraid. For this—the right to live in this way on that Land where we were born as a people—we are ready to die: Not meekly, but fighting. And if we must fight, we will try to kill our attackers, so that we may live in peace.[29]

These brave, unspoken words could well have led to total annihilation. If the American arms embargo had been obeyed, if American funds had been cut off, if the Arabs had then pushed their attacks, Israel would have been destroyed. The initiative that broke the embargo with munitions and planes, and supplied funds so that the Russian-permitted Czech airlift could be flown by the volunteers who made themselves available, guaranteed the very existence of the state. And as we established earlier, reconquest of the Negev—more than half of Israel's pre-1967 territory, its outlet to Africa and Asia—was dependent on Operation Dust; an operation which could not have taken place, then, without the physical participation of overseas volunteers.

BIBLIOGRAPHY

In English:

Acheson, Dean. *Present at the Creation.* New York: W. W. Norton & Co., 1969.
Agar, Herbert. *The Saving Remnant.* New York: Viking Press, 1962.
American Jewish Yearbook, Vol. 50 (1948–49). Philadelphia: Jewish Publication Society of America, 1949.
Bauer, Yehuda. *Flight and Rescue: Brichah.* New York: Random House, 1970.
————. *From Diplomacy to Resistance.* Phila.: Jewish Publication Society, 1970.
Begin, Menachem. *The Revolt.* New York: Henry Schuman, 1951.
Bell, J. Bowyer. *The Long War.* Englewood Cliffs, N.J.: Prentice Hall, 1969.
Berkman, Ted. *Cast a Giant Shadow.* Garden City, New York: Doubleday, 1962.
Bondy, Ruth: Zmora, Ohad; Bashan, Raphael, (ed.) *Mission Survival.* New York: Sabra Books, 1968.
Burstein, Samuel. *Rabbi With Wings.* New York: Herzl Press, 1965.
Collins, Larry and Lapierre, Dominique. *O Jerusalem.* New York: Simon and Schuster, 1972.
Edelman, Maurice. *David.* New York: G. P. Putnam's Sons, 1964.
Glubb, Sir John Bagot. *A Soldier with the Arabs.* New York: Harper & Bros., 1957.
Greenspun, Hank. *Where I Stand.* New York: David McKay Co., 1966.
Halpern, Ben (Introd). *The Jewish National Home in Palestine.* New York: Ktav, 1970.
Horowitz, David. *State in the Making.* New York: Alfred A. Knopf, 1953.
Joseph, Dov. *The Faithful City.* New York: Simon and Schuster, 1960.
Kagan, Benjamin. *The Secret Battle for Israel.* Cleveland: World Publishing Co., 1966.
Katz, Doris. *The Lady Was a Terrorist.* New York: Shiloni, 1953.
Katz, Samuel. *Days of Fire.* Garden City, New York: Doubleday & Co., 1968.
Kimche, Jon. *Seven Fallen Pillars.* London: Secker and Warburg, 1950.
Kimche, Jon and David. *A Clash of Destinies.* New York: F. A. Praeger, 1960.
Kurzman, Dan. *Genesis 1948.* New York/Cleveland: World Publishing, 1970.
Lapide, P. E. *A Century of U S. Aliya.* Jerusalem: Jerusalem Post Press, 1961.
Lorch, Netanel. *The Edge Of The Sword.* New York: G. P. Putnam's Sons, 1961.

274 AMERICAN VOLUNTEERS

Mardor, Munya M. *Strictly Illegal.* London: Robert Hale Ltd., 1964.
Munson, Kenneth C. *Aircraft Of World War II.* Garden City, New York: Doubleday & Co., 1968.
Mydans, Carl and Shelley. *The Violent Peace.* New York: Atheneum, 1968.
Nissenson, Hugh. *Notes From The Frontier.* New York: Dial Press, 1968.
O'Ballance, Edgar. *The Arab-Israeli War 1948.* London: Faber & Faber, 1956.
Pearlman, Moshe. *The Army Of Israel.* New York: Philosophical Library, 1950.
Postal, Bernard and Levy, Henry W. *And The Hills Shouted For Joy.* David McKay Co., New York, 1973.
Robinson, Donald (ed.). *Under Fire.* New York: W. W. Norton & Co., 1968.
St. John, Robert. *Shalom Means Peace.* New York: Doubleday & Co., 1949.
Safran, Nadav. *From War To War.* New York: Pegasus, 1969.
Samuel, Maurice. *Light On Israel.* New York: A. A. Knopf, 1968.
Sharef, Zeev. *Three Days.* Garden City, New York: Doubleday & Co., 1962.
Slater, Leonard. *The Pledge.* New York: Simon & Schuster, 1970.
Spicehandler, Daniel. *Let My Right Hand Wither.* New York: Beechhurst Press, 1950.
Sugrue, Thomas. *Watch For The Morning.* New York: Harper & Bros., 1950.
Swing, Julian. *God's Little Air Force.* (Unpublished: Copyright 1949.)
Truman, Harry S. *Memoirs.* (2 Volumes) Garden City, New York: Doubleday & Co., 1955.
Velie, Lester. *Countdown In The Holy Land.* New York: Fund & Wagnalls, 1969.
Vilnay, Zev. *The New Israel Atlas, Bible To Present Day.* New York/Toronto: McGraw Hill, 1969.
Weizmann, Chaim. *Trial And Error.* New York: Harper & Bros., 1949.
Zaar, Isaac. *Rescue And Liberation.* New York: Bloch Publishing Co., 1954.

Hebrew:

Ben-Gurion, David. *Behilahem Israel.* Mapai-Ahdut Press, 1951.
———. *Bamaarakha.* Tel Aviv: 1957.
———. *Mimaamad LeAm.* Tel Aviv: 1955.
Dekel, Ephraim. *Alilot Shai.* Tel Aviv: 1953.
Friedmann, A. *Lohamei Hofesh BeYisrael.* Tel Aviv: 1959.
GHQ, Army of Israel. *Atlas Gaographi-Histori Shel Eretz Israel,* Army Press.
Golomb, Eliyahu. *Hevyon Oz.* Tel Aviv: 1954.
History Department, GHQ, Army of Israel. *Toledot Milhemet Hakomemiut.* Maarahot, (12 ed.), 1964.
Kagan, Binyamin. *Hame Himreeu B'Alata.* Tel Aviv: Davar Press.
Lamdan, Yitzhak (ed.). *Yizkor.* Government of Israel Press, 1955.
Ofir, Yehoshua. *Al Hahomot.* Mahon Jabotinski Press, 1961.
Rivlin, Gershon and Sinai, Zvi. *Hateevat Alexandroni Bmilhemet Hakommiut.* Zahal, Maarahot, 1964.

Sefer Habrigada. Tel Aviv: 1957.
Sefer Hapalmach. Tel Aviv: 1953.
Sefer Toledot Hahaganah. (2 Vol.). Tel Aviv: 1960–63.
Shahan, Avigdor. *Kanfei Hanitzahon.* Am Hassefer Publishers Ltd., 1966.
Teveth, Shabtai. *Hassuffim Batzariah.* Jerusalem/Tel Aviv: Shocken Press, 1968.
Vilnay, Zev. *Gal-Ade Lagiborim.* Jerusalem: JNF/Jewish Agency, 1959.
Yakobovits, M. *Mipalmach ad Zahal.* Tel Aviv: 1953.

Periodicals

American Zionist. New York.
Bamachaneh. Tel Aviv.
Congress bi-Weekly. New York.
Davar Hashavua. Tel Aviv.
Hadassah Magazine. New York.
Haganah Speaks. New York (1948).
Maarachot. Tel Aviv.
Midstream. New York.
Jerusalem Post. Jerusalem.
Jewish Observer and Middle East Review. London.
New York Times. New York.
Palestine Information Bulletin. London
Reconstructionist. New York.
Saturday Review. New York.

Relevant Fiction (Documentary Novels): The air war as seen by three participants in the Air Transport Command.

Barber, Rowland. *The Midnighters.* New York: Crown Publishing, 1970.
Lichtman, William. *Between the Star and the Cross.* New York: Citadel Press, 1957.
Livingston, Harold E. *The Coasts of the Earth.* Boston: Houghton Mifflin Co., 1954.

NOTES

NOTES TO PREFACE

[1] In 135 C.E., Bar Kochba's rebellion was savagely put down with mass slaughter, and Jerusalem was leveled and sown with salt.

NOTES TO INTRODUCTION

[1] Country-of-origin stipend: For mail, socialization, etc., service clubs were established for "Western" overseas volunteers according to country-of-origin. These clubs maintained a register, and paid each of their volunteers a fixed additional monthly stipend. The South African Club paid the highest; the American Club, the least.

[2] Quoted from letter of April 25, 1968, Akiva Skidell to the writer; also found in Avigdor Shahan, *Kanfei Hanitzahon*, (Tel Aviv: Am Hassefer Publishing Ltd., 1966), p. 293. Actually, we consider the very last category (those who came after the start of 1949 at the request of the army) as postwar specialists rather than overseas volunteers.

[3] For a fine discussion of this problem, see the introductory essay in Jon and David Kimche, *A Clash of Destinies* (New York: F.A. Praeger, 1960).

[4] Zev Vilnay, *Gal-'Ade Lagiborim*, (Jerusalem: JNF/Jewish Agency, 1959).

[5] The original memorial plaque listed eighty names. However, detailed investigation initiated by the writer was able to verify fewer than half that total. A few of those listed were killed after the war; some had emigrated to Palestine long before the war; some could not be identified at all; and a significant number were European survivors of World War II who had gone direct to Israel—but had American next of kin. The net result of thorough re-investigation is to affirm that exactly thirty-eight Americans and Canadians were killed in the war and in its prelude. Details will be found in chapter eight. In terms of the monument, a broader caption will now head the original plaque, with a new corrected plaque erected alongside it.

[6] Israel Amir was then head of the Department of Manpower of the Army of Israel; in early 1948 he had been the first "Commander" of the fledgling Israel air arm. This writer participated directly in the discussions referred to above, as part of the Executive of the American Veterans of Israel.

NOTES TO CHAPTER 1

[1] "Jews" and "Arabs" are words that defy precise definition: Both groups are tremendously diverse, ethnically and racially. Of Jews, one may say that they are a "people" all of whose members recognize some level of affinity to

277

the historic Jewish religion. With reference to the Arabs, the word "peoples" (plural) must be used, and it must be pointed out that religious affinity is also plural (while the majority follow Islam, there are Maronites, Copts, Druze, etc.). Perhaps the only practical definitions are: Jews are those who identify themselves as Jews: Arabs are those who identify themselves as Arabs.

[2] The Haganah's initial reaction to the "Arab Revolt" (1936-1939) had been passivity, leaving security to the British. But this was clearly unsatisfactory; in 1937 the splinter IZL broke away to adopt a policy of *general* retaliation and, simultaneously, the Haganah Night Squads were formed to carry out highly selective punitive actions against guilty Arabs only. In one classic night operation, the mukhtar's house in the remote village of Sa'sa was destroyed with no loss of life on either side. Of course, the P'ulot Meyuhadot did not always operate on such a sanitary basis.

NOTES TO CHAPTER 2

[1] "Midrash" is the name given to a special genre: A story (homily, parable) —nonhistoric in nature and not necessarily literally true—but embodying one or more moral or ethical truths. Many midrashic tales are enrichments of the skeletal stories recorded in the Bible; many are quite fanciful. The Midrash is a literary art form meant to convey succinctly an observation about life, more successfully than can be done within narrow literal limits. The Talmud and many biblical commentaries are replete with such stories. Their production in Jewish tradition probably goes back more than three thousand years.

[2] Varying sources date the start as early as April 3 to as late as April 6.

NOTES TO CHAPTER 3

[1] Shaltiel's chief credential was previous service as a sergeant in the French Foreign Legion. Being an outsider with outside military experience was a most important qualification in the eyes of civilian Commander-in-Chief David Ben Gurion. The consensus is that David Shaltiel (like many of Abraham Lincoln's command appointments in the American Civil War) was a rather unfortunate choice.

[2] A detailed analysis may be found in the writer's doctoral dissertation, Appendix C, pp. 313-319. It is available in the library of the Jewish Theological Seminary, New York City.

[3] Israelis are brutally self-analytical; they have been both candid and serious in publicizing and punishing war excesses. For example, the machine-gunning (by Israeli soldiers) of Arabs at Kafr Kassem for curfew violation at the start of the Sinai Campaign (1956) was technically justifiable—the Arabs were violating the curfew—but was held to have been unnecessary on practical grounds. A court-martial for those responsible followed, with serious punishment for the guilty. Since Deir Yassin took place before the State of Israel

came into being, no punishment is possible—there is not shadow of a reason to dissemble.

⁴ Kurzman, Dan, *Genesis 1948*. New York and Cleveland: World Publishing, 1970, pp. 138–149; Collins, Larry and LaPierre, Dominique, O *Jerusalem*. New York: Simon and Schuster, 1972, pp. 266-282.

⁵ *Al Urdun*, Jordanian daily newspaper, 9 April 1955. Quoted by the Information Division, Israel Ministry of Foreign Affairs, 16 March 1969, "Background Notes on Current Themes."

⁶ Bauer, Yehuda. *From Diplomacy to Resistance*. A History of Jewish Palestine 1939–1945. Philadelphia; Jewish Publication Society, 1970, pp. 132, 309, 311–333.

⁷ History Department, General Headquarters, Army of Israel, *Toledot Milhemet Hakomemiut* (Hebrew), (Maarahot. 12ed., 1964), p. 117.

⁸ Although the name is the same, today's Jewish Agency is quite different from the quasigovernmental Jewish Agency of early 1948. Today's Agency is limited to performing nongovernmental services of philanthropic nature. The pressure of post-World War II events had made of the Jewish Agency the de facto government of Palestine's Jewish community. Once this was succeeded, in name, by the State of Israel (May 14, 1948), the Agency was able to resume the limited kind of role for which it had originally been constituted.

⁹ A letter to the writer, dated 5/5/68, from Gideon Yardain of the North American Department, Foreign Office of Israel.

¹⁰ In addition to sources already cited, see also:

Begin, Menachem. *The Revolt*. New York: Henry Schuman, 1951, pp. 162-165.

Glubb, Sir John Bagot. *A Soldier with the Arabs*. New York: Harper & Bros., 1957, p. 81.

Joseph, Dov. *The Faithful City*. New York: Simon and Schuster, 1960, pp. 71-72.

Katz, Samuel. *Days of Fire*. Garden City, New York: Doubleday & Co., 1968, pp. 214-217.

Lorch, Netanel. *The Edge of the Sword*. New York: G. P. Putnam's Sons, 1961, p. 92.

Ofir, Yehoshua. *Al Hahomot* (Hebrew). Mahon Jabotinski Press, 1961.

Schechtman, Joseph B. *"The Truth about Deir Yassin."* The American Zionist, June 1969, Vol. LIX, No. 10, pp. 17-20.

NOTES TO CHAPTER 5

¹ Harry S. Truman, *Memoirs,* 2 volumes (Garden City, New York: Doubleday & Co., 1955), vol.2, p. 166.

NOTES TO CHAPTER 6

[1] The official history lists a grand total of 10,500 rifles, 4435 automatic weapons, and 754 mortars, widely assorted as to type and very short of ammunition: History Department, *Toledot,* p. 78. David Ben Gurion (Israel's Prime Minister and Minister of Defense in 1948) gives the April 1948 total (before arrival of the arm's ship *Nora* and excluding whatever the IZL and LHI possessed) as 10,073 rifles, 1,900 light machine guns, 186 machine guns, 672 two-inch mortars, 96 three-inch mortars: "The Hagana on the Eve," *Jewish Observer and Middle East Review,* 14, No. 12, March 19, 1965, pp. 15–18.

[2] Lorch, *Edge of the Sword,* p. 90. In a subsequent chapter, we fully and critically investigate this important conclusion.

[3] History Department, *Toledot,* p. 112: The four guns are described as light German machine guns, type MG-34. Kagan, in both his books (*Himreeu,* p. 59; *Secret Battle,* p. 57) specifies 200 rifles and *40* machine guns.

[4] History Dept., *TOLEDOT,* p. 265; Lorch, *Sword,* p. 296.

[5] *The New York Times,* August 16, 1949, reported a delay in plans to detonate a large quantity of explosives which had been buried near the Old City wall by the Israelis in the summer of 1948. The *Times* of August 22 reported the blast itself (no damage was done), and the explanation that the explosives had been placed in an old abandoned tunnel as a defensive measure against possible Arab advance.

[6] This detail does not appear in any of our sources; it was related to the writer in the Spring of 1949 by Mendel Cohen, a veteran Jerusalemite who had made the furniture for King Abdullah's palace in Amman, who was reputed to be among the very few Jews allowed to visit Abdullah in early 1948, when secret negotiations were under way to try to persuade him to stay out of the developing war, and who had been Haganah's chief storekeeper in Jerusalem from the very beginning of hostilities.

NOTES TO CHAPTER 7

[1] Not unexpectedly, varying totals are given by different sources. Thus, Kurzman (*Genesis,* p. 460) lists 5,000 rifles, 300 Bren guns, 150 Spandaus, 5 tracked armored cars, 4 million bullets, several thousand air combat bombs, and other equipment.

[2] Katz, *Fire,* pp. 239–50. See also Begin, *Revolt,* pp. 166–76.

[3] Kurzman, *Genesis,* pp. 457–486.

[4] I was told verbally that some of these men refused to fire, but am unable to document this statement.

[5] Gershon Rivlin, and Zvi Sinai, *Hateevat Alexandroni B'Milhemet Hakommiut*—(Zahal, Maarahot, 1964). pp. 278-80.

[6] Lorch, *Sword,* pp. 255–6.

[7] Robert St. John, *Shalom Means Peace* (NY, Doubleday & Co., 1949), pp. 32–56. See also Thomas Sugrue, *Watch For The Morning,* (N.Y., Harper & Bros., 1950), pp. 243-245.

⁸ Even this meeting of the minds was more apparent than real: Israel Galili spoke to Begin of 20 percent going to Jerusalem—not to the Irgun forces in Jerusalem. (Kurzman, *Genesis,* p. 464.) At this point, Galili, former Commander of Haganah, was effective head of Zahal. Although his superior, Prime Minister and Minister of Defense Ben Gurion was in the process of easing him out, as part of his planned reorganization of Zahal into a regular army, the Chief of Staff, Yaacov Dori, was not well, and this kind of problem did not fall under the jurisdiction of Yigal Yadin who, as Director of Operations, may be said to have functioned as Dori's replacement in general planning and in the effectuating of plans.

⁹ These questions were not concerns of the political right alone. Several months after the *Altalena* affair, the writer was privy to a discussion by members of a left-wing kibbutz, in which they were very seriously considering illegal stockpiling of arms. The long-range development is interesting: All weapons belong to Zahal. Unlike the United States, there is no widespread private ownership of handguns in Israel. Individuals or organizations may only borrow weapons for limited periods, for legitimate self-protective purposes.

¹⁰ Lorch, *Sword,* pp. 162–163.

¹¹ This settlement has since been reestablished under another name, "Gadot." Today's Mishmar Hayarden occupies a different, neighboring area.

¹² It remains doubtful that the IZL actually turned over all the arms which had been unloaded there—although this was one of the agreed conditions of the surrender.

¹³ David Ben Gurion, *Behilahem Israel,* Mapai-Ahdut Press, 1951, pp. 165–179.

¹⁴ To complete this theory, it would be asserted that the "accidental warning shell" story was manufactured to accommodate a public opinion that otherwise would have been outraged: A large segment of the people did look askance at the leadership-fostered Agency/IZL bitterness; they felt that both approaches were patriotic and positive, and that energies directed at each other were tragically wasted.

¹⁵ Harold E. Livingston, *The Coasts of the Earth* (Boston: Houghton Mifflin Co., 1954), pp. 88–95.

¹⁶ Rowland Barber, *The Midnighters,* (New York: Crown Publishers, Inc., 1970), pp. 252–61.

¹⁷ William Lichtman, *Between the Star and the Cross,* (New York: Citadel Press, 1957), pp. 166–73.

¹⁸ Kurzman, *Genesis,* pp. 473–84.

¹⁹ Kimche, *Pillars,* p. 251 states flatly: "Ben Gurion ordered the army to fire the Irgun ship, the Altalena. . . ."

²⁰ The writer recalls the perceptive comment of one observer, upon learning of the description by the then Prime Minister, of the prowess of the Gahal at the first major battle for Latrun. Ben Gurion had stated, "They fought like lions." This critic said, "He means, they died like flies." The action, Operation Bin Nun 1, 5/25/48, was poorly prepared and badly executed. It was a night assault that failed. The following morning, New Brigade found itself penned

in by barbed wire, without water under the broiling sun, its narrow escape route under the guns of the Arab Legion.

This attack was later justified by Ben Gurion as a success in that, by directing the Arab Legion's attention to Latrun, it took deadly pressure off Jerusalem. Not everyone agrees with this assessment; it clearly failed in its obvious objective—opening the only road between Jerusalem and the coast. The attackers were largely brand-new immigrants who had had rudimentary training in the camps, but actually had to be taught to use their new Czech rifles en route to the battlefield. While it is not difficult to learn which end of a rifle to grasp and which to shoot, it was reported that a number of men never released the safety catch—and the safety prevents the rifle from firing. That such men were thrown into battle in such a way is most eloquent testimony to the desperate manpower shortage, and the desperate situation, ten days after the proclamation of the state.

[21] St. John, *Shalom,* pp. 32–56, is quite positive and detailed about this identification. Kurzman, *Genesis,* pp. 470–71, speaks only of Paul Shulman (the American commander of the Israeli navy) as being in charge of the *Wedgewood.* Since St. John did his interviewing on the spot, there can be no doubt as to the correctness of his identification. This difference in emphasis (is it the captain who commands the ship, if the Admiral of the Fleet is aboard or is the admiral then in charge?), is not overwhelmingly important from our point of view: Both men were overseas volunteers. Kurzman's account (*Genesis,* pp. 457–86) is thorough, and complements St. John's far more immediate work.

NOTES TO CHAPTER 9

[1] Kurzman, *Genesis,* p. 145; our Chapter 3.

[2] The mortar is a metal tube which rests on the ground and is aimed at an angle to the vertical. The mortar shell is dropped down the mouth of the tube and is triggered as it reaches the bottom. The angle of the tube determines the direction of the shell. When the mortar shell reaches the peak of its travel, gravity takes over, and brings it to earth. The PIAT (Projectile Infantry, Anti-Tank) is also a metal tube, but it is fired horizontally (generally, at a vehicle). "Bazooka" is the American designation for this weapon. Unlike the mortar, its shell is a rocket: That is, instead of being impelled only by an initial charge, the propellant rides with the shell and keeps it accelerating. This makes the force of impact many times greater. PIAT ammunition was manufactured in a hidden workshop at the Daniel Sieff Agricultural Institute in Rehovot. By then, this had become the site of the Weizmann Institute of Science, with Chaim Weizmann an occasional elderly visitor, making it a point to express regret at the likelihood that such activities were taking place there.

[3] Slater, *Pledge,* pp. 23, 321.

[4] Sraya Shapiro, "B-G At Home," *The Jerusalem Post Weekly,* June 23, 1969, p. 10.

⁵ It will be recalled that bitter experience had taught the Jews of Palestine that the British could not be relied upon for effective defense against marauding Arabs—only their own arms, under their own control, could be counted on. Since arms were subject to seizure when they were used, both local manufacture and an expanding "pipeline" were vital.

⁶ Slater, *Pledge*, pp. 45–50.

⁷ Slater, *Pledge*, pp. 52–55.

⁸ Slater, *Pledge*, pp. 116–117, 153–157.

⁹ Slater, *Pledge*, pp. 196–197.

¹⁰ Slater, *Pledge*, pp. 158–169, 209–218.

¹¹ *New York Times*, July 14, 1948.

¹² Shahan, *Kanfei*, p. 131.

¹³ The single major success in such procurement (at least, of machine guns) was Hank Greenspun's Hawaii/Mexico operation, which stretched over half a year. Because it began with spare aircraft engines, we tell this story in a subsequent chapter.

¹⁴ Slater, *Pledge*, pp. 256–259.

NOTES TO CHAPTER 10

¹ Burstein, *Wings*, p. 50.

² See Herbert Agar, *The Saving Remnant* (New York: Viking Press, 1962), p. 204ff, for a full appreciation of this remarkable man.

³ Slater, *Pledge*, pp. 221–224.

⁴ See Appendix J for a detailed discussion of America's paradoxical relationship with the Jewish state.

⁵ This is the conventional, surface explanation. A deeper analysis is offered in Appendix J.

⁶ Kagan, *Secret Battle*, p. 56.

⁷ Kagan, *Secret Battle*, p. 57.

⁸ For details of the fate of this ship and its arms, see Operation Pirate, Chapter 14.

⁹ Shahan, *Kanfei*, pp. 117–121; Slater, *Pledge*, pp. 250–55.

¹⁰ Balak 4 is Kagan's identification (*Himreeu*, p. 81); Shahan (who is probably correct) has an additional preceding flight (*Kanfei*, p. 140), and so calls this Balak 5.

¹¹ Kagan (*Himreeu*, p. 78) briefly refers to *two* DC-4s; no other source does so, and the weight of evidence in terms of usage supports the conclusion that just a single (rented) DC4 was involved. It does appear that a (different) DC-4 was acquired later in the year. The Constellation saw very limited service: It was disabled on a return flight from Israel July 13 (Shahan, *Kanfei*, p. 344). Slater (*Pledge*, p. 310) identifies this as its seventh flight, but says that it first arrived in Zatec July 9. Shahan (p. 119) gives the date of arrival as June 25, which would make seven flights barely possible, with a lesser number (three?) far more likely.

[12] Mardor, *Illegal*, pp. 217–18; Slater, *Pledge*, pp. 293-301, 310; Kagan, *Himreeu*, pp. 78–87; Shahan, *Kanfei*, pp. 117–127, 139–142.

[13] Kagan, *Secret Battle*, p. 111.

[14] This was not the first Arab capitol to be bombed: Damascus had been hit the night of June 10/11, just before the first truce, by throwing bombs out the door of a Dakota; and Amman, the capital of Transjordan, had been bombed earlier still—by three planes—June 1.

[15] Lorch, *Sword*, p. 363; Kagan, *Secret Battle*, p. 125; see our mitigating comment in Appendix D.

[16] Attacks on enemy capitals were checked partially by political considerations, partially by the importance of using limited resources directly against the enemy in the field, and partially by moral scruples: To bomb an enemy capital once may be a major psychological achievement; to do so repeatedly is to indiscriminately attack civilians (unless one is attacking military targets in the vicinity of a particular city).

NOTES TO CHAPTER 11

[1] We use "Americans" as an umbrella word, including citizens of the United States or Canada. No slight to the Canadians is intended—rather, it is a recognition of the similarity of culture and common usage.

[2] Oahu is the second largest of the seven major islands making up the Hawaiian chain. It is often loosely referred to as "Hawaii," which is the largest of the islands, but is otherwise less prominent. Honolulu, Diamond Head, Waikiki, and the huge naval installation called Pearl Harbor are all part of Oahu —not Hawaii.

[3] The reader may wonder at this open exposure of law breaking, including the naming of names. Neither exposure nor peril are introduced here. Greenspun himself has told the above, and what follows, in print (*Where I Stand*, New York, David McKay Co.: 1966), as have others (Kagan, Kurzman, Slater). As for peril—the statute of limitations has long since run out on any possible impropriety related anywhere in this work. (The statute of limitations states that if legal prosecution for alleged offenses is to be initiated, it must be done within a specific number of years of the alleged commitment of the offense.)

[4] Slater, (*Pledge*, p. 308), states that Schalit had bought the *Kefalos* at the Todd Shipyards in Brooklyn; Greenspun, (*Stand*, p. 132) asserts that it belonged to its captain, Adolph Sigmund Oko, who purchased it in Portland, Oregon, and with his wife had used it to smuggle illegal immigrants to Palestine.

[5] Slater, *Pledge*, p. 308, gives the total as thirty-six 75 mm howitzers, 17,000 shells, 2,000 aerial bombs, 7 million rounds of ammunition, and 500 machine guns and submachine guns, including those which had come from Oahu. The official history, *Toledot*, (p. 289), mentions 32 howitzers—and says that these "cucarachas" were of little value.

⁶ Greenspun, *Stand*, pp. 82–151; Slater, *Pledge*, pp. 198–204; Kurzman, *Genesis*, pp. 109–113, 488–493.

⁷ History Department, *Toledot*, p. 289.

⁸ Greenspun, *Stand*, p. 167.

⁹ History Department, *Toledot*, p. 289.

¹⁰ *The New York Times*, February 25, 26; March 11; June 8; September 4, 1948.

¹¹ The subject of Soviet and American attitudes is discussed in detail in Appendix J.

¹² This is detailed in chapter fourteen.

¹³ Shahan, *Kanfei*, p. 119.

¹⁴ Shahan, *Kanfei*, pp. 119–123. Heyman Shamir (Hyman Shechtman), an Israeli with American World War II aircraft experience as a navigator, was most active with the Schwimmer operations in early 1948. Being warned that the F.B.I. was looking for him Shamir, who was then in Mexico, went to Italy rather than return to the United States. In Catania, Sicily, he met the C-46s coming in from Panama—and was a passenger (and guide) on the first of the two C-46s which landed in Israel the night of May 16th.

¹⁵ Kagan, *Secret Battle*, pp. 62–63.

¹⁶ Swing, *Air Force*, pp. 38–40.

¹⁷ Slater, *Pledge*, p. 296.

¹⁸ Swing, *Air Force*, pp. 100–141.

¹⁹ Shahan (*Kanfei*, p. 146) has this final flurry taking place immediately before the closing of the base. On the other hand, Kagan (*Himreeu*, p. 136; *Secret Battle*, p. 117) states that this specific group of flights took place the final week of the truce (i.e., the first week of July). It appears to us that both would naturally be periods of maximum effort.

²⁰ Slater, *Pledge*, p. 314.

²¹ *The New York Times*, Nov. 5, Nov. 6, 1948.

NOTES TO CHAPTER 12

¹ Shahan, *Kanfei*, pp. 132–133.

² Slater (*Pledge*, p. 264) identifies the buyer as former U. S. Army Air Force Lt. Col. David Miller, then residing in Paris as a dealer in second-hand aircraft. The "front" represented itself as a Belgian company planning to operate a freight airline to Spain.

³ Shahan (*Kanfei*, p. 134) states that some of these planes came to Israel by sea. The others (e.g., Kagan, *Secret Battle*, pp. 38–39, Slater, *Pledge*, p. 266) are unanimous in indicating that all were flown in.

⁴ Swing, *Air Force*, pp. 22–29; Kagan, *Himreeu*, pp. 81–84.

⁵ Slater, *Pledge*, pp. 289–290; Swing, *Air Force*, pp. 29–30.

⁶ Shahan, *Kanfei*, pp. 135–138.

⁷ Actually, only three of these actually saw direct service: The fourth was set aside for cannibalization as a source of vital spare parts.

⁸ Kagan, *Himreeu*, pp. 133–135.

[9] See Chapter 18.

[10] Kagan, *Secret Battle,* pp. 182–184.

[11] Kagan, *Himreeu,* pp. 63–67; Shahan, *Kanfei,* pp. 158–161.

[12] In a rare, lengthy article on "Mahal," the *Jerusalem Post* of April 20, 1968, writes that the South African League for Haganah "bought three Dakotas which were used on the Marseilles-Haifa run to transport volunteers and vital equipment. When the planes turned around in Israel the pilots used the opportunity to go on a bombing mission, before returning to Marseilles."

Although it is not unlikely that communications and airlift transports on their way out of Israel during fighting periods might occasionally start off with a bombing run, this was hardly the normal, routine practice. We asked precisely this question of a participant. The reply: "I did hear of a few ATC flights which bombed enemy targets on the way out of Israel. I believe it actually was done, but I have no direct knowledge of these missions." Articles (and some books) on the War of Independence tend to romanticize and generalize at the expense of fact.

[13] Shahan, *Kanfei,* pp. 161–164.

[14] Shahan, *Kanfei,* pp. 91, 172–173. Excluded from this count are the ATC (Schwimmer) planes and those in process of being acquired, but not yet available for service in Israel.

NOTES TO CHAPTER 13

[1] Kagan, *Himreeu,* pp. 109–110.

[2] *New York Times,* Feb. 5, 1949.

[3] Kagan, *Secret Battle,* pp. 98–100; Swing, *Air Force,* pp. 58–61. There had been an alarming occurrence on one of the planes. In its earlier commercial history, an aerial camera had been installed in the floor, where a machine-gun turret had previously been. Now, this opening—the size of a manhole cover—was closed by a thin plate. In walking down the catwalk from the nose compartment, the navigator permitted the full weight of his body to rest on this plate, which suddenly gave way. Only the instinctive spreading of his arms prevented his dropping 10,000 feet into the Atlantic. His body was battered by the plane's slipstream for perhaps half an hour, until he was missed, searched for, found and rescued by his crewmates. By the time all arrived at Zatec, this near-tragedy had become a source of humor to all concerned, including the principal.

A personal footnote: Some nine months later, my wife and I were told by friends that they had been especially concerned over the newspaper reports that the B-17s were lost, since they knew we were on them. This, of course, was far from the truth: These planes had no passengers. It is a cardinal rule of "underground" operations that different channels be kept separate from each other. Thus discovery or failure of one does not bring others down with it. My wife and I (we were then married just over five months) actually did depart the United States early in June, at about the same time as this flight of B-17s, —but we left by thoroughly innocent means: A commercial Air France flight

(NY-Gander-Shannon-Paris-Rome). Proper contact was made in Rome, and we arrived in Israel (via a South African commercial charter plane) June 28. This kind of routing was not the rule; most volunteers made their way much less rapidly and directly. The usual route from Europe was by sea, as passengers or crew on one of the slow, crowded, aged refugee ships. However, as a combination electrical engineer, radar technician, and anti-radar expert, the writer was given the same top priority transportation arrangement as supplementary pilots and aircrew.

4 Kagan, *Secret Battle*, pp. 101–105; Slater, *Pledge*, pp. 312–313.

5 Shahan, *Kanfei*, pp. 126–127. Kurtz's written reports are a rich source of information; Shahan quotes many of them at length, from Israel air-force files. See also Daniel Spicehandler, *Let My Right Hand Wither*, (New York: Beechhurst Press, 1950), pp. 167–168, 196–221.

6 Kagan, *Himreeu*, pp. 143–151.

7 Shahan, *Kanfei*, pp. 147–151; Swing, *Air Force*, pp. 202–210.

8 Swing, *Air Force*, pp. 194–201.

9 Shahan, *Kanfei*, pp. 151–154.

10 Kagan, *Himreeu*, pp. 167–169. Slater (*Pledge*, p. 301) relates that a major Czech money crisis took place half a year earlier, preceeding the purchase of the second lot of ME-109s. This was a year of crises in financing.

11 Kagan, *Himreeu*, pp. 170–175.

12 Shahan, *Kanfei*, p. 156.

13 Kagan, *Himreeu*, pp. 176–179.

14 Kagan, *Himreeu*, pp. 186–188.

NOTES TO CHAPTER 14

1 P. E. Lapide, *A Century of U.S. Aliya* (Jerusalem: Jerusalem Post Press, 1961), p. 91. Another source (Bauer, *Flight*, p. 281) gives the grand total to May 1948 as 69,878. However, his figures include North Africa.

2 Lorch, *Sword*, p. 132.

3 Slater, *Pledge*, pp. 138–140, 283–285.

4 Mardor, *Illegal*, p. 197.

5 Mardor, *Illegal*, pp. 173–183. Another source describes this as a single shipment of 40 tons of arms (Slater, *Pledge*, pp. 148–149.

6 Lorch, *Sword*, pp. 312–313.

7 Mardor, *Illegal*, pp. 56–76.

8 Mardor, *Illegal*, pp. 200–211; Kurzman, *Genesis*, pp. 120–123, 549–550.

9 *Toledot*, pp. 362–363.

10 Appendix E, David Baum.

11 Appendix E, Aaron Lebow.

NOTES TO CHAPTER 15

[1] *The New York Times,* January 30, 1970, p. 45: Obituary of Basil Liddel Hart.

[2] B. H. Liddel Hart, *Strategy* (New York: 1955), Appendix II, pp. 386–391; cited by J. Bowyer Bell in *The Long War* Prentice Hall. (Englewood Cliffs, N.J.: 1969), p. 215. (The direct quotation is on p. 203).

[3] Swing, *Air Force,* pp. 166–171.

[4] During Yoav, the same crews and planes would often fly successive cargo and bombing missions.

[5] Kagan, *Himreeu,* p. 140. Mardor (*Illegal,* p. 228) gives figures of 417 flights, 4991 tons of supplies and 10,196 passengers—the latter, quite unbelievable. Slater (*Pledge,* p. 316) apparently copied these figures.

[6] History Dept., *Toledot,* p. 298.

[7] Lorch, *Sword,* pp. 350–351. Another source indicates that the majority of the trapped Egyptians successfully fled south along the beach. Kurzman, *Genesis,* pp. 605–606.

[8] Kagan, *Secret Battle,* p. 121.

NOTES TO CHAPTER 16

[1] Letter to the writer, dated March 17, 1970.

[2] Shahan, *Kanfei,* pp. 222–223, quotes the first Israeli pilot to later be attached to this squadron as rather overawed at a number of factors: The vast experience of its volunteer pilots and the opportunity to learn from such men— balanced by the negative reputation of the Norsemen (following the two fatal accidents we described much earlier, they had been nicknamed "flying coffins"). Actually, this reputation was not deserved; considering the prevailing conditions, and the fact that this plane was also involved in some accidents which were not fatal, one could suggest that its performance was quite good.

[3] Our Appendix E includes the testimony of three ATC participants: Stern, Klausner, Swing. In addition, one pilot (Kaplansky), who does not indicate his specific flying service, states of the ATC, "This whole outfit was almost exclusively foreign."

[4] One source only (Slater, *Pledge,* pp. 290–295) makes much of the hired DC-4 (C-54) Skymaster, which could carry a complete Messerschmitt fighter, and make the trip nonstop. But this plane made very few trips (two, certainly; possibly one or two more); the brunt of the airlift was the work of the ATC proper in its C-46s. Slater (alone among our sources) also sees the Czech airlift primarily in terms of delivering the fighter planes. This seems to us to be a distortion: Balak 5 was the first flight to carry a fighter—the first four carried infantry arms only. Balak 5 (May 20) was also the first flight by the hired DC4 since the critical pre-Nahshon flight March 31. And this lone "mercenary" plane is not entirely free of a volunteer aura. Slater, who emphasizes its commercial nature (*Pledge,* pp. 245, 295) also points out that a partner (and crew member) was the navigator Seymour Lerner. And Kagan (*Himreeu,* p. 238)

tells of Schwimmer's turning to the "veteran volunteer, Seymour Lerner," when a navigator was needed to join veteran volunteer pilot Ray Kurtz in flying a Mosquito from Goose Bay (Labrador, Canada) to Israel. Both men were lost: the plane took off May 17, 1951; no trace of it has ever been found.

[5] Appendix E, Kaplansky; also Bressloff, Doyle, Freundlich, Katz, Klausner, Stern, Swing, Weisberg.

[6] With the exception of the Haifa area. For an explanation of this, and a detailed discussion of Squadron 505 and radar in Israel, see chapter eighteen.

[7] Essentially, the operator of an early warning radar looks at a screen in a darkened room; she reports the existence of any moving dots which appear on the screen, reading the approximate coordinates from a sheet of transparent plastic on the face of the screen. The screen is similar to a small television screen. Thus, a single skilled operator could impart the necessary techniques and procedures to a large number of total novices and, in a very short period of time, turn out operators adequately able to cope with the very low level of air activity then prevailing in Israel.

[8] History Dept., *Toledot*, p. 362; Shahan, *Kanfei*, p. 260.

[9] Shahan, *Kanfei*, lists it as a Piper on p. 341 and an Auster on p. 345.

[10] Shahan, p. 258.

[11] Shahan, p. 275, also indicates that an additional 45 tons were deposited on neighboring Iraq el Manshiya.

[12] For a flavor of this, see Appendix E, Doyle.

[13] Lorch, *Sword*, p. 421.

[14] Shahan, *Kanfei*, pp. 276–177, 282. See also Appendix E, Doyle.

[15] Kagan (*Himreeu*, p. 182) indicates December, but the *New York Times*, January 20, 1949 quotes British Secretary for Air Arthur Henderson admitting to Parliament that the RAF had flown about twenty reconnaissance missions over Israel, until one such plane was downed off Tel Aviv November 20.

[16] Kurzman, *Genesis*, pp. 662–68.

[17] Kagan, *Himreeu*, pp. 182–185; Shahan, *Kanfei*, pp. 283–285. There remain some minor factual discrepancies concerning the January 7th action. Photo-reconnaissance was the British explanation of the purpose of the two flights. Consistent with this, the British denied that these planes had taken any offensive action against Israeli ground forces. In contradiction to this claim, we accepted the eye-witness reports of Israeli pilots. All agreed that the first RAF flight consisted of four Spitfires. With reference to the second flight, however, Kagan states that there were eight planes. Here, we accepted the British report of five. As for the total number of RAF planes destroyed, we account for four (three of the morning's four Spitfires, plus one Tempest in the afternoon.) However, it is usual to record the total as five, basing this on the first British report that all four of the Spitfires in the morning flight were lost. In our Appendix E, the testimony of one participating pilot speaks of four Spitfires destroyed and three (planes) damaged.

[18] Shahan, *Kanfei*, pp. 285–289; Kurzman, *Genesis*, pp. 692–698; Glubb, *Soldier*, pp. 229–232.

[19] Shahan, *Kanfei*, p. 286.

NOTES TO CHAPTER 17

[1] *Yizkor,* p. 684.

[2] Abraham Rabinovich, "The Saga of the 35," *Jerusalem Post* (weekend), February 2, 1970, pp. 8-9.

[3] PIAT-Projectile, Infantry, Anti-Tank—essentially the American "bazooka", a metal tube for firing rockets at tanks.

[4] *Davar Hashavua,* 18, May 12, 1949, p. 8.

[5] Mardor, *Illegal,* pp. 198–199.

[6] Tevet, *Hassufim,* pp. 49–53.

[7] In a footnote, Slater (*Pledge,* p. 266) states that 23 Jews and 12 non-Jews of the Red Army are known to have deserted immediately after VE Day (1945) and made their way to Palestine. These we would of course consider Israelis: People who came well before the war, intending to settle permanently.

[8] Shahan, *Kanfei,* p. 341.

[9] *Yizkor,* p. 747.

[10] History Department, *Toledot,* pp. 337–340.

[11] Tevet, *Hassufim,* pp. 55–63.

[12] Ted Berkman, *Cast A Giant Shadow,* (Doubleday, Garden City, N. Y., 1962). Both Kurzman (*Genesis,* p. 108) and Slater (*Pledge,* pp. 101–102) state that Marcus was originally wanted by Haganah recruiter Shlomo (Rabinovich) Shamir as junior to a combat-experienced American general. But Major General R. C. Smith demurred when the U.S. army would not guarantee his pension—and Marcus was "it."

[13] Berkman, pp. 261–2; photostat #19, following p. 158.

[14] Berkman, p. 299.

[15] *Haganah Speaks,* June 16, 1948.

[16] *Maarachot,* July, 1948, pp. 13–14.

[17] *Palestine Information Bulletin,* June 16, 1948, Jewish Agency for Palestine, London.

[18] Kurzman (*Genesis,* pp. 439–443) points out that the investigation was incomplete and left a number of apparent discrepancies unresolved.

[19] Lorch, *Sword,* p. 326.

NOTES TO CHAPTER 18

[1] Although the British were capable of leaving their living quarters in something of a mess (including crude graffiti on the walls), when it came to the radar installations in Israel they were totally neat. Outside the enormously heavy poured-concrete bases (and that metal that was an integral part of them) which had supported their large, heavy antennas, they took everything with them, down to the last screw.

[2] Roads: docking and maneuvering area in the vicinity of a coastal city, but well offshore.

[3] "Israeli" here—and throughout this work—is a catch-all term which

includes all except Mahal. Included is everyone who came before or during 1948, from the native Israeli ("Sabra") to the most recent immigrant, provided only that his presumed permanent residence was Israel. Excluded are those who, before November 29, 1947, came from a Western country on a presumably temporary basis (e.g., students) and elected to remain and serve, as well as all those, rooted in Western countries, who came during the war.

⁴ This expertise was thanks to an extra U.S. Navy course given to those designated for "beach jumping." In invading a hostile coast, a flotilla of light ships would be assembled whose task it was to simulate the invading force. The enemy would be misled and move his defenses to this area, leaving the area of the intended real invasion. This feint would necessarily take place at night using both radar and a variety of antiradar equipment (it was an important element in every genuine invasion to try effectively to disable enemy radar by a variety of jamming techniques). Beach jumping was used in the Mediterranean and in the Pacific; since its purpose was to draw maximum enemy fire, casualties could run well in the neighborhood of 90 percent. I was being trained for the invasion of the Japanese home islands, which was obviated by the surrender of Japan following the atom bombing of Hiroshima and Nagasaki.

⁵ Officially, aluminum foil did not exist in Israel, according to the Air Force Chief of Procurement. However, on the assumption that a factory could only wrap sweets with material it physically possessed, the writer went to the Elite factory in Ramat Gan, persuaded its manager to part with the amount needed (without even a written requisition—for which I have always felt friendly towards Elite chocolates), experimented successfully—and learned that the Chief of Procurement had subsequently been shifted to a position in which his bureaucratic talents would have greatly reduced scope.

NOTES TO CHAPTER 19

¹ One of our correspondents (Appendix E), an American, had harsh things to say about the volunteer American sailors; we find echoes of this elsewhere, regarding American volunteers in all branches of Israel's military service. While most volunteers conducted themselves in exemplary fashion (the brawling tendencies of some fliers were not regarded entirely in a negative way), some, particularly among the Americans, were highly critical, quick to take personal offense at general situations, and bitter and serious complainers very much out of proportion to the realities—although some complaints, of course, were justified. Perhaps this was due in large measure to the fact they did come from safe, comfortable, America, which had not been touched by war—and expected their great "sacrifice" to be visibly and continually appreciated. Instead, people who had truly suffered, greeted them as comrades-in-arms rather than as liberators, with a sincere sense of appreciation that "you have come to help us."

² In chapter seven, we suggested that the *Altalena* confrontation might not have been possible without the participation of several key (American)

volunteers. But it certainly would have been positive, not negative, had the limited tragedy of this mini-civil war not taken place at all.

[3] History Dept., *Toledot*, pp. 112–113; Lorch, *Sword*, p. 90.

[4] It appears that a modest number of Israelis had some level of World War II training flying fighters, bombers, or transports (Shahan, *Kanfei*, p. 335, lists 26 by name; we assume that this is the total number) but, particularly under the adverse conditions prevailing in the War of Independence, there is a world of difference between the realistic qualifications of one who has simply completed a course, and one who has already acquired broad experience.

[5] Kagan, *Secret*, p. 56. The two exceptions would have been Ami Cooperman, the Israeli observer, and Seymour Lerner, American navigator and partner in U.S. Overseas Airlines. Earlier, we cited a retrospective reference by Kagan to Lerner as a volunteer.

[6] Shahan, *Kanfei*, pp. 60–63.

[7] Shahan lists him as Israeli on p. 63, as South African in the table of casualties, p. 340.

[8] Shahan, *Kanfei*, pp. 63–70; p. 338.

[9] Some of the small number of Israelis with some level of previous air training served as apprentices in the transport and bomber squadrons.

[10] Kagan, *Secret*, p. 121.

[11] Burstein, *Wings*, p. 50.

[12] Shahan, *Kanfei*, pp. 340–341.

[13] We discussed earlier Shahan's misidentification of the Canadian Wilfred (Zev) Cantor as Russian. Although born in Russia, Cantor was brought to Canada at the age of five; his World War II service was in the RCAF.

[14] Ben Gurion goes further, stating, "But without the Soviet arms (e.g., the arms that the Soviets permitted the Czechs to sell) we would not have been able to survive." Sraya Shapiro, "B-G Back Home," *The Jerusalem Post Weekly,* June 23, 1969, p. 10.

NOTES TO CHAPTER 20

[1] The relative number was many times greater since Israel's Jewish population in 1948 was only about one-fourth its 1967 Jewish population.

[2] The religious imperative has, of course been a constant. But it is important to note that this ongoing religious imperative was essentially non-productive until after the reborn state was physically secure. For two millenia only isolated individuals or rare small groups returned to Zion. Modern Zionism—the politically and economically organized effort to reestablish a Jewish state in the land of Israel—was supported by some religious Jews, and articulately (even fanatically) opposed by other religious Jews. The great majority of those directly involved in modern Zionism since its inception close to the end of the 19th century, saw it as a creative *alternative* to traditional Jewish religion.

NOTES TO APPENDIX A

[1] Katz, *Fire* p. 56; Bauer, *Flight*, p. 91.

[2] For details on the rather complex origins of the Palmach, including the Special Squads, see Bauer, *From Diplomacy to Resistance,* pages 57, 129, 139ff.

NOTES TO APPENDIX B

[1] Weizmann, *Trial*, pp. 232-47. The text of Feisal's famous letter of March 3, 1919, to Felix Frankfurter is included. Also, Renee Winegarten, "T. E. Lawrence, The End of a Legend," *Midstream*, May 1970 (Vol. XVI, No. 5) pp. 61–62. The latter is a more complex view, emphasizing the ambiguous role of Lawrence of Arabia.

[2] Jordanian representative F. el Mulki to the UN Palestine Committee, as reported by *The New York Times,* November 27, 1949.

NOTES TO APPENDIX C

[1] Gil Carl Alroy, "Old Apologetics and New Realism," *Congress Bi-Weekly,* New York, April 28, 1969 (Vol. 36, no. 6), p. 9.

NOTES TO APPENDIX E

[1] At the time the questionnaires were drawn up, my thinking was to include both Gahal and Mahal in this study. As the study progressed, Gahal was eliminated so that (as we discussed elsewhere at length) our focus is on Mahal and equivalent. In terms of the replies to our questionnaire, the suggestion that Gahal be included, was universally ignored: Our replies were in terms of equating overseas volunteers with Mahal only.

[2] One only will not be quoted, since it simply refers us to the correspondent's book which is part of our bibliography.

[3] Katz, *Fire,* p. 257, writes that for the entire day of May 25, Ramat Rahel, the key to the southern flank of Jerusalem, was held by the IZL alone, under heavy attack. Ofir credits an American identified only as "Danny" with turning back one major enemy thrust there. Kurzman, *Genesis,* p. 293, names him as Moshe Brodetzky—and Moshe Brodetzky confirmed that his regular nickname was "Danny." Largely for security reasons, each underground activist routinely adopted a nickname (Hebrew: shem kinui).

[4] David Glassman is identified by Slater (*Pledge,* pp. 153–54) as being in charge of the camouflage repacking of five and a half tons of smokeless powder purchased in Mexico. *Haganah Speaks,* a semiweekly New York newspaper, in its March 1, 1948, issue, lists him as one of six men brought to trial for arms embargo violation in connection with the *Executor* (chapter nine); all were given suspended sentences.

[5] "Anglo Saxons" was the common Israeli term for Jews from the English-speaking countries.

[6] These operations were the erecting and operation of ground radar stations. All of Israel's radar (except for the Navy sector) was, administratively, part of the Air Force (the radar unit was a separate administrative "Squadron") —although there was no airborne radar in use: its primary function, then, was early warning.

[7] This probably combines the two actions in which four RAF planes were shot down on that final day of fighting by a combination of air and ground fire. See our detailed discussion, chapter sixteen.

[8] Chapter 19.

[9] The ascription to Ben Gurion is erroneous; this reference should be to *Toledot,* the official Army history.

NOTES TO APPENDIX F

[1] Lapide, *U.S. Aliya,* p. 95.

[2] History Department, *Toledot,* p. 290.

[3] Shahan, *Kanfei,* pp. 293-296.

[4] An even lower Jewish population for Denmark—5,500—is given by the *American Jewish Yearbook,* Vol. 50, (1948–1949), Jewish Publication Society, Philadelphia, Pa., 1949.

[5] As quoted in the letter of April 25, 1968: "The official definition of Mahal, promulgated by the Mahal Committee of the Manpower Section of the General Staff, 4 Feb. '49, says: Mahal are residents of the U.S., Canada, United Kingdom, S. Africa, Latin America who arrived in Israel as volunteers for the army prior to Sept. 1948; also the American students at the Hebrew University and the Technion, who had arrived on the G.I. Bill of Rights with the intention to study here and then go back home, and who left their studies after 29/11/47 and volunteered for the army; also anyone from the above countries who arrived after the respective dates specified, provided he came upon the authorized request of the army. The above definition was meant to exclude from the privilege of being repatriated at the army's expense those who came from countries where no recruitment of volunteers took place, such as Eastern Europe and North Africa, but from which people came as Olim (settlers), with the clear intention of settling in Israel, and were in due course drafted into the army."

[6] This is distinctly lower than Shahan's 750, above. Shahan's great strength is in assembling data, much of it not to be found elsewhere. His great weakness is failure to evaluate it properly. Thus, his basic American air crew figure (310) is already quite full—it does not account for the actual shortage of such personnel, nor for the fact that they were not *all* Americans. Therefore, his own data leads us to a conclusion significantly different from his conclusion.

[7] Thirty-two hundred: 1200 Americans (including Canadians), 1200 British, 800 South Africans; 3,900: 1400 Americans, 1500 British, 1000 South Africans. The total number from Australia, New Zealand, India, etc., was so

small that it disappears in the range given for "British." Zahal, the Army of Israel, included more than 90,000 by mid-October; about 60,000 at the end of the First Truce (July 9); 49,000 at the beginning of the First Truce (June 11).

[8] Appendix E, Perry.

[9] Lorch, *Sword*, p. 327.

NOTES TO APPENDIX G

[1] *American Jewish Yearbook*, Vol. 50 (1948–1949); prepared by the American Jewish Committee, Jewish Publication Society of America (Philadelphia, Pa., 1949).

[2] All figures on the number of volunteers are the best estimates of our Appendix F.

[3] See Appendix H.

[4] Dr. Louis I. Dublin and Dr. Samuel C. Kohs, *American Jews in World War II*, commissioned by the National Jewish Welfare Board (New York: Dial Press, 1947).

[5] Slater (*Pledge*, p. 232) states, "Very few of the volunteers were Zionists." Mardor (*Illegal*, p. 214) writes, "Our Jewish volunteers, many of whom had come from an assimilated background, had been shocked into a kind of practical Zionism by events in Palestine as reported in the newspapers." Burstein (*Wings*, p. 50) mentions meeting "Jerry Renov (the only pilot besides myself with a traditional Jewish and Zionist background)." Eliezer Newman, "Gachal-Israel's 7th Brigade," *The New Palestine*, August 31, 1948, writes, "Americans, Canadians, (etc.) . . . sit around the tables [in a volunteers' soldiers canteen] conversing in a score of languages. . . . The most amazing thing about most of the newcomers is that almost all of them were formerly not connected at all with the Zionist movement. A few of them vaguely belonged to what they called "the Zionist party at home," but when they were pressed for a closer definition as to what kind of Zionist party, they were at a loss to say. Few of them knew the difference between a Labor Zionist and a Revisionist, let alone the subtle distinctions between something like the Mapai and the Mapam. . . ."

[6] Quoted by Dr. Miriam K. Freund, Editor, *Hadassah Magazine*, in a written reply to the author's survey letter, summer, 1969.

[7] Interview with Ben Dorfman, surviving brother of Yaakov (Jack) Dorfman.

NOTES TO APPENDIX H

[1] As noted earlier, Eddie Cohen, who had come to Palestine from South Africa in 1947 intending to settle permanently, is an Israeli and not a volunteer by strict definition.

[2] Glen King, George (Buzz) Beurling, Spence Boyd, M. Campbell, Leonard Fitchett, Fred Stevenson, Oliver Holton. This information is extracted from a study of Shahan's tables (*Kanfei*, pp. 340–345) and each individual biography

in *Yizkor*. One small error: Fred (Steve) Stevenson is included as American above, based on printed sources. Other information insists that he was Canadian, coming from Victoria.

[3] There were a few non-Jews who served outside the Air Force from America and from other countries. However, outside the Air Force they were numerically so few that their presence does not change our general figures significantly. Non-Jews *were* significant among the postwar, hired Mahal specialists, but these are outside our focus on wartime volunteers.

NOTES TO APPENDIX I

[1] *New York Times*, Nov. 16, 1948.
[2] *New York Times*, Jan. 22, Feb. 5, 1949.
[3] *New York Times*, Nov. 25, 1948.
[4] Slater, *Pledge*, pp. 165-169, 192.
[5] *Haganah Speaks*, March, 1948; Slater, *Pledge*, p. 192.
[6] Slater, *Pledge*, p. 320; Greenspun, *Stand*, p. 170.
[7] In reporting this, the *New York Times* of Feb. 21, 1950 makes no mention of the seventh man, Abe Levin. Slater, (*Pledge*, p. 320) concurs with the Times; Greenspun, (*Stand*, p. 179) adds Levin among those found guilty.

NOTES TO APPENDIX J

[1] From the very inception of the Red regime, November 1917. While the Czars had hardly favored the Jews, they did occasionally encourage Jewish emigration to any part of the world, including Palestine.

[2] The Balfour Declaration is a letter written by Arthur James Balfour, after approval by the British War Cabinet, to Lord Rothschild, November 2, 1917. Its text is as follows:

His Majesty's Government view with favour the establishment in Palestine of a National Home for the Jewish people and will use their best endeavours to facilitate the achievement of this object, it being clearly understood that nothing shall be done which may prejudice the civil and religious rights of the existing non-Jewish communities in Palestine or the rights or political status enjoyed by the Jews in any other country.

[3] Chaim Weizmann, *"Trial and Error"* (New York: Harper and Brothers, 1949), pp. 206–208.

[4] Truman, *Memoirs*, 2:164: "I am sorry to say that there were some among them (men in the State Department) who were also inclined to be anti-Semitic."

[5] Dean Acheson, *Present At The Creation*, (New York: W. W. Norton, 1969), p. 169.

[6] Acheson (*Present*, pp. 169–70), writes, "By the time I took up my duties as Under Secretary in Sept. 1945 it was clear that the President himself was directing policy on Palestine . . . the officers of the Office of Near Eastern and

African Affairs, who under the instruction of Pres. Roosevelt and Sec. Stettinius had been following a neutral role on the Palestine issue, faithfully adapted themselves to Pres. Truman's different approach."

[7] On these same pages, Acheson asserts, "Despite my own views," he did his best to carry out the President's wishes; he similarly defends the dedication of Loy Henderson, head of the Near Eastern Office. But the fact is that with the President committed to the immediate admission of 100,000 displaced European Jews into Palestine as early as August 1945, what followed was not positive action, but endless meetings in Washington and London and the appointment of special commissions (the Anglo-American Committee of Inquiry, followed by a special Cabinet Committee)—but never any concrete action. These delays continued for more than two years, until the UN partition decision made them no longer necessary, since the independent Jewish state (if it ever really came into existence) would control its own immigration.

[8] The writer made every possible proper effort to gain access to these files, including enlisting the warm cooperation of his Congressman, Rep. John S. Monagan. But it was not possible to get beyond a conversation with the Middle East History Desk of the State Department (summer, 1969). I said that my research thus far forced the conclusion that the State Department had been quite hostile to the state of Israel in its formative years (1947–1948), and that I hoped that access to the appropriate files would mitigate this unpleasant conclusion. My anonymous discussant stated that access could not be granted, but that my conclusion was essentially correct. And the thrust of presidential adviser Clark Clifford's personal papers, to which Kurzman was granted access, is similar. (Kurzman, *Genesis,* pp. 86-97, 98-99, 213, 215-17, 251-53, 574, 635.)

[9] Truman, *Memoirs,* 2:133. Here and in subsequent quotations, emphasis has been added by the author.

[10] Truman, 2:136, 137.

[11] Truman, 2:149.

[12] Truman, 2:159–62.

[13] Acheson, *Present,* pp. 170, 181.

[14] The *New York Times,* January 24, 1948, reports on a letter from Senator Warren G. Magnuson to the State Department, asking that surplus arms be sold to the Jews, since $37,000,000 in surplus arms had already been sold to the Arab states.

[15] As late as May 11, 1948, Gen. George C. Marshall, then Secretary of State, opposed early recognition of the Jewish State, expecting that it would not prove able to stay alive. (Kurzman, *Genesis,* p. 215.)

[16] The *New York Times,* Feb. 26–27, 1948, reported the seizure of political party headquarters by police acting for the Interior Minister (and War Minister); then, that Edward Benes permitted Klement Gottwald to form a new, Communist-dominated Cabinet "to prevent chaos." March 11, the *Times* reported the "suicide" of Jan Masaryk together with a charge by Czechoslovak U.N. Representative J. Papanek that the USSR had installed a Communist government by threat of arms. Benes remained as a figurehead until early June, when he resigned; he died early in September.

[17] Interview by Sraya Shapiro, the *Jerusalem Post Weekly*, June 23, 1969, p. 10. Earlier arms shipments had apparently been largely consumed. The reinforcing airlifted Czech arms which began to come in May 12, were vital to halting the invasion of the regular Arab armies which began May 15. The first airlifted Czech fighter planes went into action May 29.

[18] *New York Times*, January 1, 1948.

[19] *New York Times*, January 29, January 31, 1948.

[20] *New York Times*, March 1.

[21] *New York Times*, March 5, March 9, March 13, March 14.

[22] *New York Times*, March 20, March 21, March 25, March 26, March 27, March 30.

[23] *New York Times*, April 10, April 21, April 29.

[24] *New York Times*, Sept. 25, Nov. 26, 1949.

[25] Velie, *Countdown*, pp. 19–32.

[26] Outsiders quickly become part of the State Dept. club. Thus, newcomers John Foster Dulles and Dean Rusk promptly agreed with Loy Henderson that support for the Jewish state would "wreck our Arab policy," and that U.S. military security "requires that we play ball with Arab military power" (Velie, *Countdown*, pp. 19–32). And Kurzman (*Genesis*, p. 215, footnote) writes: "Israelis who dealt with Rusk regard him as having opposed the creation of a Jewish State with possibly more zeal than any other top State Department official, though later he did not appear to resist the generally pro-Israel policies of Presidents Kennedy and Johnson. An unsigned memorandum in Clifford's file detailing a conversation between Rusk and the memo writer (apparently Clifford) on May 8, 1948, one week before the end of the British mandate, reflects Rusk's bitter-end stance. Rusk, the writes states, insisted that a 'simplified trusteeship' was still possible."

[27] Kimche, *Pillars*, frontispiece.

[28] In 1788 she urged the 'chiefs of the government of Cairo' to declare their independence of the Ottoman Empire, promising full military and financial assistance.

[29] General Matityahu (Mati) Peled, reminiscing over the War of Independence and, in particular, his experiences as a twenty-year-old Palmah commander bringing a single platoon to the besieged, aged, enormously outnumbered Jewish community of Safed, put it this way:

". . . And none of the Jews in Safed will forget that Saturday morning when the Palmah came with a song on their lips. . . .

"That was when there came over me the emotional memory of the stories of the Holocaust, and I thought: 'Jews were massacred once. But not here. Here, at least, we will fight. We won't be massacred.'

"You may ask anyone in Israel. I think you'll get the same answer to this day. I think that feeling controlled every mind here on the eve of the Six-Day War: that the Holocaust would never again happen. Not here. If we had to die, we would die fighting, and not like sheep."

Hadassah Magazine, New York, September 1970, p. 9; excerpted from Leonard Wolf, "The Passion of Israel" (Little, Brown, 1970).

INDEX

299

DATE DUE

APR 2 3 1998			